Instructor Guide

the STORY of the WORLD

Volume 1: Ancient Times

Instructor Guide

the STORY of the WORLD

History for the Classical Child

Volume 1: Ancient Times

From the Earliest Nomads to the Last Roman Emperor

Edited by Susan Wise Bauer, Susanna Jarrett, and Kat Stelly

WELL-TRAINED MIND PRESS

Charles City, Virginia

Well-Trained Mind Press

2006 Cover design by AJ Buffington and Mike Fretto.
2026 Cover design by Mehreen Fatima.
Book design by Itamar Katz. Composed in Hanken Grotesk.

Names:	Bauer, Susan Wise, author.
Title:	Ancient times : from the earliest nomads to the last Roman Emperor. Instructor guide / by Susan Wise Bauer.
Other titles:	Instructor guide
Description:	Charles City, Virginia : Well-Trained Mind Press, [2026] | Series: Bauer, Susan Wise. Story of the world.
Identifiers:	ISBN: 9781944481865 (paperback) | 9781944481902 (ebook)
Subjects:	LCSH: World history. | Civilization. | History, Ancient. | Nomads--History. | LCGFT: Teachers' guides. | BISAC: EDUCATION / Home Schooling. | EDUCATION / Schools / Levels / Elementary. | EDUCATION / Teaching / Subjects / Arts & Humanities.
Classification:	LCC: D20 .B35 2026 | DDC: 909--dc23

welltrainedmind.com

CONTENTS

HOW TO USE THIS BOOK

History is the most enthralling story you can tell a young child, because it's true. A good history narrative is as strange and wondrous as a good fairy tale. Kings, queens, mummies, wooden horses, knights, and castles can be as fascinating as giants and elves—but they really existed!

In classical education, history lies at the center of the curriculum. The chronological study of history allows even small children to learn about the past in an orderly way; after all, the "best way to tell a story," as the King tells Alice in *Alice in Wonderland*, "is to begin at the beginning and go on to the end." When the study of literature is linked to history, children have an opportunity to hear the stories of each country as they learn more about that country's past and its people. History teaches comprehension; young students learn to listen carefully, to pick out and remember the central facts in each story. History even becomes the training ground for beginning writers. When you ask a young student to narrate, to tell back to you the information he's just heard in his own words, you are giving him invaluable practice in the first and most difficult step of writing: putting an idea into words.

Using This Book at Home

This book is designed to accompany *The Story of the World, Volume 1: Ancient Times, 25th Anniversary Expanded Edition* by Susan Wise Bauer (it is not compatible with older editions of *The Story of the World, Volume 1*).

Required Materials:

- *The Story of the World, Volume 1, 25th Anniversary Expanded Edition* (paperback, hardcover, ebook, PDF, or audio)
- This Instructor Guide
- A Student Workbook for each student using the program (paperback or PDF)

Optional Materials:

- History Notebook (three-ring binder for storing student work)
- Tests & Answer Key (sold separately; not recommended for students under 4th grade)
- Copies of Student Page 1 (Photocopy this page as often as you like and use it for the narration exercises and other writing activities throughout the book)

For each section in *The Story of the World*, follow this pattern:

1. **Read the section (the text under one sub-heading within a chapter, not the entire chapter)** from *The Story of the World* aloud. Good readers can read the section out loud to you instead.
2. **Core Exercise:** Alternate between review questions and narration exercises for comprehension. Complete the map in each chapter. These activities are scripted for your convenience. **Bold text** is a script for the instructor to read out loud. *Italicized* text indicates a sample student answer.
3. **Interactive Activity:** Choose from a variety of engaging activities to help history come to life (not required for every lesson). Use the checklist in each lesson to plan which activities you will complete. The following symbols can help you choose the activities that will work best for you:

   activities that are classroom adaptable

   activities that are low-prep (require no materials or a few common household materials and little to no preparation)

   activities that get your students out of their seats and moving.

   Activities are also labeled by category: arts & crafts, make a model, role play, games, activity pages, math, science demonstration, coloring pages, research, cooking, memory work, storytelling, field trips, and celebrations. You can incorporate activities into different parts of your day to encourage students to make connections between disciplines (art, math, science, etc.). See Appendix Four for a list of activities organized by category. Appendix Three also includes a list of common materials used across many of the activities.
4. **Additional reading (optional):** This Instructor Guide provides library book lists for deeper exploration (RA= read aloud, IR= independent reading). When you reach a topic that your student is particularly interested in, stop and enjoy yourself. Once in a while, have students narrate a summary of the book they read or draw a relevant picture for their history notebook (do not do this for every book—your student will begin to dread it).
5. **Card Review (optional):** Every four chapters, prepare history review cards (found in the back of the Student Workbook). Photocopy onto cardstock, cut out, and color. Have students sort all of their cards into a timeline at the end of each week.
6. **Testing (optional):** If you desire a more formal evaluation or wish to develop your child's test-taking ability, use the tests (sold separately) for ages 10+.

If you would like a more detailed description of how to schedule out the program, see Appendix Six for adaptable scheduling ideas.

Multilevel Teaching

While *The Story of the World* is designed for grades 1–4, it can be adapted for older students:

- Independently read *The Story of the World*
- Supplement with an appropriate history encyclopedia such as the *Usborne History Encyclopedia*
- Track important dates on a timeline
- Explore additional readings at the appropriate level (The reading lists in this book have some suggestions for older students. You can ask your local librarian for more!)
- Where appropriate, review and evaluate primary sources with an instructor (for example, excerpts from the Pyramid Texts, excerpts from Hammurabi's Code, the Twelve Tablets of Roman Law, excerpts from *The Gallic Wars* by Julius Caesar, etc.)

For more details on teaching history to logic stage, or middle school students, refer to *The Well-Trained Mind: A Guide to Classical Education at Home* (Essential Edition, 2024).

Customizing for Your Family

Families differ in their attitudes towards teaching myths, in their willingness to view partially-clothed people in ancient art, and in their sensitivity towards the (inevitable) violence of ancient times. Preview activities, coloring pages (especially Student Pages 59, 76, and 99), and recommended books to ensure they are appropriate for your family.

Using This in the Classroom

This program is flexible and adapts well for classroom use. Below is an example of how you could use this book in a group setting:

1. **Read aloud:** The teacher reads a section while students follow along in their own books. When you reach the end of a section, ask the review questions provided in this book (or use the Review Questions Worksheets, sold separately, for older students). Students may also extend their learning with the additional history and literature books from the reading lists in each chapter.
2. **Review:** Use the review questions for an oral review or the narration prompts for a written review. To switch things up once in a while, you can make it fun by playing oral quizzing games such as "Around the World," "Last One Standing," or "Jeopardy!"
3. **Geography Work:** Have the students complete the map exercises in the Student Workbook.

4. **Interactive Activities:** Select a hands-on activity to complete (classroom-friendly ones are marked ())
5. **Chapter Review Cards:** On the last day before the test, have the students color their chapter review cards and practice organizing them into a timeline.
6. **Testing:** Review past lessons regularly and, for older students, administer tests (sold separately).

See Appendix Six for adaptable schedules, and Appendix Four for lists of activities by type.

INTRODUCTION
How Do We Know What Happened?

What is History?

Read & Review

Read pages 3-5 in *The Story of the World, Volume 1: Ancient Times* (the text). Afterward, check the student's understanding by asking the questions below. Read bold text out loud. Sample responses are provided in italics.

1. **What do we call someone who reads letters, journals, and monuments to find out about the past?** *A historian*
2. **What do we call the story that historians write about the past?** *History*

Narration Exercise

Prompt students to tell you about the lesson with the following question. Require students to answer in complete sentences.

What are two ways that historians learn about the past?

Students' narrations do not have to match the sample word for word. Write down the narration if your student is not writing independently. Good writers can write the narration down themselves. An acceptable narration may resemble:

Historians read letters and look at monuments.

or

People wrote letters and kings told people to write down stories. Historians can read them.

Note to Instructor: Student Page 1 is a reproducible template for narration exercises. You can make copies of it to use for this exercise and future narration exercises, or simply use any sheet of lined paper.

Activities

Choose from the following activities:

- ☐ Storytelling: Conduct an Interview
- ☐ Storytelling: Make a Timeline of Your Life
- ☐ Research Skills: Ask students to look up one or more related topics in their history encyclopedia or another reliable source. Read the entry together and look at the pictures. Topics could include *historians*, *what is history*, *doing history*, *oral history*, or *museums*.

Storytelling

CONDUCT AN INTERVIEW

One way historians learn about the past is by asking good questions and carefully recording what they learn. In this activity, students record the history of someone they know.

MATERIALS:

- Student Page 2
- an older relative or friend who is willing to be interviewed
- pencil
- recording device
- photograph of interviewee (optional)
- double-stick tape or glue (optional)
- extra notebook paper (optional)

DIRECTIONS:

Before the Interview:

1. Ask an elderly relative, neighbor, or family friend if they are willing to be interviewed about their life. If your interviewee does not live nearby, you can conduct this interview over the phone or on a video call. Parents can help younger students brainstorm an appropriate candidate.
2. Set up a time and place for the interview. Parents can help younger students arrange the time and place.
3. Prepare for your interview. Younger students can use the questions on Student Page 2 (they do not need to come up with extra questions). Older students can think up 2-3 extra questions to add to their Student Page.

Interview Day:

4. On the day of the interview, come prepared with a recording device, your Student Page, and a pencil. Older students may want to bring extra paper for taking notes.

Optional: Bring a helper along to be your sound person. They can manage the recording device so that you can focus on the interview

5. Before starting the recording, make sure you and your interviewee are seated comfortably.
6. After starting the recording, state your name, the date, and the name of the person you are interviewing. It is important for historians to have this information so they can keep the materials they collect organized.
7. Interview your friend or relative. Ask the questions on the top of your page first. Then ask the questions at the bottom of your page (there is no need to write these answers word for word, but older students can take notes on a separate piece of paper if they choose). Older students may also have additional questions to ask.

After the Interview:

8. When the interview is over, use the recording to finish filling out any remaining questions on your Student Page (younger students may need help with this).
9. Paste a picture of your interviewee on the page and record it in your history notebook. If you don't have a photograph, draw a picture instead. Older students may want to add their extra notes to their notebooks as well.
10. Write your interviewee a note to thank them for their time.

Note to Instructor: Provide all necessary help for younger students. It is not necessary for them to fill out the Student Page themselves.

Storytelling

MAKE A TIMELINE OF YOUR LIFE

You have a history too! In this activity, you will make a timeline of your life.

MATERIALS:

- blank paper (one sheet for each year of your life, plus one extra sheet) or a large poster board
- photographs of you (one from each year of your life, if possible)
- double stick tape or glue
- souvenirs from your life (optional)

DIRECTIONS:

1. Tape the sheets of paper together. You should have one sheet of paper for each year of your life plus one (so a 6-year-old would tape 7 sheets). Alternatively, use a poster board.
2. Start at zero and write one number in the middle of each sheet. If using a poster board, draw a line across the center of the poster board. Space the numbers evenly along the line.
3. Fill in the timeline with important dates in your life.
4. Paste a photo of yourself as a newborn at the beginning of the timeline. Paste the rest of your photos on the correct spot on the timeline.
5. You can add more photos, draw pictures, or even glue souvenirs, like theater tickets, on your timeline.

Some ideas for things to include on your timeline: when you got your first tooth, when you first sat up, crawled, your first big trip, when you started school, when you took your first music lesson or went to your first sports practice, when you met your best friend, and when your siblings were born.

Classroom Adaptation: If you plan to complete this activity with a large group, prepare a model timeline ahead of time. Have students come prepared with photos from home or have them illustrate their timeline with colored pencils or crayons instead of using pictures and souvenirs.

What is Archaeology?

Read & Review

Read pages 6–8 in the text. Afterward, check the student's understanding by asking the questions below. Sample responses are provided in italics. Encourage students to answer in complete sentences whenever possible. Answers given are approximate; accept any reasonable answer.

1. **What do *archaeologists* do?** *Archaeologists dig objects out of the ground and learn about them.*
2. **What kinds of things did people leave behind them, in the story we read?** *People left behind dishes, tools, and toys.*

Narration Exercise

Prompt students to tell you about the lesson with one or both of the following questions. Require students to answer in complete sentences.

What do archaeologists do?

Students' narrations do not have to match the sample word for word. Write down the narration if your student is not writing independently. Good writers can write the narration down themselves. An acceptable narration may resemble:

Archaeologists dig objects out of the ground and learn about them.

In the story we read, what kinds of things did people leave behind them?

People left behind dishes, tools, and toys.

Activities

Choose from the following activities:

- [ ] Role Play: A Dirty Dig!
- [ ] Research Skills: Ask students to look up one or more related topics in their history encyclopedia or another reliable source. Read the entry together and look at the pictures. Topics could include *buildings*, *archaeology*, and *excavation*.

Role Play

A DIRTY DIG!

Archaeologists carefully dig in the ground to find clues about the past. In this activity, you will practice being an archaeologist.

MATERIALS:

- items from your household that represent our civilization (see step 1 of the Setup Directions for ideas)
- a place to bury the above items
- a small shovel or garden trowel
- small brushes (old toothbrushes work well)
- bucket and containers
- a screen or sieve for sifting dirt
- plastic bags or containers (to hold artifacts)
- string
- paper or notebook
- pencil

SETUP DIRECTIONS (FOR PARENTS OR INSTRUCTOR):

1. Assemble items to bury. Try to find things that would answer these kinds of questions: What kinds of foods did these people eat? What kind of houses did they live in? What did they do for entertainment? Did they read and write? Think of some questions of your own. For older students, try to include at least one item whose purpose or use is not obvious (like a whisk, a toy, or something broken into multiple pieces).
2. Make a list of the "artifacts" to reference later.
3. Bury the artifacts in a sandbox, marked area of the yard, or large bin filled with dirt or sand.

Indoor Adaptation: If you don't have an outdoor area to bury items, try variations like a large container filled with dirt or shredded paper.

ACTIVITY DIRECTIONS:

1. You will act like you are an archaeologist in the future digging up the ruins of an "ancient civilization" — ours! Use the string to mark off sections of the dig area (make a grid with the string across the surface of the ground). For younger students, you should probably use only 2 strings to divide the ground into quarters; older students can use 3 or more pieces of string to divide the dig area into 6 or 9 spaces.
2. Excavate one section at a time using the small shovel. Work carefully so the artifacts don't get damaged.
3. Use the small brushes to gently brush dirt from the artifacts.
4. Sift the dirt you remove from the hole so the smaller artifacts aren't missed.

5. As you remove the artifacts, write down what you found and what square of the grid you found it in. Use plastic bags and containers to hold the artifacts.
6. Tell what you learned about this "ancient civilization." Compare what you wrote down to the reference questions mentioned in the setup directions.
7. Older students, try to make inferences about what archaeologists of the future might think about us (for example, might they think that you worship your dog as a god because you have so many pictures of the dog throughout the house?) .

Classroom Adaptation: Divide students into small groups (2-3 students per a group). Have each group set up an archaeological dig site (using the set-up directions above), and then have them swap sites with a different group for the activity section of the project.

Additional History Reading

A Street Through Time: A 12,000-Year Journey Along the Same Street, by Anne Millard, illus. Steve Noon (DK Children, 2012). This book helps students imagine what one street may have looked like over the course of thousands of years. (RA).

Me and My Family Tree, by Joan Sweeney, illus. Emma Trithart (Dragonfly, 2018). A picture-intensive book that explains a family tree in very simple terms. (RA [read-aloud])

The Ancient Worlds Atlas, illus. Russell Barnett (DK Publishing, 2023). This beautifully illustrated atlas has two-page spreads on many of the regions and civilizations covered in the text. It can act as an easy-to-navigate children's encyclopedia for further research throughout this curriculum. (RA 1-3, IR 4-5)

Archaeologists Dig for Clues, by Kate Duke (HarperCollins, 1997). Explains archaeological work using a cartoon format. (RA)

What is an Archaeologist?, by Libby Romero (National Geographic Partners LLC, 2019). A simple introduction to archaeology, archaeological mysteries, and a few inspiring archaeologists and what they do. It includes explanations of modern archaeological tools, like LiDAR and satellite imagery. (IR 2-4)

9000 BCE

CHAPTER ONE
The Earliest People

The First Nomads

Read & Review

Read pages 9–11 in the text. Afterward, check the student's understanding by asking the questions below. Encourage students to answer in complete sentences whenever possible. Sample responses are provided in italics.

1. **What sort of food did nomads eat?** *Plants such as grasses, leaves, grain, roots, berries; large animals such as elk, deer, reindeer, bison; other foods such as eggs, honey, lizards, snakes, and fish*

   Note to Instructor: See if your student can remember one type of food from each of the three categories. If necessary, prompt them by asking, **What kinds of plants did they eat? What kinds of large animals did they hunt? What other kinds of food could they find?**

2. **Where did nomads sleep?** *In caves or tents*
3. **Why did nomads move from place to place?** *Because they hunted all the game and ate all the plants in one place, and had to move to another to find food.*
4. **What does "nomad" mean?** *One who wanders or roams around*

Narration Exercise

Prompt the student to tell you about the lesson with the following question. Require students to answer in complete sentences.

Tell me three things you learned about nomads.

Students' narrations do not have to match the sample word for word. Write down the narration if your student is not writing independently. Good writers can write the narration down themselves. An acceptable narration may resemble:

Nomads moved around a lot. They lived in tents. They gathered grasses and berries and hunted animals for food.

or

Some people in olden times didn't have homes. They slept outside. They ate food that they picked and hunted, and they went from place to place.

Map Work: The First Nomads (Student Page 3)

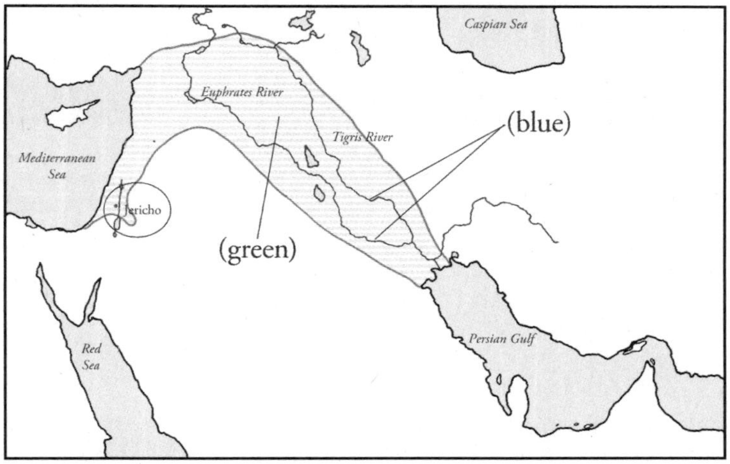

Read the instructions out loud to the student. After each step, pause and give time for students to complete the task. Provide all necessary help.

1. **Open to Student Page 3 and tear it out.**
2. **Find and circle the town of *Jericho*.**
3. **Trace the *Tigris* and *Euphrates* Rivers in blue. Lightly shade the seas blue.**
4. **Use a green crayon or colored pencil to color in the area between and around the Tigris and Euphrates Rivers. (If you need help, look at page 12 in the text). This area is known as the Fertile Crescent, and some nomads moved here because it was so easy to find food.**
5. **When you finish, place your completed map in your history notebook.**

Activities

Choose from the following activities:

- ☐ Art & Role Play: Making a Cave Painting
- ☐ Role Play: Build Your Own Hut
- ☐ Cooking: Lizard Stew
- ☐ Research Skills: Ask students to look up one or more related topics in their history encyclopedia or another reliable source. Read the entry together and look at the pictures. Topics could include *nomads*, *first people*, *earliest people*, and *early humans*.

Art & Role Play

MAKE A CAVE PAINTING

Some nomads lived in caves for shelter. They left paintings that tell us a little about their lives. In this activity, you can try your hand at making your own cave painting.

MATERIALS:

- brown paper grocery bag or other brown paper
- tape
- a wall you can tape something to
- acrylic paints in black or reddish-brown (to simulate the charcoal used by prehistoric people)
- thick paintbrush
- newspaper, an old blanket, or the brown paper that comes with packages

DIRECTIONS:

1. Cut the paper bag open so that you have a large surface area to paint on. Next, crumple the paper, and then smooth it flat. This is to add irregularities to the painting surface to simulate painting on a rough cave wall.
2. To paint standing up, like prehistoric people did, tape the crumpled paper to a wall. If you choose to do this, you will want to put down newspaper or an old blanket beneath the painting to protect the floor from spills.
3. Draw a simple outline of an animal. Draw the animal's most obvious feature (e.g. tusks or antlers) in an exaggerated way. You can also add several stick figures carrying spears to depict a hunt.

Classroom Adaptation: If you cannot paste the brown paper "cave" to the wall, have students paint on slant boards for a similar effect.

Role Play

BUILD YOUR OWN HUT

Nomads had to have homes that could move around with them, and they had to use the materials that were available, like animal skins, branches, and other things they could find. Can you build a shelter from the materials you see around you?

For an outside hut, go into your backyard and try to construct a shelter from whatever materials are available in the yard. You could try to build a small shelter for one of your favorite stuffed animals, or try to build one big enough for yourself! Use sticks and branches to make the support structures, then cover them using leaves, grass, fabric, or an old blanket. For an inside hut, use chairs, blankets, and sheets.

When you're done with your hut, make a narration page that talks about what you think it was like for prehistoric people to live outside. What dangers did they have to worry about (weather, animals, hostile people)? Would their shelter change depending on where they lived (hot, cold, windy)? Can you think of one good thing and one bad thing about living that way? Be sure to include a drawing or picture of the hut you made. For an extra challenge, try sleeping overnight in your hut!

Cooking: Lizard Stew

Remember the story about how Tarak caught some lizards for her mom to make lizard stew? We don't want to eat lizards, but we can make a fun version and pretend we're eating some delicious Lizard Stew!

INGREDIENTS:

- one pound fusilli or other twisted pasta (reserve a cup of the pasta water after boiling)
- 8 oz jar of basil pesto (or make your own)
- seasonings to taste

DIRECTIONS:

1. Boil the pasta and reserve about a cup of the pasta water before draining.
2. Put the drained pasta back into the pot and add the pesto; stir.
3. To make it more of a stew, add the reserved pasta water and stir thoroughly to mix with the pesto.
4. Enjoy your Lizard Stew!

8500 BCE

The First Nomads Become Farmers

Read & Review

Read pages 12–16 in the text. Afterward, check the student's understanding by asking the questions below. Encourage students to answer in complete sentences whenever possible. Sample responses are provided in italics.

1. **Why was the Fertile Crescent a good place to live?** *The Fertile Crescent was a good place to live because there was water, good soil, and plenty of grass and plants.*
2. **Why was it called "fertile"?** *It was called fertile because lots of plants grew there.*
3. **What was it shaped like?** *The Fertile Crescent was shaped like a crescent* OR *the new moon.*
4. **What did the first farmers grow?** *The first farmers grew wheat and barley.*
5. **Did farmers move from place to place like nomads?** *No.* **Why?** *Because they had to stay in one place long enough to tend their crops, water them, and harvest them.*
6. **How did farmers water their crops?** *They dug canals from the river and built shadufs.*
7. **Did the farmers still hunt wild animals?** *They kept their own tame animals.*
8. **What did the farmers build their houses out of?** *Farmers built their houses from mud bricks and reeds.*
9. **How did they protect their villages?** *They built stone walls around them.*

Narration Exercise

Prompt the student to tell you about the lesson with the following question. Require students to answer in complete sentences.

What are two things that nomads did differently when they became farmers?

Students' narrations do not have to match the sample word for word. Write down the narration if your student is not writing independently. Good writers can write the narration down themselves. An acceptable narration may resemble:

Some nomads settled down and grew crops. They watered the crops and built houses. They built walls around the houses. They lived in the Fertile Crescent.

or

Some people in olden times didn't have homes. They slept outside. They ate food that they picked and hunted, and they went from place to place. Farmers grew wheat and barley. They dug canals to water their plants. They lived in villages.

Activities

Choose from the following activities:

- [ ] Coloring Page: A Farmer Using a Shaduf
- [ ] Make a Model & Science: Shaduf
- [ ] Research Skills: Ask students to look up one or more related topics in their history encyclopedia or another reliable source. Read the entry together and look at the pictures. Topics could include *nomads*, *first people*, *earliest people*, and *early humans*.

Coloring Page: A Farmer Using a Shaduf
(Student Page 4)

Early farmers used a tool called a shaduf to lift water from the river and pour it onto their fields. This simple machine helped them grow crops like wheat and barley, even in dry seasons!

Make a Model & Science

SHADUF

Early farmers used a simple machine called a shaduf to bring water out of the Nile and into irrigation canals for their crops. You can build a simple shaduf model at home.

MATERIALS:

- 5 sticks of equal length (you can use craft dowels or cut sticks from your backyard)
- 1 longer stick or stem (this will be the arm of your shaduf)
- string
- mounting putty or air-dry clay (optional, but it helps make the shaduf stable)
- small rocks
- a disposable foil casserole dish or shoe box
- sand or dirt
- an individual yogurt container (emptied and cleaned)
- a bowl or tray filled with water and an empty bowl or tray (optional, but you can use these to practice transferring water using your finished shaduf!)

DIRECTIONS:

Prepare the base:

1. Fill your tray or box with sand (or dirt) and small rocks.
2. Take 2 of the equal length sticks and cross them to form a small V at the very top. Secure the sticks together by weaving string in and out of the V before tying a tight knot (if you have air-dry clay, you can secure them with clay before using the string). Leave a little string at the end to tie the crossbar on later. This will be one side of the shaduf base.
3. Repeat the process with the 2 other equal length sticks to form the other side of the shaduf base.
4. Stick both sides of the base in the dirt tray, using rocks and sand to help them stand upright. They should be the right distance apart so that the final equal length stick (or crossbar) can lay on top of them. If you have air-dry clay or tack, you can stick a small ball of clay at the base of each stick before putting them into the dirt to make the structure sturdier.

Attach the lever to the base:

5. Using string (or a combination of string and air-dry clay), fix the center of your long stick (shaduf arm) to the center of the crossbar stick. They should be perpendicular to each other. Tie the arm loosely at first (you can adjust it later). You need to be able to tilt and swing the arm on the crossbar.
6. Place the crossbar (with the lever attached) inside the V shape of your 2 standing sticks. Use the leftover string to attach the crossbar to the base.

Prepare the water bucket and counter weight:

7. Carefully pierce 2 small holes into the top of your clean yogurt container, one on each side. Cut a long piece of string and weave it through the 2 holes. Draw the ends together and tie them to the end of the arm of the shaduf. (If you have air-dry clay and want to make your shaduf look more realistic, form a small pot out of the clay. You can use the bottom of the yogurt container as a mold. Make sure to pierce your container and thread the string through before it dries.)
8. Repeat the process in step 7 to make a second yogurt cup bucket. Tie one yogurt container to the opposite side of the lever. Fill this side with small rocks or pebbles. This is your counterweight. If you have air-dry clay or tack, there is an easier way to make a counterweight: form a small ball of clay or tack. Stick the ball to the opposite side of the shaduf arm.
9. Optional: Take a picture of your shaduf to keep in your history notebook.

Optional science extension: If you like, connect this lesson to the science of simple machines. A shaduf is an example of a lever, one of the six types of simple machines. The crossbar acts as the fulcrum (or pivot point), while the long arm of the shaduf works as the lever. The bucket filled with water is the load, and the counterweight helps balance the load, reducing the effort needed to lift the water. You can read picture books about simple machines from the library or extend the activity with the following discussion questions:

1. Experiment with different weights for the counterweight or different lengths for the lever arm. What happens if the counterweight is heavier or lighter than the water bucket? What happens if the lever arm is shorter or longer? How does the counterweight affect the effort needed to lift the water?
2. Discuss other examples of levers that students may encounter, like seesaws, scissors, or crowbars.

Classroom Adaptation: Set out materials beforehand and have students work on their shaduf in teams. Have a competition to see which shaduf can transfer the most water from a bowl ("the Nile") into an empty tray ("the canal") in three minutes. For best results, place the shaduf slightly above the water source (this mimics the placement of the shaduf on a river bank) and attach a long string to the bottom of the shaduf bucket so that whoever is controlling the shaduf arm can also tilt the bucket to release water.

Additional History Reading

Discovery in the Cave (Step into Reading), by Mark Dubowski, illus. Bryn Barnard (Random House Books for Young Readers, 2010). An easy-to-read story about the young boy who discovered the Lascaux Cave paintings. (IR 2-3)

It's Disgusting and We Ate It! True Food Facts from Around the World and Throughout History, by James Solheim, illus. Eric Brace (Aladdin, 2001). Includes the foods that prehistoric peoples ate. (Possible IR [independent read])

Ancient Agriculture, by Michael Woods (Runestone Press, 1999). Chapters are divided into sections, each appropriate for reading aloud, covering the food-raising and food-gathering techniques of several different eras. The first chapter covers the nomadic lifestyle. **Out of print, but worth looking for at your local library.** (RA 1–3, IR 4–6)

Corresponding Literature Suggestions

Little Grunt and the Big Egg, by Tomie dePaola (Putnam, 1990). A light-hearted story about a nomadic family; no historical accuracy, but fun reading for beginners. (IR for most first graders)

One Small Blue Bead, by Byrd Baylor, illus. Ronald Himler (Atheneum, 1992). A boy makes it possible for an old man in their primitive tribe to go in search of other men in far-off places. (RA)

The First Dog, by Jan Brett (Harcourt Brace, 1998). A cave boy makes friends with a wolf who saves him from danger. (RA)

The First Drawing, by Mordicai Gersten (Little, Brown and Company, 2013). A picture book with a made-up story about the first kid to create a drawing.

3000 BCE

CHAPTER TWO
Egyptians Lived on the Nile River

Two Kingdoms Become One

Read & Review

Read pages 17–20 in the text. Afterward, check the student's understanding by asking the questions below. Encourage students to answer in complete sentences whenever possible. Sample responses are provided in italics.

1. **Where is the Nile River?** *The Nile River is in Africa.*
2. **What country did the Nile run through?** *The Nile River ran through Egypt.* You may have to explain the difference between a continent— a huge land mass— and a country—a certain group of people who live on the land mass.
3. **What did the Nile do every year?** *It flooded.*
4. **Why was this important?** *Because it watered the land and brought silt up onto the riverbanks.*
5. **What were the two tribes who lived in Egypt called?** *The two tribes who lived in Egypt were called Upper Egyptians and Lower Egyptians.*
6. **Who ruled them?** *The King with the Red Crown and the King with the White Crown ruled the Egyptians.*
7. **Were they friends?** *No, they fought constantly.*
8. **Who won the battle between the White Crown and Red Crown Kings?** *The White Crown King won the battle.*
9. **What kind of crown did the new king wear?** *The new king wore the double Crown.*

Narration Exercise

Prompt the student to tell you about the lesson with the following question. Require students to answer in complete sentences.

Tell me two things about Upper Egypt and Lower Egypt and their kings.

Students' narrations do not have to match the sample word for word. Write down the narration if your student is not writing independently. Good writers can write the narration down themselves. An acceptable narration may resemble:

The Egyptians fought each other until one king conquered the other and ruled the whole country. He wore both crowns.

OR

The Upper Egyptians lived along the straight part of the Nile. The Lower Egyptians lived up in the delta. The Nile flooded every year. They grew crops in the soil.

Map Work: The Two Kingdoms Become One
(Student Page 5)

Read the instructions out loud. After each step, pause and give time for students to complete the task. Provide all necessary help.

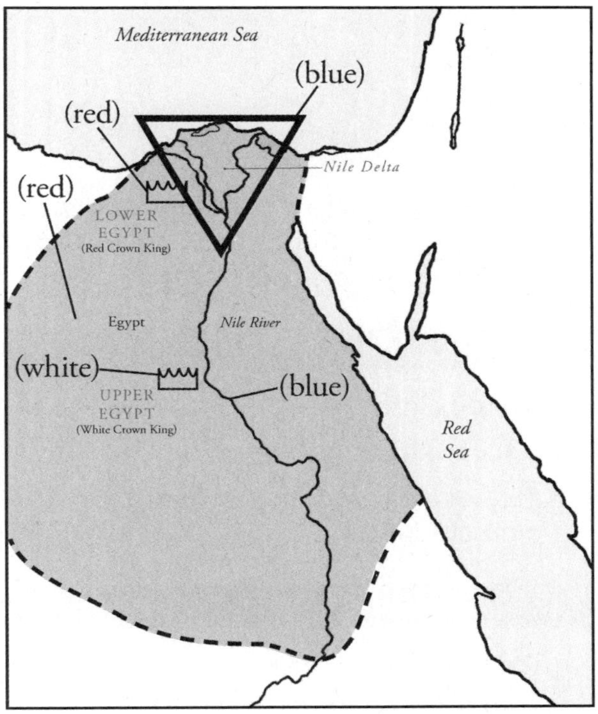

1. **Open to Student Page 5 and tear it out.**
2. **Find the *Nile River* and trace its course in blue.**
3. **Draw a blue triangle around the *Nile Delta*, where the river breaks into several smaller rivers and empties into the Mediterranean Sea.**
4. **Draw a *red crown* in the area of *Lower Egypt*. Then, draw a *white crown* in the area of *Upper Egypt*. Remember, the Lower Egyptians lived in the area of the Nile Delta, and the Upper Egyptians lived along the straight part of the river.**
5. **When King Narmer conquered the Red Crown King, he wore the red crown over his own white crown. He made Egypt into one country. To show this on your map, shade all of *Egypt* lightly in red, even coloring lightly over the white crown in Upper Egypt.**
6. **When you finish, place the completed map in your history notebook.**

Activities

Choose from the following activities:

- [ ] Craft: Make Your Own Double Crown of Egypt
- [ ] Research Skills: Ask the student to look up one or more related topics in a history encyclopedia or another reliable source. Read the entry together and look at the pictures. Topics could include the *Nile*, *King Narmer*, *Upper Egypt*, and *Lower Egypt*.

Craft

MAKE YOUR OWN DOUBLE CROWN OF EGYPT

When King Narmer united Upper Egypt and Lower Egypt, he combined the crown of each kingdom to create the Double Crown of Egypt. In this activity, you can make your own version of the double crown.

MATERIALS:

- white printer paper
- red construction paper
- gold or yellow construction paper (or pipe cleaners)
- tape or glue
- scissors
- stapler (optional)

DIRECTIONS:

1. **To create the base of the crown:** cut strips of red construction paper (about 4 inches wide) and connect them with tape, glue or staples until you have a strip long enough to fit around your head comfortably. Tape, glue, or staple the strips closed to form the base of the crown.
2. **To form the red crown of Lower Egypt:** fold a piece of red construction paper in half, and then open it again. Fold the top corners into the middle (where the fold line is), creating a triangle at the top of the paper. Attach this piece of paper (triangle up) to the back side of the base of your crown.

3. **To form the white crown of Upper Egypt:** pull and tape the top corners of a white piece of paper together to form a pointed cone. Cut off the bottom few inches of paper and roll the extra paper into a ball. Stick the ball inside the gap in the top of the cone to fill it in. Tape or glue the white cone to the red triangle section (or backside) of your crown.
4. **To form the cobra detail on the front of the crown:** cut a long narrow strip (about 1 inch wide) of red, yellow, or gold construction paper. Curl the strip up about half way and then unfold it. Attach the curl to the front of your crown. Alternatively, you could curl up a gold or yellow pipe cleaner and stick it into the front of your crown base, taping it securely in the back to keep it upright.

3000 BCE

The Gods of Egypt

Read & Review

Read pages 20–23 in the text. Afterward, check the student's understanding by asking the questions below. Encourage students to answer in complete sentences whenever possible. Sample responses are provided in italics.

1. **Did the Egyptians worship one god or many gods?** *The Egyptians worshiped many gods.*
2. **Can you name any of them?** *Ra, Horus, Isis, Osiris, the pharaoh*
3. **Do you remember the name of Osiris' evil brother?** *Set was the name of Osiris' evil brother.*
4. **How did Set get Osiris to lie down in the coffin?** *He said that he would give it to whoever fitted it best.*
5. **Did Osiris stay dead?** *No, he came back to life again.*

Narration Exercise

Prompt the student to tell you about the lesson with the following question. Require students to answer in complete sentences.

Tell me about the story of Osiris and Set.

Students' narrations do not have to match the sample word for word. Write down the narration if your student is not writing independently. Good writers can write the narration down themselves. An acceptable narration may resemble:

The Egyptians believed in many different gods. Osiris was the king of the gods. His brother tried to kill him, but he came back to life.

OR

Set wanted to kill his brother. He got him to lie down in a coffin and then threw it into the river. But Osiris didn't stay dead. That's why the Nile fills up every year.

Activities

Choose from the following activities:

- [ ] Coloring Page: Osiris and Set
- [ ] Memory Work: The Gods of Egypt
- [ ] Make a Model: Nile River
- [ ] Research Skills: Ask the student to look up one or more related topics in a history encyclopedia or another reliable source. Read the entry together and look at the pictures. Topics could include *Ancient Egypt, gods and goddesses of Egypt, Ra, Horus, Osiris,* and *Set*.

Coloring Page: Osiris and Set (Student Page 6)

Color the picture of Osiris in the coffin he won from Set. The gods Horus, Isis, and Ra are watching him try out the coffin. Everyone wouldn't look so happy, if they knew Set was going to throw Osiris into the Nile River!

Memory Work

THE GODS OF EGYPT

Egyptian mythology is embedded in our culture. Once students know the gods and their roles, they will start to see them referenced in literature, movies, video games, and music.

Note to Instructor: For detailed guidance on using memory work activities, see Appendix Two. The student's memory work reference page is available on Student Page 9. Below, you'll find the list of items to memorize, along with additional teaching ideas for your convenience.

1. Ra (RAH or RAY) - The Sun God
2. Osiris (o SYE rus) - God of the Underworld
3. Isis (EYE sis) - Mother Goddess
4. Set (SET or Seth) - God of Chaos
5. Hathor (HATH or) - Goddess of Love, Beauty, and Music
6. Anubis (uh NOO bis) - God of Mummification and the Afterlife
7. Thoth (THOHTH) - God of Writing and Wisdom
8. Horus (HORE us) - God of the Sky
9. Bastet (BAST et) - Goddess of Cats and Motherhood.

Suggested Activity: Once students have memorized the list of gods, review the knowledge with the memory work ball game. Shout out a god or goddess's name, then throw a student a large ball. Before the student catches the ball, they must shout out the deity's title. For example, say "Horus" and throw the ball to a student. The student must answer "God of the sky!" before or as they catch the ball. Switch things up by shouting out the title and having students shout out the name.

Related Reading: *Gods and Goddesses of Ancient Egypt: Egyptian Mythology for Kids*, by Morgan E. Moroney (Callisto Kids, 2020)

Make a Model

NILE RIVER

Life in Ancient Egypt centered on the Nile river; in this activity, you can make your own model of the Nile.

MATERIALS:

- grass seed
- potting soil
- rocks and pebbles
- large waterproof pan (such as a disposable aluminum roasting pan), about 3" deep. If you prefer, you can use a larger box or tub.
- tin foil
- water
- optional: your choice of clay or toy building bricks (to create decorations)

DIRECTIONS:

1. Fill the container ⅔-full with soil.
2. Push the soil away from the middle to make the riverbed. Look at your map to see what shape it should be. It should run through the center of the container, just as the Nile River ran through the center of ancient Egypt. Don't forget to split the river into a Y-shape at one end, where the delta will be located.
3. Using a double layer of aluminum foil, line the riverbed. You will need to cut and mold the foil to cover the Y-shape for the delta. Ensure the foil is long enough to fold over the top of the container at each end so it stays in place, and just high enough to slightly fold over the soil so it doesn't all fall into the river.
4. Spread some pebbles into the river to weigh down the foil. Sprinkle grass seed along the banks of the Nile.
5. Place some larger rocks along the right side of the container, to imitate the mountains in ancient Egypt.

6. Fill the river with water, letting it flood over the banks to water the seeds (be careful not to flood over the top of your pan!). Nature took care of watering the crops in ancient Egypt!
7. Each week, water your model by flooding the Nile. How long did it take for the seeds to sprout?
8. For added details, you can make clay or toy building brick replicas of the pyramids and place them on or near your model.The ancient Egyptians used reed boats, but you can float other things on your river, like leaves, seed pods, woven grass, or even a toy boat just for fun.
9. Optional: Take a picture of your Nile River model. Place it in your history notebook.

Additional History Reading

Eyewitness: Ancient Egypt, by George Hart (DK Eyewitness, 2021). Very detailed two-page spreads on Egyptian history and customs; text is fourth-grade level and up, but photographs are appropriate for all age levels. The first four pages deal with the earliest days of Egypt. (Also recommended for chapter thirteen) (RA 1–4, IR 4–6)

Egyptian Gods and Goddesses, by Henry Barker, illus. Jeff Crosby (Grossett & Dunlap, 1999). Describes each Egyptian god briefly, along with pictures. (RA)

The Nile River, by Allan Fowler (Children's Press, 2000). Pictures and descriptions of the land along the Nile. (RA)

Corresponding Literature Suggestions

Egyptian Myths: Meet the Gods, Goddesses, and Pharaohs of Ancient Egypt, by Jean Menzies (DK Children, 2022). Easy-to-read adaptations of Egyptian myths accompanied by bright illustrations and infographics about Egyptian gods. (RA)

Marcy and the Riddle of the Sphinx, by Joe Todd-Stanton (Flying Eye Books, 2017). In this fantastical fiction book, young Marcy travels to Egypt on a journey to save her father and meets an array of Egyptian gods. (RA)

Bill and Pete Go Down the Nile, by Tomie dePaola (Putnam, 1996). Bill and Pete (a little crocodile and his toothbrush-bird) go on a class trip to the museum, where they attempt to save the Sacred Eye of Isis. Will they succeed? You'll have to read to find out! (Possible IR)

Corresponding Audiobook Suggestions

Egyptian Treasures: Mummies and Myths, read by Jim Weiss (Well-Trained Mind Press, 2015). The central stories on which the Egyptian culture was based for thousands of years. In addition to these myths, the recording tells a true, modern story of scientists seeking a lost pharoah's tomb which includes information on the pyramids and the Valley of Kings. Available at welltrainedmind.com or wherever you listen to audiobooks.

2800 BCE

CHAPTER THREE
The First Writing

Hieroglyphs and Cuneiform

Read & Review

Read pages 24-27 in the text. Afterward, check the student'sunderstanding by asking the questions below. Encourage students to answer in complete sentences whenever possible. Sample responses are provided in italics.

1. **What two types of writing did we talk about?** *We talked about cuneiform and hieroglyphics.*
2. **What two countries wrote in cuneiform and hieroglyphics?** *Egypt and Sumer*
3. **What three things did the Egyptians and Sumerians write on?** *The Egyptians wrote on stone, clay, and paper (or papyrus).*
4. **Which is easiest to write on?** *Paper is the easiest to write on.*
5. **Which ones lasted the longest?** *Stone and clay last the longest.*
6. **Which one fell apart?** *Paper fell apart.*
7. **What does "Mesopotamia" mean?** *Mesopotamia means between the rivers.*
8. **Do you remember what "hippopotamus" means?** *Hippopotamus means river-horse.*

Narration Exercise

Prompt the student to tell you about the lesson with the following question. Require students to answer in complete sentences.

Tell me two differences between hieroglyphics and cuneiform.

Students' narrations do not have to match the sample word for word. Write down the narration if your student is not writing independently. Good writers can write the narration down themselves. An acceptable narration may resemble:

The Egyptians wrote on stone. These were called hieroglyphics. The Sumerians wrote on clay. These were called cuneiform.

OR

Writing on stone was called hieroglyphics. Writing on clay was called cuneiform. This writing lasted a long time. Writing on paper didn't.

Map Work: The First Writing (Student Page 8)

Read the instructions out loud to the student. After each step, pause and give time for the student to complete the task. Provide all necessary help.

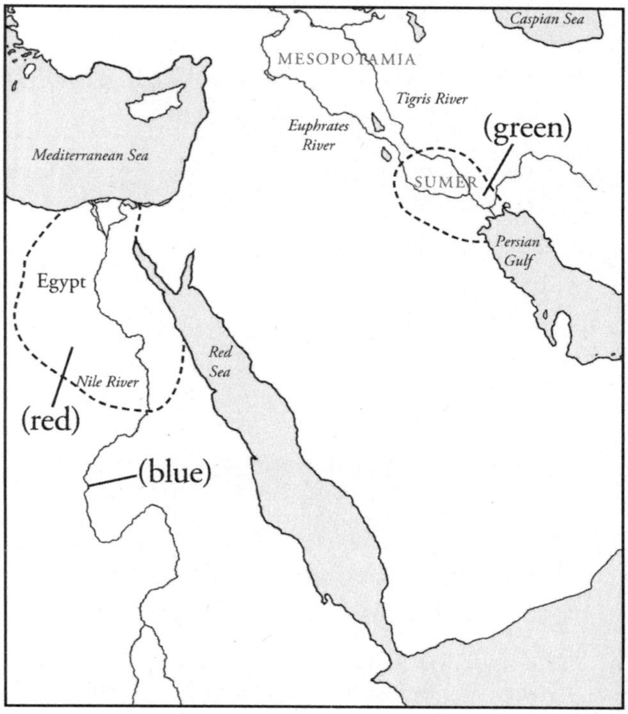

1. **Open to Student Page 8 and tear it out.**
2. **Find *Egypt* and shade it lightly in red. Remember, the White Crown King united Egypt into one country. He wore the red crown over his own white crown.**
3. **Find the *Nile River*. Trace it in blue. Many people in Egypt lived along the Nile River and near the Nile Delta.**
4. **Find *Sumer* and shade it lightly in green. Egypt and Sumer are the two countries where people first learned to write.**
5. **When you finish, place the completed map in your history notebook.**

Activities

Choose from the following activities:

- ☐ Coloring Page: Carving Hieroglyphs
- ☐ Storytelling & Craft: Make Cuneiform Tablets
- ☐ Storytelling & Craft: Make a Hieroglyphic Scroll
- ☐ Science: Clay Tablet vs Paper Scroll
- ☐ Research Skills: Ask students to look up one or more related topics in their history encyclopedia or another reliable source. Read the entry together and look at the pictures. Topics could include *hieroglyphs, cuneiform, papyrus, Mesopotamia*, and *Sumer*.

Coloring Page: Carving Hieroglyphs (Student Page 9)

This Egyptian scribe is carving hieroglyphs into stone.

Storytelling & Craft

MAKE CUNEIFORM TABLETS

Writing into stone was very difficult. The Sumerians figured out how to carve their cuneiform onto tablets of wet clay.

MATERIALS:

- air-dry clay or salt dough (recipe on page 414)
- cuneiform alphabet guide (Student Page 10)
- paper and pencil
- small wedge (a thick screwdriver would work well)
- drinking straw and heavy string (optional)

DIRECTIONS:

1. On the paper, write the message you will be translating and carving into the clay tablet. You could write your name to make a door plaque, or a simple message to a friend or relative. Use your imagination to determine what you would like to carve.
2. Roll the clay so it is a flattened rectangle, about ½-inch to ¾-inch thick. Trim the edges to make them neat.
3. Using your wedge, and following the cuneiform alphabet guide, carve your message into the clay tablet. The further you dig the wedge into the clay, the wider the mark will be. This is how the triangle shapes in the cuneiform alphabet were made by Sumerians. To make a narrower mark, press the wedge in the clay with less pressure. Alternatively, if you are using a screwdriver, press the edge into the clay, wiggle it a little bit from side-to-side to get the triangle shape, then drag it straight through the clay to get the straight line. You might want to practice this before beginning your message. Once you are comfortable making the marks, re-roll the clay and begin carving your message.
4. If you want to hang your tablet, use a straw to punch a hole in both top corners.
5. Let the clay tablet dry according to package directions.
6. If you punched holes into your tablet in order to hang it, you will need to thread some heavy string through the holes, and hang.

Storytelling & Craft

MAKE A HIEROGLYPHIC SCROLL

Ancient Egyptians invented papyrus paper and ink. In this activity, you can write your own message in hieroglyphics and store it in a scroll, just like the Ancient Egyptians did.

MATERIALS:

- paper and pencil
- firm bristled paint brush
- hieroglyphic letter guide (Student Page 10)
- water-soluble ink OR paint
- a tea bag (black tea)
- tape
- lightweight paper, several sheets, OR a brown craft paper roll OR for more historical realism, buy some sheets of papyrus paper from a craft/art supply store
- 2 wooden dowels or sticks (slightly longer than the paper); if you do not have dowels, you can use 2 empty paper towel rolls.
- twine (optional)

DIRECTIONS:

1. Using Student Page 10, plan the hieroglyphs you will use on your scroll, writing them on paper for reference. Remember to use the sounds in the words, not the actual letters (that means "Christopher" would be spelled "Kristofer"). You don't need to include silent letters (that means "night" would be spelled "nit"). If you really want to be authentic, search the internet for "Egyptian hieroglyphs."
2. If using a brown craft paper roll, cut one 22" to 32" length for your scroll, and a second length for use in the next activity. OR If using regular paper, "paint" 3 to 4 sheets of paper with a damp black tea bag. Let the paper air dry for 2-3 hours or bake in the oven at 200 degrees Fahrenheit for 2-3 minutes under adult supervision (don't overcook your paper or it will become brittle and you will not be able to roll it into a scroll).
3. Set one piece of paper to the side for use in the next activity.
4. Tape the remaining sheets of browned paper together to make one long strip. (You can skip this step if you are using craft paper roll, since it is already one long piece)
5. Using a stiff brush (the Egyptians used reeds with one end crushed into a brush) and the ink, or paint, paint the hieroglyphs onto your scroll. Also make some marks on the single piece of paper; this will be used in the next activity, and the marks do not need to be neat or mean anything.
6. Let the ink dry completely.
7. Put the single piece of paper to the side to use with the next activity.
8. Tape each end of the long paper strip onto a thin craft dowel, stick, or paper towel roll.

9. Roll each end of the scroll toward the center, ensuring roughly half the paper ends up on each end. The 2 dowels or sticks should meet in the center.
10. If you like, tie the scroll closed with twine.

Classroom Adaptation: To simplify the activity, you may want to use water-soluble markers instead of paint and skip browning your paper. Just use any blank paper. Also, you can pair students together for this activity. Once students have written a message on their scroll and rolled it back up, have them swap scrolls with a partner to translate the message.

Science

CLAY TABLET VS PAPER SCROLL

Do you think more ancient clay tablets or paper scrolls have survived to this day? In this demonstration, we will test which type of writing surface is more durable.

MATERIALS:

- Student Page 11
- pencil
- a sink
- an oven
- baking sheet
- a trivet or similar (to protect countertop)
- the single piece of paper from the "hieroglyphic scroll" activity above
- clay tablet from the "cuneiform tablet" activity above

DIRECTIONS:

Pull out a pencil and Student Page 11 to prepare for the demonstration.

Flood Simulation:

Explain to students: first we will simulate a flood, since the Egyptians lived next to the Nile.

1. Fill the kitchen sink with water. Put the clay tablet in. Now, roll up the paper scroll and put it in. Let them both sit for 5-10 minutes.
2. Pull the scroll and the tablet out of the water and document the results. Younger students should answer the discussion questions orally, then use the key on the Student Page to document the level of damage. Older students should write out answers to the questions on the back of their Student Page.

Flood discussion questions:

What does the scroll look like?
Can you still read it?
What damage has been done?
What does the clay tablet look like?

Can you still read it?
What damage has been done?

Dry Arid Desert Simulation:

Explain to students: This part of the experiment is simulating the hot, dry conditions of ancient Egypt and Mesopotamia. The paper scrolls and clay tablets of long ago spent many years in hot, dry weather.

3. Roll up the scroll again. Have an adult put both the scroll and the tablet on a baking sheet and put them in the oven at a low temperature (not more than 200 degrees F).
4. In half an hour, peek into the oven to check on the scroll. If it is charred, turn off the oven and let everything cool. If not, let the oven run for another half hour.
5. When the time is up, have an adult remove the tablet and scroll from the oven. The clay tablet will be very hot, so let it cool for an hour before touching it again.
6. Explain to students: **Hot dry air in the oven caused any changes you might see. Hot air outside will do the same thing over long periods of time. We just sped up the process!**
7. Record your results. Younger students should answer the discussion questions orally, then use the key on the Student Page to document the level of damage. Older students should write out answers to the questions on the back of their Student Page.

Arid desert discussion questions:

Does the tablet look any different?
Can you still read it as easily as before?
Unroll the scroll and look at the print. Is it any different?
Did the paper tear or break at all when it was opened?

Extended Use Simulation:

Explain to students: The unrolling and rolling of the scroll simulates the use it might get if it were a real ancient Egyptian document.

8. Re-roll the scroll. Show it to someone (your pet, baby sibling, or parent is fine). Then roll it up again. Show it to someone else, making sure you unroll it, then roll it up again. Keep showing it to other people (if you run out of live people or animals to show it to, stuffed animals would like to see it too!), making sure you unroll it to show them the hieroglyphs, and re-roll it after looking. How many times can you roll and unroll the scroll before you start to see damage? Record your answer on the Student Page.
9. Now show the clay tablet to the same number of family, friends, and stuffed pals as you did with the scroll. This won't take as long, since there is no rolling and unrolling involved.
10. Record your results:

Extended use discussion questions:

How has the paper scroll changed after showing it so many times?

How has the clay tablet changed after showing it the same amount?

Note to Parents: If the scroll remains undamaged after the extended use simulation, send the scroll and the tablet through a second flood simulation and then try the extended use simulation again with the paper wet. Or, take the test further by building a campfire. Carefully place both the clay tablet and the scroll in the fire. The scroll will burn immediately, but the clay tablet should remain in decent shape once it cools off and the soot is wiped off.

Results:

How does the paper scroll look by the end of the experiment? Is it worn, torn, or perhaps in pieces?

In contrast, the clay tablet likely looks very much the same as it did before we began this experiment.

This activity simulated the floods and hot, dry air of the Middle East that real scrolls and tablets would have been exposed to, and the damage that might have occurred. Now you can see why ancient clay tablets lasted, in general, much longer than ancient paper scrolls.

Additional History Reading

Hands-on-History! Mesopotamia, by Lorna Oakes (Armadillo, 2013). Short explanations with images as well as 15 hands-on projects for digging deeper into the history of Mesopotamia. There is a full two-page spread on the development of writing. (Also recommended for chapters seven and eight) (RA)

Hieroglyphs, by Joyce Milton (Grosset & Dunlap, 2000) A deeper dive into the history and discovery of hieroglyphs. Kids can learn about different common symbols and practice writing messages with the accompanying stencil. (RA)

Corresponding Literature Suggestions

Casting the Gods Adrift, by Geraldine McCaughrean (Cricket Books, 2005). A suspenseful story about Tutmose, an apprentice who must decide between obeying his father or the king. Set in ancient Egypt and written by a great storyteller. (IR 4–6)

Seeker of Knowledge: The Man Who Deciphered Egyptian Hieroglyphs, by James Rumford (Houghton Mifflin, 2003). The story of the quest to understand Egyptian writing. (RA)

CHAPTER FOUR
The Old Kingdom of Egypt

Making Mummies

Read & Review

Read pages 28–31 in the text. Afterward, check the student's understanding by asking the questions below. Encourage students to answer in complete sentences whenever possible. Sample responses are provided in italics.

1. **What does embalming do?** *It preserves the body.*
2. **What did priests do to a body to make a mummy?** *They took the insides out, preserved the body with salt and spices, wrapped it in linen and put it into a coffin.*
3. **Why did the Egyptians think it was important to preserve dead bodies?** *So that dead people could go on to the next world*
4. **What did the Egyptians bury with their mummies?** *Everything a dead person would need: food, clothes, toys, games, jewelry, furniture*
5. **What was this time in Egyptian history called?** *The Old Kingdom*
6. **What do "BC" and "BCE" mean?** *"Before Christ" and "Before the Common Era"*
7. **What do "AD" and "CE" mean?** *"Anno Domini" ("The Year of Our Lord" in Latin) and "Common Era"*

Narration Exercise

Prompt the student to tell you about the lesson with the following question. Require students to answer in complete sentences.

What did you learn about mummification?

Students' narrations do not have to match the sample word for word. Write down the narration if your student is not writing independently. Good writers can write the narration down themselves. An acceptable narration may resemble:

2550 BCE

The Egyptians thought that people couldn't go to the afterworld if they didn't have their bodies. So they made mummies out of the bodies. They did this during the Old Kingdom.

OR

The Old Kingdom was when the Egyptians made mummies out of dead bodies. They put all their insides into jars and put the mummies in special coffins.

Activities

Choose from the following activities:

- ☐ Craft: Make Scented Oil (PREP)
- ☐ Role Play & Science: Make a Chicken Mummy
- ☐ Role Play: Make an Apple Mummy
- ☐ Research Skills: Ask students to look up one or more related topics in their history encyclopedia or another reliable source. Read the entry together and look at the pictures. Topics could include *Ancient Egypt, mummies, embalming, canopic jars, sarcophagi, the Old Kingdom, Egyptian religion,* and *the Egyptian afterlife.*

Craft

SCENTED OIL (PREP)

Ancient Egyptians used scented oil to make mummies, but they also wore scented oil as perfume. In this activity you make your own scented oil to wear as perfume or use in the mummification project.

MATERIALS:

- small jar with lid (an empty spice bottle works well)
- carrier oil (baby oil, coconut oil, or any oil safe for skin)
- a combination of 3-4 spices that you like (for example, cinnamon, allspice, cloves, nutmeg, etc., ground or whole)
- strainer (If using whole spices, any colander should work. If using ground spices you could use a cheese cloth, coffee filter, or fine mesh strainer)

DIRECTIONS:

1. Fill the jar to the top with your choice of spices.
2. Add the unscented carrier oil to fill the jar.
3. Set it in a sunny location for a week. Shake the jar well 2–3 times per day.
4. Strain the spices out of the oil. Repeat steps 1-4 for a stronger scent.

Note: When your scented oil is ready, complete a patch test by placing a small amount of scented oil on your wrist and waiting 24 hours to ensure you do not have an allergic reaction.

5. Use as a perfume as the Egyptians did, and in the mummy-making process in the Chicken Mummy activity.

Role Play & Science

MAKE A CHICKEN MUMMY

The ancient Egyptians were famous for making mummies. When something dies, like a chicken, it will usually rot (get smelly and covered with bacteria or mold). If we dry it out quickly, it won't rot, because without water, bacteria and mold can't grow. Salt sucks water out. So we can make our own chicken mummy using lots and lots of salt!

MATERIALS:

- 3 8.1-ounce (230 grams) cans of baking powder
- 3 16-ounce (454 grams) boxes of baking soda
- one whole raw chicken (A smaller bird will take less time and require less salt. If you can find a Cornish hen, you can mummify that instead)
- 6-10 resealable plastic freezer bags (large enough to fit your chicken)
- paper towels
- disposable gloves for handling the chicken
- rubbing alcohol (or any alcohol you may have—the Egyptians used wine)
- 12-18 26-ounce canisters of plain (not iodized) salt (This amount is approximate; you need several cups of salt each time you refill the chicken bag, so it may be more economical to purchase a large bag of salt)
- scented oil (recipe above—you can use unscented, if you prefer, and just rub the chicken with the spices after rubbing in oil)
- various spices like cinnamon, allspice, cloves, nutmeg, etc. (optional)
- water, white glue
- white linen fabric, gauze, or any other fabric you have on hand.

A note on ingredients: This project requires a lot of salt. We have provided rough estimates but the amount that you need will vary depending on the size of your chicken and the wetness/dryness of your environment. We recommend using the smallest chicken you can find to make this project a bit easier and less expensive.

DIRECTIONS:

1. Put on your gloves! Chicken (and other poultry) can harbor bacteria that can make you sick.
2. Remove the neck and package of liver, heart, gizzard, etc.
3. Wash the chicken with alcohol. Don't forget to wash inside the cavity of the chicken as well. This helps to reduce the amount of bacteria that will grow on the bird. Dry the bird as much as possible before continuing with step 4.
4. Mix half a box of baking soda with half a can of baking powder and 2 boxes of salt. The addition of baking soda and powder will increase the acidity of the salt mixture, reducing the amount of bacteria that grows. The salt mixture will also be closer to the natron salt that the ancient Egyptians used (this special salt keeps germs and bacteria away!). If you like, you can add spices to the mixture as well, to make it smell a bit nicer.
5. Pour some of this mixture into the cavity of the chicken until it is full. Then, pour some into a large freezer bag. Put the chicken in the bag, and add the rest of the salt mixture. The chicken should be completely covered. If it isn't, add more salt. Seal the bag. Put the sealed bag into a second freezer bag and seal. The salt will dry out the chicken. You need lots of it because the chicken is very wet on the inside.
6. Check the chicken every day for the first week. If the salt is wet, put on some gloves, remove the chicken from the bag, dust off the salt, and repeat steps 5-6. You will likely need to do this after one day, then again 2 days later, and 2 to 4 days after that. We have to keep changing the salt because it gets wet after it pulls the moisture out.
7. After the first week, check the chicken only once per week. If the salt is wet, put on some gloves, remove the chicken from the bag, dust off the salt, and repeat steps 5-6. Likely you will need to do this at the end of the second and fourth weeks (usually every 5–10 days).
8. At the end of the 6th week, put on your gloves, remove the chicken from the bag, and dust off the salt as completely as you can. Wet a paper towel and wipe any remaining salt off the bird. Be sure to dry it immediately afterwards with paper towels.
9. Rub the fragrance oil into the chicken, inside and out. If you are using unscented oil, you may rub spices into the chicken before rubbing in the oil.
10. Stuff the inside of the bird with fabric and spices, if you like.
11. Our dried-out chicken is safe from decay, but if it touches water or anything damp, it could start to rot again. To protect it, we'll wrap it just like the ancient Egyptians did. Tear the linen into 1-inch strips.
12. Mix white glue and water (1-2 parts water to 1 part glue).
13. Dip the strips of linen into the glue, then begin wrapping. Wrap the wings and legs separately from the body. Once that is complete, wrap the body. It should be wrapped in at least 2–3 layers. If you like, wrap a few amulets into the mummy like the Egyptians did.
14. Let it dry completely.

Classroom Adaptation: If you decide to complete this with a group, let students take turns being the "high priest" or "high priestess" who checks on the chicken in steps 7-8.

Role Play

MAKE AN APPLE MUMMY

If you don't have the time to mummify an entire chicken, try this simpler version.

MATERIALS:

- small apple
- sturdy plastic bag, big enough to fit your apple
- 16 ounces of baking soda, divided
- 16 ounces of salt, divided
- vegetable peeler
- spoon
- kitchen towel (to wipe away the salt & baking soda mixture)
- craft stick or similar (for carving into the apple)
- plate

DIRECTIONS:

1. Thoroughly mix 1 cup of baking soda and 1 cup salt together in the bag, reserving the remainder.
2. Place the bag with the mixture onto the plate and set aside.
3. Peel your apple (it's okay if there's some peel at the top and bottom).
4. Using the craft stick, or the vegetable peeler (with adult assistance), carve a rough face into the apple.
5. Put your apple into the bag, completely covering it with the baking soda and salt mixture (you can use a spoon to help with this).
6. Keeping the bag open, place the plate somewhere where it won't be knocked over.
7. In 7 days, pull your apple out of the bag and see how much it has mummified. If it's not dry, proceed to step 8. If it's mummified, you can use a dry kitchen towel to wipe away any remaining mixture and skip to step 10.
8. If the apple has not dried enough, get a fresh bag and make a fresh mixture as in Step 1.
9. Put the apple into the new bag, again covering it completely, and check on it every few days until dry.
10. Admire your apple mummy! You can display it on the plate for a good while without it smelling or attracting bugs. Do you think it's bigger, smaller, or about the same as when you started?

Note to Instructor: The apple shrivels and gets smaller as the moisture is drawn out of it by the baking soda/salt mixture. For a more thorough explanation of the science of mummification, read the notes in the Make a Chicken Mummy activity.

2550 BCE

Egyptian Pyramids

Read & Review

Read pages 32–35 in the text. Afterward, check the student's understanding by asking the questions below. Encourage students to answer in complete sentences whenever possible. Sample responses are provided in italics.

1. **What kinds of tombs did pharaohs have?** *Pyramids*
2. **What were they made out of?** *Stone* [The student can also add that they were covered with white stone and capped with gold]
3. **What was Cheops's pyramid called?** *Cheops's pyramid was called the Great Pyramid.*
4. **How long did it take to build it?** *It took twenty years to build.*
5. **How did the Egyptians build the pyramids?** *Thousands of workers built the pyramids by hand.*
6. **What does the Great Sphinx look like?** *The Great Sphinx looks like it is half lion, half man.*
7. **Did the Great Pyramid keep robbers out?** *No, Cheops's mummy and treasures were still stolen.*

Narration Exercise

Prompt the student to tell you about the lesson with the following question. Require students to answer in complete sentences.

Tell me two things you learned about the pyramids.

Students' narrations do not have to match the sample word for word. Write down the narration if your student is not writing independently. Good writers can write the narration down themselves. An acceptable narration may resemble:

Cheops built the Great Pyramid out of stone. It was supposed to keep him safe, but robbers stole his treasure anyway.

OR

The Egyptians built pyramids for their pharaohs. They thought pharaohs were gods.

Map Work: Egyptian Pyramids (Student Page 12)

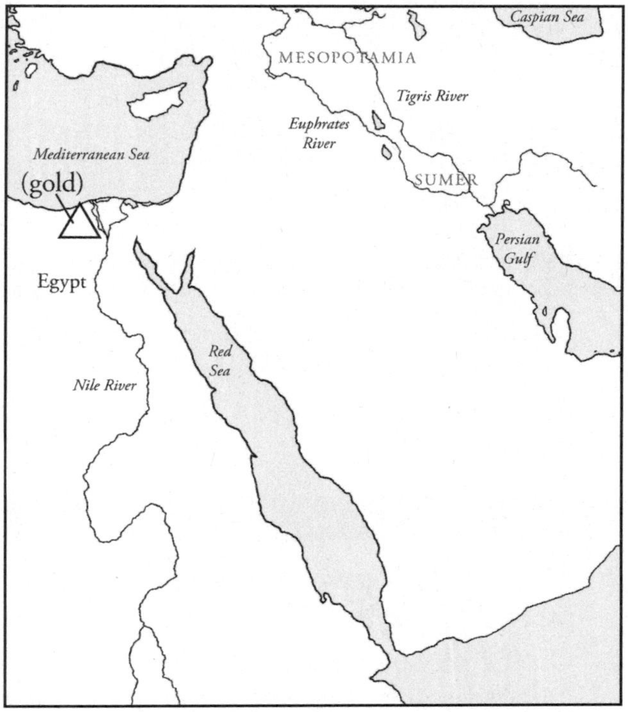

Read the instructions out loud to the student. After each step, pause and give time for students to complete the task. Provide all necessary help.

1. **Open to Student Page 12.**
2. **Find *Egypt*. Cheops's pyramid was located to the west, or on the left side, of the Nile River. On your map, draw a golden pyramid where Cheops's Great Pyramid and Sphinx were located.**
3. **When you finish, place the completed map in your history notebook.**

Activities

Choose from the following activities:

- ☐ Coloring Page: The Pyramids of Egypt
- ☐ Make a Model: Sugar Cube Step Pyramid (PREP)
- ☐ Research Skills: Ask students to look up one or more related topics in their history encyclopedia or another reliable source. Read the entry together and look at the pictures. Topics could include *Ancient Egypt*, *Pyramids*, *Cheops* or *Khufu*, *Giza*, *The Sphinx*, and *the Great Pyramid*.

Coloring Page: The Pyramids of Egypt (Student Page 13)

The pyramids of Egypt were built as tombs for pharaohs.

Make a Model

SUGAR CUBE STEP PYRAMID

Before the Ancient Egyptians built smooth-sided pyramids like the Pyramid of Giza, they built step pyramids. If you go to Egypt, you can still see ancient step pyramids standing tall.

MATERIALS:

- cardboard (a cake board works well for a clean final appearance)
- 55 square sugar cubes OR toy building bricks
- if you are using sugar cubes instead of toy building bricks: white glue or frosting

DIRECTIONS:

1. Count out 25 cubes for the base of the pyramid, 16 cubes for the second level, 9 cubes for the third level, 4 cubes for the next level, and one cube for the peak.
2. On the piece of cardboard, spread glue in the center, to form a square roughly 4 inches by 4 inches. Set the first 25 blocks on this square, in a grid of 5x5.
3. Spread glue on top of the base layer. Set 16 cubes in a 4x4-block square in the center of the bottom layer.
4. Spread glue on top of the second layer. Set 9 cubes in a 3x3-block square in the center of the second layer.
5. Spread glue on top of the third layer. Set 4 cubes in a 2x2-block square in the center of the third layer.
6. Spread glue on the final cube and place in the center of the fourth layer. Let the glue dry.
7. Optional: Take a picture of your finished pyramid. Place it in your history notebook

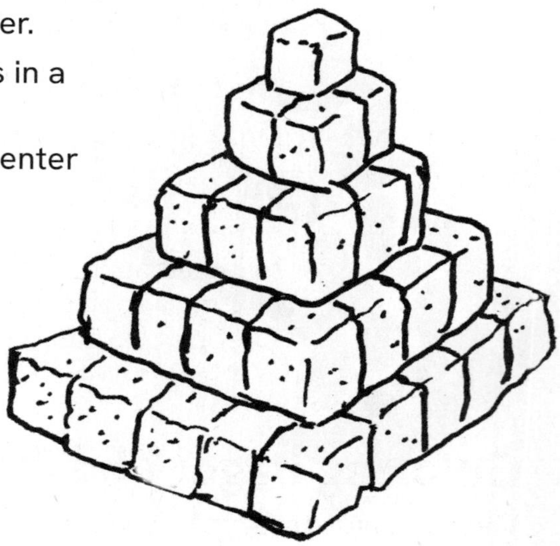

Note to Instructor: If you have 3-4 square cake pans in descending sizes, you could bake and decorate an edible step pyramid instead of using sugar cubes!

Additional History Reading

Mummies Made in Egypt, by Aliki (HarperTrophy, 1985). A very simple guide to the mummy-making process. (RA)

Mummies Unwrapped, by Victoria England (Nosy Crow, 2021). This book, written in collaboration with The British Museum, offers a step-by-step look into the mummification process. (RA)

Pyramid, by David Macaulay (Clarion Books, 1975). This book details how pyramids were built. While it may be too wordy for some younger listeners, the illustrations are fantastic and fun to flip through. (RA)

Who Built the Pyramids?, by Jane Chisholm (Usborne, 2003). An Usborne guide to life in ancient Egypt, written for first through third grade. **Out of print, but worth looking for at your local library.** (RA for all but the most advanced readers)

Curse of the Pharaohs: My Adventures with Mummies, by Zahi Hawass (National Geographic, 2004). A long but relatively simple book, written by an archaeologist and illustrated with many photos, describing his own experiences excavating in Egypt and also discussing the mythical "curse" of the mummies. An interesting appendix on "How to Become an Archaeologist," aimed at an elementary-school audience. Available used or as an audiobook. (RA 1–3, IR 4–6)

Corresponding Literature Suggestions

Pharaoh's Boat, by David Weitzman (Purple House Press, 2020). A story about Egyptian shipwrights building a boat for Pharaoh Cheops. (RA)

We're Sailing Down the Nile: A Journey Through Egypt, by Laurie Krebs, illus. Anne Wilson (Barefoot Books, 2007). A rhyming read-aloud that introduces students to landmarks along the Nile River (set in the present, but many of the landmarks come from Ancient Egypt).

Corresponding Audiobook Suggestions

Egyptian Treasures: Mummies and Myths, by Jim Weiss (Well-Trained Mind Press, 2015). The central stories on which the Egyptian culture was based for thousands of years. In addition to these myths, the recording tells a true, modern story of scientists seeking a lost pharaoh's tomb which includes information on the pyramids and the Valley of Kings. Available at welltrainedmind.com or wherever you listen to audiobooks.

CHAPTER FIVE
The First Sumerian Dictator

2330 BCE

Sargon and the Akkadians

Read & Review

Read pages 36-39 in the text. Afterward, check the student's understanding by asking the questions below. Encourage the student to answer in complete sentences whenever possible. Sample responses are provided in italics.

1. **Do you remember what "Mesopotamia" means?** You may need to prompt the student for the answer: *Mesopotamia means between the rivers.*
2. **What two rivers is Mesopotamia between?** *Mesopotamia is between the Tigris and the Euphrates rivers.*
3. **Were the cities in Sumer friends with each other?** *No, they fought each other.*
4. **What did Sargon do?** *He conquered all the city-states and made them into one country.*
5. **What was his country called?** *Akkadia* or *the Akkadian Empire*
6. **How did he keep control of it?** *He made harsh laws and put his soldiers in the conquered cities to make them obey.*
7. **What do we call it when a ruler uses an army to make sure that people obey without questions?** *A military dictatorship.* It's fine to prompt the student for this answer—this is a new concept! We'll be returning to it again.

Narration Exercise

Prompt the student to tell you about the lesson with the following question. Require students to answer in complete sentences.

What did Sargon of Akkadia do?

Students' narrations do not have to match the sample word for word. Write down the narration if your student is not writing independently. Good writers can write the narration down themselves. An acceptable narration may resemble:

The cities in Sumer all fought with each other. Sargon conquered them all. He made one empire out of them.

OR

Sargon used soldiers to make people obey. The soldiers went to cities in Sumer. They made the cities follow Sargon.

Note to Instructor: If the student uses the words "military dictatorship" in the narration, make sure he understands what this means! It isn't necessary to use this phrase in the narration since this is only the first introduction to this concept.

Map Work: Sargon and the Akkadians
(Student Page 14)

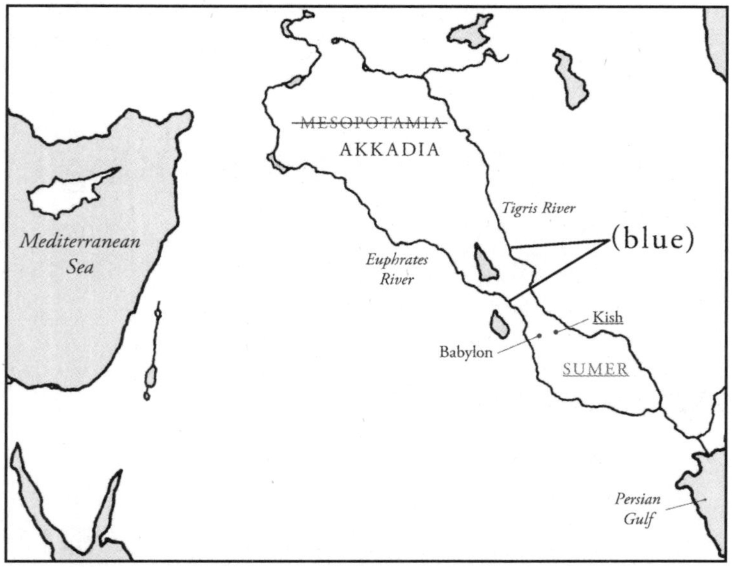

Read the instructions out loud to the student. After each step, pause and give time for students to complete the task. Provide all necessary help.

1. **Open to Student Page 14.**
2. **The area Sumerians lived in was called Sumer. Sumer was not one country, like Egypt, but was made of many city-states. Find *Sumer* on your map and underline it.**
3. **One story tells us that when Sargon was a baby, he floated down the Euphrates River in a basket. Find and trace the *Tigris* and *Euphrates* Rivers in blue.**
4. **Sargon was found at the edge of a river in the city-state called Kish. Sargon was raised in Kish, and became a servant of the king. Find *Kish* on your map and underline it.**
5. **Sargon conquered all of Mesopotamia and called his new empire Akkadia. Draw a line through the word "*Mesopotamia*," and write "*Akkadia*" to show Sargon's new empire.**
6. **When you finish, place the completed map in your history notebook.**

Activities

Choose from the following activities:

- ☐ Coloring Page: Sargon, King of Mesopotamia
- ☐ Activity Page: Sumerian Inventions Word Search
- ☐ Craft & Role Play: Make a Sumerian Cylinder Seal
- ☐ Game: The Royal Game of Ur
- ☐ Research Skills: Have students look up a related topic in their history encyclopedia or another reliable source. Read the entry together and look at the pictures. Topics could include *Mesopotamia, military dictatorship*, *Sumer*, *Sargon*, *dictators* or *dictatorships*, *Akkad*, and *Akkadia*.

Coloring Page: Sargon, King of Mesopotamia
(Student Page 15)

Sargon of Akkad was one of the world's first empire builders. His conquests united many cities under one powerful kingdom.

Activity Page

SUMERIAN INVENTIONS WORD SEARCH

Follow the instructions on Student Page 16.

Craft & Role Play

MAKE A SUMERIAN SEAL

In Sumer, very few people knew how to write their names. Instead, they signed things with special seals pressed into wet clay. Each person's seal was different so that people did not get confused.

MATERIALS:

- air-dry clay or salt dough (recipe on page 414)
- a piece of paper and pencil
- a rolling pin
- a thick crayon (alternatively you could form a cylinder out of air-dry clay)
- sculpting tool (sharp pencil, toothpick, etc.)
- play-doh or salt dough (optional)
- straw (optional)
- string or twine (optional).

DIRECTIONS:

1. Prepare your cylinder. Parents of younger students should complete this step ahead of time. If using clay, form the cylinder out of clay. If using a crayon, carefully remove the paper.
2. Plan your seal pattern on a piece of paper. Create a simple symbol that represents you: for example, you could draw a ball if you love sports or a unicorn horn shape if you like unicorns. Remember that whatever you carve onto your seal will appear backwards, so if you are using letters or numbers you have to carve them backward.
3. Use your sculpting tool to carve your design onto the cylinder. Make sure to carve the pattern deep enough so that it makes a nice impression. If using clay, allow the cylinder to dry according to the clay package instructions.
4. Use the rolling pin to roll out a small piece of clay or play-doh. Roll your cylinder seal across the clay to make your unique seal impression.
5. Draw a picture or write a note to someone special. Instead of signing your name, seal your note or picture with your clay seal, like the ancient Assyrians. Now they will know who it came from!
6. Optional: If you roll your cylinder on a small piece of clay, you can use a straw to cut a hole above the seal pattern. Cut out the clay piece and allow it to dry according to the clay package instructions. Thread a piece of string or twine through the hole. Now your seal has become a unique necklace!

Classroom Adaptation: Have students write notes to each other and sign them with their unique seal.

Game

THE ROYAL GAME OF UR

The Royal Game of Ur is one of the oldest board games in the world. It was popular in Mesopotamia. You can play a simplified version for two players using the game board on Student Page 17.

MATERIALS:

- Student Page 17
- 7 game pieces per player (you could use coins: one player uses pennies and the other player uses dimes)
- 4 craft sticks with one side marked and one side left blank. These will be your "throwing sticks."
- black, blue, and red colored pencils or crayons (optional)
- cardboard or card stock to make a sturdier game board (optional)

DIRECTIONS:

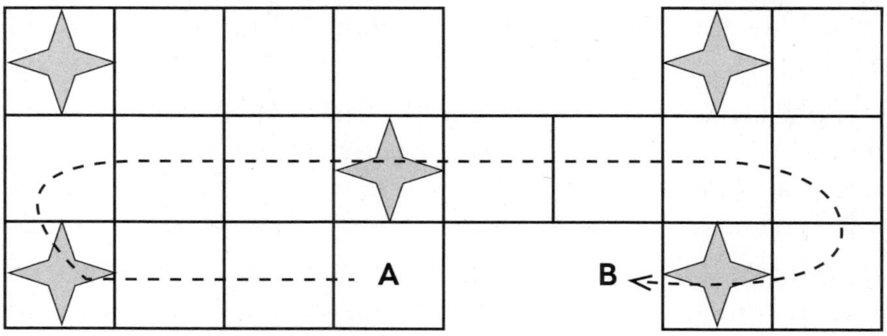

1. Pull out or make a copy of the board game on Student Page 17.
2. Optional: Color your game board with black and blue colored pencils. Paste it onto a piece of cardboard or poster board to have a sturdier board.
3. Each player tosses their throwing sticks (like you would toss a pair of dice). Count the number of sticks that land with the marked side up. The player with the higher total goes first.
4. On your turn, toss all 4 throwing sticks. Count the number of marked sides that land face up. That is the number of spaces you can move a piece. If no marked sides land face up, your turn ends without moving a piece.
5. If a marked side lands face up, choose one of your pieces to move. Move along the path shown in the illustration above (each player has their own path). You can only move a piece from the starting area onto the board if you get a total of one.
6. If you land on a space that is marked with a rosette, you can toss the sticks a second time and move again (you can move the piece on the rosette or a different piece).
7. If you land on a rosette space, your piece is safe. Your piece cannot be captured by an opponent's piece on a rosette space.
8. If you land on a space that is already occupied by an opponent's piece (except for rosettes), you can capture their piece. Their piece moves back to the starting area and the opponent has to roll a 1 to get it back onto the board.
9. To move a piece off the board, you must roll the exact number needed to land it on the finish square.
10. Once a piece reaches the finish square, it is out of the game. The first player to get all of their pieces from the starting area to the finish square wins the game.

Additional History Reading

Ancient Egyptians and Their Neighbors: An Activity Guide, by Marian Broida (Chicago Review Press, 2003). There are very few elementary-level books about Sargon and the Akkadian Empire, but this book has appropriate age-level readings and activities centered on the Akkadian people. You can look for this book at the library or purchase it used or as an ebook. (Also recommended for chapters seven, eight, and eighteen) (RA)

Ancient Mesopotamia, by Madeline Tyler (KidHaven Publishing, 2019). Covers many aspects of life in Ancient Mesopotamia, including pages dedicated to Sumer. Every page is full of photographs. (Also recommended for chapters seven, eight, and twenty-three) (RA)

The Ancient Worlds Atlas, illus. Russell Barnett (DK Publishing, 2023). This beautifully illustrated atlas has two-page spreads on many of the civilizations covered in the text, including Ancient Sumer. (Also recommended for chapters six, eight, nine, seventeen, eighteen, and twenty-two) (RA 1-3, IR 4-6)

Corresponding Literature Suggestions

Lugalbanda: The Boy Who Got Caught Up in a War, by Kathy Henderson, illus. Jane Ray (Candlewick, 2006). A retelling of an ancient Sumerian tale about a young prince who is forced to go to war. The author includes notes about how she collected and translated the story from clay tablets in Iraq. (RA) **Out of print, but worth looking for at your local library.**

CHAPTER SIX
The Jewish People

God Speaks to Abraham

2100–1900 BCE

Read & Review

Read pages 40-43 in the text. Afterward, check the student's understanding by asking the questions below. Encourage students to answer in complete sentences whenever possible. Sample responses are provided in italics.

1. **In our story, why did Terah want to leave Ur?** *He was afraid a war would start.*
2. **What was Terah's son named?** *Abram* ["Abraham" is also acceptable]
3. **Terah and his family went to another city in Mesopotamia—Haran. Why did Abram decide to leave Haran and go to Canaan?** *God told him to go.*
4. **What did God promise Abraham?** *God promised that Abraham would have a son.*
5. **Do you remember the name of Abraham's wife? It means "princess."** *Sarah*
6. **In the story, how old was Sarah when she had her baby, Isaac?** *Sarah was one hundred years old when she had her baby.*

Narration Exercise

Prompt the student to tell you about the lesson with the following question. Require students to answer in complete sentences.

Tell me three things you learned about the story of Abraham.

Students' narrations do not have to match the sample word for word. Write down the narration if your student is not writing independently. Good writers can write the narration down themselves. An acceptable narration may resemble:

Abraham lived in Ur with his father. God told him to go to Canaan. Then he had a baby when his wife was one hundred.

OR

Abraham and Sarah went to Canaan. God told them to obey him and they would have a baby. Abraham laughed because he was so old, but they had a baby.

Activities

Choose from the following activities:

- ☐ Coloring Page: The Ziggurat of Ur
- ☐ Role Play: Trade in Haran
- ☐ Research Skills: Have students look up a related topic in their history encyclopedia or another reliable source. Read the entry together and look at the pictures. Topics could include *Abraham*, *Ur*, *Ziggurat*, *the origins of Judaism*, and *the Hebrews*.

Coloring Page: The Ziggurat of Ur (Student Page 18)

Using your crayons, color the picture of the Ziggurat of Ur. This temple was originally built by the Sumerians as a place to worship their moon god.

Role Play

TRADE IN HARAN

We read in this chapter how Haran, located on the banks of the Euphrates River, was a city where many people came to trade. It was common to trade one item for another, instead of using money to buy an item.

Note to Instructor: This activity requires at least 3 students and works best with a large group of students.

MATERIALS:

- a big bowl or container to hold the trinkets (solid color, so the trinkets can't be seen)
- pencil and 2 small pieces of paper for each student
- a piece of paper that lists every trinket, with columns to record Rating 1 and Rating 2.
- one inexpensive trinket per student. Ideas include temporary tattoos, glow sticks, stickers, mini plastic animals, lollipops. Some of them should be duplicates, and at least a couple should be as unique as possible (not just the only tiger among several plastic animals, but the only tattoo or glow stick).

Low Prep Adaptation: If trinkets are not a viable option, print colorful pictures and have those be the trade items instead, keeping in mind a good variety: some cute animals, some ferocious animals, rainbows, race cars, characters. Follow the same guideline of some of them being duplicates, and at least a couple being unique.

DIRECTIONS:

1. Hand out the trinkets or pictures; it's important to do this randomly.
2. Each student should write down their trinket on a loose sheet of paper and give it a happiness rating from 1 to 5, with 5 being best and meaning they are very happy with their trinket. No one else should know how each person rates their trinket.
3. Gather the papers and record Rating 1 for each trinket, and total the ratings.
4. Tell the students they are going to trade like the ancient merchants of Haran. Explain that no one has to trade, and you can't add anything to a trade (you can't say, "I'll trade my glow stick and also share my snack at lunch," or "if you don't trade I'll be mad at you").
5. Give the students 5-10 minutes to trade.
6. When trading is complete, have the students write down the trinkets they now have, and their ratings for these.
7. Gather the papers and record Rating 2 for each one, and total the ratings.
8. Discuss the results:
   a. Compare the two ratings of the trinkets. Does a certain trinket or type of trinket have a noticeably high or low rating? How many have the same rating for 1 and 2? Which ones have the biggest difference? What are some possible reasons for being different or the same?

Note to instructor: It's unusual for all of them to be really close to the same value, but if they are, maybe it's because the class/siblings spend a lot of time together, and tend to like the same things. Differing values can be due to differing interests, rarity of item, or a popular character or theme.

   b. Is the total of the ratings higher for the randomly assigned trinkets, or is the total of the ratings higher after trading?

Note to instructor: Groups usually think they are better off after having the ability to trade (and also the ability to refuse a trade), so Column 2 is usually higher.

Joseph Goes to Egypt

Read & Review

Read pages 44–50 in the text. Afterward, check the student's understanding by asking the questions below. Encourage students to answer in complete sentences whenever possible. Sample responses are provided in italics.

1. **In the story, what did Jacob give Joseph to show that he loved him?** *Jacob gave Joseph a coat of many colors.*
2. **What did Joseph's brothers think about this?** *They were jealous; they didn't like it.*
3. **What country did Joseph's brothers send him to?** *Egypt*
4. **Joseph was the son of Jacob, and Jacob was the son of Isaac. Who was Isaac's father?** *Abraham*
5. **What did the Pharaoh dream about?** *He dreamed about seven fat cows and seven skinny cows.*
6. **What did his dream mean?** *His dream meant that seven good years would come, then seven years of famine.*
7. **After Joseph told him the answers to his dream, what did Pharaoh do?** *Pharaoh made Joseph second-in-command in Egypt.*
8. **At the end of the story, where did the Israelites live?** *They lived in Egypt.*

2100–1900 BCE

Narration Exercise

Prompt the student to tell you about the lesson with the following question. Require students to answer in complete sentences.

Tell me three things you learned about the story of Joseph.

Students' narrations do not have to match the sample word for word. Write down the narration if your student is not writing independently. Good writers can write the narration down themselves. An acceptable narration may resemble:

Joseph's brothers sold him to Egypt. He was thrown in jail. Then Joseph told the Pharaoh what his dream meant. Pharaoh made him second in command. Joseph's brothers came to get food. Then Joseph told them all to come to Egypt.

OR

Joseph's father loved him best and gave him a colored coat. Joseph's brothers were jealous. They sold him as a slave. Joseph told Pharaoh there would be a famine. He helped Pharaoh get grain and keep it. Joseph's brothers were hungry too. Joseph gave them food and they came to live in Egypt.

Map Work: Joseph Goes to Egypt (Student Page 19)

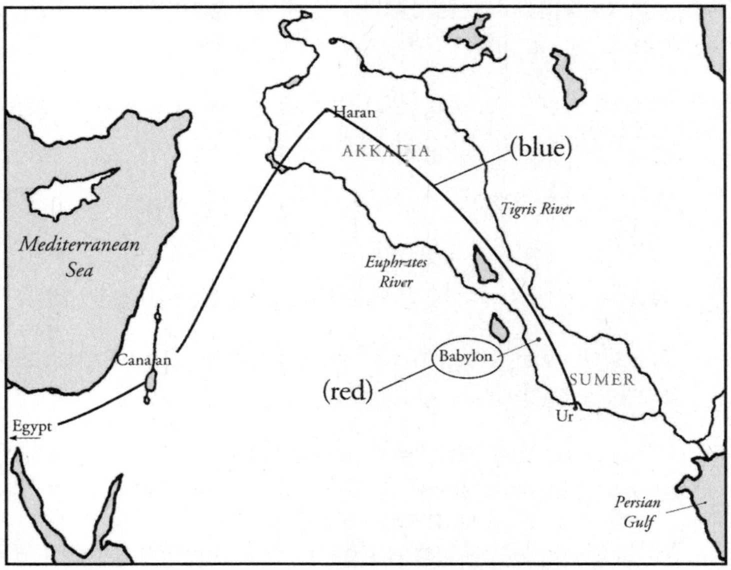

Read the instructions out loud to the student. After each step, pause and give time for students to complete the task. Provide all necessary help.

1. **Open to Student Page 19 and tear it out.**
2. **Find *Babylon* on your map. Circle the name in red, since the threat of war between Babylon and Ur was one reason Terah and his family left their home along the river.**
3. **Terah decided to move from Ur up to the city of Haran. Draw a line in blue from *Ur* up to *Haran*.**
4. **After Terah died, God told Abram to move to Canaan. Continue your blue line from Haran over to *Canaan*.**
5. **Abraham and Sarah had a child, Isaac. Isaac had a son named Jacob. Jacob had twelve sons. Joseph was Jacob's favorite son, and one of his youngest. He was sold as a slave by his older brothers and later became a governor of Egypt. Then all of his relatives moved from Canaan down to Egypt. Continue the blue line from Canaan down to *Egypt*, to show the path that the Israelites took.**
6. **When you finish, place the completed map in your history notebook.**

Activities

Choose from the following activities:

- [ ] Activity Page: The Jewish People Word Search
- [ ] Memory Work: The Twelve Sons (Tribes) of Israel
- [ ] Math: Seven Years of Famine
- [ ] Craft: Make Joseph's Coat of Many Colors
- [ ] Research Skills: Have students look up a related topic in their history encyclopedia or another reliable source. Read the entry together and look at the pictures. Topics could include *early Jewish history, Judaism, the Hebrews*, and *famine*

Activity Page

THE JEWISH PEOPLE WORD SEARCH

Follow the instructions on Student Pages 20-21.

Classroom Adaptation: Split students into groups and have each group race to come up with the answers to all of the questions to "unlock" the word search activity. Each group should have a copy of the text to refer to.

Memory Work

THE TWELVE SONS (TRIBES) OF ISRAEL

The Twelve Tribes of Israel play a significant role in the history of the ancient Middle East and the history of Judaism.

Note to Instructor: For detailed guidance on using memory work activities, see Appendix Two. The student's memory work reference page is available on Student Page 22. Below, you'll find the list of items to memorize, along with additional teaching ideas for your convenience.

Note to Instructor: Levi is not typically represented as a tribe, since the Levites served as priests and did not have their own territory. Joseph's descendants were split into two tribes, Ephraim and Manasseh (named after his two sons). Have students memorize the list of Jacob's twelve sons (including Levi and Joseph) OR the list of the tribes (remove Levi and replace Joseph with Ephraim and Manasseh).

1. Reuben
2. Simeon
3. Levi (the priests) (eliminate if you are memorizing the tribes rather than the sons)
4. Judah
5. Dan
6. Naphtali
7. Gad
8. Asher
9. Issachar
10. Zebulun
11. Joseph (or Tribe of Ephraim and Tribe of Manasseh)
12. Benjamin

Suggested Activity: Give each tribe, or son, a hand motion! OR create flashcards, mix them up, then practice putting them in order again from Reuben to Benjamin (oldest to youngest son). See how fast you can do it!

Related Reading: Read about the twelve tribes of Israel in your chosen translation of the Bible or a children's Bible. One option is *The Children's Illustrated Jewish Bible*, retold by Laaren Brown & Lenny Hort (DK Children, 2020), which has more easy-to-read abridged versions of biblical stories (RA).

Math

SEVEN YEARS OF FAMINE

During the seven years of plenty, Joseph collected grain from Egyptian farmers and stored it. He stored so much grain that the Egyptians had food to eat during the seven years of famine! How much food would your household need to survive seven lean years?

Note: Parents of younger students should complete the math ahead of time, then let their students help them scoop out ingredients. Older students can help do the math as part of the project.

MATERIALS:

- a large amount of a staple food item, such as rice, quinoa, pasta, oats, beans, or barley (use an item that you like to keep stocked in your household, as you will need at least a week's worth for your household size)

- one small bowl and one bigger bowl to measure out servings by the cup (not needed if only using packaged items like cans)
- pencil and paper

DIRECTIONS:

1. Choose a staple food item.
2. How many people are in your household? Double that number so each person gets two servings of the staple food per day, and write down the number of servings your household needs per day.
3. To see how much food that is, pour the right number of cups into the bowl or put the right number of bags/boxes/cans together. Show the day's worth of food to your student.
4. How many servings do you need for a week? Multiply the number of servings per day by 7.
5. To see how much food that is, pour the right number of cups into the bigger bowl or put the right number of bags/boxes/cans together. Compare it to the food for one day.
6. How many servings do you need for a month? Multiply the number of servings per day by 30. You can pour the right number of cups into the bigger bowl or put the right number of bags/boxes/cans together if you have enough, but you'll probably need to just picture it in your head!

Note to Instructor: For younger students, you may want to finish the activity here. Older students can move on to the final two steps.

7. How many servings do you need for a year? Multiply the number of servings per month by 12 and write this number down. Try to picture the amount.
8. How many servings do you need for seven years? Find the number of servings needed for a year (Step 7) and multiply it by 7. Try to picture the amount. If you like, draw a picture of it!

Optional discussion questions:

1. Why might it be difficult to buy and store seven years of food for your household?
2. If you bought one extra box or bag of your staple item every week for a year, how much would that cost? Multiply the cost of the item by the 52 weeks in a year.
3. How much extra food do you think you could store where you live? Is there enough room for a month's worth of food, or a year? What about seven whole years?

Bonus activity for older students: Keeping seven years' worth of food isn't practical for most people, but it's recommended to keep an emergency supply of food in case of natural disaster (anywhere from three days to two weeks). Research the recommendations for your area. What foods would you choose to keep? How would you make sure you kept a sufficient amount without anything expiring?

Craft

MAKE JOSEPH'S COAT OF MANY COLORS

Joseph's brothers were jealous of his beautiful coat. You can make your own coat of many colors at home.

MATERIALS:

- button down shirt (If oversized, it will drape down the body more. Use an old shirt you don't need any more or buy one from the thrift store)
- paint (Fabric paint is best, but tempera paint can be used—it will be more rigid. You could also use fabric markers or permanent markers. If you use permanent markers, set the shirt's color by drying it for 30 minutes before washing).
- scissors

DIRECTIONS:

1. Cut the collar off the shirt (younger students may need help with this step).
2. Paint the shirt in many colors. Let it dry completely.
3. Put it on, and pretend to be Joseph.

Alternatively, you could:

1. Cut a large paper grocery bag into a vest, instead of using a shirt.
2. Use fabric scraps instead of paint. Sew or glue them in place.

Additional History Reading

Ancient Worlds: Travel Back in Time and Discover the First Great Civilizations (DK Children, 2024). This book has illustrated depictions of ancient cities. It has a two-page spread on Ur, the city Abraham moved out of. (RA)

The Ancient Worlds Atlas, illus. Russell Barnett (DK Publishing, 2023). This beautifully illustrated atlas has a spread on Canaan and other lands discussed in the Bible. (Also recommended for chapters five, eight, nine, seventeen, eighteen, and twenty-two) (RA 1-3, IR 4-5)

Dance, Sing, Remember: A Celebration of Jewish Holidays (HarperCollins Juvenile Books, 2000). A page or two of text explains the significance and traditions of each of the eleven holidays included in the book—a crash course in basic Jewish history! Most include a story, song, activity, or recipe. **Out of print, but worth looking for at your local library.** (RA) LFA

Corresponding Literature Suggestions

A is for Abraham: A Jewish Family Alphabet, by Richard Michelson, illus. Ron Mazellan (Sleeping Bear Press, 2013). An introduction to Jewish history and customs for younger students. (RA 1-3).

God's People: Stories from the Old Testament, by Geraldine McCaughrean, illus. Anna C. Leplar (Margaret K. McElderry, 1997). Well-told tales ranging from Creation to Esther. **Out of print, but worth looking for at your local library.** (RA 1–3, IR 3–5)

Plays for Learning: Ancient Israel by L.E. McCullough (Smith and Kraus, 2001). Twelve brief plays, written for young children to read or perform, based on stories from the Hebrew Bible and the Apocrypha. Some of the plays include stories from the Midrash as well (e.g., Falsehood and Wickedness hitch a ride on Noah's ark). Clear explanations of the origins of each story. Not appropriate for parents who prefer to avoid Biblical paraphrase. (RA 1–3, IR 3–5)

The Children's Illustrated Jewish Bible, retold by Laaren Brown & Lenny Hort, illus. Eric Thomas (DK Children, 2020). More easy-to-read abridged versions of biblical stories (RA).

Corresponding Audiobook Suggestions

Bible Stories: Great Men and Women from Noah Through Solomon, as told by Jim Weiss (Well-Trained Mind Press, 2019). An exciting introduction to the Bible. Features nondenominational portraits of biblical characters as caring, understandable humans facing extraordinary situations. Available at welltrainedmind.com or wherever you listen to audiobooks.

CHAPTER SEVEN
Hammurabi and the Babylonians

Hammurabi's Code

1790 BCE

Read & Review

Read pages 51–55 in the text. Afterward, check the student's understanding by asking the questions below. Encourage students to answer in complete sentences whenever possible. Sample responses are provided in italics.

1. **Why did Hammurabi want to be king?** *Hammurabi wanted to be king so that people would be treated fairly.*
2. **What city did Hammurabi rule?** *Hammurabi ruled in Babylon.*
3. **What did Hammurabi write down on a stone monument?** *He wrote down laws.*
4. **What were these laws called?** *They were called the Code of Hammurabi.*
5. **Who had to obey these laws?** *Everyone in Babylonia had to obey the laws.*
6. **Can you tell me about one of these laws?** Allow the student to summarize any of the laws in the chapter.

Narration Exercise

Prompt the student to tell you about the lesson with the following question. Require students to answer in complete sentences.

Tell me two things you learned about King Hammurabi.

Students' narrations do not have to match the sample word for word. Write down the narration if your student is not writing independently. Good writers can write the narration down themselves. An acceptable narration may resemble:

Hammurabi lived in Babylon. He built an empire like Sargon. But he wanted to be fair.

or

Hammurabi was the king of Babylon. He made the Code of Hammurabi. These were laws for everyone to obey.

Map Work: Hammurabi's Code (Student Page 23)

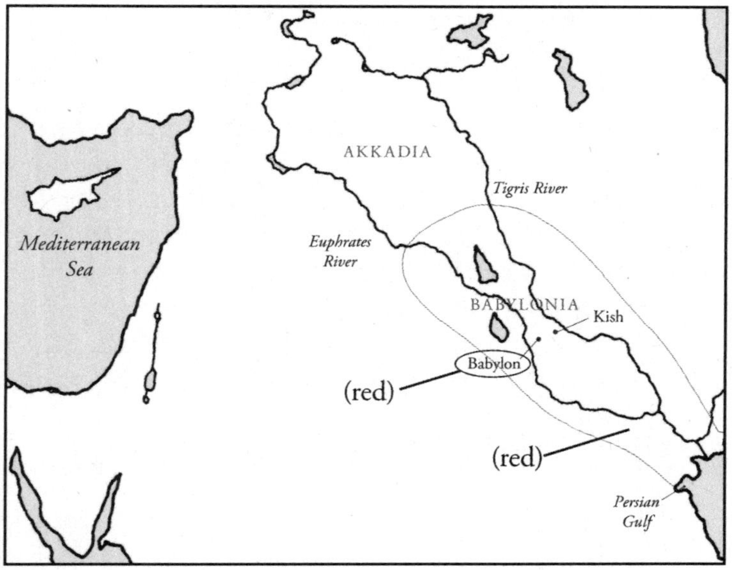

Read the instructions out loud to the student. After each step, pause and give time for students to complete the task. Provide all necessary help.

1. **Open to Student Page 23 and tear it out.**
2. **Find Hammurabi's city of *Babylon*, and circle it in red.**
3. **Hammurabi began by ruling over the city of Babylon, but he soon conquered the southern part of Mesopotamia and named it Babylonia. Find and lightly shade *Babylonia* in red.**
4. **When you finish, place the completed map in your history notebook.**

Activities

Choose from the following activities:

- [ ] Activity Page: Name That Place Crossword Puzzle
- [ ] Art: Make Your Own Law Code Stele
- [ ] Role Play: Hammurabi's Court
- [ ] Research Skills: Have students look up a related topic in their history encyclopedia or another reliable source. Read the entry together and look at the pictures. Topics could include *ancient laws, the Code of Hammurabi, Hammurabi,* and *Babylon.*

Activity Page

NAME THAT PLACE CROSSWORD PUZZLE

Follow the instructions on Student Page 24. Answers: Akkadia, Ur, Jericho, Babylon, Tigris, Kish.

ART

MAKE YOUR OWN LAW CODE STELE

A stele is a carved stone. Hammurabi had many of these markers carved to display his Law Code around his empire. This way, his people would know what the laws were and would obey them. Pretend you are Hammurabi. You need to decide on the rules that everyone in your house must follow and write them down for all to see. You can even draw a picture at the top showing someone, seated in a chair, handing them to you—just like Hammurabi received them from the god of justice, Shamash. A children's book called The Rules, *by Marty Kelley (Zino Press, 2000), might be fun to read before doing this project. This book is about the confusing or silly rules that adults teach to children.*

MATERIALS:

- a large sheet of paper (10 inches x 18 inches)
- scissors
- a saucer
- a ruler
- colored pencils or crayons

DIRECTIONS:

1. Using a saucer, or other round object, draw a curved line on the corners at the top of the paper. Use scissors to trim the pointed parts.
2. Measure down 9 inches from the top of the page and draw a straight line across the page with your ruler. The top curved portion of the page will be where you draw your picture and the bottom portion will be where you write your rules. Drawing extra lines with your ruler on the bottom portion of the page will make it easier to keep your writing straight.
3. When you're finished, hang your stele in your room so that you don't forget the rules!

Classroom Adaptation: Work together as a group to come up with a set of class rules. Create a model law code stele based on the classroom rules. Then have each student create their own stele for their family at home or for their room, clubhouse, or backyard.

Role Play

HAMMURABI'S COURT

Hammurabi was famous for setting a code of law that everyone, even the king, had to follow. In this activity you get to use Hammurabi's code to decide the punishment for various crimes.

MATERIALS:

- Hammurabi's Court cards (Student Page 25)
- Hammurabi's Court comparison page (Student Page 26)
- pencil
- glue

DIRECTIONS:

1. Cut out the cards on Student Page 25. Glue the front and back of the cards together so that one side shows the scenario and the other side shows Hammurabi's punishment.
2. Stack the cards with the scenario side facing up. Read the front side of the top card out loud.
3. You be the judge. What do you think would be the right punishment for the crime? Write your answer on the matching box on your Hammurabi's Court Student Page (younger students can dictate their answer and have an adult or older sibling write it down).
4. Once you have written your idea, flip the card over and read Hammurabi's punishment. Older students can write Hammurabi's punishment next to their own on their Student Page; younger students can paste the back side of the card to their Student Page.
5. Compare your ideas. Was your punishment similar to Hammurabi's? Which one was harsher? Why do you think that is?
6. Repeat with a new scenario card.

Classroom Adaptation: After reading out the scenario card, give students a few minutes to jot down their idea for a fair punishment. Invite a few students to share. Then read Hammurabi's actual punishment. Ask: Would your punishment change if the person on trial were your best friend? A stranger? A family member? Discuss how the students' answers differed. Does having one fixed law for everyone make things more fair or less fair? Why?

Additional History Reading

Ancient Egyptians and Their Neighbors: An Activity Guide, by Marian Broida (Chicago Review Press, 1999). There are no easy-to-locate books about Hammurabi written on an elementary level, but this book (also recommended for Chapters Five, Eight, and Eighteen) contains age-appropriate information and activities centered on the early Babylonian civilization. You can look for this book at the library or purchase it used or as an ebook. (RA)

Ancient Mesopotamia, by Madeline Tyler (KidHaven Publishing, 2019). Covers many aspects of life in Ancient Babylon, including pages dedicated to the Old Babylonian Empire. It makes the distinction between the old and later Babylonian empires clearer than other books in this category. Every page is full of photographs. (RA) (Also recommended for chapters five, eight, and twenty-three) (RA 1-3, IR 4-6)

Hands-on-History! Mesopotamia, by Lorna Oakes (Armadillo, 2013). Short explanations with images as well as 15 hands-on projects for digging deeper into the history of Mesopotamia. There is a full two-page spread on the rise of Babylon and King Hammurabi as well as references to Babylon throughout the book. (Also recommended for chapters three and eight) (RA)

Corresponding Literature Suggestions

The Lifeboat that Saved the World, by Irving Finkel (Thames & Hudson, 2017). A picture book retelling of the Ancient Babylonian flood story. Sidebars describe details about life in ancient Mesopotamia. Note: this is not the story of Noah from the Bible; it is an ancient Mesopotamian flood story with many parallels to the biblical story (RA 2-3, IR 4)

The Winged Cat: And Other Tales of Ancient Civilizations, by Deborah Nourse Lattimore (HarperTrophy, 2002). Three short tales, one of which is set in ancient Babylon. Written and illustrated by Lattimore. **Out of print, but worth looking for at your local library.** (RA 2-3, IR 4)

CHAPTER EIGHT
The Assyrians

Shamshi-Adad, King of the Whole World

1800 BCE

Read & Review

Read pages 56–58 in the text. Afterward, check the student's understanding by asking the questions below. Encourage students to answer in complete sentences whenever possible. Sample responses are provided in italics.

1. **What Assyrian king did we read about?** *Shamshi-Adad*
2. **What city did he live in?** *He lived in Assur.*
3. **What was the name of his empire?** *The Assyrian Empire*
4. **How did he build his empire?** *He built the empire through conquering other cities, through cruelty, and through fear.*
5. **How was the Assyrian king, Shamshi-Adad, different from the Babylonian king, Hammurabi?** Discuss the answer with the student: *Shamshi-Adad was a dictator who ruled by fear and cruelty. Hammurabi ruled by a code of laws.*

Narration Exercise

Prompt the student to tell you about the lesson with the following questions. Require students to answer in complete sentences.

Tell me two things about Shamshi-Adad.

Students' narrations do not have to match the sample word for word. Write down the narration if your student is not writing independently. Good writers can write the narration down themselves. An acceptable narration may resemble:

The king of Assyria was a dictator. He made people obey him.

or

Shamshi-Adad wanted to be king of the whole world. He conquered cities and was very cruel.

What happened to Shamshi-Adad's empire?

Assyria became part of Babylon.

or

Hammurabi took his kingdom.

Map Work: Shamshi-Adad, King of the Whole World (Student Page 27)

Read the instructions out loud to the student. After each step, pause and give time for students to complete the task. Provide all necessary help.

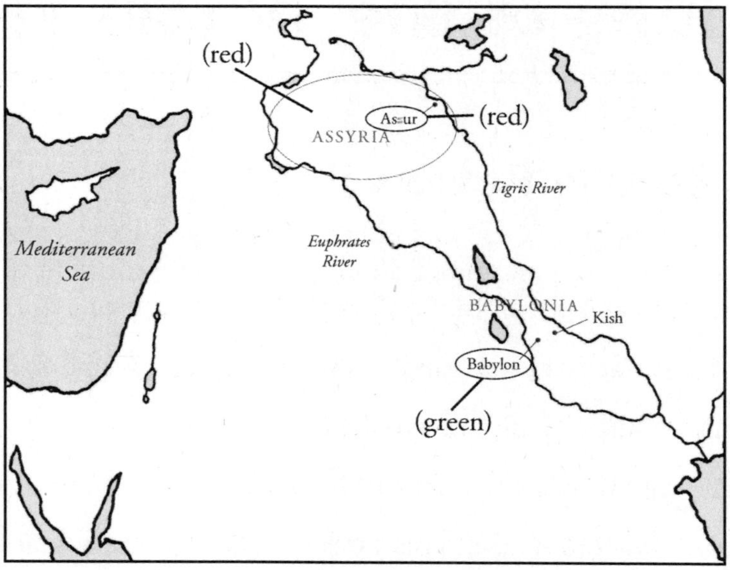

1. **Open to Student Page 27 and tear it out.**
2. **Shamshi-Adad lived in a city called Assur, in the north part of Mesopotamia beside the Tigris River. Find *Assur* and circle it in red.**
3. **Find the area that Shamshi-Adad conquered. Shade the area in red.**
4. **Assyria was in the north part of Mesopotamia. But Shamshi-Adad and the Assyrians never tried to conquer Babylon, in the south of Mesopotamia. Find the city of *Babylon* and circle it in green.**
5. **When you finish, place the completed map in your history notebook.**

Activities

Choose from the following activities:

- [ ] Role Play: Dictator for the Day
- [ ] Game: Assyrian Battle
- [ ] Research Skills: Have students look up a related topic in their history encyclopedia or another reliable source. Read the entry together and look at the pictures. Topics could include Assyria, Assur, dictatorship, and Shamshi-Adad.

Role Play

DICTATOR FOR THE DAY

Shamshi-Adad was one of the first dictators. He was not kind to the people he ruled. In this activity you will get a tiny taste of what it is like to live under a dictatorship.

Each student should be given a slot of time (15-30 minutes) when they get to be the dictator. Everyone has to do what they say (within limits - parents or instructors still have to approve of the dictator's commands). Example commands could include commanding everyone to call the dictator a special name, making everyone except the dictator hop on one foot for thirty seconds, or ordering one student to bring the dictator a glass of water or a snack.

Once everyone has had their turn, debrief the experience with the following questions:

1. What did you like about being the dictator? What did you dislike about it?
2. What did you like about being under a dictatorship? What did you dislike about it?
3. Would you want to live under a dictatorship all the time?

Note to Instructor: If you have just one student, have the student be the dictator for 15 minutes and then have a parent or instructor be the dictator for 15 minutes. For group settings or with young students, it may work better to have the instructor be the dictator the entire time. To make it more fun, the instructor could use a puppet or stuffed animal. The puppet could order students to chant a special pledge of allegiance, bow whenever the puppet passes by, give the puppet items that he asks for, etc.

Game

ASSYRIAN BATTLE

Shamshi-Adad conquered many city-states to build his empire. In this game, imagine that each card represents a city-state. Whoever controls all of the cards should be crowned Shamshi-Adad, King of the Whole World!

MATERIALS:

- a deck of playing cards

DIRECTIONS:

1. Divide a deck of cards evenly between players. Each card in your deck represents a city state that you control.
2. Each player should hold their deck face down.
3. When it comes time to "battle," each player turns up the next card on their deck, revealing the value. The player whose card has the highest value wins all of the cards in that round and adds them to the bottom of his or her deck.
4. If 2 cards have the same value, the players with the tied cards should draw another card from their deck. The person with the higher value card collects all of the cards from that round.
5. The game ends when one player has won all the cards. This player should be crowned Shamshi-Adad, King of the Whole World.

Note to Instructor: Play it like a normal game of War.

The Story of Gilgamesh

Read & Review

Read pages 58–63 in the text. Afterward, check the student's understanding by asking the questions below.

1. **Was Gilgamesh a good king, or a bad king?** *He was a bad king (although he was very strong).*
2. **When Gilgamesh's people asked Anu the sky-god for help, what did he send?** *The monster Enkidu*
3. **Enkidu was half man and half what?** *Animal*
4. **What did the trapper's son do when he met Enkidu?** *Took him home, taught him how to talk, eat, and wear clothes*
5. **When Enkidu and Gilgamesh fought, who won?** *Gilgamesh, but he was too tired to keep fighting!*
6. **What did Enkidu do to make the gods angry?** *He killed the bull of the gods.*
7. **Why did Gilgamesh decide to go see Utnapishtim, the only immortal man on earth?** *He wanted to find the secret of eternal life OR He wanted to beat death.*
8. **What is the first thing Utnapishtim told Gilgamesh to do, so that he would live forever?** *Stay awake for six days and seven nights OR Stay awake for a very long time*
9. **Did Gilgamesh stay awake?** *No*
10. **What did Utnapishtim tell Gilgamesh to do then?** *Pick a magic plant from the bottom of the sea*
11. **Who ate the magic plant after Gilgamesh picked it?** *A snake*

1800 BCE

Narration Exercise

Note to Instructor: This is a long and complex story for a young student to remember! Ask your student to tell you about Gilgamesh and Enkidu, or about Gilgamesh and Utnapishtim, but don't require her to do both. Remind her what the characters are named, since these names are strange and unfamiliar.

Tell me about either Gilgamesh and Enkidu, or Gilgamesh and Utnapishtim.

Gilgamesh was a strong king, but he was very bad. The sky god sent a monster down to punish him. The monster was Enkidu. He learned how to talk. He almost beat Gilgamesh in a fight. They got to be friends. Enkidu got sick because he killed the bull of heaven.

or

Gilgamesh was sad because his friend was dead. He went to see a man who had lived forever. The man (Utnapishtim) told him to stay awake for a week. He couldn't. So the man told him to pick a magic plant. He did, but a snake ate it, so he got old and died like everyone else.

Activities

Choose from the following activities:

- ☐ Coloring Page: Gilgamesh and the Lion
- ☐ Art: Draw a Picture of Enkidu
- ☐ Storytelling: Compose Your Own Fairy Tale

Coloring Page: Gilgamesh and the Lion (Student Page 28)

This picture is based on a carving 16 feet high, found in Assyria at the entrance of a doorway.

Art

DRAW A PICTURE OF ENKIDU

Because the story of Gilgamesh is a fairy tale, there's no one way to represent Enkidu. Although *The Story of the World* features one artist's picture of Enkidu, you can draw your own version of what you think he looked like. Remember, Enkidu was supposed to be a wildman—half man and half animal. What do you think he looked like? Did he have fur? Did he have claws? Use your imagination, and draw a picture of Enkidu.

Storytelling

COMPOSE YOUR OWN FAIRY TALE

The Epic of Gilgamesh is one of the first fairy tales. Use your imagination and write a fairy tale of your very own. Your story could be another adventure for Gilgamesh and Enkidu to embark on. Or, you could start from scratch and make up completely new characters and adventures. When you have decided what your tale will be about, tell a parent and they will write it down for you (older students can write the story down by themselves). To make your fairy tale complete, draw a picture to go with it. When you are done, be sure to place your finished story in your notebook to keep it safe.

Additional History Reading

Ancient Egyptians and Their Neighbors: An Activity Guide, by Marian Broida (Chicago Review Press, 2003). Early Assyria, like early Babylonia and Akkadia, isn't popular with the publishers of children's books, but this activity book (also recommended for chapters five and seven) contains good basic information about the earliest Assyrian people. You can look for this book at the library or purchase it used or as an ebook. (RA)

Ancient Mesopotamia, by Madeline Tyler (KidHaven Publishing, 2019). Covers many aspects of life in Ancient Mesopotamia, including pages dedicated to Assyria. Every page is full of photographs. (Also recommended for chapters five, seven, and twenty-three) (RA)

Hands-on-History! Mesopotamia, by Lorna Oakes (Armadillo, 2013). Short explanations with images as well as 15 hands-on projects for digging deeper into the history of Mesopotamia. There are references to Assyrian history throughout the book, including a two-page spread on the City of Ashur (where Assyria began), information about running the Assyrian Empire, Assyrian palaces, Assyrian furniture, Assyrian art, and more. (Also recommended for chapters three and seven) (RA)

The Ancient Worlds Atlas, illus. Russell Barnett (DK Publishing, 2023). This beautifully illustrated atlas has a two-page spread on the Assyrians. (Also recommended for chapters five, six, nine, seventeen, eighteen, and twenty-two) (RA 1-3, IR 4-5)

Corresponding Literature Suggestions

Gilgamesh the King, by Ludmila Zeman (Tundra, 1998). The cruel tyrant, Gilgamesh, learns the true meaning of friendship from Enkidu. (RA)

The Revenge of Ishtar, by Ludmila Zeman (Tundra, 1998). When Gilgamesh and Enkidu slay monsters that threaten the city of Uruk, the goddess Ishtar becomes angry. (RA)

The Last Quest of Gilgamesh, by Ludmila Zeman (Tundra, 1998). Gilgamesh sets out on a quest to conquer death. (RA)

Stone Age Tales: The Great Monster, by Terry Deary (Bloomsbury Education, 2018). A young Mesopotamian boy retells Gilgamesh stories. An easy-to-read fictional story by the author of the *Horrible Histories* series. (IR 2-4)

CHAPTER NINE
The First Cities of India

The River-Road

1900 BCE

Read & Review

Read pages 64–67 in the text. Afterward, check the student's understanding by asking the questions below.

1. **Why did ancient people use the river as a road?** Acceptable answers: *It was easier than traveling on sand or rocks; it was faster than walking or using carts pulled by cows.*
2. **Why did people in ancient Mesopotamia and India build cities near rivers?** Acceptable answers: *There was plenty of water for drinking and for crops; it was easier to send food and other things down the water; the rivers were good roads for trade; the rivers were good for fishing.*

Narration Exercise

Tell me two things about the Indus River.

People lived near the Indus River. They also used it for travel.

or

The Indus River is in India. Ancient people used the river to get around. Sailing on the river was easier than going over the mountains.

Activities

Choose from the following activities:

- [ ] Memory Work: Rivers and Their Civilizations
- [ ] Science: Friction!
- [ ] Research Skills: Have the student look up a related topic in a history encyclopedia or another reliable source. Read the entry together and look at the pictures. Topics could include *the Indus River*, *the Indus Valley civilization*, *the Harappan Civilization*, *Ancient India*, and *Arabian Sea*.

Memory Work

RIVERS AND THEIR CIVILIZATIONS

The earliest civilizations sprouted up around major rivers. Memorizing this list of important rivers and their associated civilizations can help solidify a student's mental map of the world. All of these rivers are still important today.

Note to Instructor: For detailed guidance on using memory work activities, see Appendix Two. The student's memory work reference page is available on Student Page 29. Below, you'll find the list of items to memorize, along with additional teaching ideas for your convenience.

1. Tigris and Euphrates - Mesopotamia
2. Nile - Egypt
3. Indus River - Indus Valley Civilization or Harappan Civilization
4. Yellow River - Ancient China
5. Ganges River - Mauryan Empire

Suggested Activity: Print out or purchase a paper map of the world (or a map of Eurasia that includes at least the top of Egypt). Have the student use a thick marker or pen to trace the lines of the six rivers. Using the same thick pen or marker, mark and write out the names of each river and its associated early civilization. Let the student draw one picture for each river/civilization combo. For example, near the Nile/Egypt, a student could draw a pyramid or a hieroglyph. If you don't have a large map, you can draw the pictures on Student Page 29 instead.

Related Reading: *The Ancient Worlds Atlas*, by Russell Barnett (DK Children, 2023).

Science

FRICTION

Introduce this activity with the following explanation. In this lesson, we read about how the Assyrians and the people of Ancient India used boats to travel for trading, because it would be difficult or impossible to go that far in a cart on sandy or rocky ground due to friction (an unseen force that hinders the movement of a sliding object).

This activity will demonstrate the effect of friction. Smooth surfaces, like a smooth road, have less friction than rougher surfaces, like a sandy path. Friction keeps things from sliding or moving easily.

MATERIALS:

- toy car (or small ball, such as a ping-pong ball)
- measuring tape or ruler
- cardboard or poster board for the ramp
- books (to help build the ramp)
- foil
- kitchen towel or hand towel
- pencil and paper

DIRECTIONS:

1. Create a ramp on a table or on the floor by stacking several books, placing one end of the cardboard or poster board on the books, and then stacking more books on top to hold the ramp in place.
2. Use your pencil to make a mark at the top of the ramp, in the center, so that you are always releasing your car from the same spot.
3. Release the car. Make sure you just release it; don't push it.
4. Measure the distance the car traveled and write it down, or just mark the stopping point with a small object.
5. Cover the middle of the ramp (where the car will be traveling) with foil, making sure to keep the foil smooth and the ramp at the same angle.
6. Release the car.
7. Measure the distance it traveled and write it down or mark it.
8. Cover the middle of the ramp with the towel, making sure to keep the ramp at the same angle.
9. Release the car.
10. Measure the distance it traveled and write it down or mark it.
11. When did the car go the furthest? Foil is smoother than cardboard or poster board, so it probably went a bit further than it did on the plain ramp. The towel is rougher than cardboard or poster board, so it probably didn't go nearly as far as it did on the plain ramp.

Optional extension: Can you think of other materials that might make the car go faster or slower? Try them out!

The Mystery of Mohenjo-Daro

Read & Review

Read pages 61–70 in the text. Afterward, check the student's understanding by asking the questions below.

1. **What is a citadel?** *A circular mound in the center of a city*
2. **Tell me some of the things that the people of the Indus Valley built.** *Citadels, drains, houses from mud bricks, toilets, public baths*
3. **What happened to the citadel cities?** *No one knows for sure, but they were deserted.*
4. **What did the quail decide to do, so that they could escape the hunter?** *Stay all together*
5. **Did it work?** *Yes!*
6. **Did the quail keep on cooperating with each other?** *No, they started to argue and scattered.*
7. **What did the hunter do then?** *Caught them for supper*

1900 BCE

Narration Exercise

Tell me about Mohenjo-Daro OR tell me the story of the hunter and the quail.

People in the Indus Valley built big cities. They had wells, baths, and citadels. One of the cities was Mohenjo-Daro. Then all the cities disappeared, but we don't know why.

or

The quail wanted to escape from a hunter and his net. They decided to stay together in one bunch. When the hunter threw his net on them, they all flew up together and got away. But then they started to fight with each other and the hunter caught them one at a time.

Map Work: The Mystery of Mohenjo-Daro (Student Page 30)

Read the instructions out loud to the student. After each step, pause and give time for the student to complete the task. Provide all necessary help.

1. **Open to Student Page 30 and tear it out.**

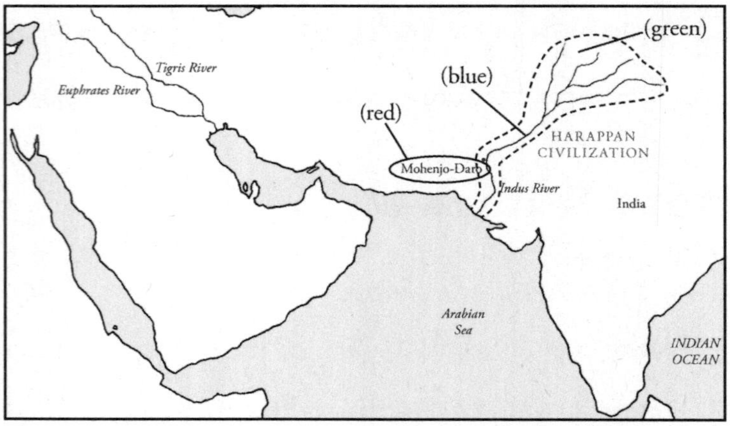

2. **On your map, find the Indus River and trace its path in blue.**
3. **Find the town of *Mohenjo-Daro*. Circle it in red.**
4. **The area around the Indus River became known as the *Indus River Valley*. You've already traced the Indus River in blue. Now color the area to either side of the river green.**
5. **When you finish, place the completed map in your history notebook.**

Activities

Choose from the following activities:

- ☐ Coloring Page: A Statue from Mohenjo-Daro
- ☐ Make a Model: Mohenjo-Daro Dwelling
- ☐ Storytelling: What Happened at Mohenjo-Daro?
- ☐ Research Skills: Have the student look up a related topic in a history encyclopedia or another reliable source. Read the entry together and look at the pictures. Topics could include *Mohenjo-Daro, Citadels, Harappan cities, the Indus Valley*, and *Ancient India.*

Coloring Page: A Statue from Mohenjo-Daro
(Student Page 31)

This picture of the Indus King is based on a sculpture found at Mohenjo-Daro.

Make a Model

MAKE A MOHENJO-DARO DWELLING

The people at Mohenjo-Daro built simple houses from bricks baked in ovens. You can practice making your own structure out of miniature bricks in this activity.

MATERIALS:

- 1lb of air-dry clay or 1lb salt dough (recipe on page 414)
- a rolling pin
- a sculpting tool or blunt knife
- white glue
- ruler
- a paint brush
- 2 thin pieces of cardboard
- wax paper
- reddish-brown paint (optional)

DIRECTIONS:

1. Roll the clay out on a piece of wax paper.
2. Using a ruler as a straight edge, cut the clay into ½-inch wide strips. Then, cut the strips into 1-inch long bricks. Let them air dry according to the package instructions.
3. For a more realistic mud-brick look, paint your building with a brownish colored paint.
4. When the bricks are dry, start building. Use your first thin piece of cardboard as a base. The houses in Mohenjo-Daro were small rectangular buildings, with flat roofs. Many of them had no windows at all. White glue can be used as cement to hold your building together. Use a piece of thin cardboard for the roof.
5. **Optional:** Take a picture of your finished project. Place it in your history notebook.

Note to Instructor: Please note that if you plan to complete all four years of *The Story of the World*, there will be more opportunities for students to build models of homes from around the world. Your student may want to keep this project and collect other model homes that she makes as she works through the final three volumes.

Storytelling

WHAT HAPPENED AT MOHENJO-DARO?

"It was a dark and windy night as the town of Mohenjo-Daro slept. Little did anyone know that this was their last night..."

No one knows what happened to the people of Mohenjo-Daro. Why did they leave their beautiful city and never return? Was it a flood? Was it an earthquake? Or was it an invading army? Only you know the answer.

Use your imagination and decide what happened to the people of Mohenjo-Daro. When you've decided what your story will be about, tell a parent and they will write it down for you (older students can write their story by themselves). Make your tale complete by drawing a picture to go with it.

For a detailed explanation on how to use creative writing prompts with younger students, see Appendix One.

Additional History Reading

The Ancient South Asian World, by Jonathan M. Kenoyer and Kimberly Heuston (Oxford University Press, 2005). For grades five and up, a good introduction to the history and culture of ancient India. Of the twenty-three chapters, five deal with the Harappan civilization. (IR 5–up)

The Ancient Worlds Atlas, by DK, illus. Russell Barnett (DK Publishing, 2023). This beautifully illustrated atlas has a two-page spread on the Indus Valley Civilization. (Also recommended for chapters five, six, eight, seventeen, eighteen, and twenty-two) (RA 1-3, IR 4-5)

The Indus Valley, by Madeline Tyler (KidHaven Publishing, 2019). Covers many aspects of life in the Indus River Valley civilization, including their plumbing innovations, daily life, and writing system. Every page is full of photographs. (RA)

Corresponding Literature Suggestions

Once a Mouse, by Marcia Brown (Aladdin, 1989). As it changes from mouse, to cat, to dog, to tiger, the pet of an Indian hermit becomes increasingly vain. (IR for strong readers)

One Grain of Rice, by Demi (Scholastic, 1997). A reward of one grain of rice doubles day by day into millions of grains of rice when a selfish raja is outwitted by a clever village girl. (RA)

The Elephant's Friend: And Other Tales from Ancient India, by Marcia Williams (Candlewick Press, 2014). A short book with eight ancient Indian folk tales told in an easy-to-read graphic novel format. (RA 1-4)

Desert Girl, Monsoon Boy by Tara Dairman, illus. Archana Sreenivasan (G. P. Putnam and Sons, 2020). A short, rhyming picture book about a girl and her family escaping drought in the desert and a boy escaping the waters of a monsoon. Set in modern-day India, it illustrates the Indian subcontinent's disparate climates. (RA)

CHAPTER TEN
The Far East: Ancient China

2600 BCE

Lei Zu and the Silkworm

Read & Review

Read pages 71–74 in the text. Afterward, check the student's understanding by asking the questions below.

1. **Why is China called "the Far East"?** *Because it is all the way to the east on the map, if you live in the Fertile Crescent*
2. **The Chinese people lived between two rivers. Do you remember the name of one of them?** The student can answer either *"The Yellow River"* or *"The Yangtze River"*; be sure to tell the student the name of the river she doesn't guess.
3. **What was their valley called?** *The Yellow River Valley*
4. **The Chinese first settled in many small villages. Do you remember the name of the emperor who united them into one empire?** *Huang Di* (be sure to supply the answer if the student can't remember)
5. **What did Huang Di's wife, Lei Zu, discover?** *She discovered the silkworm and learned how to make silk.*

Narration Exercise

Tell me about how the Empress discovered silk.

The Empress was eating in the garden. A worm fell into her tea. It was covered with threads! Then the Chinese people learned how to make silk from the threads.

Map Work: Lei Zu and the Silkworm
(Student Page 32)

Read the instructions out loud to the student. After each step, pause and give time for the student to complete the task. Provide all necessary help.

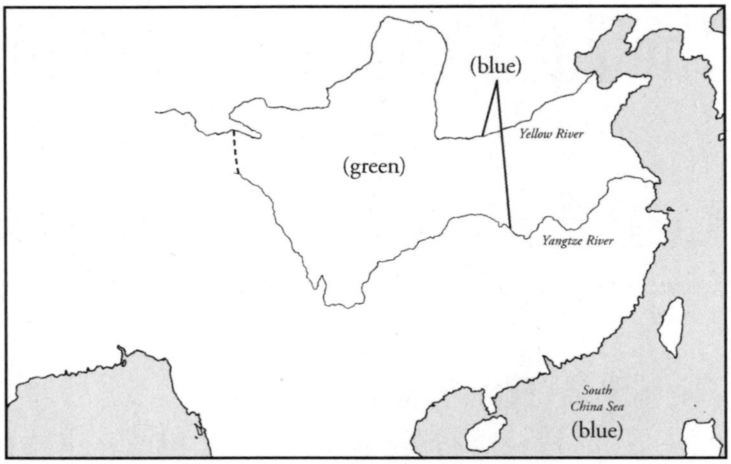

1. **Open to Student Page 32 and tear it out.**
2. **Find the *Yellow River* and the *Yangtze River*. Use a blue crayon to trace the course of the rivers.**
3. **Lightly shade the *South China Sea* in blue.**
4. **Color the area between the two rivers in green. This was called the *Yellow River Valley*, and it is where the first Chinese settled down and started to farm.**
5. **When you finish, place the completed map in your history notebook.**

Activities

Choose from the following activities:

- ☐ Activity Page: Life Cycle of a Silkworm
- ☐ Storytelling: The Story of Lei Zu
- ☐ Research Skills: Have the student look up a related topic in a history encyclopedia or another reliable source. Read the entry together and look at the pictures. Topics could include *Ancient China, the Yangtze River, the Yellow River, the Yellow Emperor, Lei Zu* or *Xi Ling-shi, Huang Di* or *Huangdi, silk*, and *silkworms*.

Activity Page

LIFE CYCLE OF A SILKWORM
(Student Page 33)

Have the student color in the pictures that show each stage in a silkworm's life. Older students can write the name of each stage by its picture. Younger students can write the stage number by each picture.

Storytelling

THE STORY OF LEI ZU

Read through the story of Lei Zu one more time. Act out the story of the discovery of silk. Make sure to include how silk was discovered and why it is special. Get creative with your props. What could you use for silk worms? Cotton balls? Pipe cleaners? What could you use for silk? A scarf? A ribbon? Fancy fabric? What about mulberry leaves? Could you draw or cut out paper leaves or collect leaves from the park? Practice your play with your group (or by yourself if you're working solo), then perform it for your class, family, friends, or record on a phone or video camera. It doesn't have to be perfect. The goal is to have fun and tell the story in your own creative way.

The Pictograms of Ancient China

1700–1200BCE

Read & Review

Read pages 75–77 in the text. Afterward, check the student's understanding by asking the questions below.

1. **What Chinese dynasty did we read about today?** *The Shang dynasty*
2. **What is a dynasty?** *A family that rules one country for years and years*
3. **How long did the Shang dynasty rule?** *Around five hundred years*
4. **During the Shang dynasty, the Chinese people began to use a special kind of writing. Do you remember what their picture-words are called?** *Pictograms*
5. **In pictograms, what do words look like?** *Pictures!*
6. **Do you remember any of the pictograms we looked at?** *Sun, water, house, bow-and-arrow, soldier*

Narration Exercise

Instead of telling me about what we read, practice drawing one or two of the pictograms from the lesson.

Activities

Choose from the following activities:

- [ ] Art: Draw Your Own Pictograms
- [ ] Research Skills: Have the student look up a related topic in a history encyclopedia or another reliable source. Read the entry together and look at the pictures. Topics could include *Ancient China*, *T'ang*, *the Shang Dynasty*, and *pictograms*.

Art

DRAW YOUR OWN PICTOGRAMS

In Ancient China, people used pictograms—simple pictures that stood for words—to record their language. In this activity, you'll create your own pictograms and see if your family or classmates can guess their meanings.

MATERIALS:

- black paint
- a thin paintbrush
- white cardboard or construction paper

DIRECTIONS:

Ancient Chinese pictograms looked like the things they stood for. What would the pictogram for "table" look like? How about pictograms for "brother," "sister," or "dog"? Make up your own pictograms and paint them in black paint on the white paper. Can your siblings or parents figure out what the pictograms stand for?

Low-Prep/Classroom Adaption: To avoid messes, you can have students work with black markers instead of paint. Play a game where each student draws a pictogram and then the rest of the class, or their group, has to guess what word the pictogram stands for.

Farming in Ancient China

Read & Review

Read pages 77–80 in the text. Afterward, check the student's understanding by asking the questions below.

1. **What valley did Chin live in?** *The Yellow River Valley*
2. **What two rivers ran on either side of the Yellow River Valley?** *The Yellow River and the Yangtze River*
3. **What crop did the ancient farmers of China grow?** *Rice*
4. **Why did Chin get up so early in the morning?** *He was going to help his father in the fields for the first time.*

1700-1200BCE

5. **What kind of ground did the rice grow in?** *Wet ground*
6. **What was Chin supposed to do for his father, first thing in the morning?** *Find out whether his father was well, and whether he needed food or water*
7. **What story did Chin's grandfather tell?** *About a time when the Yellow River flooded*

Narration Exercise

Tell me about Chin and his family's farm.

Chin lived in ancient China. He helped his father grow rice. The rice grew where the river flooded.

Activities

Choose from the following activities:

- [ ] Sequencing Events: Farming in Ancient China
- [ ] Research Skills: Have the student look up a related topic in a history encyclopedia or another reliable source. Read the entry together and look at the pictures. Topics could include *Ancient China, the Shang Dynasty, the Yellow River*, and *rice farming.*
- [ ] Field Trip Idea: Take your student on a tour of a local farm. If there are rice farms in your area, go to one of those. Otherwise, your student can still learn a lot about the farming process from any local farm.

Sequencing Events

FARMING IN ANCIENT CHINA

This activity introduces sequencing (putting events in order) and is designed for younger students. We recommend completing it if you plan to complete later sequencing activities in the book, as they build and become slightly more complicated throughout the year. Older students may be able to complete later sequencing activities without this introduction, but younger students may need more scaffolding.

You can use toys as props if you like, but no supplies are required; the student can just act out the events.

DIRECTIONS:

1. Say: **We're going to act out three things Chin did in the lesson, using the words *first, next,* and *finally* to help us remember.**
2. ***First,* Chen fed the animals** (student pretends to reach into a bucket and toss food to the animals.)
3. ***Next,* he pulled weeds out of the field** (student bends over and pulls imaginary weeds with exaggerated motions.)
4. ***Finally,* he got to eat a good lunch** (student takes big bites of imaginary food.)
5. Repeat steps 2, 3, and 4.
6. See if the student can now fill in the blanks: the teacher says **"first, Chen -"** and lets the student fill in *"fed the animals."* Repeat for each step, prompting as needed.

Additional History Reading

All About China: Stories, Songs, Crafts and Games for Kids (Tuttle Publishing, 2018) by Allison "Aixin" Branscombe. This book has lots of great information about China's geography and culture, modern and ancient. There is a timeline with a quick overview of each of the major dynasties, as well as recipes, games, activities, and stories. (Also recommended for chapter thirty-nine) (RA)

Ancient China, by Dale Anderson (Raintree, 2005). One of the "History in Art" series, this book discusses how historians can use art as a source, and then briefly covers the histories of four dynasties (Shang, Zhou, Qin, and Han), examining artifacts from each era. **Out of print, but worth looking for at your local library.** (RA 1–3, IR 3–6)

DK Eyewitness Books: Ancient China, by Arthur Cotterell (DK Kids, 2005). Packed with information and beautiful photographs of actual clothing, weapons, statues, and more.

D is for Doufu: An Alphabet of Chinese Culture, by Maywan Shen Krach (Shen's Books, 2000). An introduction to elements of modern and ancient Chinese culture. (RA)

Corresponding Literature Suggestions

Chinese Children's Favorite Stories: Fables, Myths and Fairy Tales by Mingmei Yip (Tuttle Publishing, 2020). Easy-to-read illustrated adaptations of popular Chinese stories for children. (RA)

The Master Swordsman—The Magic Doorway: Two Legends from Ancient China, by Alice Provensen (Simon & Schuster Books for Young Readers, 2014). A very entertaining picture book about the wiles of a master teacher and a master artist. **Out of print, but worth looking for at your local library.** (RA 1–2, IR 1–3)

The Story About Ping, by Marjorie Flack (Penguin Young Readers, 2000). A classic children's story; Ping is an adventurous duck who lives on the Yangtze River. (RA, possible IR for some advanced readers)

The Weather's Bet, by Stephen Cowan, illus. Ed Young (Philomel Books, 2020). This rhyming picture book retells Aesop's fable "The Wind and The Sun" and incorporates Chinese seal character pictograms of heavenly elements into each illustration. (RA 1-3)

3500 BCE

CHAPTER ELEVEN
Ancient Africa

Ancient Peoples of West Africa

Read & Review

Read pages 81–84 in the text. Afterward, check the student's understanding by asking the questions below.

1. **Do you remember what a continent is?** *A large piece of land with many countries on it*
2. **What continent is the Nile River in?** *Africa*
3. **Do you remember the name of the large desert in North Africa?** *The Sahara Desert*
4. **Was the Sahara Desert always hot and sandy?** *No, once it had water and grass and animals in it.*
5. **What did archaeologists find when they dug down into the hard, dry dirt of the Sahara?** *Pollen, seeds, bones of animals, turtle shells*
6. **Why did the people of ancient Africa go south?** *Because the Sahara began to dry up.*

Narration Exercise

Tell me three things you learned about ancient Africa.

Answers may vary but may include any of the following facts:

The Nile River is in Africa. The Sahara Desert is in Africa. The Sahara Desert used to be grassy and have water in it. People in Africa had to go south when their land dried up. Archaeologists found seeds and animal bones in the desert. People in Africa made cave paintings.

Map Work: Ancient Peoples of West Africa
(Student Page 34)

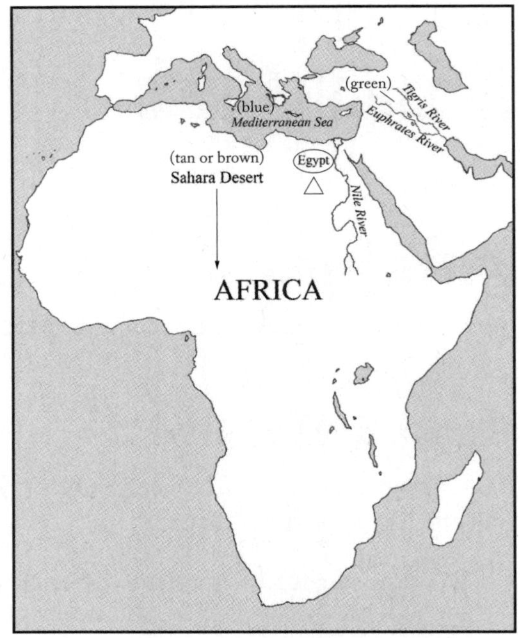

Read the instructions out loud to the student. After each step, pause and give time for the student to complete the task. Provide all necessary help.

1. **Open to Student Page 34 and tear it out.**
2. **On your map, put your finger between the Tigris and Euphrates Rivers. The area between the rivers is called "*Mesopotamia.*" Color this area green. Nomads first settled here.**
3. **Now put your finger on Mesopotamia and go left—that's west on your map. You'll run into a big sea. What is this sea called? *The Mediterranean Sea.* Color it blue.**
4. **Follow the shore of the Mediterranean Sea down to the Nile River. Circle the label on the map which identifies *Egypt*. Draw a little *pyramid* next to the name "Egypt."**
5. **Move your finger to the left from the Nile River and find the area marked "Sahara Desert." First, color the area in tan or brown.**
6. **Now look at the entire continent of *Africa*. Draw an arrow down from the Sahara Desert into the rest of Africa to remind you that the people and animals that lived in that region migrated south to escape the growing desert. The Sahara Desert became a huge divide. People lived in Egypt and along the Mediterranean Sea and people lived below the Sahara in the rest of Africa, but they didn't talk to each other or interact for a long time because of the treacherous desert between them.**
7. **When you finish, place the completed map in your history notebook.**

Activities

Choose from the following activities:

- ☐ Science: Erosion
- ☐ Craft: Sand Art
- ☐ Cooking: African Recipes
- ☐ Research Skills: Have the student look up a related topic in a history encyclopedia or another reliable source. Read the entry together and look at the pictures. Topics could include *Ancient Africa, the Sahara Desert, the history of West Africa, desertification,* and *oases*.

Science

EROSION

The Sahara Desert is one of the largest deserts in the world—and it's still getting bigger! One reason it keeps growing is erosion. Erosion happens when wind or water carries away the top layer of soil. Without this rich topsoil, plants can't grow, and the land begins to dry out. Let's take a closer look at how erosion works—and why plants are so important for protecting the land.

MATERIALS:

- 2 paper plates or trays
- loose dirt or soil (from your yard is fine!)
- a patch of sod (you can purchase from a garden center, nursery, or home improvement store, or cut out a small piece of earth from your yard that has grass, weeds, or other plants growing in it)
- cup of water
- measuring cup or spoon (optional for controlled pouring)

DIRECTIONS:

1. Place a large pile of loose dirt on your first plate (there should be minimal to no vegetation or rocks in this pile).
2. On the second plate, place your small patch of sod.
3. The first plate represents land without plants (which happens when too many trees are cut down or too many animals are eating the same grass). The second plate represents land with plants growing on it.
4. Pour a glass of water on the first mound and observe what happens. Then pour a glass of water onto the sod and observe what happens. How does the first plate change? How does the second plate change?
   - On the first plate, the water should start washing away the dirt, making little streams and muddy puddles.
   - On the second plate, the plant cover will slow the water down. There should be much less dirt moving or erosion.

Note to Instructor: Complete the activity with a simple explanation of erosion. For example: **Erosion happens when wind or water moves dirt away. If there are no plants, the dirt washes away, and the ground can start to dry out and get empty. When plants grow, their leaves and roots help hold the dirt together, and the ground stays strong!**

Craft

SECRETS OF THE SAHARA SAND ART

To celebrate learning about the Sahara desert, let's play with some sand and make a desert in a jar!

MATERIALS:

- small clear plastic bottle, spice jar, or baby food jar.
- colored play sand
- small funnels or paper cones
- spoon or scoop
- items from around the house to represent what archaeologists found deep in the Sahara:
    - for bones: dry elbow noodles, small white beads, dry rice, or plastic dinosaur bones (from party stores)
    - for turtle shells you could use pistachio shells
    - for pollen and seeds you could use birdseed, quinoa, millet, or whole spices like fennel and coriander
    - for plant remains you could put in tiny bits of green moss or tiny pieces of twigs.
- hot glue or tape

DIRECTIONS:

1. Place your archaeological finds at the bottom of your clear container. These are going to be covered up by the layers of sand!
2. Use spoons or funnels to pour layers of different colored sand into the plastic container. Alternate the colors to make "stripes" of color, like desert layers. Gently tap the container after each layer to settle the sand.
3. Add a lid and secure it with hot glue or tape.
4. Can you see the evidence of life at the bottom of the layers of sand? Does it make a difference if you look from the side or the bottom? Or have they been completely covered up by the desert sand above?

Cooking

AFRICAN RECIPES

While we don't have any recipes from ancient West Africa, we do know what foods grew in the area long ago. These foods include black-eyed peas, watermelon, yams, okra, tamarind, kola nut, sorghum, pearl millet, and African rice.

Below are a few recipes that are popular in West Africa today and that use crops that Ancient Africans may have eaten. Take note that since people across the world have been sharing foods and recipes for thousands of years, some of the ingredients in these modern African dishes would not have been available to ancient Africans.

Note to Instructor: There is an additional cooking activity for this chapter in the "Anansi and the Make-Believe Food" lesson. You may want to review both activities and choose one to complete, or prepare extra plantains to use later in the "African Taste-Test" activity.

Sorghum Porridge

Sorghum is a grain native to West Africa. In this recipe you can make a breakfast porridge out of this ingredient.

INGREDIENTS:

- 1 cup sorghum
- 2 cups milk
- 1 cup water
- blender
- flavoring of choice: sugar, maple syrup, or honey
- toppings of choice: traditionally it is served with cinnamon and peanut butter, but you can try it with whatever toppings you typically enjoy on your porridge.

DIRECTIONS:

1. Add the sorghum to a blender and blend or pulse until it becomes a coarse flour.
2. Add the sorghum with all the other ingredients into a small pot.
3. Heat until it comes to a low boil. Reduce heat to low and allow it to simmer for about 25 minutes, stirring occasionally.
4. Take the porridge off the heat and let it sit for 5 minutes (it will thicken some more).
5. Eat like a breakfast porridge! You can add yogurt, fruit, or other toppings.

"Red Red" Black-Eyed Pea Stew

Red Red Stew is a popular West African dish made with black-eyed peas, tomatoes, and spices. It's called "Red Red" because of its rich red color from palm oil and tomatoes—delicious, hearty, and full of flavor! Tomatoes are not native to West Africa, but black-eyed peas are!

INGREDIENTS:

- 2 14.5 oz cans of black-eyed peas
- ½ cup palm oil or another cooking oil
- 1 onion
- 1 tablespoon of minced ginger or ginger paste
- ½ tablespoon of minced garlic
- 2 tablespoons of tomato paste

- 1 can of diced tomatoes (even though this stew has a tomato-based broth, tomatoes originated in South America and were not available in Western Africa until the 19th century)
- 1 tablespoon of paprika
- 2-3 cups of chicken stock
- 2-3 green onions, chopped
- salt and pepper
- fried plantains or cooked rice to serve with the stew

DIRECTIONS:

1. Heat oil in a large saucepan. Sauté the onions over medium-high heat until they are caramelized, scraping any browned bits off the bottom of the pot.
2. Add in the tomato paste, canned tomatoes, minced ginger, minced garlic, and paprika, and cook for about 60 seconds, stirring thoroughly.
3. Add in chicken stock and let it cook for 10 minutes.
4. Add the beans and green onions. Let everything simmer for about 15 minutes. If it becomes too thick, add more stock or water.
5. Adjust seasoning to taste. Serve with fried plantains and/or rice.

Fried Plantain

Plantains are not native to Africa; they come from Southeast Asia. Some historians believe that they were introduced to Africa by the Portuguese in the Middle Ages. Other historians believe that plantains came to Africa thousands of years ago. Either way, they are a staple food in West Africa today.

INGREDIENTS:

- ¼ cup cooking oil
- 1 plantain

DIRECTIONS:

1. Preheat the oil in a large skillet over medium high heat.
2. Peel and cut the plantain into rounds, a bit thicker than ¼″.
3. Very carefully, fry the pieces till the edges are very lightly golden brown. Flip them over, and fry the other side. As a guideline, one minute per side should be sufficient. Don’t let them get too dark.
4. Place plantains on a plate lined with a paper towel to absorb excess oil. Serve immediately.

3500 BCE

Anansi and Turtle

Read & Review

Read pages 84–88 in the text. Afterward, check the student's understanding by asking the questions below.

1. **What are yams like?** *Sweet potatoes*
2. **Why didn't Anansi want to share with Turtle?** *He was too hungry!*
3. **What did Anansi tell Turtle to do before he ate?** *Wash his hands*
4. **Where did Turtle set his supper table when Anansi came to visit him?** *Under the water*
5. **How did Anansi get down to the bottom of the water?** *He put rocks in the pockets of his coat.*
6. **What did Turtle tell him to do?** *Take his jacket off before he ate*
7. **What happened when Anansi took his coat off?** *He popped back up to the surface of the water!*

Narration Exercise

Tell me the story of Anansi and Turtle.

Anansi the Spider didn't want to share his supper with Turtle. He told Turtle to keep washing his hands until the supper was all gone. Then Anansi went to see Turtle. Turtle didn't want to share either! He put his supper at the bottom of the river. Anansi couldn't get down to the bottom to eat it!

Activities

Choose from the following activities:

- ☐ Coloring Page: Anansi and Turtle
- ☐ Craft: Make Anansi the Spider
- ☐ Craft: Make Anansi's Friend, Turtle
- ☐ Storytelling: Act out an Anansi the Spider Story

Coloring Page: Anansi and Turtle (Student Page 35)

Color the picture of Anansi being tricked by Turtle.

Craft

MAKE ANANSI THE SPIDER

Bring Anansi the Spider to life with this craft activity! If you like, you can use the Anansi that you create in this activity to recreate an Anansi story (see the "Act out an Anansi the Spider Story" activity below).

MATERIALS:

- 1 1″ styrofoam ball
- 1 2″ styrofoam ball
- glue
- scissors
- googly eyes
- paint
- pipe cleaners
- a toothpick

DIRECTIONS:

1. Paint (with brush or spray paint) both styrofoam balls. Let them dry.
2. Attach the smaller ball (head) to the larger ball (body) using part of a toothpick and/or glue.
3. Cut the pipe cleaners into 8 appropriate lengths. Attach 4 per side to the body of the spider and shape them to look like legs.
4. Glue on the eyes and draw or paint a mouth.

Craft

MAKE ANANSI'S FRIEND, TURTLE

If you like, you can use Turtle, along with the Anansi you created in the prior activity, to recreate an Anansi story (see the activity below).

MATERIALS:

- 8.5″x11″ sheet of brown paper
- 8.5″x11″ sheet of green paper, or enough green paper to make:
  - 5 strips of green paper, 1.5" by 3"
  - 1 strip of green paper, 1" by 2"
- small bowl or saucer for tracing
- glue stick
- ruler
- scissors
- crayons or colored pencils

DIRECTIONS:

1. Fold the brown piece of paper in half from bottom to top.

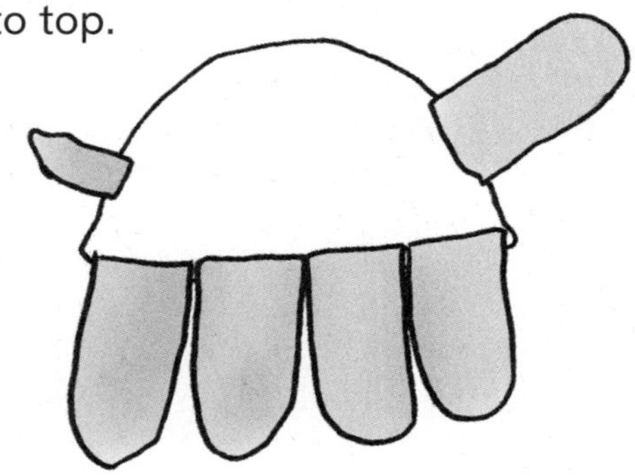

2. Take the bowl or saucer and put it about halfway over the closed side of the paper and trace a semi-circle.
3. Keeping the paper folded, cut along the trace line.
4. Now cut across the fold line so you have 2 pieces; these will form your turtle's shell.
5. Measure and cut the strips of green paper as above.
6. Take the 5 strips of 1.5″ by 3″ green paper and use scissors to round one end.
7. Take the 1″ by 2″ piece of green paper and cut one end down to make a pointy tail.
8. Make the legs by gluing 4 of the large green strips to the bottom of one of the brown pieces of paper.

9. Make the face by gluing the fifth large strip in about the 2 o'clock position, pointing it a bit upwards.
10. Glue the tail on.
11. Glue the second half of the shell on top.
12. Add eyes and a mouth with your crayons or colored pencils.
13. Alternating sides, bend each leg upward so that your turtle has 2 legs on each side. Your turtle can stand!
14. If you like, you can add a pattern to your shell.

Storytelling

ACT OUT AN ANANSI THE SPIDER STORY

Use the turtle and spider you created in the previous activities to bring an Anansi story to life! If you did not make a turtle and a spider craft, you can use stuffed animals or action figures instead. Choose a tale that we read in this chapter or one of the tales found in the Literature List. Share your performance with classmates, siblings, or grandparents, or record it on video to keep as a fun memory.

Classroom Adaptation: Read 1-3 short Anansi the Spider stories to the class. Place students in groups and have them create a short performance of either a story they just heard or their own made-up Anansi story.

Anansi and the Make-Believe Food

Read & Review

Read pages 88-92 in the text. Afterward, check the student's understanding by asking the questions below.

1. **Do you remember the three kinds of food that Anansi found in the villages?** If necessary, prompt the student for the answers: *Yams, plantains, and rice*
2. **What do yams look like?** *Potatoes*
3. **What do plantains look like?** *Bananas*
4. **Why did Anansi keep on leaving the villages to go to the next one?** *Because he thought he would find something better*
5. **Did he get a wonderful meal at the end of the story?** *No, he didn't get anything!*
6. **What was the moral of this tale?** *Don't be greedy—eat what you're given.*

Narration Exercise

Instead of a narration exercise, draw a picture of Anansi the Spider with a banana, a potato, and several grains of rice. Use your imagination - remember that the food was talking to Anansi!

Activities

Choose from the following activities:

- [ ] Cooking: African Foods Taste Test
- [ ] Storytelling: If your student is particularly interested in Anansi stories, read a few more stories (there are suggestions in this chapter's reading list).

Cooking

AFRICAN FOOD TASTE TESTS

In the story "Anansi and the Make-Believe Food," Anansi tries lots of delicious ingredients from Africa. In this activity, you will read the story again while tasting new foods along the way!

INGREDIENTS:

- yams
- a baking sheet
- paprika
- garlic powder
- plantains (see recipe above)
- a large skillet
- rice
- a small pot
- your favorite savory dipping sauce (optional)

DIRECTIONS:

1. Prep your foods (you will need adult supervision and help):

   For the yams: Peel the yams and cut them into short fat sticks. Drizzle them in oil or butter and your choice of spices (paprika, garlic powder, or both). Spread the yam sticks on a baking sheet in a single layer. Roast at 400F for 20-30 minutes, flipping halfway, until golden and crispy on the edges. Place the sticks on a plate and serve with your favorite savory dipping sauce.

   For the plantain: Preheat some oil in a large skillet over medium high heat. Peel and cut the plantain into rounds, a bit thicker than ¼". Very carefully, fry the pieces till the edges are very lightly golden brown. Flip them over, and fry the other side. As a guideline, one minute per side should be sufficient. Alternatively: many grocery stores sell frozen sweet plantains in the freezer section. You can bake them in the oven, fry them in a pan, or heat them up in an air fryer. When your plantains are done, place them on a plate with a napkin or paper towel beneath them to soak up the excess oil.

   For the rice: Boil a cup of rice according to the package directions. Once the rice is cooked, dump it on a plate.

2. Read the story of "Anansi and the Make-Believe Food." Whenever Anansi encounters food, pull the plate with that food out and taste it. You can taste all the yummy foods that Anansi missed out on!

3. Once you are finished reading, decide which of the foods Anansi passed up was your favorite.

Additional History Reading

Africana: An Encyclopedia of an Amazing Continent, by Kim Chakanetsa (Wide-Eyed Editions, 2022). An illustrated encyclopedia that includes a timeline page, wildlife and landscapes page, and more for each region of the continent. (RA)

Ancient West African Kingdoms, by Jane Shuter (Heinemann, 2002). An easy-to-read guide to the history and culture of Ghana, Mali, and Songhai, with a brief section on modern West Africa. **Out of print, but worth looking for at your local library.** RA 1–2, IR 2–4)

Great African Kingdoms, by Sean Sheehan (Raintree Steck-Vaughn, 1998). This book gives a great overview of the first kingdoms of Africa; a timeline and glossary are also included. **Out of print, but worth looking for at your local library.** (RA)

Corresponding Literature Suggestions

Anansi and the Magic Stick, retold by Eric Kimmel, illus. Janet Stevens (Holiday House, 2002). A brightly illustrated picture-book tale of Anansi. (RA 1–2, IR 2–4)

Anansi the Spider: A Tale from the Ashanti, by Gerald McDermott (Henry Holt, 1987). This tale, which tells how mischievous Anansi and his six brave sons helped place the moon in the sky, won a Caldecott Award. (IR for most readers, RA for beginners)

The Pot of Wisdom: Ananse Stories, by Adwoa Badoe, illus. Baba Wague Diakite (Groundwood, 2008). More tales about the trickster spider, written to be read out loud. (RA 1–3, IR 3–5)

Zomo the Rabbit: A Trickster from West Africa, by Gerald McDermott (Voyager, 1996). Zomo the rabbit, an African trickster, sets out to gain wisdom. This tale originated in Nigeria. The pictures are colorful and enticing, adding to the excitement of the story. (RA)

Corresponding Audiobook Suggestions

Tales From Cultures Far and Near, as told by Jim Weiss (Well-Trained Mind Press, 2015). Classics of many lands—wisdom from China and Japan, an African romance, wildly funny Native American, Arabian and Spanish tales—show that the human beings who tell them all are related. Stories include: A Guest Who Ran (Native American), Two Monks (Japan), The Three Friends of Manuel (Spain), Courting the Wind (West Africa/Senegal), The Secret Weapon (China), and Djuha: Two Stories (Arabic).

CHAPTER TWELVE
Life in Early Crete

1800 BCE

Bull-Jumpers and Sailors

Read & Review

Read pages 93–96 in the text. Afterward, check the student's understanding by asking the questions below.

1. **Why did the Minoans hold bull-jumping festivals?** *To honor the gods of Crete*
2. **Were the bull-jumpers treated well?** *Yes; they were given food, beautiful clothes, jewelry, and gold.*
3. **Was bull-jumping dangerous?** *Yes; bull-jumpers were often killed.*
4. **What did pirates do in the Mediterranean Sea?** *They attacked and robbed people who tried to sail on the sea.*
5. **What did the Minoans build to get rid of the pirates?** *Ships*
6. **What is a navy?** *An army that fights on water*

Narration Exercise

Tell me what you learned about bull-jumping.

The Minoans had festivals and jumped over bulls to honor their gods. Bull-jumpers started training when they were just kids! They were given beautiful clothes and jewelry, but it was very dangerous.

or

Tell me what you learned about ship-building.

Pirates in the Mediterranean Sea attacked and robbed other people sailing on the sea. The king of the Minoans wanted a navy. He built ships to drive pirates away.

Map Work: Bull-Jumpers and Sailors (Student Page 36)

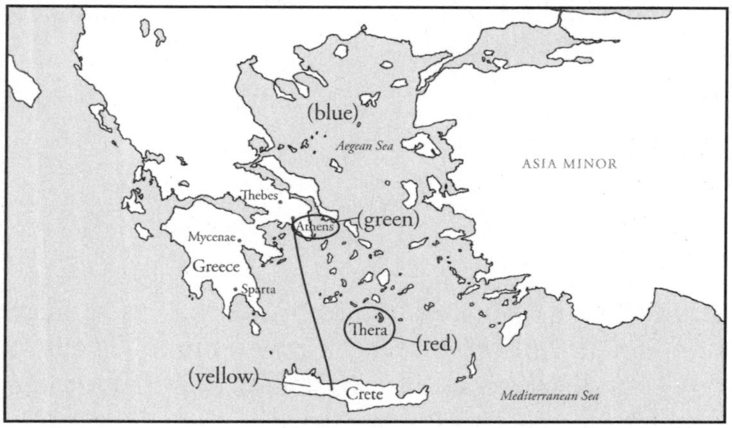

1. **Open to Student Page 36 and tear it out.**
2. **On your map, find the *Aegean Sea*. Shade it lightly in blue.**
3. **Find the island of *Crete* and color it yellow.**
4. **Find *Athens* and circle it in green. Then draw a line from Athens to Crete. This is the path that Theseus took.**
5. **Can you find the island of *Thera*? Circle it in red to remind you that a volcano erupted there!**
6. **When you finish, place the completed map in your history notebook.**

Activities

Choose from the following activities:

- [ ] Coloring Page: Bull Jumper
- [ ] Role Play: Bull-Jumping Practice
- [ ] Research Skills: Have the student look up a related topic in a history encyclopedia or another reliable source. Read the entry together and look at the pictures. Topics could include *Crete, Minoans, Minoan Civilization, Minoan Age,* and *bull-leaping* or *bull-jumping*.
- [ ] Field Trip Idea: If you live near a body of water, visit a marina. What kind of ships are there? Do you see any sailboats? Learn about the design of boats. What makes them float? What is *buoyancy*? What makes a ship *buoyant*? Sample answers at a first grade level: *Buoyancy is the ability to float. A boat floats because it pushes water down and the water pushes back up! That invisible push from the water is called buoyancy. Buoyancy helps things like boats stay on top of the water instead of sinking. The special shape of a ship or boat helps make it buoyant. Even though it's heavy, it pushes down a lot of water - and the water pushes back up enough to hold it.*

Coloring Page: Bull Jumper (Student Page 37)

In ancient Crete, athletes practiced bull-leaping, a daring sport where they vaulted over the backs of charging bulls.

Role Play

BULL-JUMPING PRACTICE

Young Cretan boys and girls practiced doing acrobatic tricks, like somersaults, spins, and flips, off of the backs of moving bulls. In this activity, you will pretend you are a young bull-jumper. It is your first day at practice. What are some tricks you can practice in your house or yard?

MATERIALS:

- A large safe spot for completing acrobatic tricks (mats on the floor or a trampoline are perfect for this!)
- A cardboard box or large stuffed animal

DIRECTIONS:

1. Start by practicing your tricks. Here are a few things to try: When you jump in the air, can you spin all the way around before landing? How high can you jump? How long can you jump? Can you hold your legs straight and land? Can you spread your legs out when you jump and then put them back together before landing? Can you make up one trick all on your own?
2. Now create a routine. A routine should include 4-6 tricks that you do in a row. Practice your routine in a safe spot.
3. Now it is time for the big day at the bull-jumping festival. Place a medium size cardboard box on a soft space in your house or yard. You can paint eyes and a nose on it to remind you that it represents the bull. Alternatively, you can use a large stuffed animal. Do your tricks with the stuffed animal or box beneath you. For example, jump over the prop and spin in the air. Jump over the prop as high as you can. Jump over it and go as far as you can.

King Minos and the Minotaur

Read & Review

Read pages 96–100 in the text. Afterward, check the student's understanding by asking the questions below.

1. **What kind of monster was the Minotaur?** *Half man and half bull*
2. **Why did King Minos tell Athens to send him seven girls and seven boys every year?** *To feed them to the Minotaur*
3. **Where did the Minotaur live?** *Under the palace, in a maze*
4. **How did Theseus get out of the maze?** *With a ball of wool that Ariadne gave him*
5. **What color sail was Theseus supposed to put on his ship?** *A white sail*
6. **What happened when he forgot to put on the white sail?** *His father jumped off a cliff.*
7. **The father of Theseus was called King Aegeus. What sea was named after him**? *The Aegean Sea*

1800 BCE

Narration Exercise

Tell me the story of Theseus and the Minotaur.

Note to Instructor: Aim for a narration of four to six sentences; if the student wants to include every detail, guide them to a more condensed version of the story. A lot happens, but the student only needs to include a few main points.

Theseus found out that kids were being sent to Crete for the Minotaur to eat, so he went to kill it. The Minotaur lived in a big maze, so the princess gave him a ball of wool so he could find his way back out again. She gave him a torch to see, too, and a sword to help him fight. Theseus killed the Minotaur and everyone was saved.

or

Draw a scene from the story. When you're done, tell me about it and I will write your description at the bottom of the page.

Activities

Choose from the following activities:

- [ ] Activity Page: The Minotaur's Maze
- [ ] Craft: Build Your Own Labyrinth
- [ ] Research Skills: Have the student look up a related topic in a history encyclopedia or another reliable source. Read the entry together and look at the pictures. Topics could include *Crete*, *Knossos*, *King Minos*, *Minotaur*, *King Aegeus*, *Ariadne*, and *labyrinth*.

Activity Page

THE MINOTAUR'S MAZE

(Student Page 38)

Help Theseus slay the Minotaur—color the maze and help Theseus find his way through the labyrinth to the Minotaur at the center.

Craft

BUILD YOUR OWN LABYRINTH

Build your own labyrinth and then help a marble escape the maze, just like Ariadne helped Theseus.

MATERIALS:

- 2 flat sheets of cardboard (they can be cut from a cardboard box)
- scissors
- a glue gun
- ruler
- a marble

DIRECTIONS:

Note for Adults: For this activity, you will need a glue gun. Older students can use a low-heat glue gun, but they may still need help figuring out where to draw their maze wall lines. Younger students will need help for most of this activity. However, they can participate by coloring the base and walls of the maze before you glue things together, by helping decide where the maze walls should go, and by playing the final game!

1. Take your first flat sheet of cardboard and cut it into the size you want your maze base to be.
2. Use a ruler to draw lines mapping out where the walls of your maze will go. These lines should form a path with right-angle turns.
3. Draw a small dot on the place where you want the maze to start and an X on the spot where you want it to finish.
4. Measure the 4 sides of your maze base. Cut 4 strips of cardboard, half an inch tall and the right lengths to go around the perimeter of the maze base, creating a wall around the base. Attach the walls using a glue gun. Leave about an inch of opening in front of the X marking the end of the maze, so the marble can come out.
5. Measure the lines you drew inside your maze. Cut more cardboard strips (half an inch tall) to fit the lines of your maze. Attach the maze walls using a glue gun.

6. Punch a small hole through the dot, indicating the start of the maze. This is where you will rest your marble before working it through the labyrinth.
7. Play with your labyrinth! Place a marble on the starting hole, then using two hands to rotate the labyrinth, move the marble through the maze. You can time yourself and your friends to see who can get the marble through the maze fastest!

Instead of using cardboard, use toy building bricks, clay, or another creative material to create a labyrinth.

The Mysterious End of the Minoans

1600 BCE

Read & Review

Read pages 100–101 in the text. Afterward, check the student's understanding by asking the questions below.

1. **Why did the Minoans leave Crete?** *Because a volcano erupted nearby*
2. **What island did the volcano erupt on?** *Thera*
3. **What happened to Thera?** *It sank beneath the sea.*
4. **What did the volcano do to the air and land of Crete?** *A tidal wave hit Crete; ash, dust, and rock covered the fields and towns, so that people couldn't breathe and crops couldn't grow.*

Narration Exercise

Tell me why the Minoans had to leave Crete.

A volcano erupted near Crete. All the people on Crete had to leave.

or

A volcano blew up the island of Thera. The ash and the dust fell all over Crete, and the people couldn't grow crops any more. So they had to leave.

Activities

Choose from the following activities:

- ☐ Science & Make a Model: Erupting Volcano
- ☐ Research Skills: Have the student look up a related topic in a history encyclopedia or another reliable source. Read the entry together and look at the pictures. Topics could include *volcanoes*, *Crete*, *Minoan Civilization*, and *Thera*.

Science & Make a Model

MAKE AN ERUPTING VOLCANO

The Minoans may have left Crete because the effects of a volcanic eruption ruined the air and land. This model volcano mimics the eruption of lava due to some simple chemistry: when you mix vinegar (an acid) with baking soda (a base), there is a chemical reaction that creates a new substance, carbon dioxide gas. Carbon dioxide is the same gas that's used to create carbonation in soda, and the reaction you see here is similar to the one you see if you shake up a can of soda!

MATERIALS:

- plastic cup, 8 oz or bigger, depending on how big you'd like your volcano to be (adjust other supplies accordingly)
- air-dry clay or salt dough (recipe on page 414)
- baking soda, a teaspoon or more for each time you want your volcano to erupt
- vinegar, ¼ cup or more for each time you want your volcano to erupt
- dish soap
- red food coloring (to dye the lava)
- old clothes to wear
- baking sheet or something else that is easily cleaned
- old tablecloth or cardboard if you'd like to further protect your work area

DIRECTIONS:

1. Set the plastic cup onto the baking sheet.
2. Using the plastic cup as your base, use clay to form a volcano, leaving an open crater at the top.
3. Let the volcano dry as per the instructions for your particular clay (creating an eruption in a wet volcano might ruin your model).
4. Mix vinegar with a few drops of dish soap and red food coloring.
5. Add a tablespoon of baking soda into the crater of your volcano.
6. Pour in the vinegar mixture and watch your volcano erupt! A model volcano is fun to make and watch, but imagine that the volcano was bigger than your house and that the lava was blazing hot!
7. Optional: Take a picture of your volcano. Keep it in your history notebook.

Additional Investigation: What happens if you increase or decrease the amount of baking soda, keeping the amount of vinegar the same? What if you increase or decrease the amount of vinegar, keeping the baking soda the same? Does it make a difference if you add the vinegar to the volcano first?

Additional History Reading

Atlantis: The Lost City (DK Eyewitness Readers: Level 4), by Andrew Donkin (Sagebrush, 2001). This 2nd–3rd grade reader begins with Plato telling the story of Atlantis, and then discusses the possible evidence. (RA 1–2, IR 2–4)

Eyewitness: Ancient Greece, by DK Children (DK Children, 2023). This book is packed with information bites that make it a good reference. Descriptive of many aspects of ancient Greece, using pictures, drawings, costumed actors, and more. Fantastic pictures of artifacts! There is a helpful two-page spread on the Minoans. (Also recommended for chapters sixteen, twenty, twenty-one, and twenty-seven) (RA)

Digging Up the Past: The Palace of Knossos, by Emily Rose Oachs (Bellwether Media, Inc, 2020). This easy-to-read book takes kids on a journey to discover the Minoan palace of Knossos, including its history, the story of its excavation, and its special architectural features. (IR 2-4)

Corresponding Literature Suggestions

D'Aulaires' Book of Greek Myths, by Edgar Parin d'Aulaire (Delacorte, 1992). A classic in its own right, this introduction to the gods and goddesses of Ancient Greece has beautiful illustrations by Caldecott Award winners. There is a myth about Theseus that includes the story of the Minotaur and other Greek legends set in Crete. (RA)

Usborne Greek Myths, by Heather Amery (Usborne, 2024). Simplified retelling of Greek myths, including the story of Daedalus and Icarus and the story of Theseus and the Minotaur, both set in Crete. These stories are shorter than D'Aulaire's version listed above. (RA, possible IR for advanced readers)

Corresponding Audiobook Suggestions

Heroes in Mythology, as told by Jim Weiss (Well-Trained Mind Press, 2021). Three of the world's greatest adventures—Theseus and the Minotaur, Prometheus, Bearer of Fire, and Odin and the Norse Men—each featuring a quest for wisdom.

CHAPTER THIRTEEN
The Middle Kingdom of Egypt

Egypt Invades Nubia

1800 BCE

Read & Review

Read pages 102–104 in the text. Afterward, check the student's understanding by asking the questions below.

1. **What happened to the Old Kingdom of Egypt?** *It became weak and powerless.*
2. **When Amenemhet became pharaoh, what country did he decide to conquer?** *Nubia*
3. **Why was Nubia valuable to the Egyptians?** *It had gold.*
4. **What new name did the Egyptians give to Nubia?** *Kush*
5. **What do we call this time in Egyptian history?** *The Middle Kingdom of Egypt*

Narration Exercise

Tell me at least two things you learned about in this lesson.

Egypt was weak. Then it became strong again. This was called the Middle Kingdom. The Egyptians conquered Nubia.

or

The Egyptians invaded part of Africa. It was called Nubia. It had iron and gold in it. This was during the Middle Kingdom of Egypt.

or

"The Egyptians took over part of Africa. They called it Kush. Then the people of Kush became Egyptian. Some even became pharaohs!"

Activities

Choose from the following activities:

- ☐ Coloring Page: Ancient Nubians
- ☐ Craft: Make a Golden Bracelet
- ☐ Craft: Make an Incense Holder
- ☐ Research Skills: Have the student look up a related topic in a history encyclopedia or another reliable source. Read the entry together and look at the pictures. Topics could include *Nubia*, *Ancient Africa*, *Queen Tiye*, *Kush*, *Amenemhet*, and *Queen Tiye*.

Coloring Page: Ancient Nubians (Student Page 40)

A Nubian soldier guards a Nubian noblewoman. Nubian soldiers were known for their archery skills.

Craft

MAKE A GOLDEN BRACELET

The Nubians traveled along the Nile and sold many things, including gold jewelry.

MATERIALS:

- gold paint and brushes
- scissors
- toilet paper tube
- sticker gems (optional)

DIRECTIONS:

1. Cut the toilet paper tube in half, making 2 shorter tubes.
2. Cut each of the smaller tubes lengthwise (end to end).
3. Paint the outside of the tubes gold. Let them dry completely.
4. Optional: decorate your new bracelet with sticker gems.
5. To wear your gold bracelets, gently open the tube, where it has been split, and wrap around your upper arm. It will fit tightly enough that it shouldn't fall off. If it is too tight, take it off, and gently open the tube wider, bending the cardboard a bit. Try it on again. Wear one bracelet on each arm. What a nice gift from the Nubians!

Classroom Adaption: Have students decorate their bracelets and then exchange them.

Craft

MAKE AN INCENSE HOLDER

Tomb pictures show Nubians carrying incense, among other things, to the Egyptians to give as gifts. In this activity you can make a lovely incense holder to keep for yourself or give as a gift to someone special.

Note to Instructor: This activity involves lighting a match to burn incense and requires adult supervision.

MATERIALS:

- air-dry clay or salt dough (recipe on page 414)
- a tool for cutting clay (cookie cutters work great, or you can freestyle your shapes with a craft stick)
- a clay roller (or a drinking glass can work for this)
- craft paint, including gold paint if possible!
- small paintbrushes
- incense (can be purchased at some grocery and drug stores, and at many gift stores)
- matches
- gilding paint (this will add a fancier gold look to your final creation, but is not necessary. It is great if you plan to give this incense holder as a gift!)
- clay glaze (again, this gives the final product a glossy finish but is not necessary)

DIRECTIONS:

1. Work a small amount of clay in your hands until it is soft. Then roll it out to about ¼ inch thick.
2. Cut out the shapes you want for your incense holder using cookie cutters, craft sticks, or a blunt knife.
3. Stick one piece of incense into the clay and then twist it around one time. Then carefully remove the incense by pulling it straight up. This will create the hole for your incense holder.
4. Dry your clay according to the package instructions.
5. Once your incense holders are dry, decorate them with paint. Use small thin brushes to paint simple geometrical shapes and lines. Optional: Use gold paint or gilding paint to add gold touches, since the Nubians liked to use gold to decorate.
6. Let the paint dry thoroughly.
7. Optional: If you are using clay glaze, paint the glaze on and let dry according to the package instructions.

8. Once your incense holder is ready, try burning incense! Place one stick of incense in the tiny hole in your clay incense holder. Have an adult light the incense with the matches, as directed on the package. After burning, be sure to put out the ember completely. If the package doesn't direct you as to the best way to do this, douse it in water.

9. With the assistance of an adult, try a few different scents of incense. Which do you like best?

Classroom Adaptation: Make an example incense holder ahead of time that students can use as a model. Rather than allowing each student to burn their own incense, use the example holder to show how it works; then, send students home with empty incense holders. Encourage students to give their incense holder as a gift to a special adult they know, or work with their trusted adult at home to use their new incense holder.

The Hyksos Invade Egypt

Read & Review

Read pages 104–106 in the text. Afterward, check the student's understanding by asking the questions below.

1. **What happened to the Middle Kingdom of Egypt?** *It became weak because of bad pharaohs.*
2. **Who invaded Egypt and took over the Egyptian throne?** *Wandering nomads* [It is nice (but not essential) if the student can remember the name "Hyksos."]
3. **Where were they from?** *Canaan*
4. **Did the Egyptians like having the Hyksos for kings?** *No! They thought the Hyksos were unclean shepherds.* 1750–1550BCE
5. **How did the Egyptians get rid of the Hyksos?** *Egyptian princes got together and used the Hyksos' own weapons to drive them out.*

Narration Exercise

How did the Middle Kingdom of Egypt end and the New Kingdom begin?

Egypt became weak again. Nomads came from Canaan and took over. They had good weapons and fought with chariots. Then the Egyptians chased them out.

or

The Middle Kingdom ended because nomads invaded. They ruled Egypt. Then Egyptians used bows and arrows and chariots to drive them out.

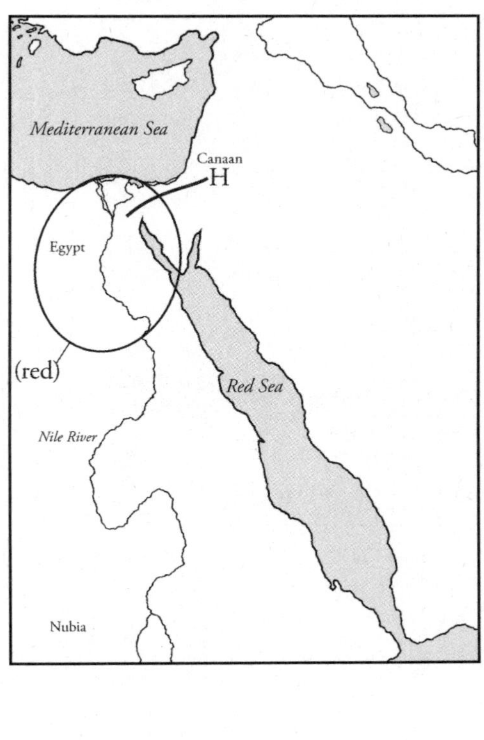

Map Work: The Hyksos Invade Egypt
(Student Page 39)

1. **Open to Student Page 39 and tear it out.**
2. **On your map, circle the area around the Nile (*Egypt*) with a red crayon.**
3. **Nubia is south of Egypt, in Africa. Label *Nubia* at the bottom of your map, just to the left of the *Nile River*.**

4. **Find *Canaan*. Draw an H for Hyksos in Canaan. Then draw a line from Canaan down into Egypt. The Hyksos came down from Canaan when they conquered Egypt.**
5. **When you finish, place the completed map in your history notebook.**

Activities

Choose from the following activities:

- [ ] Make a Model: Egyptian War Chariot
- [ ] Research Skills: Have the student look up a related topic in a history encyclopedia or another reliable source. Read the entry together and look at the pictures. Topics could include *Amenemhet*, *Hyksos*, *The New Kingdom of Egypt*, and *Ahmose*.

Make a Model

EGYPTIAN WAR CHARIOT

The Egyptians learned many fighting methods from the invading Hyksos. They developed their own version of the small, fast war chariots used by their conquerors, and eventually drove the Hyksos out of Egypt.

MATERIALS:

- 8-ounce paper cup
- 2 wheels (wooden or plastic) about 1.5-inch to 2-inch diameter
- axle for wheels (straw, dowel, lollipop stick, about 3.5 inches long)
- handle to pull chariot (straw, dowel, lollipop stick, craft stick)
- hole punch
- ruler
- scissors
- hot glue gun, hot glue stick
- pen or marker
- cardstock
- paper, markers, glue stick to decorate chariot (optional)

DIRECTIONS:

1. You can start heating your glue gun while doing the other steps. You can also use regular glue; you will just have to wait much longer for it to dry.
2. Cut about a quarter of the cup away from top to bottom in a U-shape, stopping just before the bottom of the cup.

3. Punch a hole on either side of the open part of the cup, just above the bottom.
4. If you are decorating your chariot, now is a good time to do so. Based on ancient artifacts, red, green, and beige were the colors most often used.
5. Put your axle through the holes in the cup.
6. Using your hot glue gun, glue each wheel in place. Let glue dry.
7. Make a small notch at the front bottom of the cup so that your handle fits more smoothly.
8. Glue your handle to the bottom of the cup.
9. Pull your chariot along by the handle! You can also tape the handle to a toy horse if you like.
10. Optional: Take a picture of your chariot. Keep it in your history notebook.

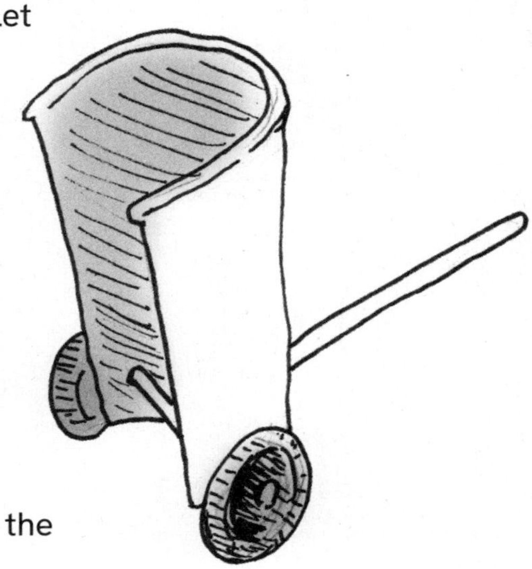

Classroom Adaptation: Have a model built ahead of time that students can reference as they work through the activity. This will work better with older students.

Additional History Reading

Ancient Worlds: Travel Back in Time and Discover the First Great Civilizations, by DK (DK Children, 2024). This book has illustrated depictions of ancient cities and scenes. It has a two-page spread on Kush. (Also recommended for chapter six) (RA)

Life in Ancient Egypt: A Coloring Book, by John Green (Dover, 1989). Detailed and interesting pictures of life in ancient Egypt, along with brief descriptions. (RA and activity)

The Pharaohs of Ancient Egypt, by Elizabeth Payne (Sagebrush, 1999). This read-aloud book has a brief chapter about the life of each important pharaoh of Egypt. (RA)

Corresponding Literature Suggestions

Egyptian Gods and Goddesses, by Henry Barker (Grossett & Dunlap, 1999). A Penguin Young Readers Level 4 book with stories about the most important gods and goddesses of Egypt's Middle Kingdom. (RA, but probably an IR for advanced readers)

Be a Scribe! Working for a Better Life in Ancient Egypt, by Michael Hoffen, Christian Casey, Janet Thum (Callaway Children's Classics, 2024). Translated from a papyrus from Egypt's Middle Kingdom, this book tells the story of Pepi, a boy training to become a scribe. Pepi's father introduces him to 18 trades in Ancient Egypt. Students get a first-hand glimpse into daily life in the Middle Kingdom. There are illustrations and pictures of artifacts on each page.

Temple Cat, by Andrew Clements (Clarion, 2001). A temple cat in ancient Egypt runs away from his temple and catches fish like a normal cat. (RA)

CHAPTER FOURTEEN
The New Kingdom of Egypt

The General and the Woman Pharaoh

Read & Review

Read pages 107–110 in the text. Afterward, check the student's understanding by asking the questions below.

1530-1480BCE

1. **We've already learned about the Old Kingdom and the Middle Kingdom of Egypt. What is this time in Egypt's history called?** *The New Kingdom*
2. **We read about two pharaohs today. Do you remember their names?** Prompt the student if necessary: *Thutmose and Hatshepsut*
3. **What did Thutmose do?** *He made Egypt bigger.*
4. **What did Hatshepsut do?** *She became a pharaoh even though she was a woman.*
5. **What did Hatshepsut wear?** *Men's clothes and a false beard!*

Narration Exercise

Retell the story of EITHER Thutmose OR Hatshepsut.

Thutmose wanted to make Egypt bigger. He fought the Nubians and he even fought the Hyksos. He made Egypt twice as big!

or

Hatshepsut wanted to be pharaoh. The Egyptians didn't think a woman could be pharaoh. So Hatshepsut pretended to be a man. She put on a false beard and ruled Egypt for years.

Activities

Choose from the following activities:

- [ ] Craft: Make Hatshepsut's False Beard
- [ ] Role Play: Make One of Hatshepsut's Monuments (NO PREP)
- [ ] Research Skills: Have the student look up a related topic in a history encyclopedia or another reliable source. Read the entry together and look at the pictures. Topics could include *the New Kingdom of Egypt, Thutmose I, Thebes, Hatshepsut,* and *the Golden Age of Egypt* or *Egypt's golden age.*

Craft

MAKE HATSHEPSUT'S FALSE BEARD

Hatshepsut was a woman, but she wore a false beard while on the throne. In this activity, you can create a false beard like Hatshepsut's.

MATERIALS:

- colored tissue paper
- fabric elastic, ¼-inch to ½-inch width (the sort used in clothing)
- white glue
- a paint brush (for glue)
- a toilet paper tube
- A piece of cling wrap or scrap paper

DIRECTIONS:

1. The toilet paper tube will be the "base" for your false beard. Cover it with thin strips of tissue paper, glued to the tube at one end and hanging free at the other. To avoid getting your hands sticky, you can use a paint brush to paint glue onto the tissue paper, and then apply the tissue to the tube. Let the beard dry by setting one end of the tube on a piece of cling wrap or scrap paper.
2. Once the beard is dry, punch 2 holes opposite each other at one end of the tube. Thread the fabric elastic through one hole, and tie a knot on the inside of the tube.
3. Put the beard up to your chin, and measure how long the elastic needs to be to reach around your head to the other side of the tube. An older sibling or adult could help you with this task. Cut the elastic at the appropriate length (this will keep the beard on your face, so you don't want it to be too loose or too tight).

4. Thread the free end of the elastic into the open hole in the tube. Tie a knot on the inside of the tube. Try the beard on. If it is too loose, pull the knot tighter. You may need to undo the original knot first, or perhaps just tie a second knot to take up the slack.
5. Wear your beard and pretend to be Hatshepsut, the first woman Pharaoh.

Role Play

MAKE ONE OF HATSHEPSUT'S MONUMENTS

Instructor: Lead the student through the following imaginative exercise.

During Queen Hatshepsut's reign, she had many monuments built.

Do you know what a monument is? A monument is usually built to serve as a memorial to a person or group of people who have died. An ancient monument could be a statue of a person, a statue of a god, a large building, a pillar with a story written on it, or a large stone with words carved on it. In ancient times, monuments were often statues of people; sometimes they were also large buildings, or pillars with words written on them.

Imagine that you were a king or queen in ancient times. What important things did you do? What do you want to be remembered for? What would you want your monument to look like? Would it be colorful? What shape would it have? Would there be words on it—if so, what would they say?

Design and build your monument. If it helps, draw a picture of your monument before you begin building it. For building, you can use any material you have around the house including cardboard boxes, toy building bricks, or other building toys.

Amenhotep and King Tut

Read & Review

Read pages 110-116 in the text. Afterward, check the student's understanding by asking the questions below.

1. **What is polytheism?** *The worship of many different gods*
2. **What is monotheism?** *The worship of just one god*
3. **Did the Egyptians worship just one god, or many gods?** *Many gods.* That means that they were polytheists.
4. **Did Amenhotep worship just one god, or many gods?** *Just one god*
5. **Did the Egyptians like this?** *No! They wanted all their gods back.*
6. **Where was King Tut buried?** *In the Valley of the Kings*
7. **Who discovered his tomb?** *A man named Howard Carter*

1350-1325BCE

8. **Did robbers steal Tut's treasure?** *No.* **Why not?** *They couldn't find his tomb.*
9. **Why did people think there was a curse on the tomb?** *Because some people who opened it died, and Howard Carter's canary was swallowed by a cobra*

Narration Exercise

What did Amenhotep want his people to do?

The Egyptians worshipped many different gods. Amenhotep wanted them to worship just one god. But they didn't want to.

or

The Egyptians had lots of gods. A pharaoh tried to make them be monotheists. That means having just one god.

or

Draw a picture of King Tut's mummy or of Howard Carter discovering the tomb full of treasure. When you're done, tell me about it and I will write your description at the bottom of the page.

Map Work: Amenhotep and King Tut (Student Page 41)

Read the instructions out loud to the student. After each step, pause and give time for the student to complete the task. Provide all necessary help.

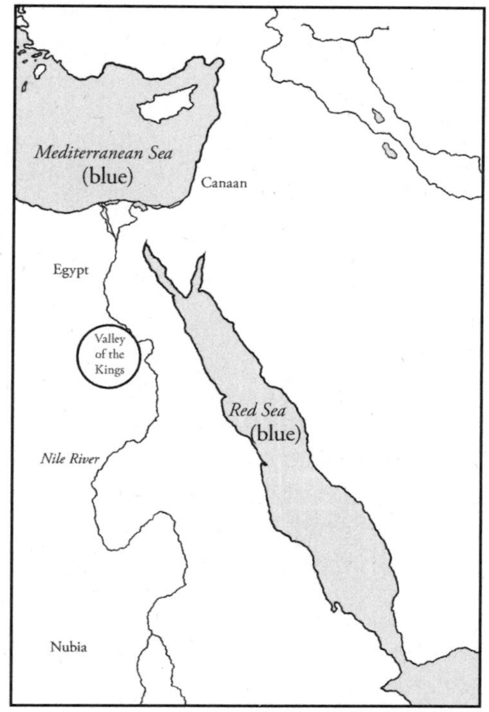

1. **Open to Student Page 41 and tear it out.**
2. **On your map, circle the area that is known as the *Valley of the Kings*.**
3. **Review the location of *Canaan*. Color Canaan yellow.**
4. **Review the location of the *Mediterranean Sea*. Color it blue to remind yourself that it is a body of water.**
5. **Review the location of the *Red Sea*. Color it blue too because it is a body of water and is not really red; that is just its name.**
6. **When you finish, place the completed map in your history notebook.**

Optional extension: If your student is interested, do some research about how the Red Sea got its name. There are a few different theories.

Activities

Choose from the following activities:

- ☐ Coloring Page: The Mask of King Tut
- ☐ Craft: Make an Egyptian Death Mask
- ☐ Role Play: Be an Archaeologist
- ☐ Storytelling: Pharaoh For Dinner
- ☐ Research Skills: Have the student look up a related topic in a history encyclopedia or another reliable source. Read the entry together and look at the pictures. Topics could include *Amenhotep, Polytheism, Monotheism, King Tutankhamen, Howard Carter*, and *the Valley of the Kings*.

Coloring Page: The Mask of King Tut (Student Page 42)

King Tutankhamen became king when he was only seven years old. When he died, he was buried in a tomb full of treasure, like this mask of his face. The mask was made of gold and jewels.

Craft

MAKE AN EGYPTIAN DEATH MASK

Kings, queens, and other people of nobility and high class in ancient Egypt were mummified and buried in highly decorated coffins. Each mummy wore a "death mask" which was made in the likeness of the person being buried. The Egyptians believed that every person had a spirit called "ka" which separated from the body at death. To live in the afterlife, the ka would need to find the body it belonged to. The death masks (and the coffins, which were also crafted to look like the person within) helped the ka to recognize the body it belonged with.

MATERIALS:

- circular balloon
- paper mache paste (made of 1 part glue to 1 part water; it will be runny).
- strips of newspaper, paper, or construction paper.
- scissors
- craft knife (this makes cutting out the eye holes easier, but you can also use scissors)
- paint, gold glitter, etc. (optional)

DIRECTIONS:

1. Make the paste. You can use a glue and water mixture (1 part glue to 1 part water).
2. Blow up the balloon.
3. Soak the strips of paper in the paste mixture. Remove strips one at a time, remove excess paste, and paste onto the surface of the balloon. Repeat until the entire front surface of the balloon is covered and you can no longer see the surface of the balloon on the covered section. Let dry completely.
4. Pop balloon.
5. Carefully cut out holes for your eyes.
6. You can now paint the mask with bright colors and gold glitter, so that it resembles the death mask of a pharaoh.

Role Play

BE AN ARCHAEOLOGIST

Archaeologist Howard Carter discovered King Tut's tomb and its treasures after years of searching. Pretend to be an archaeologist discovering a tomb! You'll need a parent or older sibling to help you out.

DIRECTIONS:

1. **Parent or older sibling:** Choose a small, out-of-the-way, secret place in the house (or outdoors, if the weather is nice) to be "King Tut's Tomb." Select a number of small treasures from around the house (toys from the student's room, stuffed animals, small pieces of candy or other approved treats—a new toy is nice but not essential). Don't choose too many treasures, since the student will need to draw pictures of the treasures as soon as he finds them. Arrange these treasures in the "tomb." Draw a simple map for the student to follow, and tell him to go find the tomb!

2. **Student:** Find the tomb using the provided map. Before an archaeologist can move anything in a tomb, he has to draw a picture of its original place. When you discover your "tomb," don't touch any of the treasures! Instead, get a piece of paper and a crayon or pencil. Draw each item in the tomb, just as you see it. After you've drawn your "tomb picture," you can play with the treasures!

Classroom Adaptation: Create a fancy "tomb" in the classroom with a few cheap trinkets that kids can take home (party favors work great for this!). Place students in groups and have them take turns drawing their picture of the tomb, one group at a time. Display the drawings in the classroom and then divide up the treasure!

Storytelling

PHARAOH FOR DINNER

In this chapter, you read about 4 famous pharaohs. Choose one. Dress up as that pharaoh as best as you can using materials from around your house (if you choose Hatshepsut, you can make yourself a fake beard in the activity above). If you have time, read an additional biography about your chosen pharaoh (there are options listed in the reading list below). Alternatively, review their section in the text. Then come to dinner acting like your pharaoh. See if you can act like your character throughout the entire meal!

Additional History Reading

The Great and the Terrible: The World's Most Glorious and Notorious Rulers and How They Got their Names by Joanne O'Sullivan (Running Press Kids, 2020). This book includes a short but engaging biography of Hatshepsut and other important rulers of the ancient world like Cyrus the Great (chapter twenty-four of *The Story of the World*), Alexander the Great (chapter twenty-eight), Asoka the Great (chapter twenty-nine), and Attila the Hun (chapter forty-one). (RA 1-2, IR 3-5)

The Pharaohs of Ancient Egypt, by Elizabeth Payne (Sagebrush, 1999). This read-aloud book has a brief chapter about the life of each important pharaoh of Egypt. (RA)

Amazing Women of the Middle East: 25 Stories from Ancient Times to the Present Day, by Wafa' Tarnowska (Crocodile Books, 2020). This colorful collection of biographies includes an entry about Nefertiti, wife of Amenhotep IV. (Also recommended for its biography of Semiramis, chapter eighteen) (RA 1-3, IR 4-6)

Tut's Mummy—Lost...and Found, by Judy Donnelly (Random House, 1988). A simple account of the mummy's discovery. (IR for many readers, RA for beginners)

Corresponding Literature Suggestions

Mara, Daughter of the Nile, by Eloise McGraw (Puffin, 1985). Mara is a young slave girl who escapes from her cruel master and finds herself in the hands of two new enemies. The story takes place during Hatshepsut's reign. Too long to read in one day, but this might make a good family reading project, especially if an older child can take on the project of reading to the younger ones. (RA)

Tales of Ancient Egypt, selected and retold by Roger Lancelyn Green (Puffin, 2011). Green's stories, first published in 1967, are classics in their own right. This collection of tales includes a story about Hatshepsut, as well as fables about the Egyptian gods. (RA 1-3, IR 3-6)

Tutankhamen's Gift, by Robert Sabuda (Aladdin, 1997). The story of King Tut's childhood—especially good for the youngest children in the family who may feel left out at times. (RA)

Tut, Tut (The Time Warp Trio), by Jon Scieszka (Puffin, 2004). A silly but entertaining trip through time. For advanced readers to tackle alone. (IR for advanced readers)

Corresponding Audiobook Suggestions

Pharaohs and Queens of Ancient Egypt, told by Jim Weiss (Well-Trained Mind Press, 2024). Engaging tales from ancient Egypt, including stories about Hatshepsut, Akhenaten, and the discovery of King Tut's tomb.

CHAPTER FIFTEEN
The Israelites Leave Egypt

The Baby Moses

1250 BCE

Read & Review

Read pages 117–120 in the text. Afterward, check the student's understanding by asking the questions below.

1. **Who were the Israelites descended from?** *Abraham.* [Take a moment to talk about what a "descendant" is, if necessary.]
2. **Did the Israelites worship one god or many gods?** One god
3. **Were they monotheists or polytheists?** Monotheists
4. **Why did they go to Egypt?** Because of a famine in Canaan
5. **What happened to them in Egypt?** They became slaves.
6. **Who led them back out of Egypt?** Moses
7. **What terrible command did the pharaoh give?** To kill all the baby boys of the Israelites
8. **What did Moses's mother do to save his life?** Put him in the Nile River in a basket
9. **Who took him out?** The princess of Egypt

Narration Exercise

What's an important thing that happened in this story?

Note: The narration should EITHER say that the Israelites went to Egypt, and were made into slaves by the pharaoh, OR should retell the story of Moses. (If the student wants to include both parts of the lesson in the narration, that's fine, but don't require this.)

The Israelites went to Egypt because of a famine. There were many of them and the Egyptians were afraid of them. The Egyptians made them into slaves.

or

Moses' mother wanted to keep him safe. She hid him. Then she put him in a basket on the river. The daughter of the pharaoh found him. Then his mother got to take care of him again.

Activities

Choose from the following activities:

- ☐ Craft: Make Baby Moses' Basket
- ☐ Science Challenge: Will It Float?
- ☐ Research Skills: Have the student look up a related topic in a history encyclopedia or another reliable source. Read the entry together and look at the pictures. Topics could include *the Hebrews*, *Judaism*, *Israelites*, and *early Jewish history*.

Craft

MAKE BABY MOSES' BASKET

Moses' mother hid him in a basket made of reeds. In this activity you can practice making a basket like the one Baby Moses hid inside!

MATERIALS:

- a paper or styrofoam cup
- craft sticks
- glue
- embroidery floss or friendship thread
- scissors

DIRECTIONS:

1. Have an adult cut the top off of a paper cup, leaving about 2 inches of cup to be the base of your basket.
2. Glue a craft stick on the cup base, standing it straight up. Repeat until you have craft sticks all around and covering the cup base. The amount of craft sticks you need will vary based on cup size, but make sure you end up with an odd number.

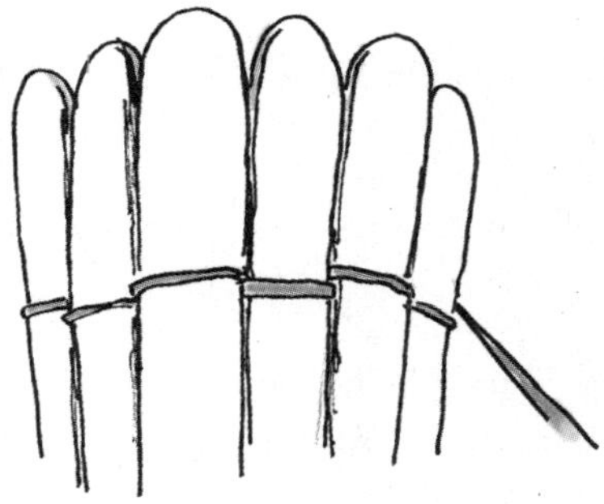

3. Pick your first thread color. Tie the end of the thread around one of the craft sticks. Weave the thread around all of the craft sticks following this pattern: go behind one stick, then in front of another. Once you have woven the thread around all the sticks once, continue weaving another line of thread right above the first one. Repeat until you have enough of that color on your "basket." Cut off the thread with about 3 to 4 inches to spare and tie a knot on the end. Weave the final piece of thread until the knot is hidden behind one of the craft sticks.
4. Choose another color of thread and repeat the process until you are satisfied with the design.
5. When you are done weaving, cut off any extra cord. Glue the ends of the cord in place on the inside of the basket.
6. You can use your basket to hold a small plant, pens, or something else!

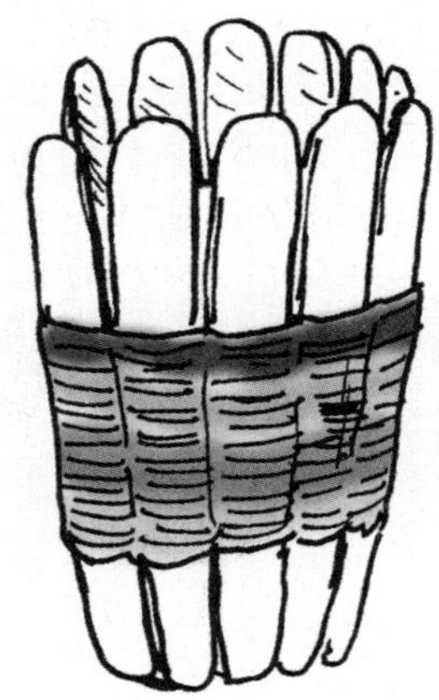

Science Challenge

WILL IT FLOAT?

In this lesson's story, Baby Moses floated down the river in a basket made of reeds. In this activity, you will try to build a boat that can continue to float, even while holding heavy loads.

MATERIALS:

- a source of water (large sink, bathtub, wading pool, lake, or waterproof container)
- building materials (this can vary depending on what you have available; ideas include aluminum foil, craft sticks, straws, tape, plastic wrap, paper or cardboard, glue, scissors, toilet paper or paper towel rolls, empty water bottles, plastic tubs)
- a scale
- marbles

DIRECTIONS:

1. Ask a parent how much you weighed when you were born. Or if you do not have this information, use 7 pounds. Your goal will be to build a boat that can float while holding as many marbles as pounds you were when you were born (or 7 marbles)
2. Use materials from around the house to create a boat or flotation device. It can be any shape. Test different things if you like! You will need a base that floats and is sturdy and then something to hold your marbles and keep them dry.

3. Once you finish building it, fill a small pool or bathtub with water.
4. Place your boat on the water and observe it. Does it float? Does it stay steady? Place the marbles onto your boat one at a time until it starts to sink. How many marbles can it hold?
5. Optional: when you finish, read a picture book or watch an online video for kids about buoyancy. What could you have done differently based on the science of buoyancy? If you like, try building your boat or tweaking it to see if you can get it to hold more weight.

Classroom Adaptation: Separate students into groups. Provide each group with the exact same set of materials (for example: one 12x18 sheet of aluminum foil, 10 craft sticks, 5 plastic straws, one roll of masking or duct tape, one 12x12 inch piece of plastic wrap, one sheet of paper, 3 rubber bands, one container of glue, one pair of scissors, one small styrofoam cup). Give them thirty minutes to build their boats. Once the timer runs out, bring the boats to a testing space (a small blow-up pool or tub). The team with the boat that holds the most marbles wins a prize.

The Exodus from Egypt

Read & Review

Read pages 120–123 in the text. Afterward, check the student's understanding by asking the questions below.

1. **How many plagues did God send on Egypt?** *Ten*
2. **Did the pharaoh finally let the Israelites go?** *Yes*
3. **What happened when they got to the Red Sea?** *The water parted* OR *God parted the water OR Moses parted the water.*
4. **What was this great escape from Egypt called?** *The Exodus*
5. **Where did the Israelites go next?** *Back to Canaan!*

Narration Exercise

Tell me about the Israelite flight from Egypt.

Note: Prompt her to use the word "Exodus."

1250 BCE

The Israelites were in Egypt. The pharaoh didn't want to let them go, so God made them have plagues. Then they left Egypt. This was called the Exodus.

or

Israel was in Egypt. They were slaves. Moses led them out of Egypt to Canaan. They went across the Red Sea. This was the Exodus.

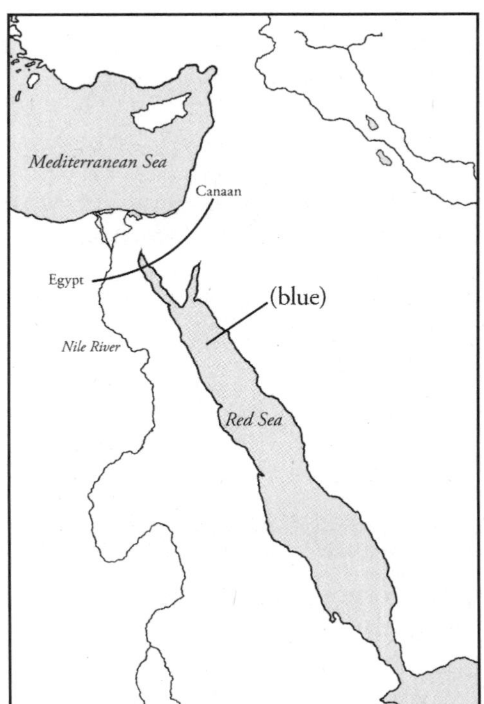

Map Work: The Exodus from Egypt (Student Page 43)

Read the instructions out loud to the student. After each step, pause and give time for the student to complete the task. Provide all necessary help.

1. **Open to Student Page 43 and tear it out.**
2. **On your map, draw a line from *Egypt* up to *Canaan*. The Israelites fled from Egypt up to Canaan, the land God promised to Abraham.**

3. **Find the *Red Sea* on your map and shade it in blue. Remember that when Moses led the Israelites away from Egypt, he led them through the Red Sea.**
4. **When you finish, place the completed map in your history notebook.**

Activities

Choose from the following activities:

- ☐ Coloring Page: Moses Parting the Red Sea
- ☐ Craft: Make a Red Sea Diorama
- ☐ Research Skills: Have the student look up a related topic in a history encyclopedia or another reliable source. Read the entry together and look at the pictures. Topics could include *monotheism, the Hebrews, Judaism, Israelites*, and *early Jewish history*.

Coloring Page: Moses Parting the Red Sea
(Student Page 44)

Use color pencils or crayons to color in this depiction of one of the most famous stories in the Bible.

Craft

MAKE A RED SEA DIORAMA

Make a diorama of the story of Moses and the Israelites crossing the Red Sea.

MATERIALS:

- large shoebox
- construction paper
- tissue paper
- crayons or markers
- glue or tape
- string
- scissors
- small rocks
- small plastic figures (plastic soldiers will do in a pinch!)

DIRECTIONS:

1. Decorate the inside of your shoebox to look like the Red Sea—glue blue construction paper onto the walls of your box, or color them blue with markers (or paint).

2. Add brown paper on the shoebox bottom, for the sea floor.
3. Glue or tape down a few rocks on your sea floor. Draw fish on the walls and floor, if you want to.
4. Glue the feet of the small plastic figures in a line down the middle of the shoebox. These are the Israelites, walking through the sea. (If you use plastic soldiers, you might want to cut or twist their weapons off!)
5. Cut a small square hole in one end of the shoebox, to use for a peephole.
6. Cut a larger square hole in the far end of the shoebox. Glue or tape one layer of tissue paper across it. (This allows light to come in).
7. Put the shoebox lid on. Now hold the shoebox up to a light and peer in. You'll see an underwater scene!

Additional History Reading

Eyewitness: Bible Lands (annotated edition), by Jonathan N. Tubb (DK Publishing, 2016). A guide to the geography, customs, and history of Israel. Much of the text is too difficult for elementary children, but the pictures are beautiful. (RA)

Exodus, by Brian Wildsmith (Eerdmans, 1998). A simple retelling of the Exodus story with spectacular illustrations. **Out of print, but worth looking for at your local library.** (RA)

The Story of Passover, by David A. Adler, illus. Jill Weber (Holiday House, 2015). A short illustrated retelling of the Passover story. (RA)

Corresponding Literature Suggestions

Angels Sweep the Desert Floor: Bible Legends About Moses in the Wilderness, by Miriam Chaikin, illus. Alexander Koshkin (Clarion, 2002). Stories set during the 40 years of Moses' wanderings in the desert. Not appropriate for parents who want to avoid biblical paraphrase. **Out of print, but worth looking for at your local library.** (RA 2–3, IR 4–6)

Baby Moses in a Basket, by Caryn Yacowitz , illus. Julie Downing (Candlewick, 2021). A picture-book retelling of the Biblical story of Moses' birth and journey down the Nile with beautiful watercolor illustrations. As Moses drifts in his basket, he meets Curious Ibis, Mama Hippo, and Mighty Crocodile who watch over him until morning breaks and he meets Pharaoh's daughter. (RA 1, IR 2–3)

Miriam at the River, by Jane Yolen, illus. Khoa Lee (Lerner Publishing Group, 2020). This well-illustrated retelling comes from Miriam's point of view. (RA 1–2, IR 3–4)

CHAPTER SIXTEEN
The Early Greeks

The Mycenaeans

1450-700 BCE

Read & Review

Read pages 124–125 in the text. Afterward, check the student's understanding by asking the questions below.

1. **What were the people who came from Greece to conquer Crete called?** *The Mycenaeans*
2. **What were the Mycenaeans good at?** *Fighting*
3. **Where did the Mycenaeans build colonies?** *Around the Aegean Sea*
4. **Can you tell me a little bit about how the Mycenaean Greeks lived?** Prompt the student if necessary for the following answers: *They lived in houses, had jobs, and went to school.*

Narration Exercise

Tell me what happened after the volcano erupted near Crete.

The Minoans were weak and other people took over. They were called Mycenaeans. They used helmets and shields and chariots to fight.

Map Work: The Mycenaeans (Student Page 45)

Read the instructions out loud to the student. After each step, pause and give time for the student to complete the task. Provide all necessary help.

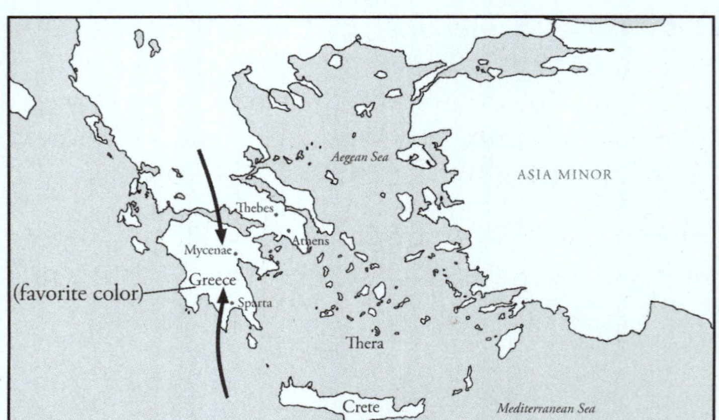

1. **Open to Student Page 45 and tear it out.**

2. **On your map, find the cities of *Mycenae*, *Thebes*, and *Athens*.**
3. **Choose your favorite color, and color *Greece*.**
4. **Draw an arrow from the *Mediterranean Sea* up into Greece. This shows that the Sea People invaded Greece.**
5. **On your map, find the land above and to the left (that is, north and west) of Thebes. Draw an arrow from this land down into Greece. This shows that *Dorians* came from the north to invade Greece.**
6. **When you finish, place the completed map in your history notebook.**

Activities

Choose from the following activities:

- ❑ Coloring Page: Greek War Chariot
- ❑ Craft: Make a Mycenaean Shield
- ❑ Storytelling: How Would You Sneak into Troy?
- ❑ Research Skills: Have the student look up a related topic in a history encyclopedia or another reliable source. Read the entry together and look at the pictures. Topics could include *Minoans, the Mycenaean Age, the Aegean Sea, Crete, the Greek Bronze Age, early Greek civilizations*, and *Ancient Greece*.

Coloring Page: Greek War Chariot (Student Page 46)

This picture of a warrior in his chariot is based on a fresco found in Pylos.

Craft

MAKE A MYCENAEAN SHIELD

The Mycenaeans were famous for their armor that helped protect them in battle! In this activity, you can make your own model of a Mycenaean figure-eight shield.

MATERIALS:

- a large piece of cardboard (ideally about the same height as the student)
- scissors
- pencil
- glue
- duct tape or a glue gun
- paint
- bronze paint, animal print fabric, stapler (optional)

DIRECTIONS:

1. Use a pencil to draw the shape of your shield on a piece of cardboard. Draw circles on top of each other (the largest you can fit) and a section to connect them. See illustration.
2. Carefully cut along the outline (younger students should have an adult or older sibling help with the cutting). Save the excess cardboard for handles.
3. Cut out a strip of cardboard (about 1.5 inches wide and 8 inches long) to be the handle. Bend it slightly to form an arch. Attach both ends to the narrow section in the back of the shield, using strong tape or a glue gun. This will create a loop to grip onto.
4. Decorate the front of your shield with paint or fabric! Many shields from this period had either geometric designs or animal skin on the front. So you can paint designs, paint an animal skin pattern, or staple animal print fabric across the front of the shield. Many shields were reinforced with bronze edges. Paint the edges of your shield with metallic paint.
5. Optional: Save your shield for use in the Iron vs. Bronze activity in the next chapter!

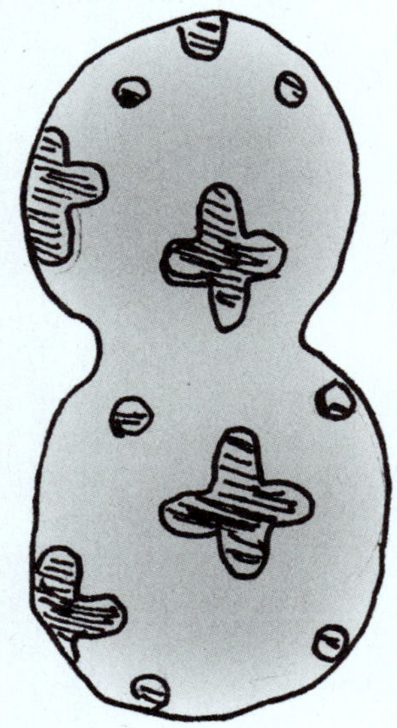

Storytelling

HOW WOULD YOU SNEAK INTO TROY?

Years after the Mycenaean period, a famous Greek storyteller named Homer wrote down the myth of the Trojan Horse. In Homer's story, the Mycenaean Greeks hid inside a giant hollow wooden horse to sneak into Troy. Read *The Trojan Horse* by Emily Little (or find a different version of the story at your local library). Then ask your student "If you were a Greek soldier who needed to sneak behind the walls of Troy, how would you get in?" Younger students should narrate their answer to an instructor. Older students can write their answers on their own.

For detailed instructions on using the creative writing prompts with younger students, see Appendix One.

The Greek Dark Ages

Read & Review

Read pages 125-128 in the text. Afterward, check the student's understanding by asking the questions below.

1. **How did the barbarians live?** Prompt the student if necessary for the following answers: *They wandered around, couldn't read or write, and spent their time fighting other people.*
2. **What did the Mycenaean Greeks have that made them such strong fighters?** *Bronze weapons and chariots*
3. **What kind of weapons did the barbarians have?** *Iron weapons that were stronger than bronze weapons*
4. **When the Greeks and the barbarians fought, who won?** *The barbarians*
5. **Do you remember why we call this time the Dark Ages?** *Because the barbarians didn't leave us any written history or records about the time that they lived in Greece!*

1450-700 BCE

Narration Exercise

What happened in this lesson?

The Greeks thought they were strong. But barbarians were stronger. They took over Greece. This was the 'Dark Ages,' when they didn't write anything.

or

Greeks lived like regular people. Barbarians wandered around fighting. The barbarians conquered the Greeks, but they didn't keep histories. This was the 'Dark Ages.'

Activities

Choose from the following activities:

- ☐ Coloring Page: A Greek Vase
- ☐ Storytelling: Tell a Story Without Writing
- ☐ Role Play: Iron vs. Bronze
- ☐ Research Skills: Have the student look up a related topic in a history encyclopedia or another reliable source. Read the entry together and look at the pictures. Topics could include *Grecian Dark Ages*, *Sea Peoples*, *Dorians*, *early Greek civilizations*, *Late Bronze Age*, and *Ancient Greece*.

Coloring Page: A Greek Vase (Student Page 47)

Much of what we know about the Ancient Greeks comes from the pictures they painted on their beautiful pottery. Use the vase template on Student Page 47 to draw an important scene from your life.

Storytelling

TELL A STORY WITHOUT WRITING

After the Mycenaeans, new groups of people moved into Greece. These people didn't know how to read or write, so we don't have much written history about them. In this activity we are going to find out what it's like to live in a time when people couldn't write things down. Can we tell a story and remember it, without writing it down?

Have all of the players sit in a circle. Start a story about a brave child or hero in ancient Greece. If you like, you can use the following sentence starter:

"Once upon a time in Ancient Greece, there was a..."

The next player adds one sentence. Take turns adding one sentence at a time. Keep going until a natural ending has been reached, or stop after a set number of sentences.

Wait a day or two, then try to remember all of the details in the story. It is pretty hard! Imagine how much of the story you will remember in a week! What about a year? What about 10 years? Remind students that when there was no writing, people had to pass important messages and stories orally. Sometimes details may have gotten lost or changed.

Note to Instructor: If you like, record the story on your phone or write down the details so that you can quiz students on the story a few days later. Do not let students listen to the recording or read the notes.

Alternative Idea/Classroom Adaptation: If you have a large group, instead of creating your own story, try playing the game "telephone." Have students sit in a line or circle. The teacher whispers a short message into the first student's ear. It could be a silly sentence, a short fact, or even a tongue twister (ex: "The hero hid the golden goat in a garden" or "A sneaky sailor sang songs to a sleepy cyclops."). Each student whispers what they heard to the next person, one at a time. No repeating, and it must stay quiet! The last student says the sentence out loud for everyone to hear. Reveal what the original sentence was—and have fun comparing how much changed along the way!

Role Play

IRON VS BRONZE

The Mycenaeans were able to conquer the city-states around the Aegean Sea because they had superior weapons. They ruled for a few hundred years before barbarians came along with even better weapons and defeated them. In this simulation, you will feel how hard it must have been to fight against enemies with better weapons.

MATERIALS:

- A large area where you can run around
- If you made a Mycenaean shield in the last lesson, wear it during this game!

DIRECTIONS:

1. Choose one student to be the Mycenaean soldier and one student to be the Athenian soldier. If completing with more than 2 students, divide them into pairs. If you have just one student, have the student act as the Athenian soldier and the instructor act as the Mycenaean soldier.
2. Read the following script to set-up the game:

   This game is simple. One of you is a Mycenaean soldier and one of you is an Athenian soldier. Mycenaean soldier/s, give your battle cry!

   Student or instructor sound out their battle cry.

   Now, Athenian soldier/s give your battle cry!

   Student sounds out a battle cry.

   Instead of actually fighting each other, we will play tag. Whoever tags the other person first wins the battle. Ready, set...

   Oh wait one second. The Mycenaean had bronze armor. So the Mycenaean soldier can only be tagged on their right shoulder, but the Athenian soldier can be tagged anywhere. Okay, now we are ready...

Oh wait... the Mycenaean soldiers had chariots and horses, so they could move faster than the Athenians. So the Athenian soldier must choose one foot to hop on but the Mycenaean soldier gets to use both feet. Okay, now we are ready. Ready... set...go!

3. Let the game play out. If there are multiple pairs "fighting" each other, wait until each pair has a winner. Tally the score to see which group won, the Mycenaeans or the Athenians. In almost all cases, the Mycenaeans will win. If you want, you can add more advantages to the Mycenaean side (for example: having a student help the Mycenaean soldier, making it 2 against one; this could represent that Mycenaeans had warships).

4. Once the game is over, explain:

   The Mycenaeans conquered many city-states around the Aegean Sea. They had bronze weapons and armor, horses, chariots, and warships. They spread their power and ruled for several hundred years, but then things changed. Barbarians came.

5. Set things up for the next round with the following script:

   Now we will play another round. Whoever was a Mycenaean soldier will still be a Mycenaean soldier, but whoever was an Athenian soldier will now be a barbarian soldier. This time, the barbarian has iron weapons, while the Mycenaean only has bronze. So the Mycenaean can be tagged anywhere, but the barbarian can only be tagged on their right shoulder. The barbarians also had javelins and could hit their enemies from a distance. So the Mycenaean soldier has to clasp their hands together, but the barbarian soldier can use both hands.

6. Once again, let the game play out. If you have multiple pairs, tally the total points for the Mycenaean team vs the barbarian team.

7. Once everyone has had a turn to win and a turn to lose, complete the activity with a discussion.

   a. Ask the Mycenaeans: **How did it feel when you fought the Athenian? How did you feel when you fought the barbarians?**
   b. Ask the Athenian/barbarians: **How did it feel when you were an Athenian? How did it feel when you were a barbarian?**
   c. **Was this game fair? Why or why not?**
   d. **Imagine you are a Mycenaean soldier. What would it be like to fight in a battle with someone who has iron weapons when you only have bronze weapons?**

Additional History Reading

Eyewitness: Ancient Greece, by DK Children (DK Children, 2023). This book is packed with information bites that make it a good reference. Descriptive of many aspects of ancient Greece, using pictures, drawings, costumed actors, and more. Fantastic pictures of artifacts! There are helpful two-page spreads on the Mycenaeans and the Greek Dark Age. (Also recommended for chapters twelve, twenty, twenty-one, and twenty-seven) (RA)

The Best Book of Ancient Greece, by Belinda Weber (Kingfisher, 2005). Colorful and easy-to-read sections on the Minoans, Mycenaeans, Trojans, Spartans, Athenians, and various aspects of daily life. Excellent for young students (some parents may wish to preview the picture of the Minotaur on p. 28). (RA)

You Wouldn't Want to Be a Slave in Ancient Greece: A Life You'd Rather Not Have, by Fiona MacDonald (Franklin Watts, 2000). An entertaining guide to the life of an ancient Greek slave, with cartoon-like illustrations. Good historical information. (RA 1–2, IR 3–5) You can look for this book at the library or purchase it used or as an ebook.

Corresponding Literature Suggestions

The Trojan Horse, by Emily Little (Random House, 1988). This legendary Greek assault on Troy took place during the Mycenaean period; this retelling can be read independently by strong readers. (IR, RA for beginners)

D'Aulaires' Book of Greek Myths, by Edgar Parin d'Aulaire (Delacorte, 1992). A classic in its own right, this introduction to the gods and goddesses of Ancient Greece has beautiful illustrations by Caldecott Award winners. (RA)

Usborne Greek Myths, by Heather Amery (Usborne, 2024). Simplified retelling of Greek myths. The stories are shorter than D'Aulaire's version listed above. (RA, possible IR for advanced readers)

CHAPTER SEVENTEEN
The Phoenicians

Phoenician Traders

1200-800 BCE

Read & Review

Read pages 129–131 in the text. Afterward, check the student's understanding by asking the questions below.

1. **Where did the Phoenicians live?** *In Canaan*
2. **What were they good at?** *Sailing their boats*
3. **The Phoenicians made glass. Do you remember what two things they made glass from?** *Sand and lye*
4. **What special way of shaping glass did the Phoenicians invent?** *Glass blowing*
5. **What did they make their purple dye from?** *Snails*
6. **Why was purple called "the color of kings"?** *Because it was so expensive.*

Narration Exercise

List four things that the Phoenicians sold to other countries.

Cedar trees, logs, beautiful furniture, salt, dried fish, embroidered cloth, tin, metals, glass, purple dye, and purple cloth.

Map Work: Phoenician Traders (Student Page 48)

Read the instructions out loud to the student. After each step, pause and give time for the student to complete the task. Provide all necessary help.

1. **Open to Student Page 48 and tear it out.**
2. **On your map, find the Phoenician cities of *Tyre* and *Carthage* and circle their names using a red pencil.**

3. **With a green pencil, color in the area known as *Phoenicia*. Then, using the same green pencil, color the areas that were controlled by the Phoenicians. These areas are already marked on your map. If you need a reminder, see the map in your book.**

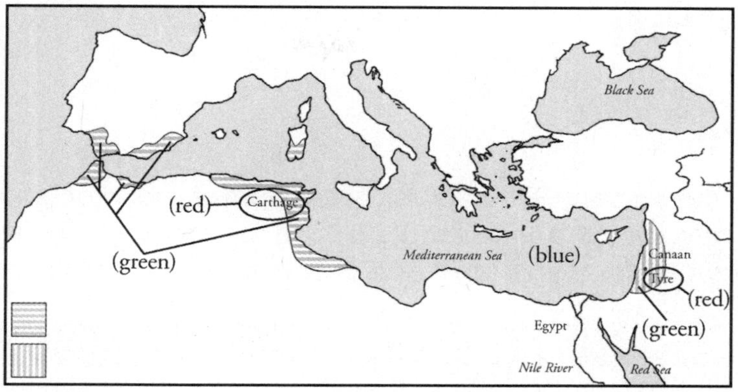

4. **Color the *Mediterranean Sea* in blue. This is where the Phoenician sailors did most of their trading.**
5. **When you finish, place the completed map in your history notebook.**

Activities

Choose from the following activities:

- ☐ Coloring Page: A Phoenician Ship
- ☐ Craft: Faux Colored Glass
- ☐ Science: Make Purple Dye and Use as an Acid/Base Indicator
- ☐ Craft: Make a Colored Pasta Necklace (with Homemade Purple Dye)
- ☐ Research Skills: Have the student look up a related topic in a history encyclopedia or another reliable source. Read the entry together and look at the pictures. Topics could include *the Phoenicians, glassmaking, glassblowing, the alphabet*, and *Tyre*.
- ☐ Field Trip Idea: Visit a glass studio and watch artists blow glass, or watch an online video about glass blowing.

Coloring Page: A Phoenician Ship (Student Page 49)

The Phoenicians were expert sailors who built strong, fast ships to trade goods across the Mediterranean Sea.

Craft

PAINT FAUX COLORED GLASS

The ancient Phoenicians often added red, blue, and yellow dyes to their sand and lye mixture before making glass. In this activity, we will imitate this and decorate a glass jar. Note: this is strictly a decorative item; don't store food or beverages in it.

MATERIALS:

- craft paint: red, blue, yellow
- short, clear glass jar with a removable top (such as some jams and salsa come in, or a baby food jar—the jar needs to be short enough for the paintbrush to reach the bottom)
- paint brush
- paper plate to hold paint
- oil and baking soda to remove sticky residue as needed (you can also use commercial products for this)
- paper and glue stick to cover top of jar (optional)

DIRECTIONS:

1. Remove the label from your jar.
2. If there's a sticky residue, form a paste of oil and baking soda and spread it on the sticky part. Let sit for a few minutes, then scrub. Wash off with dish soap and warm water.
3. If the lid has writing you wish to cover, cut a circle out of paper and glue it on top.
4. Think about how you want your jar to be colored. Do you want one main color and 2 accent colors? Do you want a more equal mix of colors?
5. Put some of each color paint onto your paper plate.
6. Use your paint brush to start painting the inside of your jar with the first color, leaving clear spaces for adding the next 2 colors.
7. Wash your paint brush and proceed to the second color. The colors will bend and swirl where the 2 colors meet, and you can add some more intentional swirls with the paint brush if you like.
8. Wash your paint brush and proceed to the third color.
9. Look at your jar from the outside and see if there are any blank spots you need to fill in.
10. Let the paint dry with the lid off.
11. Find a place to display your colorful glass jar, or give it as a gift!

Science

MAKE PURPLE DYE AND USE AS AN ACID/BASE INDICATOR

***The Phoenicians boiled snails with salt water and lemon juice for ten days to make purple dye. In this activity, you'll make a simple purple dye in just twenty minutes! Then, you can use that dye in a fun science demonstration, and to dye pasta and make a necklace. Note:** wear old clothing, as the purple dye can leave stains.*

MATERIALS FOR THE PURPLE DYE:

- red cabbage (also called purple cabbage)
- water, about 8 cups
- pot big enough for both cabbage and water
- colander or strainer
- bowl or container to hold the dyed water

MATERIALS FOR THE SCIENCE DEMONSTRATION:

- vinegar
- baking soda
- additional items to test, such as lemon juice, other juices, baking powder, milk of magnesia, milk, soda (optional)
- 2 clear cups or containers (more if you'd like to test additional items)

DIRECTIONS FOR MAKING PURPLE DYE:

1. Chop about a third of the red cabbage into small pieces.
2. Put it in a pot and add about 8 cups of water, making sure to cover the cabbage.
3. Boil, uncovered, for about 20 minutes (until the water turns purple).
4. Let cool.
5. Strain the purple water into the container.

DIRECTIONS FOR SCIENCE DEMONSTRATION:

Note to Instructor: Do not allow the student to taste any of the items set aside for the experiment, either before or after mixing them. This is an important safety precaution that should be used in all experiments.

You can add different things to your purple dye to create chemical reactions - mixing things together to make something new!

Red cabbage juice is an acid-base indicator, meaning that its color will change to shades of pink and red if you add an acid to it, and to shades of blue and green if you add a base to it. Acids that you can eat usually taste sour or tart, and bases that you can eat usually taste bitter.

1. Pour about ¼ cup of the cabbage juice into each of 3 clear cups.
2. Put one of the cups to the side so you can compare the original color.
3. Add about a teaspoon of lemon juice to one of the cups and stir.
4. Note the color. Is it an acid or a base?
5. Add about a teaspoon of baking soda to another cup and stir.
6. Note the color. Is it an acid or a base?
7. Investigate further by testing additional items.

Craft

MAKE A COLORED PASTA NECKLACE (WITH HOMEMADE PURPLE DYE)

Purple dye was so expensive in ancient times that it was called "the color of kings." Red cabbage dye is much less expensive and we can dye pasta with it and make a necklace!

MATERIALS:

- purple dye (from the activity above)
- uncooked pasta (hollow for stringing)
- string or yarn

DIRECTIONS:

1. Add a handful of pasta to the remaining purple dye. Keep the pasta in the dye until it has changed its color. This will take a few minutes.
2. Remove the pasta from the dye and set it to dry in a safe place.
3. If needed, add more pasta to the dye and repeat until there is enough colored pasta to make a necklace.
4. After the pasta is completely dried, string onto a length of string or yarn that is long enough to fit easily over your head.
5. Securely tie the ends together.

The Founding of Carthage

Read & Review

Read pages 132–133 in the text. Afterward, check the student's understanding by asking the questions below.

1. **What is a colony?** Prompt student for the answer: *A little settlement of people*
2. **Do you remember the name of the little Phoenician colony that grew into a big city?** *Carthage*
3. **What queen helped to start Carthage?** *Dido*
4. **Why did Dido have to leave her home?** *She was afraid of her brother.*
5. **Why did Dido want to start the city of Carthage near the water?** *So that ships would visit her city and trade with her*

Narration Exercise

How did Dido use the bull-hide to get the land she wanted?

She told the man who owned the land that she only wanted enough to go under a bull hide. Then she cut it up into lots of small pieces and laid it all around a big piece of land.

1200–800 BCE

Activities

Choose from the following activities:

- ☐ Coloring Page: Queen Dido
- ☐ Sequencing Events: The Founding of Carthage
- ☐ Math: Queen Dido's Perimeter Trick
- ☐ Research Skills: Have the student look up a related topic in a history encyclopedia or another reliable source. Read the entry together and look at the pictures. Topics could include *Carthage*, *Tyre*, and *Dido* (sometimes also called *Elissa*).

Coloring Page: Queen Dido (Student Page 50)

Dido, the legendary founder and ruler of Carthage, tricked the landowner by asking for "a bull's-hide worth of ground" and then cutting the hide into a very thin strip that could surround a large piece of land.

Sequencing Events

THE FOUNDING OF CARTHAGE

In this activity, the student will put four events in the correct order. No supplies are needed; the student can act it out.

DIRECTIONS:

1. As the instructor reads out the rhyming sequence, the student should act out the events in the chapter.
2. We're going to act out four things Dido did in the lesson, using rhymes and the words *first*, *next*, *then*, and *finally* to help us remember.
3. First, Dido slipped from the palace at night, took her friends and fled from sight (student silently tip-toes across the room, pretending to escape).
4. Next, they sailed across the sea, looking for a place to be (student "jumps" into a boat and puts his hands on his eyes to scan the horizon).
5. Then, Dido cut the bullhide nice and thin, laid out the strips so she could win (student mimes cutting and laying out the bullhide).
6. Finally, they built with stone and sand, a brand new city on the land (student pretends to lift and stack heavy stones, and then admires his building).
7. Repeat steps 3-6.
8. Challenge: see how few words the student needs to hear before they can begin acting out each step.

Math

QUEEN DIDO'S PERIMETER TRICK

Queen Dido founded Carthage by using a math trick to enlarge the perimeter of her bull hide. The perimeter of a shape is the measurement of all the lines or edges of a shape. In this activity, you can practice your own perimeter trick, similar to the one Queen Dido used to found Carthage. You will be able to walk through a piece of paper!

MATERIALS:

- Student page 51
- Scissors

DIRECTIONS:

1. Pull out Student Page 51.
2. Fold the paper in half lengthwise (vertically), ensuring that the template stays visible and the center line becomes the seam.
3. Cut the dashed lines that start at the seam and have arrows pointing toward the edge of the paper. Make sure to stop cutting when you reach the arrowheads.
4. Now cut the dashed lines that start on the edge of the paper and have arrows pointing toward the seam. Cut from the edge of the paper to the arrowheads.
5. Cut the seams, except the one at the top of the page and the one at the bottom of the page (there should be seven of them).
6. Carefully stretch the paper out. There will be a hole in the middle that you can carefully step through!

Perimeter is the distance around the shape. To find the perimeter of a piece of paper, you add the length of all the sides together. So if you have a rectangle that has two 4-inch sides and two 2-inch sides, the perimeter would be 4 + 4 + 2 + 2 = 12 inches!

Surface area is the entire area contained within the shape. To find the surface area of a piece of paper you multiply the length of the paper by the width of the paper.

By carefully cutting the paper, you increased the perimeter and allowed for a hole big enough for you to walk through. However, the surface of the area remained the same; you didn't actually magically change how big the paper was. You distributed the surface area in a different way. That's the power of math!

Queen Dido did the same thing when she cut the bull hide into thin strips and stretched it across a large piece of land to found the city of Carthage.

Classroom Adaptation: Make a few extra copies of the student page ahead of time in case a student makes a mistake and needs a replacement page.

Additional History Reading

The Ancient Worlds Atlas, by DK (DK Publishing, 2023). This beautifully illustrated atlas has a two-page spread on the Phoenicians. (Also recommended for chapters five, six, eight, nine, eighteen, and twenty-two) (RA 1-3, IR 4-5)

Ancient Israelites and Their Neighbors: An Activity Guide, by Marian Broida (Chicago Review Press, 2003). This book contains a few activities related to ancient Phoenicia—very little is available for elementary children on this subject. (RA)

Ox, House, Stick: The History of Our Alphabet, by Don Robb, illus. Anne Smith (Charlesbridge, 2007). An illustrated history of how the Sinaitic, Phoenician, Greek, and Roman alphabets evolved. (RA)

Corresponding Literature Suggestions

In Search of a Homeland: The Story of the Aeneid, by Penelope Lively, illus. Ian Andrew (Frances Lincoln, 2006). Aeneas meets Dido, among other adventures; you may not want to read all of the text to a young child, but the illustrations are lovely. (RA)

The Orchard Book of Roman Myths, by Geraldine McCaughrean (Orchard, 2003). This collection of myths includes two short tales about Aeneas, Dido's husband, the story of Romulus and Remus (see chapter twenty-two), and the kidnapping of the Sabine women. (RA 1-3, IR 3-6).

CHAPTER EIGHTEEN
The Return of Assyria

Ashurbanipal's Attack

Read & Review

Read pages 134–137 in the text. Afterward, check the student's understanding by asking the questions below.

1. **Can you tell me two countries that Assyria conquered?** *Egypt, Canaan* [the answers Mesopotamia, Babylon, and Asia Minor are also acceptable]
2. **What did Ashurbanipal like to do for fun?** *Hunt lions with bows and arrows*
3. **What kind of shields did the Assyrians use?** *Basket shields tied together with leather*
4. **How did the Assyrian soldiers break through city walls?** *They built ramps out of dirt and pushed wooden towers on wheels up the ramps.*
5. **Did the people in the Assyrian Empire like their king?** *No, they hated him for his cruelty.*

675–600 BCE

Narration Exercise

Tell me two things you learned about the Assyrians.

The Assyrians wanted to make their empire big again. They conquered everyone around them. Their king knew how to break into cities with walls. The Assyrians were very cruel to the cities they beat.

Activities

Choose from the following activities:

- [ ] Coloring Page: A Bas-Relief From Ancient Assyria
- [ ] Make a Model: Make an Assyrian Siege Tower (PREP)
- [ ] Research Skills: Have the student look up a related topic in a history encyclopedia or another reliable source. Read the entry together and look at the pictures. Topics could include *Ashurbanipal*, *siege tower*, *Assyria*, and *Nineveh*.

Coloring Page: A Bas-Relief From Ancient Assyria
(Student Page 52)

Ancient Assyrian bas-reliefs were detailed stone carvings. This carving from Nineveh shows King Ashurbanipal hunting lions.

Make a Model

ASSYRIAN SIEGE TOWER (PREP)

The Assyrians are gearing up to take over another city – and they need your help to build a siege tower! These towers protected the Assyrian army as they used battering rams to smash through enemy walls. Grab your toy building bricks and create your own siege tower.

Note to Parents: Use whatever type of building toy you have around the house. For example, Tinker Toys, K'nex, LEGO, or magnetic building sets.

DIRECTIONS:

1. Build a 3-sided tower, using wheels if you have them (if you don't have wheels, building on a piece of cardboard will allow for sliding the tower across a smooth surface, such as the table or floor).
2. The siege tower was built on a wheeled base and had a 3-sided tower built on the front portion of the vehicle. If you have small action figures (for example LEGO figures or Playmobil), you can place them inside the tower and pretend they are the archers, shooting arrows as the tower gets pushed closer and closer to the city walls.
3. Make your battering ram out of bricks and place it sticking out from the front of your tower.
4. Build a city wall (or tower) out of blocks. Attack!
5. Optional: Take a picture of your siege tower. Keep it in your history notebook.

The Library of Nineveh

Read & Review

Read pages 137–140 in the text. Afterward, check the student's understanding by asking the questions below.

1. **What city did Ashurbanipal live in?** *Nineveh*
2. **Can you tell me two things that Ashurbanipal did to make Nineveh beautiful?** *He built a beautiful palace, decorated the gates of the city, planted gardens, and made sculptures.*
3. **Why did Ashurbanipal decide to collect a library?** *So that people would remember him*
4. **Were the library books made out of paper?** *No, they were made out of clay.*
5. **Some of the clay tablets had the history of Assyria written on them. Can you tell me two other kinds of writing from Ashurbanipal's library?** *Stories, prayers, facts about the sun, moon and sky; medicine, law, and science*
6. **Can we still read Ashurbanipal's library today?** *Yes, some of the clay tablets can still be read today.*

Narration Exercise

Tell me about Nineveh and the king.

Ashurbanipal lived in Nineveh. It was a beautiful city with gardens in it. He wanted to be remembered. He made a library out of clay tablets.

or

The first library was in Nineveh. The king collected stories and other writings. He kept them in big rooms so that people could read them a long time afterwards.

Map Work: The Library of Nineveh
(Student Page 53)

Read the instructions out loud to the student. After each step, pause and give time for the student to complete the task. Provide all necessary help.

1. **Open to Student Page 53 and tear it out.**
2. **On your map, find Ashurbanipal's city, *Nineveh*, and circle the name in red.**

3. **Use a green crayon or pencil to underline *Assyria*—the area that Ashurbanipal ruled.**
4. **Use a blue crayon to color in all of the seas. See if you can read all of their names.**
5. **When you finish, place the completed map in your history notebook.**

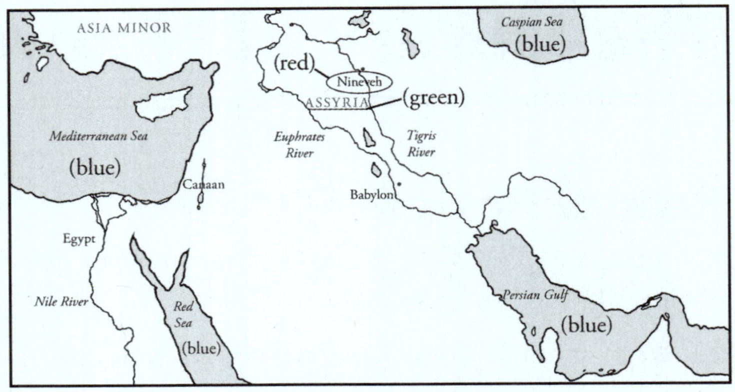

Activities

Choose from the following activities:

- ☐ Storytelling: Record a Family Story
- ☐ Game: Library of Nineveh Scavenger Hunt
- ☐ Research Skills: Have the student look up a related topic in a history encyclopedia or another reliable source. Read the entry together and look at the pictures. Topics could include *Ashurbanipal*, *Assyria*, *Nineveh*, and *The Library of Nineveh*.
- ☐ Field Trip Idea: To celebrate learning about the Library of Nineveh, try visiting your local library. If you want, add a library challenge. Here are some ideas: (1) Most public libraries in the United States use the Dewey Decimal Classification system to organize their books. Help the student figure out the Dewey Decimal number for Ancient Civilizations. See if you can find any books about Ancient Assyria. (2) Ask a librarian or look up the Dewey Decimal number for a topic of your choice. See if you can find a book on that topic. (3) Find a book that starts with the same first letter as your name. (4) Find a book with a red cover. (5) Ask a librarian how they choose which books to add to their collection.

Storytelling

RECORD A FAMILY STORY

King Ashurbanipal had his scribes go throughout the kingdom and write down stories that families had told to each other orally (that means through spoken words, not written words) for generations. He made his scribes write them down and bring the tablets back to his library.

Every family has stories that they tell over and over again, but we don't always write them down. In this activity, pretend you are one of King Ashurbanipal's scribes. Choose a favorite family story to record for future generations. Younger students should narrate the story to an adult and have the adult write it down. Older students can write it down on their own. Alternatively, you could tell the story orally and record it as an audio or video recording. Keep your recorded story in a safe place so that it can be preserved for future generations!

Classroom Adaption: Younger students can work in small groups to record each other telling their family story into an audio recording device. Have students prepare and practice their story before they record it. Limit each story to a set time, 2 to 5 minutes. Older students can write down their family story independently and then exchange the story with a partner for review.

Game

LIBRARY OF NINEVEH SCAVENGER HUNT

King Ashurbanipal had his scribes go throughout the land and collect clay tablets to keep in his grand library. In this activity, you will pretend to be one of King Ashurbanipal's scribes. You must collect all of the clay tablets before the time runs out!

MATERIALS:

- 7 index cards or pieces of paper ("tablets")
- crayons or pencil
- 7 books
- a basket or box for collecting "tablets"
- a reward (for example, a few chocolate chips, outside play-time, or a sticker)

DIRECTIONS:

1. On each index card, or "tablet," write one letter: N, I, N, E, V, E, H). If you like, write a clue about where to find a tablet on the back of each index card (for example, draw a picture of an egg carton as a clue for the book hidden in the refrigerator. Or draw a picture of a jug of milk.)

2. Place each index card so that it is sticking out of a book. Then hide the books in places around the house where you don't normally find books (for example in the refrigerator, underneath a couch cushion, etc...).
3. Set a timer for 10 minutes. See if the student can collect all "tablets" before the time runs out.
4. Once the tablets are collected, help younger students arrange the letters to spell the word NINEVEH. Older students can unscramble the letters on their own.
5. Collect the cards and offer a reward!

Additional History Reading

Ancient Egyptians and Their Neighbors: An Activity Guide, by Marian Broida (Chicago Review Press, 1999). This book contains a few activities related to ancient Assyria—very little is available for elementary children on this subject. You can look for this book at the library or purchase it used or as an ebook. (RA)

The Ancient Worlds Atlas, by DK (DK Publishing, 2023). This beautifully illustrated atlas has a two-page spread on the Assyrians. (Also recommended for chapters five, six, eight, nine, seventeen, and twenty-two) (RA 1-3, IR 4-5)

Amazing Women of the Middle East: 25 Stories from Ancient Times to the Present Day, by Wafa' Tarnowska (Crocodile Books, 2020). This colorful collection of biographies includes an entry about Semiramis, a semi-legendary queen who is based on Shammuramat. (Also recommended for its biography of Nefertiti, chapter fourteen) (RA 1-3, IR 4-6)

Corresponding Literature Suggestions

The Children's Illustrated Jewish Bible (New Edition) by Laaren Brown and Lenny Hort, illus. Eric Thomas (DK Publishing, 2020). Includes a beautifully illustrated version of Jonah's journey to Nineveh. (RA)

The Hard to Swallow Tale of Jonah and the Whale, by Joyce Denham, illus. Amanda Hall (Lion Cub Books, 2024). Jonah was sent to Assyria's capital city, Nineveh, but he didn't want to go! (RA 1-2, IR 3 and up)

Sinbad: From the Tales of the Thousand and One Nights, retold and illustrated by Ludmila Zeman (Tundra Books, 1999). A kid-friendly and beautifully illustrated adaptation of the Sinbad story from One Thousand and One Nights. The Sinbad stories, though they took place in a much later time period, are from the same part of the world as the Assyrian Empire. (RA)

OPTIONAL LESSON
The Story of Shammuramat, Warrior Queen of Assyria

Read & Review

Read pages 141–143 in the text. Afterward, check the student's understanding by asking the questions below.

1. **What did Queen Shammuramat do after her husband died?** *She ruled Assyria alongside her son.*
2. **What is something Queen Shammuramat did that Assyrian queens before her did not do?** Answers may vary. Acceptable answers include: *She decided how to spend money. She made laws. She went to battle.*
3. **What is one story that people made up about Queen Shammuramat?** Answers may vary. Acceptable answers include: *She was raised by doves. She invented pants for women. She conquered an army of elephants. She built a palace in 7 days. She dug a river to keep her people from becoming thirsty.*

Activities

Choose from the following activities:

- ☐ Coloring Page: Queen Shammuramat (Student Page 54)
- ☐ Creative Writing Prompt: Pretend you are one of Queen Shammuramat's subjects. Write her a letter to thank her for something she did. (If needed, review the instructions on how to use the creative writing prompts in Appendix One.)

800 BCE

CHAPTER NINETEEN
Greece Gets Civilized Again

Greece Gets an Alphabet

800–700 BCE

Read & Review

Read pages 144–147 in the text. Afterward, check the student's understanding by asking the questions below.

1. **What happened to the barbarians who lived in Greece?** *They became civilized—built houses, learned how to read, etc.* (any details the student wants to repeat from the lesson are fine).
2. **Did they kill their neighbors for fun?** *No*
3. **What did they do instead?** *Wrestled, raced, danced*
4. **Did the women go out and find food?** *No, they stayed indoors.*
5. **The barbarians were now called Greeks. They learned to read and write. Can you tell me about the letters that they used?** Ask the student to point back to some of the Greek letters and tell you what they represent.

Narration Exercise

What happened to the barbarians in this chapter?

They learned to farm. They learned to play sports and dance. They were no longer barbarians. They became Greeks.

Activities

Choose from the following activities:

- ☐ Memory Work: The Greek Alphabet
- ☐ Activity Page: Write Your Name with Greek Letters
- ☐ Craft: Make a Greek Loom
- ☐ Research Skills: Have the student look up a related topic in a history encyclopedia or another reliable source. Read the entry together and look at the pictures. Topics could include *Dorians*, *Ancient Greece*, *the history of alphabets*, and *the Archaic Age*.

Memory Work

THE GREEK ALPHABET

The Greek alphabet is the foundation of many modern writing systems and has influenced mathematics, science, and philosophy. Memorizing these letters can help students recognize Greek-derived words and symbols and provide early appreciation for the legacy of ancient Greece in modern culture.

Note to Instructor: For detailed guidance on using memory work activities, see Appendix Two. The student's memory work reference page is available on Student Pages 55-56. Below, you'll find the list of items to memorize, along with additional teaching ideas for your convenience.

Note to Instructor: Have the student learn the names of the letters and their corresponding symbols. They do not need to learn the significance or modern use of each letter; that information is provided just for fun.

1. Alpha (Α, α) - The first letter of the Greek alphabet! We sometimes use alpha to describe something that's the first or most important. For example, scientists call the brightest star in a constellation the alpha star!
2. Beta (Β, β) - The second letter. It is used when something is almost ready but not quite finished, like a "beta version" of a new video game.
3. Gamma (Γ, γ) - This letter looks like an upside-down L. It is famous for representing gamma rays in science, a type of light we cannot see.
4. Delta (Δ, δ) - This triangle-shaped letter means "change." Scientists use it to show when things are different, like how much you've grown since last year.
5. Epsilon (Ε, ε) - This letter is used by scientists to talk about very small amounts, like a drop of water in a big ocean.

6. Pi (Π, π) - This letter looks like a table and represents a special number (3.14) used to measure circles.
7. Sigma (Σ, σ) - In mathematics, this letter is used to show when you are adding a bunch of numbers.
8. Omega (Ω, ω) - The last letter of the Greek alphabet. It is used to talk about the end of things or something that is complete.

If older students want an additional challenge, have them memorize the entire Greek alphabet:

1. Alpha (Α, α)
2. Beta (Β, β)
3. Gamma (Γ, γ)
4. Delta (Δ, δ)
5. Epsilon (Ε, ε)
6. Zeta (Ζ, ζ)
7. Eta (Η, η)
8. Theta (Θ, θ)
9. Iota (Ι, ι)
10. Kappa (Κ, κ)
11. Lambda (Λ, λ)
12. Mu (Μ, μ)
13. Nu (Ν, ν)
14. Xi (Ξ, ξ)
15. Omicron (Ο, ο)
16. Pi (Π, π)
17. Rho (Ρ, ρ)
18. Sigma (Σ, σ, ς) - (Note: ς is used as the lowercase final form of sigma.)
19. Tau (Τ, τ)
20. Upsilon (Υ, υ)
21. Phi (Φ, φ)
22. Chi (Χ, χ)
23. Psi (Ψ, ψ)
24. Omega (Ω, ω)

Suggested Activity: Create your own flashcards with the name of the letter on one side and the symbols for that letter on the other side!

Related Reading: Look for a "Greek alphabet for kids" book or a Greek alphabet coloring book! If you are interested in using this memory work to jump-start a deeper dive into learning Greek, Memoria Press publishes a variety of useful resources including a Greek alphabet workbook (for older students), flashcards, and wall and desk charts.

Activity Page

WRITE YOUR NAME WITH GREEK LETTERS

Using Student Page 57, write your name—and the names of your friends and family—in Greek.

Classroom Adaptation: Have students create decorative name cards with their English and Greek names. Display their names in the classroom.

Craft

MAKE A GREEK LOOM

The Ancient Greeks had to make all their own clothes. They even had to weave their own cloth! In this activity you will try a simplified weaving activity.

MATERIALS:

- a ruler
- a small to medium rectangular piece of cardboard
- string or strong thread
- scissors (for adult use)
- a variety of materials for weaving: paper strips, yarn, ribbon, pipe cleaners, or dried grasses.
- dowel rod for hanging (optional)

DIRECTIONS:

1. **For the Instructor:** Use the scissors to cut evenly spaced slots or small Vs along both shorter ends of the cardboard rectangle. Each slot should be about half an inch deep and half an inch apart from the next one. The slots on the top of the cardboard should line up with the slots on the bottom of the cardboard. Use a ruler to make the cuts even.

2. **For the Student:** Secure one end of the string at the top left corner of the cardboard. You can knot it around the edge or tape it securely to the back.

3. Wind the string around the cardboard by slipping it into each slit or V, then stretching it tightly across the front. Continue wrapping the string down the cardboard until you reach the bottom. The result should be a series of parallel strings forming the "warp" for your loom. Secure the end of the string at the bottom right corner, using a knot or tape to keep it in place.

4. Choose your materials for weaving. Starting at one side, weave the material over the first warp string, under the next, and so on. Pull the material gently to the side after each row to keep it snug but not too tight. Alternate the pattern for the next row (under the first string, over the second, etc.).

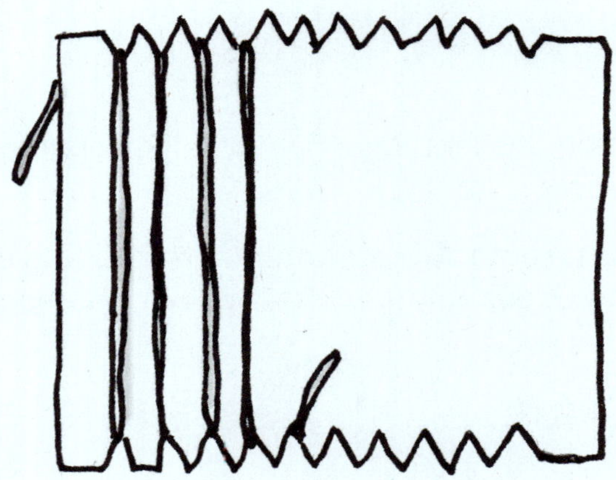

5. Continue weaving until your loom is filled or you are satisfied with your design.
6. To finish your weaving project, cut the warp strings carefully on both sides of your woven piece. Make sure to leave about an inch of extra string on each side.
7. Tie the loose warp strings in small knots to secure the ends of your weaving and keep it from unraveling. You can also tape them down if you prefer.
8. Gently slide the woven piece off the cardboard loom, making sure not to pull too hard, so your weaving stays intact.
9. Optional: Display by attaching the top of your woven piece to a dowel rod and hanging it on the wall.

The Stories of Homer

Read & Review

Read pages 147–154 in the text. Afterward, check the student's understanding by asking the questions below.

1. **What hero is the Odyssey named after?** *Odysseus*
2. **Why did Poseidon get angry at Odysseus and his men?** *Because they forgot to thank him for their victory over Troy*
3. **What was the one-eyed monster called?** *Cyclops*
4. **How did the Greeks know the stories of Odysseus and Troy, in the days when they couldn't read and write?** *They told them to their children and grandchildren.*
5. **Who first wrote down these stories?** *The poet Homer*
6. **How did Odysseus get revenge on the Cyclops?** *He blinded him/put his eye out.*
7. **How did the men get out of the cave?** *They held on to the Cyclops' sheep when he let them out in the morning.*
8. **Why did Odysseus tell the Cyclops that his name was Noman?** *So that anyone who came to rescue the Cyclops would think that no man was hurting him*
9. **After Odysseus made fun of the Cyclops, what did the Cyclops do?** *Asked Poseidon to keep him from reaching home*
10. **Why do you think Odysseus decided to make fun of the Cyclops? Why didn't he just sail quietly away?** Discuss this with the student. Possible answers: *Pride, foolishness, he wanted to boast*
11. **Would it have been better if he'd just left without making any more noise?** *Yes*

800-700 BCE

Narration Exercise

What happened after Odysseus and his men won the Trojan War?

Odysseus and his men were headed home. They landed on an island where a monster lived. The monster ate two of the men. Odysseus tricked the monster into going to sleep and put his eye out. Then he and his men sneaked out of the cave. The Cyclops cursed Odysseus before he left.

or

Odysseus landed on an island. A monster who lived there ate two of his men. Odysseus was trapped in the monster's cave and couldn't get out. Odysseus told the monster that his name was Noman, and then put out his eye. The monster told everyone that Noman was killing him. Then Odysseus and his men held on to the sheep to get out of the cave.

Map Work: The Stories of Homer (Student Page 58)

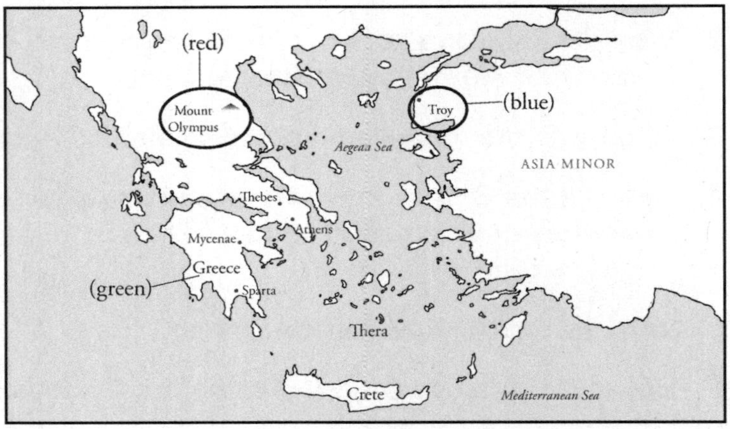

Read the instructions out loud. After each step, pause and give time for students to complete the task. Provide all necessary help.

1. **Open to Student Page 58 and tear it out.**
2. **On your map, find the country of *Greece* and color it green.**
3. **Find *Mount Olympus* and circle it in red.**
4. **Find *Troy* and circle it in blue.**
   What sea did the Greeks cross to find the Trojans? *The Aegean Sea*
5. Optional: **Color all the islands of Greece in your favorite color. How many islands are there?**
6. **When you finish, place the completed map in your history notebook.**

Activities

Choose from the following activities:

- ☐ Coloring Page: The Cyclops
- ☐ Craft: Make a Simple Cyclops Puppet
- ☐ Storytelling: The Stories of Homer
- ☐ Research Skills: Have the student look up a related topic in a history encyclopedia or another reliable source. Read the entry together and look at the pictures. Topics could include *Greek mythology, The Trojan War, Homer, the Iliad, the Odyssey, Odysseus, Poseidon,* and *Cyclops.*

Coloring Page: The Cyclops (Student Page 59)

PARENTS, PLEASE PREVIEW. Odysseus encounters the fierce one-eyed Cyclops.

Craft

MAKE A SIMPLE CYCLOPS PUPPET

Create your very own one-eyed monster on a stick!

MATERIALS:

- white paper plate
- crayons OR markers
- wooden craft stick OR wooden paint stick
- tape OR glue

DIRECTIONS:

1. Draw the Cyclops's face on the paper plate, remembering that he has one eye in the center of his forehead.
2. Tape or glue the completed paper plate onto the craft stick/paint stick; this is your handle to carry your Cyclops around.
3. Your Cyclops is a giant, so lift him up high, way over your head, as he steps out of his cave and walks around the island.
4. Here's a rhyme you can say as you walk with your Cyclops: I've got one eye, don't ask me why, I stomp around and reach the sky!
5. **Optional extension:** Take turns being the Cyclops and searching for Odysseus and his men! Find a safe space to play—like a room without sharp furniture. One player holds the Cyclops puppet and becomes the Cyclops. The Cyclops closes their eyes (to pretend he has been blinded by Odysseus). The other players scatter quietly. The Cyclops calls out: "Noman, where are you?" All other players must reply: "I'm here, Cyclops!" The Cyclops tries to tag someone by following their voices. When a player is tagged, they become the next Cyclops.

Storytelling

THE STORIES OF HOMER

Choose one of Homer's stories to work with. See this chapter's Corresponding Literature List and Corresponding Audiobook list for suggestions. Then pick one of the following activities:

- **Illustrate the Story:**

Listen to an audiobook adaptation (or have an adult read the story aloud). As you listen, draw your own pictures to go with the story.

- **Dramatic Reading:**

  Choose a scene or story to present dramatically.

  Have an older student or adult read the text aloud while younger students:

  - Make pre-planned sound effects (like wind, waves, or sword fights)
  - Hold up pre-drawn illustrations
  - Mime motions silently in the background

Classroom Adaptation: For younger students, try the "illustrate the story" project and staple all of the students' drawings together into a classroom illustrated epic. For older students, try dramatic reading. Separate students into groups of 3-5 students and have each group plan a dramatic reading of one scene from the same story.

The First Olympic Games

Read & Review

Read pages 155–157 in the text. Afterward, check the student's understanding by asking the questions below.

1. **What god was honored by the first Olympic games?** *Zeus, the king of the gods*
2. **What places was the Olympics named after?** *Mount Olympus, where the gods were supposed to live, and Olympia, Zeus's second home*
3. **What is a virtue?** *Something good about a person*
4. **What virtues did the Olympic Games reward?** *Strength and courage*
5. **Who was allowed to compete in the Olympic games?** *Men from Greece*

Narration Exercise

Draw a picture of an Olympic competition. When you're done, you can tell me about it and I will write your description on the bottom of the page.

or

Tell me three things about the Olympic games.

The Olympics started in ancient Greece. They were held to worship Zeus. Only men could go.

or

The Olympics started because two cities made peace. They were held every 4 years. The winners got olive wreaths to wear.

800–700 BCE

Activities

Choose from the following activities:

- [ ] Craft: Make Greek Instruments
- [ ] Craft: Make an Olympic Wreath
- [ ] Role Play: Host the Olympic Games
- [ ] Cooking: Host a Greek Feast
- [ ] Research Skills: Have the student look up a related topic in a history encyclopedia or another reliable source. Read the entry together and look at the pictures. Topics could include *Ancient Greece, the Olympics*, and *pentathlon, Zeus, Greek gods*.
- [ ] Celebration: Combine all of the activities in this chapter for a fun day celebrating what you've learned so far about Ancient Greece! Invite friends over to compete in the Olympic Games. Award wreaths to the winner of each event. Afterward, enjoy music with your Greek instruments or play Greek music and dance. Of course, enjoy some delicious Greek food! You can make your own food with the recipes below or purchase food from a restaurant or Greek festival (often hosted by Greek Orthodox churches).

Craft

MAKE GREEK INSTRUMENTS

The Greeks loved music and dancing. There are very few records of the songs the Greeks played, but we do know about the instruments that they used because they painted pictures of them on pottery.

Make a Timpanon

A timpanon is a tambourine that the Greeks used to provide rhythm. It was made from animal skin stretched tightly over a frame.

MATERIALS:

- 2 disposable pie pans
- glue
- hole punch
- ribbon
- paints or markers

DIRECTIONS:

1. Glue the 2 plates together at the rim, so that they form a hollow "shell."
2. Paint or decorate as desired.
3. Punch evenly spaced holes around the edges of the plates.
4. Lace ribbon through the holes and tie ends together leaving streamers. Tap your timpanon for rhythm!

Make a Greek Flute

MATERIALS:

- cardboard roll from toilet paper or paper towels
- wax paper
- rubber band
- markers
- pencil or ice pick

DIRECTIONS:

1. Punch 3 holes on one side of the cardboard roll using a pencil or ice pick (adult help required!).
2. Decorate your flute with markers.
3. Stretch a small piece of wax paper over one end and fasten with a rubber band.
4. Hum in your flute. Using your fingers, cover the holes one at a time to make different sounds.

Now put on your favorite music and pretend you are in Ancient Greece. Make up a dance and play your instruments while dancing.

Craft

MAKE AN OLYMPIC WREATH

The winners at the ancient Olympics received olive branch wreaths as a prize.

MATERIALS:

- green construction paper
- glue
- stapler
- scissors
- construction paper leaves, real leaves, or artificial leaves

DIRECTIONS:

1. To create the base of the wreath: cut strips of green construction paper (about 2 inches wide) and connect them with glue or staples until you have a strip long enough to fit around your head comfortably. Glue or staple the strips closed to form the base of the wreath.
2. Go outside and pick green leaves to paste to your base. Alternatively, you can cut leaves out of green construction paper. Cut 6-8 leaves with one shade of green construction paper and 6-8 leaves with a second shade of green construction paper. If you don't have green construction paper, cut the leaf shapes out of regular paper and color them in.
3. Glue or staple your leaves to the base of the wreath, alternating different leaf colors or types. Now you have an olive wreath crown that you can award to the winner of the Olympic games!

Role Play

HOST THE OLYMPIC GAMES

Invite several friends over to your backyard or a park to participate in some fun games. Award the winners an olive branch wreath (see activity above) or provide the materials and let each participant make their own wreath.

SUGGESTED GAMES:

- Discus throw - in ancient Greece, athletes threw heavy discs. For this version, take turns throwing a frisbee and see who can throw it the farthest.
- Javelin throw - in ancient Greece, athletes had to throw a spear as far as they could. You can use pool noodles or broom handles instead. Whoever throws their "spear" the farthest wins.
- Long jump - ancient Greek athletes competed to see who could jump the farthest. To recreate this, mark a starting line and make sure you have a soft place to land!
- Wrestling - the ancient Greek athletes had a wrestling competition. For our version, mark out a soft play area (on grass or carpet). Competitors cannot step outside of the marked lines! Two competitors go into the marked area and try to tap their competitor on either shoulder. Whoever manages to tap their competitor on the shoulder 3 times is the winner.
- Chariot Racing - ancient Greek athletes competed in chariot races. Since we don't have horses, we will make our own version. Divide into teams of 2. Each team needs one "horse" and one "driver." The "horse" must place their hands on the ground. The "driver" grabs the "horse" by their ankles, holding their legs up while the "horse" supports their weight with their hands. Mark a starting line and have teams race to cross the finish line.

You can add your own games to the Olympics if you like! For example, play tug-of-war, set up an obstacle course, or see who can hula hoop the longest.

Cooking

HOST A GREEK FEAST

After completing your Olympic games, you may want to celebrate with some Greek food and dancing. You can also look in your area for Greek festivals hosted by Greek Orthodox churches.

Hummus

INGREDIENTS:

- 2 15-ounce cans of chickpeas rinsed and drained
- 6 tablespoons tahini (sesame seed butter)
- 2 to 3 garlic cloves pressed
- ¼ cup olive oil
- lemon juice
- salt
- pepper
- food processor or potato masher
- pita bread or pita chips

DIRECTIONS:

1. Mix all of the ingredients (except pita chips or bread) together in your food processor or mash with a potato masher. Serve with warmed pita bread or pita chips.

Greek Pilaf

INGREDIENTS:

- 2 tablespoons olive oil
- 1 small onion, finely chopped
- 3 cloves of garlic, minced
- 2 cups of long-grain rice (such as basmati or jasmine)
- 4 cups chicken or vegetable broth
- 1 teaspoon salt
- ½ teaspoon pepper
- 1 teaspoon dried oregano
- 1 teaspoon cinnamon (optional, but adds depth)
- ½ cup golden raisins or currants (optional)
- 2 tablespoons fresh lemon juice
- ½ cup fresh parsley or dill
- optional add-ins: ½ cup slivered almonds or pine nuts, ½ cup crumbled feta cheese

DIRECTIONS:

1. In a medium saucepan, heat olive oil over medium heat. Add the chopped onion and sauté until soft and translucent (about 3-4 minutes). Stir the garlic and cook for another 30 seconds until fragrant. Stir in the garlic and cook for another 30 seconds (or until fragrant).
2. Add the rice to the pan and stir to coat it with oil. Toast for about 2 minutes until slightly golden.
3. Pour in the broth and spices. Bring to a boil, then reduce to low heat, cover, and let simmer for about 20 minutes or until the liquid is fully absorbed in the rice.
4. Remove from heat and let the pilaf sit, covered, for 5 minutes. Stir in lemon juice and fresh herbs.
5. Fluff with a fork and garnish with extra herbs, feta cheese, or nuts (if desired).

Stuffed Grape Leaves

INGREDIENTS:

- about 24 grape leaves 3 to 4 inches wide (Grape leaves can be found in larger grocery stores or specialty food stores.)
- Greek pilaf (see recipe above)
- spaghetti sauce

DIRECTIONS:

1. Preheat the oven to 350 degrees and lightly grease a baking dish.
2. Place a heaping spoonful of Greek Pilaf on each leaf and roll it up, tucking in the ends.
3. Place the stuffed leaves in the baking dish and bake for 20 minutes.
4. Serve with spaghetti sauce or squeeze lemon juice on top.

Additional History Reading

Eyewitness: Ancient Greece, by DK Children (DK Children, 2023). This book is packed with information bites that make it a good reference. Descriptive of many aspects of ancient Greece, using pictures, costumed actors, and more. Fantastic pictures of artifacts! (Also recommended for chapters twelve, sixteen, twenty-one, and twenty-seven) (RA)

Hide and Seek History: Ancient Greeks, by Jonny Marx (Little Tiger Press, 2024). A large lift-the-flap board book with information about ancient Greece hidden under flaps on every page. (RA)

The Librarian Who Measured the Earth, by Kathryn Lasky, illus. Kevin Hawkes (Little, Brown, 1994). Describes the life and work of Eratosthenes, the Greek geographer and astronomer who accurately measured the circumference of the Earth. (RA)

Corresponding Literature Suggestions

Black Ships Before Troy: The Story of the Iliad, by Rosemary Sutcliff (Laurel Leaf, 2005). A simple and beautifully illustrated (but lengthy) retelling of the Trojan War; good for a read-aloud project that extends over a couple of weeks. (RA)

The Trojan Horse, by Emily Little (Sagebrush, 1999). A retelling of the Trojan War with simple sentences and vocabulary (on a second or third-grade reading level). (RA, IR for advanced readers)

The Wanderings of Odysseus: The Story of the Odyssey, by Rosemary Sutcliff (Frances Lincoln, 2005). Fascinating and beautifully illustrated, but not long. Some scary pictures. (RA)

Corresponding Audiobook Suggestions

Greek Myths, by Jim Weiss (Well-Trained Mind Press, 1997). Make Hercules, King Midas, and Perseus and Medusa understandable to children, with strong emphasis on character over violence.

She and He: Adventures in Mythology, by Jim Weiss (Well-Trained Mind Press, 1999). Upbeat and exciting yet deeply moving, this unique collection of myths addresses respect between men and women and the value of love and honor.

Galileo and the Stargazers, including Archimedes and the Golden Crown, by Jim Weiss (Well-Trained Mind Press, 1999). This audio collection of true stories about bold scientists includes chapters on Archimedes and Ptolemy.

CHAPTER TWENTY
Sparta and Athens

Life in Sparta

Read & Review

Read pages 158–160 in the text. Afterward, check the student's understanding by asking the questions below.

1. **Did the Greek cities all obey the same king?** *No, each city had its own king.*
2. **What did all Spartan boys grow up to be?** *Soldiers*
3. **What did they learn in school?** Acceptable answers: *How to fight; how to be tough; how to be strong*
4. **If you were a Spartan boy and you hurt yourself, what would you do?** *Be brave and silent! You wouldn't cry. You would pretend that you were fine.*
5. **What were Spartan girls supposed to do?** *Have children who would be good fighters.*

Narration Exercise

Tell me two interesting things about Sparta. Answers will vary but may include:

500 BCE

Boys were supposed to be soldiers.

Spartan boys went away to camp to learn how to fight.

Men were supposed to be tough (or brave, or strong, or silent).

Spartans weren't supposed to complain.

The Spartans didn't obey the same king as other Greeks.

Activities

Choose from the following activities:

- ☐ Coloring Page: A Spartan Warrior
- ☐ Role Play: Make "No-Sew" Greek Clothes
- ☐ Craft: Make Spartan and Greek Paper Dolls
- ☐ Research Skills: Have the student look up a related topic in a history encyclopedia or another reliable source. Read the entry together and look at the pictures. Topics could include *Sparta*, *Greek city-states*, and *classical Greece*.

Coloring Page: A Spartan Warrior (Student Page 60)

Spartan warriors were fierce warriors, trained from a young age to be strong and disciplined.

Role Play

MAKE "NO-SEW" GREEK CLOTHES

How do we know how the Greeks dressed in ancient days? Archaeologists get a pretty good picture from the artwork that has been left to us. Bowls, beautifully carved statues, and letters give us peeks into their daily lives. Spartan soldiers were depicted in their uniforms. Their long red cloak was their most prized possession. If you want to be a Spartan, make sure you use an old red T-shirt!

MATERIALS:

- old white pillowcase
- a large colorful old T-shirt (adult size!)
- scissors
- twine or rope

DIRECTIONS:

1. Place a white pillowcase flat on a table. Cut out a hole in the middle of the folded edge on the short side. This will be the neck hole.
2. On the longer, folded sides, cut out arm holes at the top corner edge on the side close to the neck hole. Slip it over your head. Voila! This is your chiton (KAI-ton). Adjust it to drape nicely.
3. Use the rope as a belt for the chiton.

4. To make your cloak, use the old T-shirt and make a cut down the middle of the front, from the neck to the bottom seam. Slip it on over your chiton.
5. Do your hair like a Greek! Girls often wore their hair in ponytails or buns. Sometimes they would wrap a ribbon in a criss-cross fashion around their heads. Boys wore a band of material around their heads.
6. Add sandals and you're ready to visit ancient Greece!

Craft

MAKE SPARTAN AND ATHENIAN PAPER DOLLS

Make your own paper dolls of Spartans and Athenians. You can use them to play out your own scenes from Ancient Greece.

MATERIALS:

- colored pencils, scissors
- removable double sided tape photocopy of the paper dolls (Student Pages 61-63) on card stock, and clothes on regular white paper
- stick-on laminate sheets (optional, available at most office supply stores)

DIRECTIONS:

1. Color the figures and their clothes and then cut them all out. The Spartan soldier's pride was his flaming red wool cloak, and the helmets of the Athenian soldiers were passed down from generation to generation.
2. Use the removable double sided tape to keep the outfits on your dolls.
3. Optional: Laminate your dolls and their clothes. Photocopy the dolls and clothes twice or more for a family or army.

Life in Athens

Read & Review

Read pages 160–163 in the text. Afterward, check the student's understanding by asking the questions below.

1. **What is a democracy?** [Prompt the student for the answer:] *A country where people vote on the laws and on who becomes the leaders.*
2. **Did Athens think fighting was the most important thing for boys to learn?** *No*
3. **What kinds of things did Athenian boys learn in school?** *Mathematics, reading, writing, poetry, and music*
4. **What did Athenian girls learn how to do?** *Keep house*
5. **What happens to ignorant people who don't know the laws?** *Other people can make them do things.*
6. **Why is it important to be educated?** [Discuss the answer with your student:] *So that you know what the laws are; so that you know how to vote on laws and leaders; so that tyrants can't tell you what to do.*

Narration Exercise

Tell me two important things about Athens. Answers will vary but may include:

Athens was a democracy.

In Athens, people voted on the laws and on the leaders.

People in Athens were educated.

Boys learned how to read and write (or do math, or play music, or memorize poetry).

Girls learned how to keep house.

Plato was a famous man in Athens.

They didn't want tyrants to be in charge.

500 BCE

Map Work: Athens and Sparta (Student Page 64)

Read the instructions out loud to the student. After each step, pause and give time for the student to complete the task. Provide all necessary help.

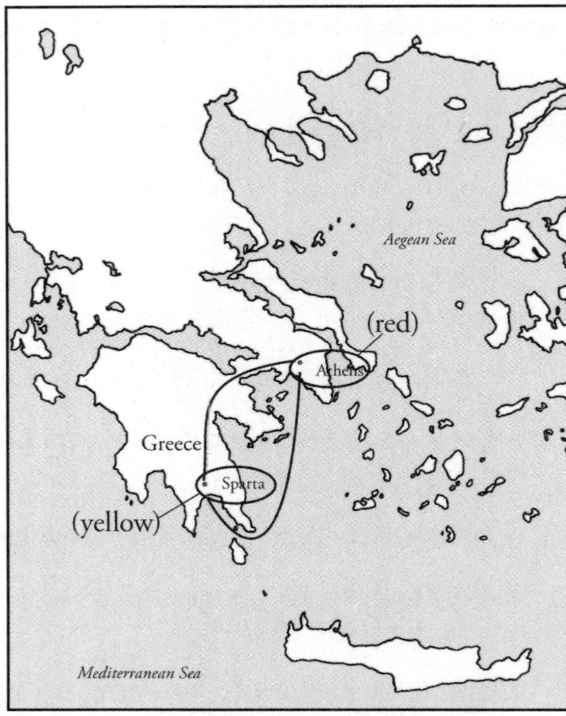

1. **Open to Student Page 64 and tear it out.**
2. **On your map, find the city of *Athens*. Circle it in red.**
3. **Now find *Sparta*, and circle it in yellow.**
4. **The Athenians and Spartans could reach each other in two ways—by land and by sea. Draw a blue line to show the sea route between the two. If the Athenians wanted to sail over to Sparta, they would use this path.**
5. **Now draw a green line to show the land route between the two. If the Spartans wanted to march an army over to Athens, they would use this path.**
6. **When you finish, place the completed map in your history notebook.**

Activities

Choose from the following activities:

- ☐ Role Play: Write on an Athenian Wax Tablet
- ☐ Role Play: Vote at an Agora
- ☐ Research Skills: Have the student look up a related topic in a history encyclopedia or another reliable source. Read the entry together and look at the pictures. Topics could include *Athens*, *democracy*, *Greek city-states*, and *classical Greece*.

Role Play

WRITE ON AN ATHENIAN WAX TABLET

Wax tablets were a common writing tool in ancient Greece. Boys used them for schoolwork, while girls often used them to assist with household tasks. This reusable method of writing was practical, durable, and an essential part of daily life in Athens!

MATERIALS:

- a small brick of softened lard or shortening, or plasticine non-hardening clay
- plastic lid from a yogurt or margarine tub
- a toothpick
- table knife

DIRECTIONS:

1. An hour before you plan to use your wax tablet, spread the lard or margarine on the inside of the plastic lid so that the edges provide a frame for your tablet. Place in the refrigerator and let it solidify.
2. When you're ready, take it out of the fridge. Write a message or draw a picture on the lard with a toothpick. See if someone else can read your words or recognize your picture.
3. When you're finished, smooth it over with the knife and write something new. This is similar to how the sturdy wax tablets were used. You're ready for school in ancient Athens!

Role Play

VOTE AT AN AGORA

The Agora was a public gathering space where Athenian citizens debated and decided on important issues. Later, the Romans would call this kind of meeting place a forum. In this activity, we will create and vote on new laws in our own forum.

MATERIALS:

- a group of friends, siblings, or classmates
- a speaking stick (or any object to designate a speaker)
- pen and paper
- a timer (optional)

DIRECTIONS:

1. Have each friend, sibling, or classmate write down one new rule they would like to propose. Younger students can narrate their rule to an adult and have the adult write it down.
2. Select one student to act as chairperson (if in a larger group, have an adult act as chairperson). This person will call the meeting to order, ensure every "citizen" gets a chance to speak, and count the votes.
3. Once the chairperson calls the meeting to order, her or she will call on one citizen to read their proposed law. The citizen explains why their idea is a good one.
4. Have a 5 minute discussion. Citizens take turns sharing their opinions. Use a speaking stick to ensure only one person speaks at a time.
5. When the debates are finished, the chairperson calls for a vote. All citizens vote on the law by a show of hands. The chairperson announces the decision.
6. Repeat the process until you have 1-3 special rules for the day. These laws can be fun, creative, or practical, as long as the majority agrees on them (of course the supervising adult always gets final say and can veto a law if it is not safe).
7. Finish the activity with a wrap-up discussion (suggested prompts below)

Discussion Questions

- Was it easy or hard to agree on laws?
- How would it be different if we were making laws for an entire city?
- What made some laws more popular than others?
- How does this compare to how decisions are made normally in your home or classroom?
- For older students: How does this compare to how laws are made today?
- Discuss how in ancient Athens, only male citizens age 18 and older could participate in the forum. Over time, modern democracies have expanded to include people of all genders, races, and backgrounds, ensuring more voices are heard in decision-making.

Classroom Adaptations: If completing in a classroom, have students make new classroom rules for the day. They can be silly! Just make sure students know that the teacher has full veto power. They need to make wise laws! Students may come up with great laws you want to write out and display in the classroom.

Additional History Reading

A Coloring Book of Ancient Greece (Bellerophon Books, 2000) is available at bellerophonbooks.com. Real Greek art, simplified for young artists to color, along with interesting explanatory text. (RA and activity)

Eyewitness: Ancient Greece, by DK Children (DK Children, 2023). This book is packed with information bites that make it a good reference. Descriptive of many aspects of ancient Greece, using pictures, drawings, costumed actors, and more. Fantastic pictures of artifacts! (Also recommended for chapters twelve, sixteen, twenty-one, and twenty-seven) (RA)

Spend the Day in Ancient Greece! Projects and Activities that Bring the Past to Life, by Linda Honan (Jossey Bass, 1998). Weave on a loom, paint an amphora, and build a racing chariot—these are a few of the fun projects taught in this book. Each section centers around a child in ancient Greece and the tasks he or she has to do. (RA and activity)

Top Secret: A Handbook of Codes, Ciphers, and Secret Writing, by Paul B. Janeczko, illus. Jenna Leau (Candlewick Press, 2004). Pages 48–54 cover two ciphers developed by the ancient Greeks: the Greek square, invented by Polybius, and the Greek scytale, a cipher that comes from ancient Sparta. (RA 1–3, IR 3–6)

Corresponding Literature Suggestions

Bright-Eyed Athena: Stories from Ancient Greece, by Richard Woff (Getty Museum Publications, 1999). A group of weaving women in Athens tell stories about the city's protector. **Out of print, but worth looking for at your local library.** (RA)

D'Aulaires' Book of Greek Myths, by Edgar Parin d'Aulaire (Delacorte, 1992). A classic in its own right, this introduction to the gods and goddesses of Ancient Greece has beautiful illustrations by Caldecott Award winners. (RA)

Usborne Greek Myths, by Heather Amery (Usborne, 2024). Simplified retelling of Greek myths.The stories are shorter than D'Aulaire's version listed above. (RA, possible IR for advanced readers)

Corresponding Audiobook Suggestions

Courage and a Clear Mind: True Adventures of the Ancient Greeks, created and told by Jim Weiss (Well-Trained Mind Press, 2016). A collection of stories from Ancient Greece, including stories about Socrates, the Spartan 300, and day-to-day life in Athens and Sparta.

OPTIONAL LESSON
The Story of Draco and Solon, The Two Lawgivers of Athens

Read & Review

Read pages 164–167 in the text. Afterward, check the student's understanding by asking the questions below. Sample responses are provided in italics.

1. **What did the poor Athenians ask for?** *They wanted all the laws written down.*
2. **What did Draco do after writing his laws?** *He ran away to an island.*
3. **What did Solon do after writing his laws?** *He traveled the world for ten years.*

Activities

Choose from the following activities:

- ☐ Coloring Page: Draco Flees Athens (Student Page 65)
- ☐ Creative Writing Prompt: If you could make up one law that everyone in your family had to follow, what would it be? (If needed, review the instructions on how to use the creative writing prompts in Appendix One.)

622-600 BCE

CHAPTER TWENTY-ONE
The Greek Gods

The Golden Apple

Read & Review

Read pages 168–171 in the text. Afterward, check the student's understanding by asking the questions below.

1. **Were the Greeks monotheists?** *No*
2. **Were they polytheists?** *Yes*
3. **Does a polytheist believe in one god or many gods?** *Many gods*
4. **Why did Zeus start a war on earth?** *Because there were too many people on earth*
5. **Can you name any of the other gods from the story?** *Hera, Aphrodite, Athena, Eris, Poseidon*

800 BCE

Narration Exercise

Tell me the story of the Golden Apple.

Zeus wanted to get rid of some of the people on earth. So he started a war on earth. All the gods took sides.

or

Paris had to say which goddess was the most beautiful. He picked Aphrodite. The other goddesses got mad. A war started.

Map Work: Ancient Greece (Student Page 66)

Read the instructions out loud to the student. After each step, pause and give time for the student to complete the task. Provide all necessary help.

1. **Open to Student Page 66 and tear it out.**

2. **This map is the same map of Greece you've seen in recent chapters (sixteen and nineteen). But on this map, the names are missing. Can you find them? Try to find:**
   - **The country of *Greece***
   - **The island of *Crete***
   - **The *Aegean Sea***
   - **The city of *Athens***
   - **The city of *Sparta***
   - **The city of *Troy***
   - ***Mount Olympus***

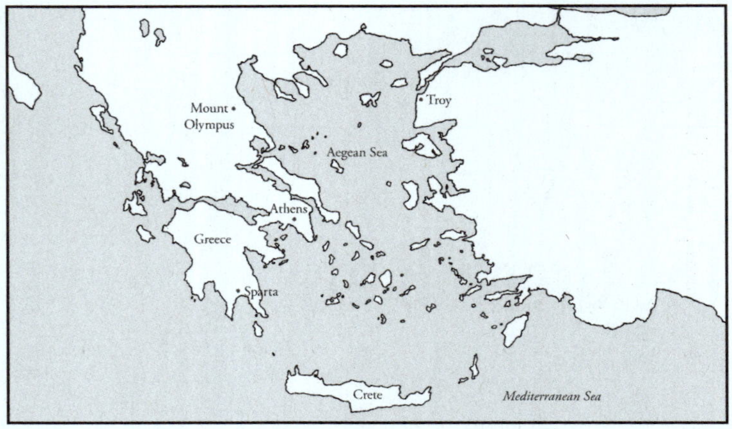

3. **When you finish, place the completed map in your history notebook.**

Note to Instructor: You can offer a small reward—a chocolate chip, for example—for each name the student can identify. Offer the student a chance to look back at the map of Greece before trying to identify places on the new map.

Activities

Choose from the following activities:

- [ ] Coloring Page: Athena and Zeus
- [ ] Activity Page: Greek Gods and Goddesses Word Search
- [ ] Memory Work: The Greek Gods
- [ ] Craft: Make an Olympus Family Tree
- [ ] Art: Draw A Home for the Greek Gods

Coloring Page: Athena and Zeus (Student Page 67)

Athena the goddess of war and wisdom, and Zeus the mighty king of the gods.

Activity Page

GREEK GODS AND GODDESSES WORD SEARCH

Follow the instructions on Student Page 68. Answers are below:

G	S	P	A	P	H	R	O	D	I	T	E
R	Z	I	P	F	E	Q	L	O	O	K	X
E	A	H	P	G	O	T	W	G	H	Z	A
E	U	W	L	Z	E	R	I	S	E	E	T
C	S	M	E	B	V	O	X	I	L	Y	H
E	X	J	R	E	D	Y	P	N	E	M	E
Y	K	I	Z	A	P	L	J	G	N	O	N
B	J	M	S	U	T	S	U	N	R	M	A
M	O	U	N	T	O	L	Y	M	P	U	S
B	P	T	E	I	Y	C	T	O	Y	S	C
O	W	P	J	F	P	A	R	I	S	I	F
Y	O	U	R	U	Z	Q	M	X	B	T	G
H	E	R	A	L	O	N	G	Z	E	U	S

Memory Work

THE GREEK GODS

Greek mythology permeates modern media, culture, and language. Memorizing the important Greek gods and goddesses will certainly come in handy as your student will begin to notice references to Greek mythology all around them.

Note to Instructor: For detailed guidance on using memory work activities, see Appendix Two. The student's memory work reference page is available on Student Page 69. Below, you'll find the list of items to memorize, along with additional teaching ideas for your convenience.

1. Zeus - (ZOOS) King of gods
2. Poseidon - (po SYE din) God of the sea
3. Hera (HEER uh or HAIR uh) - Queen of the gods, wife of Zeus
4. Demeter - (duh MEE ter) Goddess of the harvest
5. Hestia - (HESS tee uh) Goddess of the hearth and fire

6. Aphrodite (A fro DITE ee or AH fro DITE ee) - Goddess of love and beauty
7. Athena (ath EE nuh) - Goddess of wisdom and warfare
8. Artemis - (AR tuh miss) Goddess of the hunt, wilderness, and childbirth
9. Apollo - (uh POL oh) God of the sun, music, and poetry
10. Ares - (AIR eez) God of war
11. Hermes - (HER meez) Messenger of the gods, god of trade
12. Hephaestus (heh FESS tuss) - God of fire, metalworking, and sculpture

Suggested Activity: Chant each Olympian's name and title. Have the student repeat the chant while drumming to a beat or jumping up and down

Related Reading: *A Child's Introduction to Greek Mythology: The Stories of the Gods, Goddesses, Heroes, Monsters, and Other Mythical Creatures*, by Heather Alexander (Black Dog & Leventhal, 2011).

Craft

MAKE AN OLYMPUS FAMILY TREE

Once you have read through The Gods and Goddesses of Olympus *by Aliki or another one of the recommended books about the Greek gods, consider making a family tree of the Greek and Roman gods and goddesses. The Greeks imagined their gods as a big, complicated family—often full of disagreements and drama!*

MATERIALS:

- large twig with several branches
- small clay pot, coffee can, or other container
- rocks, sand, or modeling clay
- green construction paper
- string, ribbon, or hot glue
- double stick tape or glue
- markers, crayons, or colored pencils

DIRECTIONS:

1. Find a sturdy branch with multiple smaller twigs to represent the "branches" of your family tree.
2. Stabilize your tree branch in a pot using rocks, sand or clay. Make sure it can stand upright. You can decorate the pot if you like!
3. Go outside and find your favorite leaf shape. Trace one leaf shape onto your green construction paper for each Greek god and goddess you will include.
4. Write the name of the god or goddess on the green leaf. You can also draw a picture of the character on the other side of the leaf (use chart on Student Page 69).

5. Using string, ribbon or hot glue, attach the leaf for the god who is in charge, Zeus, at the top of your "tree." Place the other leaves in order, from the most important gods near the treetop down to the least important near the bottom.

6. Save this project! You may want to come back to it and add the Roman names for these gods when you get to Chapter 31.

Art

DRAW A HOME FOR THE GREEK GODS

According to Greek legends, the gods lived on Mount Olympus. In this activity you will imagine what it was like to live like a Greek god.

MATERIALS:

- long sheet of kraft paper, poster board, OR a piece of white construction paper, 11″ x 14″
- colored pencils or thin markers
- an ink pad and your thumb
- a book about Greek mythology from the library (one option is *The Gods and Goddesses of Olympus*, by Aliki)

DIRECTIONS:

1. Imagine what it might be like to live on the top of a mountain. Illustrators for books about the Greek gods and goddesses had to imagine this. Take your piece of paper and think through how you want to set up your home for the Greek gods. You may want to draw it in pencil first. What would you include in your home for the Greek gods? Maybe their thrones, or the fire that Hestia might be stoking, a valley for Pan's sheep, a bed for Hypnos or a long road for Nike to race on? If you need ideas, go through Aliki's book or another of the recommended readings on the Greek gods and goddesses.

2. After you've set up their home, use your thumb-print to make your gods and goddesses. Put your thumb on the ink pad, and then on the paper where you want the head of your character to be.

3. Now add eyes, nose, and mouth with your markers. Add a body to each head with another thumb-print, or draw a body with your markers. Add arms and legs with your markers.

4. Decorate each character so that you remember who they are. Zeus might carry a lightning bolt and have a beard; Cupid could have a heart in his hand, while Helios might have sun-rays coming out of his head!

Classroom Adaptation: Cut out a few long sheets of kraft paper and have students work on their drawings in small groups.

Additional History Reading

An Ancient Greek Temple: The Story of the Building of the Temples of Ancient Greece, by John Malam, illus. Mark Bergin (Peter Bedrick Books, 2001). A beautifully illustrated look at the building of a Greek temple from the quarry to the finished product. (RA)

Eyewitness: Ancient Greece, by DK Children (DK Children, 2023). This book is packed with information bites that make it a good reference. Descriptive of many aspects of ancient Greece, using pictures, drawings, costumed actors, and more. Fantastic pictures of artifacts! There is a helpful two-page spread on Greek gods and religious beliefs. (Also recommended for chapters twelve, sixteen, twenty, and twenty-seven) (RA)

Corresponding Literature Suggestions

The Gods and Goddesses of Olympus, by Aliki (HarperTrophy, 1997). Colorful pictures and lively, short tales of the central Greek gods. (RA) Note: This book is the basis for the "Olympus Family Tree" project in this chapter.

D'Aulaires' Book of Greek Myths, by Edgar Parin d'Aulaire (Delacorte, 1992). A classic in its own right, this introduction to the gods and goddesses of Ancient Greece has beautiful illustrations by Caldecott Award winners. (RA)

Usborne Greek Myths, by Heather Amery (Usborne, 2024). Simplified retelling of Greek myths. The stories are shorter than D'Aulaire's version listed above. (RA, possible IR for advanced readers)

Corresponding Audiobook Suggestions

Aesop's Fables, read by Jim Weiss (Well-Trained Mind Press, 2023). Eighteen of Aesop's fables performed by Jim Weiss.

Greek Myths, read by Jim Weiss (Well-Trained Mind Press, 2021). Makes Hercules, King Midas, and Perseus and Medusa understandable to children, with emphasis on character over violence.

She and He: Adventures in Mythology, read by Jim Weiss (Well-Trained Mind Press, 2023). Upbeat and exciting yet deeply moving, this unique collection of myths addresses the equality of the sexes and the value of love and honor.

CHAPTER TWENTY-TWO
The Rise of Rome

Romulus and Remus

Read & Review

Read pages 172–175 in the text. Afterward, check the student's understanding by asking the questions below.

1. **Can you tell me the names of three empires that came before Rome?** Acceptable answers include *Assyria, Babylon, Media, Persia, Greece*
2. **Who founded the city of Rome in the legend that we read?** *Romulus*
3. **Who raised Romulus?** *First a wolf, then a shepherd*
4. **What was Romulus's twin brother named?** *Remus*
5. **Why did Romulus name his city Rome?** *He named it after himself* OR *Rome sounds like Romulus.*
6. **How many hills was Rome built on?** *Seven hills*

700 BCE

Narration Exercise

Tell me the story of Romulus and Remus. Note: Make sure the student includes the information that Rome was named after Romulus.

Romulus and Remus were twins. A wolf raised them. They built a town at Rome. Romulus killed Remus and became king. He named Rome after himself.

or

Draw a scene from the story. When you're done, tell me about it and I will write your description at the bottom of the page.

Activities

Choose from the following activities:

- [ ] Coloring Page: Romulus and Remus
- [ ] Storytelling & Art: Illustrate a Story Book
- [ ] Make a Model: Salt Dough Map of Italy
- [ ] Research Skills: Have the student look up a related topic in a history encyclopedia or another reliable source. Read the entry together and look at the pictures. Topics could include *Romulus and Remus, the founding of Rome, the city of Rome, peninsula, the Tiber River*, and *early Rome*.

Coloring Page: Romulus and Remus (Student Page 70)

According to legend, Romulus and Remus, twin brothers, were raised by a she-wolf and later founded the city of Rome.

Storytelling & Art

ILLUSTRATE A STORY BOOK

In this activity you will retell the myth of Romulus and Remus with your own words and pictures!

MATERIALS:

- A few sheets of blank paper OR photocopies of Student Page 1 (no less than 4, no more than 10)
- pencil
- colored pencils, markers, or crayons
- hole punch
- string

DIRECTIONS:

1. Have the student retell the story of Romulus and Remus in their own words (Note to Instructor: If you have already written down the student's narration, you can use that narration for this activity. Simply write each line of the narration down on a separate piece of paper and have the student create simple illustrations for each sheet).

2. As the student/s narrate, write one line of the story on the bottom of each sheet of paper. Older students can write it down on their own.

3. Repeat until you have the entire story written down across several pieces of paper (4-10).

4. Draw illustrations for each page. Make them vibrant using lots of colors! Add as many details as you like!
5. Once the illustrations are complete, stack the pages in order. Add one blank page to the top of the stack.
6. Write "The Story of Romulus and Remus as told by [student's name]" on the blank sheet. This will be the front cover of your book. Decorate it however you like. You can add an extra illustration or border.
7. Punch holes on the left edge using the hole punch and use string to bind the pages together into a book. Now you have your own illustrated version of the Romulus and Remus myth!

Classroom Adaptation: Students can each create their own book OR work with the whole class to retell the story. Each student should provide one sentence and then pause, allowing another student to continue. As students retell the story, the teacher should write down their retelling, verbatim, across several pieces of blank paper, numbering the pages as she goes. Divide up the pages of the story to individual students or groups of students to illustrate. Once all of the illustrations are complete, compile them into a classroom book.

Make a Model

A SALT DOUGH MAP OF ITALY

Italy's shape and location as a peninsula have had a profound impact on its history. In this activity, you can make your own map of Italy and learn more about its coastlines and other geographic features!

MATERIALS:

- a printed map of Italy (you can use the map from this chapter)
- a large thin piece of cardboard or clean pizza box
- salt dough (recipe on page 414)
- pencil and paints
- atlas or globe with geographical features marked on it
- shaping tool, like a craft stick or dull knife

DIRECTIONS:

1. On the cardboard, draw an outline of Italy. You can enlarge the map from Chapter 22 and use it as a stencil or pattern or find a different map of just the Italian peninsula. Younger students will need help with this.
2. Note the coastlines on the map or globe you are using as a reference. Italy is a peninsula; it is surrounded by water on three sides. Use green paint to draw the land that connects to Italy, and blue paint to represent the sides surrounded by water.

3. Now it is time to fill in your outline! Make your salt dough according to the instructions on page 414. Spread dough onto the outline.
4. Consult your encyclopedia or globe. Do you see the mountains of Italy? Make peaks where the mountain ranges belong, using your finger or a shaping tool. Do you see the rivers of Italy? Make grooves for major rivers like the Po and Tiber.
5. Put the salt dough map in a warm, sunny spot and let it dry. This may take a day or two.
6. Paint your map! Use colors to represent geographic features like rivers, mountains, and plains.
7. Optional: Take a picture of your finished map. Keep it in your history notebook.

The Power of Rome

Read & Review

Read pages 176–177 in the text. Afterward, check the student's understanding by asking the questions below.

1. **What important tribe of people lived in Italy?** *The Etruscans*
2. **Whose alphabet and gods did they borrow?** *The Greeks*
3. **Did the Romans fight with the Etruscans?** *Yes*
4. **Did they learn anything from them?** *Yes*
5. **Do you remember anything that the Roman kings borrowed from the Etruscans?** Any of the following are acceptable: *How to dress, about the Greek gods, painting, music, special robes called togas, fasces (the rods with axe blade)*
6. **In a democracy, who makes the laws and chooses the leaders?** *The people*
7. **How do they do this?** *They vote.*
8. **What does monarchy mean?** *Rule by a king*
9. **What two symbols of power did the Roman kings have?** *The fasces (bundle of rods with an axe in the middle) and the purple-bordered robe*
10. **How many kings did Rome have?** *Seven*
11. **Who ruled Rome once the Romans got rid of their kings?** *Two consuls*
12. **Was Rome a democracy?** *No*

700 BCE

Narration Exercise

How did the Romans change how they were ruled?

Note: The student should include the information that Rome was ruled by kings first, and that the kings were followed by consuls.

At first Rome had kings. Rome got rid of the kings and had consuls instead. There were two of them.

or

The Etruscans lived in Italy. They taught the Romans about painting and other things. Rome had kings, but then the people wanted to help with the government. They had consuls instead of kings.

Map Work: The Power of Rome (Student Page 71)

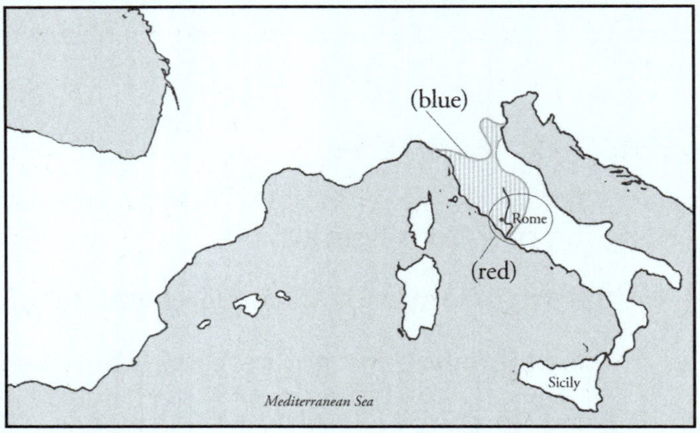

Read the instructions out loud to the student. After each step, pause and give time for the student to complete the task. Provide all necessary help.

1. **Open to Student Page 71 and tear it out.**
2. **On your map, circle *Rome* with a red crayon. Rome is in Italy.**
3. **The Etruscans lived and ruled the area north of Rome. Find the borders on your map, and outline them in blue.**
4. **When you finish, place the completed map in your history notebook.**

Activities

Choose from the following activities:

- ☐ Craft: Make the Fasces
- ☐ Craft: Make a Saturnalia Gift Out of Clay
- ☐ Research Skills: Have the student look up a related topic in a history encyclopedia or another reliable source. Read the entry together and look at the pictures. Topics could include *the Etruscans, togas, fasces, republic, patricians, Roman consuls, early Rome, kings of Rome*, and *the Roman Republic*.

Craft

MAKE THE FASCES

In Ancient Rome, fasces were a symbol of authority and power. Etruscan kings wore fasces to show they could punish anyone who did wrong. In this activity, you can make your own fasces.

MATERIALS:

- Student Page 72
- handful of long sticks (12-18 inches each, straight and sturdy)
- string or ribbon
- cardboard
- aluminum foil

- scissors
- glue (craft glue or glue gun)
- tape (optional)

DIRECTIONS:

1. Use the template on Student Page 72 to trace the shape of an axe blade onto a piece of cardboard. Carefully cut the blade shape.
2. Cover the axe blade (both sides) with aluminum foil.
3. Arrange the sticks into a neat bundle, ensuring they are aligned at the bottom. Hold the bundle in place, firmly, as you move on to the next step.
4. Starting at the bottom of the bundle, wrap the string or ribbon tightly around all the sticks. Make sure the string covers the sticks completely and is wound snugly to keep them secure. Gradually wind the string upward, continuing to wrap tightly until you reach the top of the sticks. At the top, wrap the string or ribbon a few extra times to secure it, and glue or tie the ends to prevent unraveling.
5. Insert the axe blade between 2 sticks near the top of the bundle. Glue to secure the blade in place. Hold it steady until the glue dries.
6. Check to ensure all components are secure. You can add extra glue to any loose areas if needed.
7. Carry your *fasces* around and make sure everyone in the house completes their chores for the day!
8. Optional: for a more polished look, trim any uneven edges of the sticks at the top or bottom of the bundle.

Craft

MAKE A SATURNALIA GIFT OUT OF CLAY

Saturnalia was a festival to honor Saturn, the god of agriculture. Romans celebrated this festival by exchanging gifts and eating. The most common gifts were small clay figures.

MATERIALS:

- air-dry clay or salt dough (recipe on page 414)
- baking sheet, wax paper
- cookie cutters (small ones, if available—animal shapes work great!)
- rolling pin
- pencil, plastic knife

DIRECTIONS:

1. Roll out about ¼ block of clay until flat on wax paper. Use a cookie cutter to cut out a shape. Trim with a plastic knife, if needed.
2. Use a pencil to poke eyes or any details. You may also wish to add small pieces of another color clay for features on your shape.
3. Bake or let dry according to package instructions.
4. Choose someone to give your Saturnalia gift to!

Classroom Adaptation: You may want to use air-dry clay or any other clay that does not require baking. After completing their Saturnalia gifts, make time for students to exchange their gifts with classmates.

Additional History Reading

Eyewitness: Ancient Rome by Dr. Simon James (DK Children, 2022). This book is packed with short information bites and pictures of artifacts. It focuses on daily life in Rome, including going to the theater, arts, entertainment, life for children and families, crafts, cooking, and more. (Also recommended for chapters thirty-one and forty-two) (RA)

The Ancient Worlds Atlas, illus. Russell Barnett (DK Publishing, 2023). This beautifully illustrated atlas has a two-page spread on the rise of Rome from a village to an empire and another spread on daily life in Rome. (Also recommended for chapters five, six, eight, nine, seventeen, and eighteen.) (RA 1-3, IR 4-5)

The Romans, by Peter Hicks (Thomas Learning, 1995). Illustrates the culture and history of ancient Rome. **Out of print, but worth looking for at your local library.** (Also recommended for chapter thirty-five)(RA)

Corresponding Literature Suggestions

Romulus and Remus (Building Fluency through Reader's Theater), by Melissa Fitzgerald (Teacher Created Materials, 2009). A script for kids to act out the Romulus and Remus myth. Each role is written at a different reading level.

Romulus and Remus (Ready to Read, Level 2), by Anne Rockwell (Aladdin, 1997). In this young-reader version of the legend of the twin founders of Rome, Romulus does not kill Remus; instead, Remus goes away to hunt with the wolves. Available as a board book. **Out of print, but worth looking for at your local library.** (IR for many children, RA for very early beginners)

The Orchard Book of Roman Myths, by Geraldine McCaughrean (Orchard, 2003). Colorful, engaging read-aloud tales include two about Aeneas, Romulus and Remus, and the kidnapping of the Sabine women. **Out of print, but worth looking for at your local library.** (RA 1–3, IR 3–6)

OPTIONAL LESSON

The Story of Tullia Minor and Tarqin the Proud, The Last King and Queen of Rome

Read & Review

Read pages 179–181 in the text. Afterward, check the student's understanding by asking the questions below.

1. **What did Tullia tell her husband Tarquin to do to become King?** *Tullia told Tarquin to kill her father.*
2. **What is one cruel thing that Tullia and Tarquin did as king and queen?** Answers may vary. Acceptable answers include: *They put people to death. They stole land from their subjects. They used Rome's wealth for their own comfort.*
3. **What change did the people of Rome make after Tarquin and Tullia were gone?** *They decided not to have kings anymore.*

Activities

Choose from the following activities:

- ☐ Coloring Page: The King and Queen of Rome (Student Page 73)
- ☐ Creative Writing Prompt: If you were king or queen of the land for a day, what is the first thing you would do? (If needed, review the instructions on how to use the creative writing prompts in Appendix One.)

530 BCE

CHAPTER TWENTY-THREE

Babylon Takes Over Again!

Nebuchadnezzar's Madness

Read & Review

Read pages 183–184 in the text. Afterward, check the student's understanding by asking the questions below.

1. **What did the Assyrians do to Babylon when they conquered it?** *They flooded it (destroyed it).*
2. **What did the Babylonians do to Nineveh when they conquered Assyria?** *They destroyed it and smashed some of Ashurbanipal's clay tablets.*
3. **Was the Babylonian empire as big as the Assyrian empire?** *No*
4. **Do you remember the name of Babylon's most famous king? He built the Ishtar Gate in Babylon.** *Nebuchadnezzar*
5. **What happened to Nebuchadnezzar after he thought he was a god?** *He went mad (thought he was an animal).*
6. **Did he get better?** *Yes*

600 BCE

Narration Exercise

Tell me about Nebuchadnezzar.

Assyria was destroyed by Babylon. The king of Babylon thought he was a god. Then he went mad and ate grass like a cow. Finally he got better again.

or

Nebuchadnezzar was the king of Babylon. He was a great king, but he thought he was greater than God. So he lost his mind. He thought he was an animal. When he said that he was only a man, he got better.

Map Work: Nebuchadnezzar's Madness (Student Page 74)

Read the instructions out loud to the student. After each step, pause and give time for the student to complete the task. Provide all necessary help.

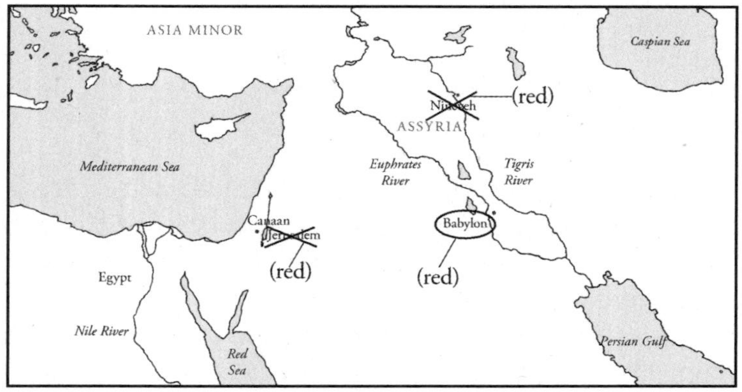

1. **Open to Student Page 74 and tear it out.**
2. **On your map, find Nebuchadnezzar's city of *Babylon* and circle it in red.**
3. **Find the city of *Nineveh* on your map. Put a red X across the name Nineveh to show that Nebuchadnezzar destroyed it.**
4. **Find the city of *Jerusalem*, also destroyed by Nebuchadnezzar. Just like you did with Nineveh, put a red X across the name Jerusalem.**
5. **When you finish, place the completed map in your history notebook.**

Activities

Choose from the following activities:

- ☐ Coloring Page: Ishtar Gate
- ☐ Storytelling: Nebuchadnezzar's Charades
- ☐ Research Skills: Have the student look up a related topic in a history encyclopedia or another reliable source. Read the entry together and look at the pictures. Topics could include *Nebuchadnezzar*, *Babylon*, *Ishtar Gate*, and *Nineveh*.

Coloring Page: The Ishtar Gate (Student Page 75)

One of Nebuchadnezzar's grand building projects was the Ishtar Gate, named after Babylon's chief goddess.

Storytelling & Art

NEBUCHADNEZZAR'S CHARADES

Note to Instructor: Write charade prompts (see ideas below) on slips of paper ahead of time and place them in a bowl.

In this game, you will take turns acting out scenes from today's lesson. When it is your turn, draw a slip of paper and act out the prompt without speaking or making any noise. The rest of the group—whether classmates, siblings, or the instructor—will try to guess what part of today's lesson you are acting out. Participants do not need to guess the exact wording—just figure out what the acting student is trying to show from the lesson.

Note to Instructor: Younger students may need extra help when it is their turn to act. You can whisper the prompt to them and/or provide a suggestion for how to act it out (see ideas below).

Prompt Ideas:

- **Medes and Babylonians attack Assyria** - Pretend to march forward with weapons, sneak up, or act out a battle.
- **Babylonians build the Ishtar Gate** - Pretend to stack bricks, paint designs, or admire a finished gate.
- **Babylonians parade through the Ishtar Gate** - March proudly, wave to an imaginary crowd, and gesture as if playing musical instruments.
- **Nebuchadnezzar boasts about his kingdom** - Stand tall, puff out your chest, point to yourself, and gesture to an imaginary city.
- **Nebuchadnezzar eats grass like a bull** - Get on all fours, pretend to munch on grass, and shake your head like an animal.
- **Nebuchadnezzar realizes God's power** - Look up at the sky, stretch out your arms, and kneel in humility.

Classroom Adaptation: If you have multiple students, allow 2-3 students to act out a charade prompt together while the rest of the class guesses.

The Hanging Gardens of Babylon

Read & Review

Read pages 184–188 in the text. Afterward, check the student's understanding by asking the questions below.

1. **Why was Nebuchadnezzar afraid of Media?** *He thought Media would attack him.*
2. **Why was Media afraid of Nebuchadnezzar?** *The Medians thought Nebuchadnezzar would attack them.*
3. **Why was Amytis homesick?** *Because she missed the mountains*
4. **What did Nebuchadnezzar build to make Amytis happy?** *The Hanging Gardens of Babylon*
5. **We've studied three of the Seven Wonders of the Ancient World. What three have we learned about?** *The Great Pyramid, the statue of Zeus at Olympia, and the Hanging Gardens of Babylon*

Narration Exercise

Tell me about Nebuchadnezzar and Amytis.

Nebuchadnezzar married a princess who missed her home. He built her a big garden on a hill to make her happy. It was called the Hanging Gardens of Babylon.

600 BCE

Activities

Choose from the following activities:

- [ ] Coloring Page: Marduk and Tiamat
- [ ] Memory Work: The Seven Wonders of the Ancient World
- [ ] Art: Draw The Hanging Gardens of Babylon
- [ ] Science: Build a Simplified Babylonian Mountain Garden
- [ ] Research Skills: Have the student look up a related topic in a history encyclopedia or another reliable source. Read the entry together and look at the pictures. Topics could include *Nebuchadnezzar*, *the Babylonian Empire*, and *the Hanging Gardens of Babylon*.
- [ ] Field Trip Idea: Visit a botanical garden! Think about how the garden is designed. If you could design a garden for yourself or someone you love, what would it look like? Draw a picture.

Coloring Page: Marduk and Tiamat (Student Page 76)

PARENTS, PLEASE PREVIEW. Marduk was the most important god to the Babylonians. Here he's fighting another god, named Tiamat, who's in the form of a dragon. This scene comes from an ancient Babylonian story that explains how Marduk defeated Tiamat, became the ruler of the gods, and created the world, a myth that was important to the people of Nebuchadnezzar's time.

Memory Work

THE SEVEN WONDERS OF THE ANCIENT WORLD

The Seven Wonders of the Ancient World introduces students to remarkable achievements in ancient architecture. If your student is interested, he can research and come up with an eighth wonder of the Ancient World or make his own list of seven modern wonders.

Note to Instructor: For detailed guidance on using memory work activities, see Appendix Two. The student's memory work reference page is available on Student Page 77. Below, you'll find the list of items to memorize, along with additional teaching ideas for your convenience.

1. The Temple of Artemis at Ephesus (Greek colony)
2. The Great Pyramid of Giza (Egypt)
3. The Hanging Gardens of Babylon (Babylon)
4. The Statue of Zeus at Olympia (Greece)
5. The Mausoleum at Halicarnassus (Persian Empire)
6. The Colossus of Rhodes (Greece)
7. The Lighthouse of Alexandria (Egypt)

Suggested Activity: Make up a hand motion for each of the Seven Wonders of the Ancient World. For example, for the Great Pyramid of Giza, make a triangle over your head, or for the statue of Zeus at Olympia, pretend to throw a lightning bolt.

Related Reading: *Seven Wonders of the Ancient World*, by Michael Woods and Mary B. Woods (Twenty-First Century Books, 2009) or Where *Were the Seven Wonders of the Ancient World?* by Yona Zeldis McDonough (Penguin Workshop, 2020)

Art

DRAW THE HANGING GARDENS OF BABYLON

You have just finished reading the story of why Nebuchadnezzar built the Hanging Gardens in Babylon. But no one knows what the gardens actually looked like. We only know of their existence because we have copies of ancient Greek and Roman texts that describe them. Many people believe that the gardens were made up of terraces stacked one on top of another. It probably resembled a ziggurat with plants! Trees, shrubs and flowers were brought in from all around the vast empire and planted in the garden. The finished result was like a magnificent green emerald in the desert landscape.

Use your crayons and your imagination to draw a picture of how you think the Hanging Gardens of Babylon looked. Your drawing just might be the one that best depicts how the gardens really looked so long ago.

Science

BUILD A BABYLONIAN MOUNTAIN GARDEN

The Hanging Gardens of Babylon were renowned far and wide for their beauty. In this activity, you will plan and grow your own miniature layered garden to explore how plants grow on different levels, just like in ancient terraces and natural landscapes.

MATERIALS:

- large bucket (optional, but it will help with moving the dirt and filling the pots)
- potting soil or garden dirt
- water
- 3-4 plastic or terra cotta plant pots in small, medium, and large sizes (or similar containers; they must have drainage holes in the bottom)
- grass seed, wildflower seeds, small flowers, or herbs (let your student help you plan what to plant!)
- a piece of paper and pencil

DIRECTIONS:

1. Plan your tiered garden; after all, Nebuchadnezzar's gardeners must have planned their garden carefully to make it so beautiful! If you like, use paper and pencil to draw a picture of your garden and decide what you will plant. Work with your trusted adult to choose plants that grow well in your climate. If you are planting multiple things, make sure they require about the same amount of sun and water.
2. If you are using lightweight pots, consider pouring some rocks into the bottom of each pot to help stabilize the final product.
3. Place the largest pot in the area you chose for your garden. Level it on the ground and fill it with soil.
4. Fill the next biggest pot with soil and place it on top of the first pot, centering it and ensuring it is level. You may want to press the pot into the soil a bit to keep it stable.
5. Repeat with the rest of your pots.
6. Plant your plants or seeds!
7. Check your garden daily and make sure your plants have the right amount of water and sun.
8. Observe how the plants grow!
9. Optional science demonstration: Keep a garden journal to track how many days it takes each plant to germinate. Draw pictures of your plants as they grow! Look up the names of each part of the plant to add labels to your drawings.

Additional History Reading

Ancient Mesopotamia, by Madeline Tyler (KidHaven Publishing, 2018). Covers many aspects of life in the Neo-Babylonian Empire. It makes the distinction between the older and later Babylonian empires much clearer than other books in this category. Every page is full of photographs. (Also recommended for chapters five, seven, and eight.) (RA)

Seven Wonders of the Ancient World, by Mary Hoffman, illus. M.P. Robertson (Frances Lincoln, 2003). The tale of a fictional slave who travels to see the real Wonders of the World. Includes a map, good illustrations, and historical details. **Out of print, but worth looking for at your local library.** (RA 1-3, IR 3-6)

Where Were the Seven Wonders of the Ancient World?, by Yona Zeldis McDonough (Penguin Workshop, 2020). A short chapter book on the Seven Wonders of the World. It includes a colored fold-out map in the back of the book. (IR 3-4)

Corresponding Literature Suggestions

1001 Arabian Nights (Oxford Story Collections), by Geraldine McCaughrean, illus. Rosamund Fowler (Oxford University Press Children's Books, 2000). A long and fascinating collection of stories from the ancient Near East. (RA)

The Children's Illustrated Jewish Bible, retold by Laaren Brown & Lenny Hort, illus. Eric Thomas (DK Children, 2020). More easy-to-read abridged versions of biblical stories, including three additional stories about Nebuchadnezzar and one about his son (RA). Most children's Bibles should have at least a few stories about King Nebuchadnezzar (2 Kings 24:10-16 discusses Nebuchadnezzar besieging Jerusalem, 2 Kings 25: 1-12 discusses the exile to Babylon; Daniel 2:1-49 discusses Daniel interpreting Nebuchadnezzar's dream; Daniel 3:1-30 discusses Nebuchadnezzar building a golden image that Daniel's friends refused to worship; and Daniel 4:1-37 discusses Nebuchadnezzar's period of madness).

The Legend of the Persian Carpet, by Tomie dePaola (Putnam, 1993). A traditional folk-tale from Nebuchadnezzar's part of the world, retold in picture-book form. **Out of print, but worth looking for at your local library.** (RA 1-2, IR 2-4)

CHAPTER TWENTY-FOUR
The Medes and the Persians

A New Empire

Read & Review

Read pages 189–193 in the text. Afterward, check the student's understanding by asking the questions below.

1. **What was the name of the shepherd tribe at the edge of Media?** *Persia, or the Persians*
2. **What country ruled over the Persians at this time?** *The Medes, or Media*
3. **Why did the Median king, Astyges, want to get rid of his grandson?** *He dreamed that the baby would grow up and take his throne away.*
4. **What was the baby's name?** *Cyrus*
5. **After Cyrus grew up, what did he do?** *He took power away from his grandfather and became the ruler of the Medes and the Persians.*

560–529 BCE

Narration Exercise

Tell me three things you learned in this lesson. Note: The student should know the name Cyrus, but she doesn't need to know the other proper names of characters in the story.

The king of Persia was afraid of his grandson. The baby was named Cyrus. When he grew up, he took over the throne. Then he conquered the Medes.

or

Cyrus grew up and became king of the Persians. Then he also took over Media. He became a great ruler.

Map Work: A New Empire (Student Page 78)

Read the instructions out loud to the student. After each step, pause and give time for the student to complete the task. Provide all necessary help.

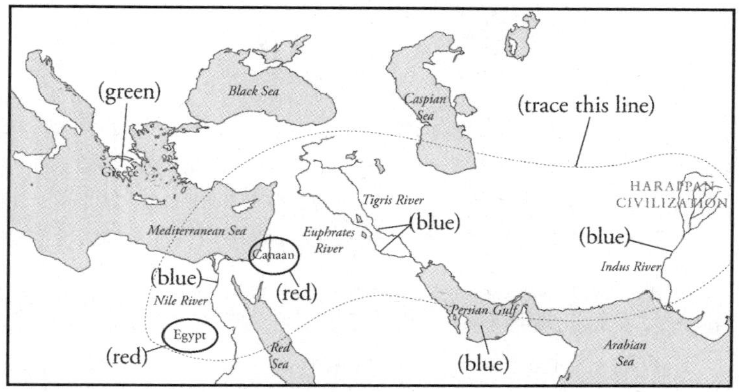

1. **Open to Student Page 78 and tear it out.**
2. **On your map, trace the dotted line that goes all the way around the *Persian Empire*. Remember that the Persian Empire swallowed up the empires of Media and Babylonia.**
3. **Find the *Persian Gulf* and color it blue. Why do you think it is called the *Persian* Gulf?**
4. **The ancient Persian Empire had four big rivers in it. Trace each one in blue. What are the names of the *four rivers*?**
5. **Two countries we have already studied—*Egypt and Canaan*—fall within the boundaries of the Persian Empire. Find those two countries and circle their names in red.**
6. **Persia was becoming the most powerful country in the east. Soon, they would meet the Greeks in battle. Find *Greece* on your map and color it in green.**
7. **When you finish, place the completed map in your history notebook.**

Activities

Choose from the following activities:

- ☐ Coloring Page: Cyrus the Great
- ☐ Storytelling: Persian Puppets
- ☐ Research Skills: Have the student look up a related topic in a history encyclopedia or another reliable source. Read the entry together and look at the pictures. Topics could include *the Persian Empire*, *Medes*, *Cambyses*, *Astyges*, *Harpagus*, and *Cyrus the Great*.

Coloring Page: Cyrus the Great (Student Page 79)

This picture of Cyrus the Great is based on a carving found in Pasargadae, the capital city of Persia founded by Cyrus.

Storytelling

PERSIAN PUPPETS

Use your creativity and whatever materials you have around to build puppets depicting the major characters in today's lesson! You don't need to create a puppet for every character. Just choose the characters and events that you think are most important to tell the story of Cyrus the Great's rise to power.

MATERIALS:

- several paper lunch bags (one for each puppet)
- crayons, markers, or colored pencils
- construction paper, fabric scraps
- buttons, felt, glitter, or sequins
- glue
- scissors

DIRECTIONS:

1. Read over the story of Cyrus and how he became king of the Persians. Decide which characters in the story would make good puppets.
2. Use the paper bags as puppet bases. Put your hand into each one and open and close the fold for a mouth. Draw lips around each "mouth" and use buttons, sequins, or construction paper circles to make eyes.
3. Glue strands of yarn on the top crease of the puppet for hair.
4. Use your other art materials to decorate the puppets.
5. Get behind your sofa, put your hand into the puppet, and push the puppet up above the back of the sofa. Now you have a stage! Act out part of the story of Cyrus for your parents, grandparents, or a video camera.

Classroom Adaptation: Place students in groups and have them work together to make puppets and then plan and perform a short puppet show about Cyrus (1-2 scenes or 5 minutes per a group).

Cyrus the Great

Read & Review

Read pages 193–195 in the text. Afterward, check the student's understanding by asking the questions below.

1. **Was Cyrus a good king?** *Yes, he was very fair.*
2. **Can you tell me one of the fair things Cyrus did?** *He let the Medes have some power in his empire* OR *He let the Jews go back to Palestine.*
3. **What was King Croesus known for?** *His gold—he was richer than anyone else.*
4. **Why did the Babylonians let Cyrus into their city?** *Because they did not like their own king*

Narration Exercise

Tell me about Cyrus's conquests. Note: Use the above questions to prompt the student if necessary. The narration should include the information that Cyrus conquered Babylon.

Cyrus conquered lots of other nations. One was ruled by a rich king named Croesus. He had lots of gold. He also conquered Babylon.

or

Cyrus was a good king. His people liked him. Babylon let him in because he was better than their king. Cyrus ruled a large empire.

560-529 BCE

Activities

Choose from the following activities:

- [ ] Craft: Make the Persian Ruler's Silver Plate
- [ ] Game: Play Mesopotamian Conquest!
- [ ] Research Skills: Have the student look up a related topic in a history encyclopedia or another reliable source. Read the entry together and look at the pictures. Topics could include *the Persian Empire*, *Medes*, *Croesus*, *Belshazzar*, *Asia Minor*, and *Cyrus the Great*.

Craft

MAKE THE PERSIAN RULER'S SILVER PLATE

The Persian kingdom was full of silver. To us, silver is valuable. Silver was valuable to the Persians as well. Workers of this precious metal made beautiful silver plates and bowls, decorating them with pictures of their favorite warriors or heroes—some of whom were famous hunters. They also made beautiful silver crowns. Some were so heavy that the kings couldn't even wear them! In this activity, we'll make a silver plate with foil instead of actual silver.

MATERIALS:

- cardboard
- dinner plate
- foil (heavy duty works best)
- pencil
- craft knife
- scratch paper

DIRECTIONS:

1. Put the dinner plate face down on a large piece of cardboard and trace the plate.
2. Using a craft knife, cut out the plate shape from the cardboard.
3. Wrap the cardboard plate with foil. Tack down the foil on the back of your cardboard plate with glue or tape. Cut away any extra foil, making sure that it lies down flat.
4. Using your scratch paper, draw some pictures of heroes: a king on a throne, a hunter, or a warrior on a horse. Stick figures are just fine!

5. When you have a drawing that you like, place the paper on the silver plate, right where you want your picture to be. Trace over the lines of your drawing with your pencil, pushing medium-hard so that your pencil tip dents the foil beneath.
6. Take the scratch paper off. See your picture on your Ruler's Plate!

Game

PLAY MESOPOTAMIAN CONQUEST!

Review what you've learned about the history of Mesopotamia with this game!

MATERIALS:

- 2-4 players
- your copy of *The Story of the World, Volume 1* text
- 1 instructor or "reader"
- 1 die
- the "Mesopotamian Conquest" gameboard (Student Page 80)
- small objects to represent each player (coins, buttons, beans, small plastic animals, etc.)
- cardboard or card stock to glue to your board (optional, but it makes it a lot sturdier and easier to play on)
- crayons or colored pencils to color in your game board (optional)

DIRECTIONS:

1. Pull out Student Page 80. We highly recommend coloring it in and gluing it to card stock or cardboard to make it sturdier.
2. The object of the game is to be the first one to the FINISH line!
3. Keep your copy of *The Story of the World, Volume 1* nearby for quick answer checks.
4. Players should select different objects to represent them on the board. All playing pieces should be placed on START.
5. Roll the die. The highest number goes first.
6. Going clockwise, each player should throw the die and move the prescribed number of spaces. When a player lands on a square that contains a symbol, the instructor, or "reader," reads the instructions for that symbol:
    - **Star: Shamshi-Adad conquers another city. What kind of king was Shamshi-Adad? Was he kind or cruel? If you can remember without the book, advance 3 spaces. If you need to reference the book to find the answer, find it in chapter Eight, then advance 1 space.** *He was a cruel king.*
    - **Tablet: Can you remember one of King Hammurabi's laws? If you can remember without the book, advance 3 spaces. If you need to reference the book to find the answer, find it in chapter Seven, then advance 1 space.** Answers may vary.
    - **Moon: What were the two main rivers in Mesopotamia? If you can remember without the book, advance 3 spaces. If you need to reference the book to find the answer, find it in chapter Three or Twenty-Four, then advance 1 space.** *Tigris and Euphrates.*

- **Globe: Babylonians watched the sky and discovered that the earth travels around the sun. What did they call the amount of time it takes for the earth to travel around the sun? If you can remember without the book, advance 3 spaces. If you need to reference the book to find the answer, find it in chapter Seven, then advance 1 space.** *One year.*
- **Sword: Who is Gilgamesh? If you can remember without the book, advance 3 spaces. If you need to reference the book to find the answer, find it in chapter Eight, then advance 1 space.** *A legendary king that the Babylonians and Assyrians told stories about.*
- **River: The Assyrians rebel against their masters, the Babylonians! They rage up and down the Tigris and Euphrates Rivers, and invade Canaan and scatter the Jews. And one of the greatest Assyrian kings of all, Ashurbanipal, leads his soldiers all the way down to Egypt to take over. Advance 1 space.**
- **Tower: What does Ashurbanipal build in Nineveh? If you can remember without the book, advance 3 spaces. If you need to reference the book to find the answer, find it in chapter Eighteen, then advance 1 space.** *A library.*
- **Spear: Babylon wants revenge! Now they rule Mesopotamia! What city did they destroy? If you can remember without the book, advance 3 spaces. If you need to reference the book to find the answer, find it in chapter Twenty-Three, then advance 1 space.** *Nineveh.*
- **Heart: Oh no! Nebuchadnezzar's wife wants to return home to Media. What does he build for her? If you can remember without the book, advance 3 spaces. If you need to reference the book to find the answer, find it in chapter Twenty-Three, then advance 1 space.** *The Hanging Gardens of Babylon.*
- **Walls: Nebuchadnezzar was not a happy king. What happened to Nebuchadnezzar the Great after he rebuilt Babylon? If you can remember without the book, advance 3 spaces. If you need to reference the book to find the answer, find it in chapter Twenty-Three, then advance 1 space.** *He lost his mind.*
- **Two figures holding hands: Babylon makes friends with the Medes. Now Babylon and the Medes are in charge! What empire do they work together to destroy? If you can remember without the book, advance 3 spaces. If you need to reference the book to find the answer, find it in chapter Twenty-Four, then advance 1 space.** *Assyria.*
- **Leaf: The Babylonians and the Medes are getting very proud! But who is the next nation to take over? If you can remember without the book, advance 3 spaces. If you need to reference the book to find the answer, find it in chapter Twenty-Four, then advance 1 space.** *Persia.*

- **C: Cyrus the Great gains the Persian throne and leads the Persians against the Medes. What do the Medes and Persians think about having Cyrus for a king? If you can remember without the book, advance 3 spaces. If you need to reference the book to find the answer, find it in chapter Twenty-Four, then advance 1 space.** *They think he is a good and fair king.*
- **Happy face: Cyrus the Great wants to conquer another enemy, Babylon! What big advantage did Cyrus have over the Babylonian king? If you can remember without the book, advance 3 spaces. If you need to reference the book to find the answer, find it in chapter Twenty-Four, then advance 1 space.** *The Babylonians hated their king.*

Additional History Reading

Discover Ancient Persia, by Neil D. Bramwell (Enslow Publishers, Inc., 2014). A history of Ancient Persia including the rule of Cyrus, best suited for older elementary students. (IR 4-6)

My Name is Cyrus, by Nazila Fathi (Susa Inc, 2020). In this short picture book with simple illustrations, Cyrus the Great tells the story of his life in the first person. (RA 1-4)

The Great and the Terrible: The World's Most Glorious and Notorious Rulers and How They Got their Names, by Joanne O'Sullivan (Running Press Kids, 2020). This book includes a short but engaging biography of Cyrus the Great and other important rulers of the Ancient world like Hatshepsut (Chapter Fourteen), Alexander the Great (chapter twenty-eight), Asoka the Great (chapter twenty-nine) and Attila the Hun (chapter forty-one). (RA 1-2, IR 3-5)

Corresponding Literature Suggestions

King Midas and the Golden Touch, by Charlotte Craft (HarperCollins, 2003). The legend of King Midas may be based on Croesus, the rich king of Asia Minor. For a longer project, listen to the unabridged audio of Lynne Reid Banks's *The Adventures of King Midas* (try your local library). (RA)

The Persian Cinderella, by Shirley Climo and Robert Florczak (HarperCollins, 2001). This retelling sets the story in ancient Persia, with beautiful detailed paintings for illustrations. (RA)

Corresponding Audiobook Suggestions

Esther's Story, by Diane Wolkstein (HarperCollins, 1996). The story of Esther took place during the expansion of the Persian Empire, among the Jews who were in exile in the Persian capital city. (RA)

CHAPTER TWENTY-FIVE
The Aryans of India

Life on the Ganges River

Read & Review

Read pages 196–199 in the text. Afterward, check the student's understanding by asking the questions below.

1. **What were the people who settled in ancient India called?** *Aryans*
2. **Where did they come from?** *Asia*
3. **Do you remember the names of the two big rivers that they settled near?** *Ganges and Indus*
4. **Why did they settle near the Ganges and Indus Rivers?** *Because they needed water for crops and animals*
5. **What was the name of the chief god of the Indian Aryans?** *Shiva*
6. **Why did the river-goddess Ganga get angry at Shiva?** *He told her to go down to earth and give water to the people who were thirsty.*

1500-483 BCE

7. **What did Shiva do when he saw that Ganga was getting ready to jump down on the earth?** *He jumped down ahead of her so that she landed on top of him.*
8. **Which river was named after Ganga?** *The Ganges*
9. **What do we call people who believe in Shiva and Ganga?** *Hindus*

Narration Exercise

Tell me about the Aryans coming to India.

After the citadel cities disappeared, other people came to India. They were called Aryans. They lived near the Ganges River and the Indus River.

or

Tell the story of Shiva and Ganga.

Once the people on earth were thirsty. Shiva told the river goddess Ganga to go down to earth. She didn't want to, so she tried to drown everyone. Shiva stopped her and she turned into the Ganges River.

Map Work: Life on The Ganges River (Student Page 81)

Read the instructions out loud to the student. After each step, pause and give time for the student to complete the task. Provide all necessary help.

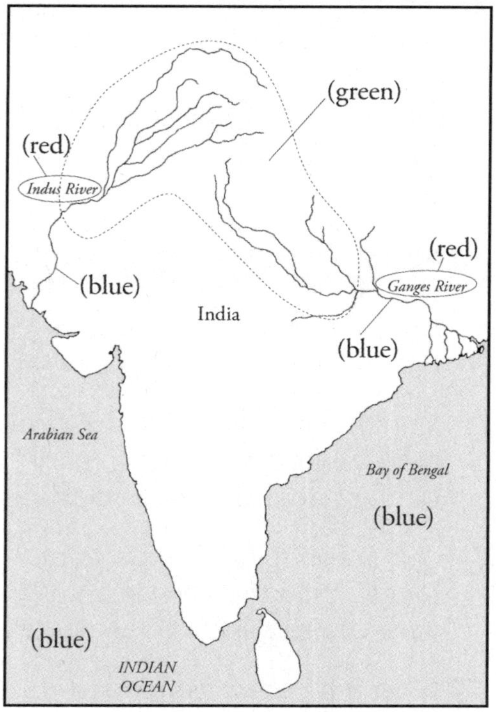

1. **Open to Student Page 81 and tear it out.**
2. **On your map, find the *Ganges* and *Indus* Rivers and circle their names in red. Then, trace their paths with a blue crayon.**
3. **Notice that the Ganges River has a delta just like the Nile River does. Make sure that you traced the delta in blue.**
4. **Color in the area that made up the *Aryan Empire* in green. The Aryan Empire is the area inside the dashed lines.**
5. **Lightly shade the *Bay of Bengal* and the *Indian Ocean* in blue.**
6. **When you finish, place the completed map in your history notebook.**

Activities

Choose from the following activities:

- ☐ Craft: Shiva and the Ganges River
- ☐ Game: Catch Ganga!
- ☐ Research Skills: Have the student look up a related topic in a history encyclopedia or another reliable source. Read the entry together and look at the pictures. Topics could include *Ancient India, the Ganges River, Aryans, Shiva*, and *Hinduism*.

Craft

SHIVA AND THE GANGES RIVER

In the story we read today, Shiva saved the people of earth. Ganga landed on his head and water flowed down Shiva's head in seven gentle streams to the earth below. With this craft, we will recreate that scene from the story.

MATERIALS:

- brown, black, or gray yarn or ribbon (for hair)
- blue ribbon or yarn (for Ganga)
- a paper plate
- a piece of paper
- glue or tape
- crayons, markers, or colored pencils
- scissors

DIRECTIONS:

1. Decorate the paper plate to look like Shiva's face. Shiva is often depicted with light blue skin and a third eye in the middle of his forehead.
2. Cut long strands of black, brown, or gray yarn. Glue or tape them to the top of the plate to be Shiva's long hair (if using tape, tape the strands behind the lip of the plate so that the tape doesn't show).
3. Cut seven long strands of blue ribbon to be the Ganges River. The ribbon should be longer than the yarn used for Siva's hair. If you don't have ribbon, you can use blue yarn braided into seven separate strands that stand out from the rest of the hair.
4. Glue the back of the paper plate (Shiva's head) to the top of a vertical sheet of paper.
5. On the bottom of the paper, draw the Earth: people, trees, animals, villages—whatever you imagine was saved by Ganga's gentle rivers.

Game

CATCH GANGA!

Ganga, the mighty river goddess, is rushing down from the heavens! Her powerful waters could flood the whole earth. Can Shiva catch her in time and help her flow gently instead?

MATERIALS:

- a large play area
- 2 or more players
- optional: a large cup or jug filled with water

DIRECTIONS:

1. Choose a point in your yard or play area to be "Earth," or the base.
2. Choose one player to be Ganga and one to be Shiva.
   - If you have more than two players, match up players who are about the same age and ability and take turns until everyone has had a turn to compete.
3. Set-up the players so that Shiva, Ganga, and "Earth" form a triangle—Shiva and Ganga should both start the same distance from Earth, but a little ways apart from each other.
4. f you do not have students of the same age or ability—for example, if you have a younger student competing against his older sibling—give the younger player a head start by placing him a bit closer to "Earth."
5. When the instructor says "GO!", Ganga races toward Earth while waving or twirling her arms to act like rushing water.
6. Shiva races to tag Ganga before she reaches Earth! If Shiva tags Ganga in time, Ganga must slow down and finish the race with gentle, flowing movements. Shiva wins! If Ganga reaches Earth first, Ganga wins!

Optional challenge: if you're playing on a sunny day, give Ganga a large cup or jug filled with water. The instructor or students waiting to play next sit in the spot marked Earth. Ganga races toward Earth with her water, trying not to spill! If Shiva tags her, she must gently pour out the water on the ground and walk slowly to "Earth." If Ganga makes it to Earth without being tagged, she gets to splash the people sitting in "Earth" with her water!

The Castes of Ancient India

Read & Review

Read pages 199–202 in the text. Afterward, check the student's understanding by asking the questions below.

1. **What were the four different castes of ancient India?** *Priests, warriors, farmers and traders, servants*
2. **How did you know what caste you belonged in?** *You were born into it OR your family belonged to it.*
3. **What was the best caste to be in?** *The priests or Brahmins*
4. **What were the people called who didn't belong to any caste?** *Untouchables*
5. **What kind of work did they do?** *Dirty work: burying dead animals, cleaning streets, picking up garbage, working in the fields*
6. **What story did the Hindus tell to explain castes?** *The story of Purusha, the first man*

Narration Exercise

Tell me about the caste system.

People in India belonged to four different groups. Some groups were better than others. People who didn't belong to any of the groups were called Untouchables. They had to do dirty work.

1500–483 BCE

Activities

Choose from the following activities:

- ☐ Game: Play Tiger Hunt
- ☐ Craft: Make a Rakhi
- ☐ Research Skills: Have the student look up a related topic in a history encyclopedia or another reliable source. Read the entry together and look at the pictures. Topics could include *Ancient India*, *Rig Veda*, and *Hinduism*.
- ☐ Field Trip Idea: Look to see if there is a Hindu temple open for visitors in your town. Call ahead to ensure you know the proper etiquette for visiting. Most temples are welcoming and open to non-Hindus who want to visit and learn more about Hindu culture.

Game

PLAY TIGER HUNT

In ancient India, royalty hunted tigers for entertainment.

MATERIALS:

- yellow construction paper or thin cardboard
- markers, paints, glitter
- yellow, black, or striped T-shirt

DIRECTIONS:

1. Make a crown for the "king." Cut a strip of yellow construction paper or thin cardboard with a serrated edge, long enough to fit around the student's head. Tape the ends together. You can decorate the crown with your paints and art materials if you want to.
2. One student will be the "tiger" and another student the "king." If you have just one student, the student can be the tiger! The "tiger" should put on the T-shirt. The "king" should wear the crown.
3. Choose a place in the house or yard to serve as "base."
4. Now the "king" should count to ten while the "tiger" hides. Can the king find the tiger and catch him (by tagging him) before the tiger can sneak back to base?

5. If you have additional students, they should serve as the king's servants—they should also try to find the tiger. When they find the tiger, they can't touch him. Only the king can catch the tiger! Instead, they should try to "herd" the tiger back towards the king so that the king can catch him.

Craft

MAKE A RAKHI

One special day in India is called Raksha Bandhan. This celebrates the bond of love between brothers and sisters. During this celebration the sister ties a rakhi (like a bracelet) on her brother's wrist. The brother promises his sister he will look after her.

MATERIALS:

- yarn, ribbon, or needlepoint floss
- cardboard or poster board cut into round shapes
- glue
- beads, sequins, glitter, foil, gel pens, and/or anything else to decorate

DIRECTIONS:

1. Knot the ends of the yarn, ribbon, or floss together, and divide the number of strands by 3. Braid as you would braid hair. You want this to be the size of a bracelet. Attach the ends together but leave the bracelet large enough to slip over your hand.
2. Decorate a small circle of cardboard or poster board with foil, beads, sequins, etc.
3. Sew or glue the decorated circle to the middle of the braided band.
4. Give your Rakhi to someone special!

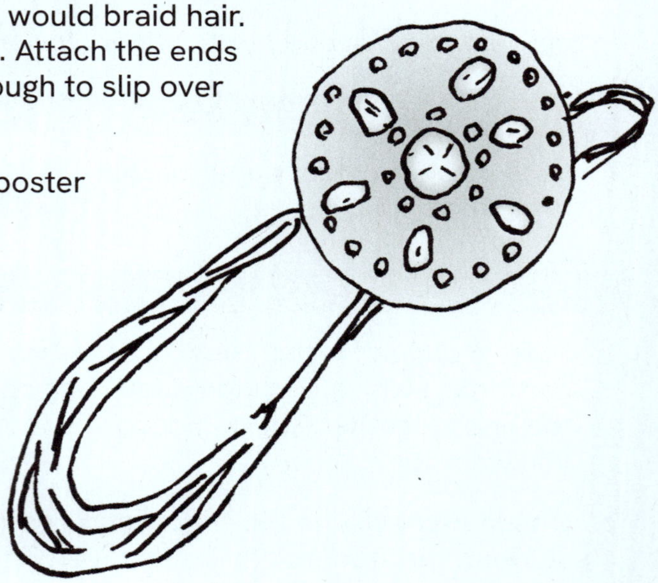

Siddhartha

Read & Review

Read pages 202–205 in the text. Afterward, check the student's understanding by asking the questions below.

1. **Why did Siddhartha decide to move out of his palace and live the life of a beggar?** *Because he saw sick, poor, and old people*
2. **What did Siddhartha teach all men to do?** *To live good lives; to be honest, make peace, and to avoid violence*
3. **What was Siddhartha's new name?** *Buddha*
4. **What were his followers called?** *Buddhists*

Narration Exercise

Tell me about Siddhartha.

Siddhartha was a prince. He lived in a great palace. Finally he saw that some people were poor and sick. He left the palace. He taught people to be good, and he was called Buddha.

1500-483 BCE

Activities

Choose from the following activities:

- ☐ Cooking: Indian Recipes
- ☐ Research Skills: Have the student look up a related topic in a history encyclopedia or another reliable source. Read the entry together and look at the pictures. Topics could include *Ancient India*, *Siddhartha*, *Buddha*, and *Buddhism*.
- ☐ Field Trip Idea: Many cities have Buddhist temples and centers that offer educational programs and tours. Call ahead to ensure you know the proper etiquette for visiting. Respect for others is a key value of Buddhism, so temples and centers tend to be very welcoming to non-Buddhist visitors.
- ☐ Celebration: Complete all of the activities in this lesson to celebrate what you've learned about ancient Indian history and culture! Make a Rakhi to give to one of your siblings (or a friend if you don't have siblings). Cook Indian food (or purchase food from a local Indian restaurant). Play Indian music and dance! Finish off by reading some stories from ancient India (see suggestions in the reading list below).

Cooking

INDIAN FOOD

Try some traditional Indian recipes that reflect the flavors and ingredients that may have been used during the Mauryan Empire!

Masala Rice

Rice is a staple food in India, as well as in China and other Asian countries. Each country, and even many regions within countries, have their own favorite way to cook it. Here is one simple recipe inspired by South Indian cuisine.

INGREDIENTS:

- 2 tablespoons oil or ghee
- 1 small onion, diced
- 3 cloves of garlic (minced)
- 2 teaspoons fresh ginger (crushed or use pre-made ginger paste)
- 1 teaspoon turmeric
- 1 teaspoon ground cumin
- 1 teaspoon ground coriander
- 1 teaspoon salt
- 2 cups rice
- 4 cups water or broth

DIRECTIONS:

1. Rinse your rice and set aside (optional, but will help rice be fluffier and less sticky once cooked)
2. Sauté onion in oil or ghee until the pieces are translucent.
3. Add ginger, garlic, and spices and stir for about 30 seconds.
4. Add rice and stock/water to the pot.
5. Bring to a simmer then cover and reduce heat to low. Allow the rice to continue cooking until all the liquid has been absorbed by the rice.
6. Remove from heat and let sit for 5 minutes.
7. Fluff with a fork and serve.

Red Lentil Dal

Lentils are a staple food in India and have been for thousands of years. Among Buddhists, vegetarianism and plant-based diets became popular, making lentils an essential protein source.

INGREDIENTS:

- 1 tablespoon ghee or oil
- 1 large yellow onion, chopped
- 1 tablespoon minced garlic
- 1 tablespoon fresh ginger paste or minced ginger
- 1 teaspoon ground turmeric
- 1 ½ cups red lentils
- 1 (14 oz) can diced tomatoes
- 4 cups vegetable broth (for a vegetarian version) or chicken broth
- 1 teaspoon salt
- 1 lemon, juiced
- 1 cup baby spinach
- 1 tablespoon garam masala (your local grocer may have this, or you can find this at the Indian grocery store or international store. Alternatively, substitute with ground cumin and a pinch of cinnamon)

DIRECTIONS:

1. Heat the ghee or oil in a pot over medium heat. Add the chopped onion and sauté until soft and translucent, about 3-5 minutes.
2. Stir in the garlic and ginger and cook for 30 seconds, until fragrant.
3. Add the turmeric, stirring constantly for another 30 seconds to release their flavors.
4. Stir in red lentils, diced tomatoes (with juices), and broth. Increase the heat to high and bring the mixture to a boil.

5. Reduce the heat to low, cover, and let the dal simmer for about 20 minutes, stirring occasionally, until the lentils are soft and fully cooked.
6. Stir in the baby spinach and cook until wilted.
7. Season with salt, garam masala, and fresh lemon juice to taste before serving.
8. Serve with rice or roti flatbread.

Besan Chilla (Savory Chickpea Pancakes)

Besan chilla is a popular everyday dish in North India. Made from chickpea flour (besan), spices, and water, it cooks like a pancake — no rolling or special equipment needed. It's quick, healthy, and fun for kids to help make.

INGREDIENTS:

- 1 cup chickpea flour (besan) OR 1 cup of dried chickpeas (you can buy besan from an Indian grocery store or you can make your own chickpea flour using the directions below. It just adds a few extra steps to the recipe)
- Food processor, high-power blender, or coffee/spice grinder (if you are making your own flour)
- 1 teaspoon ground cumin
- ½ teaspoon turmeric
- ½ teaspoon salt
- 1 cup water (add more if needed for a pourable batter)
- ½ small onion, finely chopped (optional)
- 1 small tomato, finely chopped (optional)
- A handful of chopped spinach or cilantro (optional)
- 2 tablespoons oil or ghee (for cooking)

DIRECTIONS:

1. **Making the Flour** (skip if you purchased chickpea flour): Rinse your dried chickpeas. Spread them out on a baking sheet for a few hours or lightly roast in a 300F oven for 10-15 minutes to dry them out. Place chickpeas in a high power blender, food processor, or coffee/spice grinder. Pulse until you have a fine, powdery flour. If you like, you can sift your flour through a fine-mesh sleeve to remove larger bits and get an extra smooth flour.

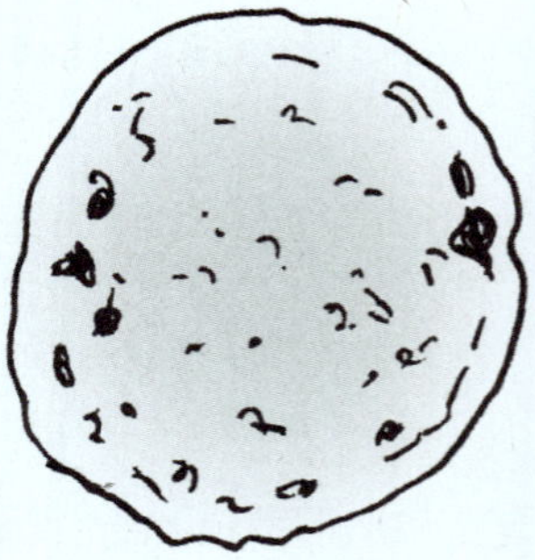

2. In a mixing bowl, whisk together chickpea flour, cumin, turmeric, and salt.
3. Gradually add water while whisking until you have a smooth, pourable batter (like pancake batter).
4. Stir in chopped onion, tomato, and spinach if using.
5. Heat a little oil or ghee in a nonstick skillet over medium heat.

6. Pour ¼ cup of batter into the skillet and spread it gently with the back of a spoon into a thin circle.
7. Cook until the edges look set and the bottom is golden, about 2 minutes. Flip and cook the other side for 1-2 minutes.
8. Repeat with remaining batter, adding a little oil or ghee as needed.
9. Serve warm alongside dal and rice.

Additional History Reading

The Ganges (Rivers of the World), by David Cumming (World Almanac Library, 2002). An overview of the Ganges River, one of the largest waterways in the world, valued not only for trade and irrigation but also for its religious importance to Hindus. (RA)

Buddha, by Demi (Henry Holt, 1996). The story of Siddhartha's life and a brief introduction to the teachings of Buddhism. (RA)

Prince Siddhartha: The Story of Buddha, by Jonathan Landaw (Wisdom Publications, 2000). The story of Prince Siddhartha and how he became Buddha. (RA)

Religion Around the World: A Curious Kid's Guide to the World's Great Faiths, by Sonja Hagander, Matthew Maruggi, and Megan Borgert-Spaniol (Beaming Books, 2022). Pages 8-15 cover Hinduism, and pages 16-23 cover Buddhism. (RA)

The Kids Book of World Religions by Jennifer Glossop (Kids Can Press, 2013). A great introduction to religions around the world, including the origins of Buddhism and Hinduism. (RA 1-3, IR 4-5).

Corresponding Literature Suggestions

Animal Tales from India: Ten Stories from the Panchatantra, by Nikita Gill, illus. Chaaya Prabhat (Nosy Crow, 2023). Ancient animal tales to read out loud.

Ganesha's Sweet Tooth, by Sanjay Patel and Emily Haynes (Chronicle Books, 2012). A playful take on the well-known story of how the god Ganesha became the scribe for an important Hindu epic poem, the Mahabharata. This book was developed and illustrated by a Pixar animator and story artist, and the illustrations are fantastic. However, the story veers significantly from the original tale and thus is just for fun and not a faithful retelling. (RA 1-3)

The Gita and You, by Sheila Dhir (HarperCollins, 2019). A child-friendly introduction to the Bhagavad Gita, one of Hinduism's most important holy texts. The book presents eight simple stories, each highlighting a key teaching from the Gita, along with interactive activities. This is a good choice if you want to dive deeper into learning about Hinduism with your children.

Prince of Fire: The Story of Diwali, by Jatinder Verma (Barefeet Books, 2016). A chapter book retelling of the origin story of Diwali, a Hindu holiday. (IR 3-5)

Buddha Stories, by Demi (Henry Holt, 1997). A collection of ten tales told by the Buddha. (RA)

I Once Was a Monkey: Stories Buddha Told, by Jeanne Lee (Farrar, Straus and Giroux, 2016). This book covers some of the basic teachings of Buddha, through a collection of six classic tales. (RA)

Princess of India: An Ancient Tale (30th Anniversary Edition) by Aaron Shephard (Skyhook Press, 2020). A brave and resourceful Indian princess saves her husband from death. (RA)

OPTIONAL LESSON
The Story of Ajatashatru the Expander, The First Empire-Builder in India

Read & Review

Read pages 206–210 in the text. Afterward, check the student's understanding by asking the questions below.

1. **What did Ajatashatru do to his father?** *Ajatashatru put his father in jail and let him starve.*
2. **What is one of the new things that Ajatashatru did in war?** Acceptable answers include: *He created the first professional army in India. He invented a new kind of war chariot. He built a rock-throwing catapult.*
3. **Whose teachings did Ajatshatru protect for future generations?** *Ajatashatru preserved the Buddha's teachings.*

Activities

Choose from the following activities:

- [ ] Coloring Page: Ajatashatru Travels to Meet the Buddha (Student Page 82)
- [ ] Creative Writing Prompt: Pretend you are a friend of Ajatashatru. Write him a letter to try to convince him NOT to throw his father in jail. (If needed, review the instructions on how to use the creative writing prompts in Appendix One.)

492-460 BCE

CHAPTER TWENTY-SIX
Writing, Fighting, and Thinking in China

Calligraphy in China

Read & Review

Read pages 211–215 in the text. Afterward, check the student's understanding by asking the questions below.

1. **What was the earliest Chinese writing called—where words looked like the things they named?** *Pictograms*
2. **What do we call later Chinese writing?** *Calligraphy*
3. **Can you tell me the names of several lines used in Chinese calligraphy?** You can look back at the lesson as you answer. *Horizontal line, vertical line, dot, downward stroke, sweeping downward stroke, hook*
4. **What kinds of hair did scribes use for their brushes?** *Mouse, rabbit, sheep, wolf*
5. **The Chinese developed a faster way to print books. What did they use?** *Ink and blocks of wood*

500 BCE

6. **Had anyone else ever done this?** *No, the Chinese were the first.*

Narration Exercise

Tell me what you learned about writing in ancient China.

The Chinese used to use pictures for writing. Then they wrote characters instead. They didn't look as much like pictures. They used seven different lines.

or

At first the Chinese wrote by hand. They used special brushes made out of mouse hair, rabbit hair, and wolf hair. It took a long time. Then they figured out how to use wood blocks instead.

Activities

Choose from the following activities:

- ☐ Art: Practice Chinese Calligraphy
- ☐ Research Skills: Have the student look up a related topic in a history encyclopedia or another reliable source. Read the entry together and look at the pictures. Topics could include *Ancient China, Chinese calligraphy, Diamond Sutra*, and *printing.*

Art

PRACTICE CHINESE CALLIGRAPHY

Practice what you've learned about calligraphy with this simple activity.

MATERIALS:

- *The Story of the World, Volume 1* text to reference pictograms in this chapter
- several different sizes and types of paintbrushes
- black ink or paint
- several sheets of white paper

DIRECTIONS:

1. Practice painting the different lines shown in the chapter. Experiment to find the brushes you like best. It's easier if you use bigger strokes.
2. Now try combining the lines together into the characters shown in the chapter, continuing to use big strokes.
3. Pictograms for mountain, fire, man, horse, field, tree, and woman are shown in the chapter. Can you make up some of your own characters? What do you think the character for "bird" should look like? How about "fish" or "flower?" Try any words you like, and then see if a sibling or parent can guess the meaning of any of the words.
4. Optional: look up modern forms of Chinese writing and try to copy a few words! Do you see any that are similar to the ancient pictograms?

Classroom Adaptation: If paint is too messy, have students use pens or markers instead. Have students create their own characters and write the word that each character represents on the back of the page. The teacher can collect a few characters from students and have the class try to guess their intended meanings.

Confucius: China's Wise Teacher

Read & Review

Read pages 215–217 in the text. Afterward, check the student's understanding by asking the questions below.

1. **Who was the great teacher of ancient India?** *Buddha*
2. **Who was the great teacher of ancient China?** *Confucius*
3. **Tell me one thing that Confucius taught.** *Obey people in authority, don't do anything to another person that you wouldn't want done to yourself, try to fix your mistakes, giving is more fun than getting, don't be greedy.*
4. **When did Confucius live?** *During the Period of Warring States*

Narration Exercise

Tell me what you learned about Confucius.

Confucius lived in China. He taught people to obey their rulers and children to obey their parents. He had many followers.

500 BCE

Map Work: Confucius: China's Wise Teacher
(Student Page 83)

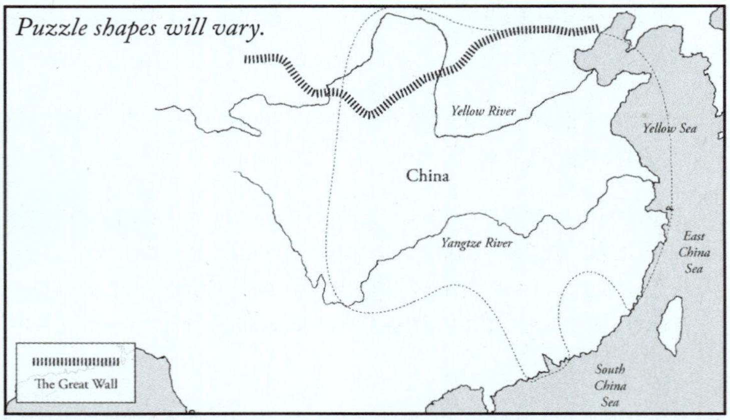

Read the instructions out loud to the student. After each step, pause and give time for the student to complete the task. Provide all necessary help.

1. **Open to Student Page 83 and tear it out.**
2. **Look at the map of China in this chapter. Confucius lived during the Period of the Warring States. China was split into many kingdoms that fought each other.**

3. **Let's make a puzzle to simulate China's fracture. Spread a thin layer of glue over the entire back side of the map. Place on a thin piece of cardboard and press down firmly. With a black marker, draw "puzzle" shaped lines on the cardboard side. See if you can cut it into seven pieces, one for each of the strong warlords.**
4. **Have an adult cut out the pieces.**
5. **When the cutting is finished, mix up the pieces and see how quickly you can put the Qin Empire back together.**
6. **Keep the pieces of your China puzzle in a bag so that you can practice putting it back together again and again.**

Activities

Choose from the following activities:

- [ ] Coloring Page: Confucius, China's Wise Teacher
- [ ] Cooking: Chinese Tea
- [ ] Storytelling: Confucius's Teachings
- [ ] Art: The Golden Rule Poster
- [ ] Research Skills: Have the student look up a related topic in a history encyclopedia or another reliable source. Read the entry together and look at the pictures. Topics could include *Confucius*, *Confucianism*, and *the Period of the Warring States*.

Coloring Page: Confucius, China's Wise Teacher
(Student Page 84)

Confucius was a great teacher and philosopher of ancient China whose ideas about respect, wisdom, and kindness shaped Chinese culture for thousands of years.

Cooking

CHINESE TEA

Confucius said, "Let your palate be your guide." What is your palate? It's your sense of whether something tastes good or not! Read "The Legend of the Tea" and then make some simple tea. Does your palate approve?

The Legend of the Tea

One afternoon, very long ago, Emperor Shen Nung was enjoying a cup of boiling water. The Emperor felt that drinking very hot water made him feel better. There was a gentle breeze this afternoon, and a few leaves from a nearby tree floated down and landed in his hot water. The Emperor thought the leaves made the water smell nice. He decided to take a sip of the water with leaves and found he enjoyed the taste. He proclaimed the leaves to be sent from heaven. This is believed to be the first cup of green tea.

Mint Tea

Note to Instructor: Most students seem to prefer mint herb tea to black or green tea. You can often buy fresh mint in the produce section of a grocery store. Another option is to buy some loose tea. Put it into an infusing basket, add it to the water, and steep. Or, for a more authentic tasting experience, try green tea bags or see if you can find some Chinese tea at the store. aware that green tea and black tea are caffeinated.

INGREDIENTS:

- fresh or dried mint leaves
- boiling water
- teacup

DIRECTIONS:

1. Pour boiling water into the teacup and have your student add a few mint leaves. Let steep for 3–5 minutes, then remove mint leaves.
2. Let cool slightly and drink.

Storytelling

CONFUCIUS'S TEACHINGS

Choose one of Confucius's sayings from the passage. Using puppets, stuffed animals, or yourselves, act out a short scene that shows someone not following the rule at first, then realizing their mistake and making a better choice. For example, a puppet refuses to share, but then learns that generosity brings him more friends and thus more happiness. After the performance is complete, discuss the following:

1. What was the problem?
2. How did the character fix it?
3. How can we follow this rule in real life?

Classroom Adaptation: Divide students into small groups and assign each group one of Confucius's sayings. Groups must plan a 2-5 minute sketch based on their assigned saying.

Art

THE GOLDEN RULE POSTER

Let's consider one of Confucius's most important teachings: Do not do unto others what you would not want others to do to you. On a large blackboard, whiteboard, or piece of paper, write "What actions would you not want done to you?" and "What kind actions could you do instead?" Take turns sharing ideas while the instructor writes them down. Choose one of the ideas in the chart and have the student draw a picture of themselves doing the kind action. Save the picture in the student's history notebook.

Classroom Adaptation: Create a class "Golden Rule Collage" by pasting together each student's drawing.

Additional History Reading

Chinese Menu: The History, Myths, and Legends Behind Your Favorite Foods, by Grace Lin (Little, Brown and Company, 2023). This unique book offers an illustrated legend or historical story for a variety of common Chinese foods. There is an outline in the front so that you can find food stories connected to whatever dynasty you are studying. Recipes are not included, but can easily be found online. (Also recommended for chapter thirty-nine) (RA)

Eyewitness: Ancient China, by Arthur Cotterell (DK Children, 2005). Geared toward older students, this book has great illustrations, with each chapter covering a two-page spread (one is titled "The Teachings of Confucius"). Sections will be suitable as a read-aloud; the timeline across the bottom of the first several pages is also very helpful. (RA 1–3, IR 4–7)

Long is a Dragon: Chinese Writing for Children, by Peggy Goldstein (Pacific View Press, 1992). Explains how Chinese writing developed and demonstrates how to write seventy-five Chinese characters, using detailed instructions and examples. **Out of print, but worth looking for at your local library.** (RA)

Confucius: Great Teacher of China, by Demi (Shen's Books, 2018). A picture book that introduces kids to the life and teachings of Confucius. (RA)

Who Was Confucius? By Michael Burgan (Penguin Workshop, 2020). A chapter book biography of Confucius with lots of illustrations. (IR 3-7).

World Religions, by John Bowker (DK, 2021). Beautifully illustrated, with a section on Chinese beliefs. (RA)

Corresponding Literature Suggestions

Peng's Vase: A Chinese Folktale, by Angus Yuen-Killick, illus. Paolo Proietti (Red Comet Press, 2023). This picture book adaptation of a famous Chinese folktale explains the value of honesty. (RA 1-3

Scroll, by Hui Li (Little, Brown and Company, 2023). In this cute picture book, a young girl is transported into a world made up of Chinese characters. (RA 1-3)

The Legend of Lao Tzu and Tao Te Ching, by Demi (Margaret K. McElderry Books, 2007). This book tells the legend of Lao Tzu, known as the father of Taoism. (Lao Tzu's existence is debated. Some think he was a contemporary of Confucius. Although he was not specifically mentioned in the chapter, this book would act as a quick introduction to Taoist beliefs if you are interested in diving deeper into the history of different religions.) (RA)

OPTIONAL LESSON
The Story of Mencius, The Greatest Follower of Confucius

Read & Review

Read pages 218–221 in the text. Afterward, check the student's understanding by asking the questions below.

1. **What ancient Chinese teacher did Mencius learn about?** *Mencius learned about Confucius.*
2. **What was the first important idea that Mencius taught?** *Mencius taught that people are good.*
3. **What was the second important idea that Mencius taught?** *Mencius taught that a king can only rule if God approves.*

Activities

Choose from the following activities:

- ☐ Coloring Page: Mencius (Student Page 85)
- ☐ Creative Writing Prompt: Pretend that you live in a country ruled by an evil king or queen. The king or queen is getting ready to come through your village, and you can go and protest! (That means you can tell the king or queen what a bad ruler they are.) What will you tell the ruler about your life? How will you prove that the ruler doesn't have the Will of Heaven on his or her side? (If needed, review the instructions on how to use the creative writing prompts in Appendix One.)

320 BCE

CHAPTER TWENTY-SEVEN
The Wars of the Greeks

Greece's War with Persia

Read & Review

Read pages 222–225 in the text. Afterward, check the student's understanding by asking the questions below.

1. **Why did Athens and Sparta decide to be friends and allies?** *Because they were afraid of the Persians*
2. **What did the Athenians and Spartans do to the messenger sent by the Persian king?** *They threw him down a well.*
3. **What did Persia do then?** *Attacked!*
4. **What two armies fought the Battle of Marathon?** *Persia and Athens*
5. **Who won?** *Athens*
6. **Why didn't the Spartans come help the Athenians?** *They were having a religious festival.*

490–480 BCE

7. **What happened to the runner who took the good news to Athens?** *He died of exhaustion.*
8. **Was the Battle of Marathon the end of Greece's war with Persia?** *No*
9. **The last battle in the war with Persia was the Battle of Salamis. Who won—the Greeks or the Persians?** *The Greeks, and the Greek cities stayed independent!*

Narration Exercise

Tell me about Greece's war with Persia. Note: The narration should include the information that Athens and Sparta united to fight the Persians, and that the Persians eventually lost the war.

Athens and Sparta weren't friends. But they fought the Persians together. They won a famous battle at Marathon. Persia lost the war.

or

Persia attacked Greece. The Greek cities fought back all together. Persia was defeated. One of the battles was at Marathon.

Map Work: Greece's War with Persia (Student Page 86)

Read the instructions out loud to the student. After each step, pause and give time for the student to complete the task. Provide all necessary help.

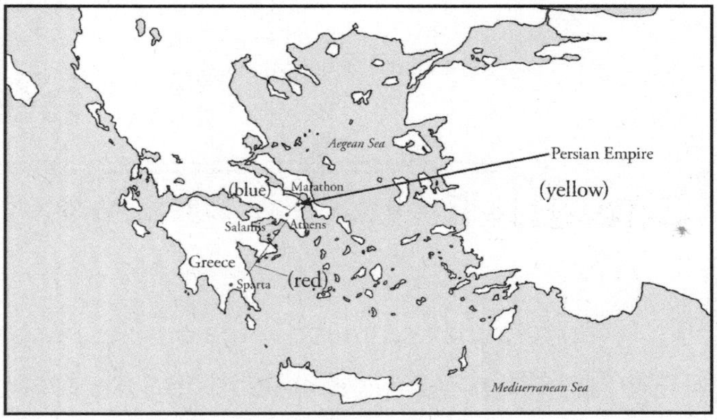

1. **Open to Student Page 86 and tear it out.**
2. **On your map, find *Sparta* and *Athens*. Draw a red line connecting them to show that they often fought each other.**
3. **The Persian Empire wanted to conquer Greece. Athens and Sparta decided to stop fighting against each other, and become friends and allies so that they could defend themselves against the Persians. Color the *Persian Empire* yellow. Then, draw an arrow from the Persian Empire across the *Aegean Sea*, toward *Marathon*.**
4. **After the Battle of Marathon, a messenger ran from Marathon to Athens to bring the news that the Athenians had driven back the Persian threat. Draw a blue line to show his path.**
5. **The Persians and Greeks went on fighting until the Greeks finally defeated the Persians, once and for all, in a great sea battle at a place called Salamis. After this battle, the Persians finally gave up attacking Greece. Find *Salamis* on your map.**
6. **When you finish, place the completed map in your history notebook.**

Activities

Choose from the following activities:

- [ ] Cooking & Make a Model: Make an Ice Cream Boat
- [ ] Role Play: Run a Marathon!
- [ ] Research Skills: Have the student look up a related topic in a history encyclopedia or another reliable source. Read the entry together and look at the pictures. Topics could include: *Darius the Great, the Persian Empire, the Greco-Persian Wars*, and *the Battle of Marathon*.

Cooking & Make a Model

MAKE AN ICE CREAM BOAT

In this activity you will build your own ice cream ship. You will have to build your ship fast, before it melts, just like the Greeks had to build their ships quickly to prepare for a Persian invasion.

MATERIALS:

- inexpensive box of ice cream, frozen hard
- table knife and spoon
- glass of warm water
- toothpicks
- 2 skewers or chopsticks
- white paper cut in the shape of a sail x2
- cookie sheet or brownie pan
- heavy whipping cream or an alternative whipped dairy topping
- blue food coloring
- black, red, and white cans of icing (optional)

DIRECTIONS:

1. Before you begin, look at the illustration of the Greek warship. It is long and rectangular with 2 sails and lots of oars coming out of the sides. This is what you will be shaping your ice cream to look like. It won't be perfect!

2. Wash your hands! Open the box of ice cream and peel the paper away from the ice cream block.

3. Ask an adult to use a large knife to cut the block lengthwise into 2 long rectangles. Put the rectangles end-to-end on the cookie sheet.
4. Work fast! Dip the table knife and spoon in the warm water. Use the knife for carving and the spoon for scooping. Carve sharp ends into your ice cream, and scoop a hollow out of the middle. Use your hands if you need to! Keep dipping the knife and spoon into the warm water. You should also keep a warm damp towel nearby to warm your hands now and then. If the ice cream begins to melt, slide your cookie sheet back into the freezer and take a break until the ice cream refreezes. Remember, the goal is to have fun, not to make it perfect!
5. Once your ice cream is shaped, place it in the freezer for at least 15 minutes before moving on. While you wait, decorate your paper sails and attach them to the skewers to be ready for your ship.
6. Pull your ship out of the freezer and decorate! Slide toothpicks into the sides for "oars." Push the sail into the middle of the boat. Mix a few drops of blue food coloring with your whipped cream. Spread the whipped cream over the cookie sheet and around the boat for "water." Optional: use the frosting to decorate your ship. Line the sides and edges. Paint an "eye" on the bow of the ship like Greek ships had (see illustration).
7. Take a picture (quick!), and then eat! Keep the picture in your history notebook.

Note to Instructor: This is an exciting but messy project. A perfectly-shaped boat is impossible, and the frosting tends to slide off, especially if the ice cream is melting.

Role Play

RUN A MARATHON!

The most famous runner in Ancient Greek history was Pheidippides, who ran from the battlefield of Marathon to Athens to announce the Greek victory over the Persians. His legendary run inspired the modern marathon! Your challenge is to run as far as Pheidippides. Use Student Page 87 to track your progress, and run a little each day until you complete your tracker. It's okay if you miss a day—just keep going until you reach your goal! And don't run until you feel exhausted-just run the distance that's comfortable for you. When you finish, reflect on how long that took, and imagine doing it all in one day like marathoners do!

The Greeks Fight Each Other

Read & Review

Read pages 225–229 in the text. Afterward, check the student's understanding by asking the questions below.

1. **What kind of building was the Parthenon?** *A temple*
2. **In one of the wall friezes, or carved pictures, on the walls of the Parthenon, Greek soldiers are fighting strange creatures. What were they?** *Centaurs—half man, half horse.*
3. **Did the Greeks go on making beautiful art in peace?** *No, they fought with each other.*
4. **What two cities fought the Peloponnesian War?** *Sparta and Athens*
5. **When Sparta was attacking Athens, what happened inside the city of Athens that made it weaker?** *The plague*
6. **What did Alcibiades do when he realized the Athenians would lose the fight?** *He left OR he switched sides.*
7. **Which Greek city won the fight?** *Sparta finally conquered Athens.*

Narration Exercise

Tell me what happened after the Greeks defeated the Persians. Note: The narration should include the information that the Greeks made lifelike art, and that Sparta and Athens fought until both cities were weak.

The Greeks knew how to make statues that looked like real people. They built beautiful buildings. But they kept on fighting with each other.

431–404 BCE

or

Athens and Sparta were at peace for a little while. They did beautiful art. Then they started fighting with each other again. They got weak from fighting.

Activities

Choose from the following activities:

- ☐ Coloring Page: The Parthenon
- ☐ Coloring Page: Design a Greek Temple
- ☐ Make a Model & Art: Build Greek Columns out of Clay
- ☐ Research Skills: Have the student look up a related topic in a history encyclopedia or another reliable source. Read the entry together and look at the pictures. Topics could include *Classical Greece*, *Acropolis*, *Sparta*, *Athens*, and *the Peloponnesian War*.
- ☐ Field Trip Idea: Visit the Parthenon in Nashville, Tennessee, the only exact-size replica of the original Parthenon in the world. The re-creation of the 42-foot statue of Athena, also full-scale, is the focus of the building just as it was in ancient Greece. The plaster replicas found in the west room are direct casts of the original sculptures. This makes for a great day trip or long weekend.

  If you're too far away, search for a virtual field trip or tour of the Parthenon. Then, visit a local city center or university and look for the three types of Greek columns on buildings: Doric, Ionic, and Corinthian. Greek architecture influenced early American architecture and is still commonly used in government buildings, universities, and old mansions.You can explore without a plan or search online for "Greek architectural influences in [your city]" to plan your route. Don't forget to grab some Greek food to make the outing extra special!

Coloring Page: The Parthenon (Student Page 88)

The Parthenon was a temple built to honor Athena, the goddess of war.

Coloring Page: Design a Greek Temple (Student Page 89)

The Greeks used three types of columns to hold up their buildings. Finish this picture of a Greek temple by drawing in the columns. Try to copy one of the famous Greek designs on the top of the page, or design your own style of column!

Note to Instructor: this page is also used for the "Build Greek Columns Out of Clay" activity.

Make a Model & Art

BUILD GREEK COLUMNS OUT OF CLAY

Ancient Greeks were known for their architecture, particularly their strong, beautiful columns. They had three different styles of columns: Doric, Ionic, and Corinthian. If you look closely, you may notice that these three styles of columns are still commonly used in fancy buildings today!

MATERIALS:

- Student Page 89
- air-dry clay or salt dough (recipe on page 414)
- toothpicks or craft sticks

DIRECTIONS:

1. Review the images of Doric, Ionic, and Corinthian columns on Student Page 89:
   - Doric: Simple and plain at the top
   - Ionic: Elegant, with a scroll (or spiral) on either side of the top
   - Corinthian: The fanciest, with carvings of leaves and flowers adorning the top
2. After discussing all three types, choose one to try to sculpt. Encourage younger students to try a simpler style, like Doric or Ionic. Challenge older students to try the Corinthian style.
3. Sculpt the body of the column by rolling a piece of clay into a thick cylinder.
4. Use a toothpick or craft stick to impress vertical grooves into the sides of the column (these grooves are called the "fluting"). Doric and Ionic columns usually have straight grooves, while Corinthian columns may have more ornate ones.

Note on Fluting: Columns are an example of engineering and physics in action! The ancient Greeks designed them to support the heavy weight of buildings by distributing force evenly. The grooves (fluting) on columns weren't just decorative—they helped reduce material while keeping the column strong.

5. Create the top (called the "capital"):
   - Doric column: roll a small piece of clay into a thick disc. Flatten it slightly and place it on the top of the column.
   - Ionic column: roll 2 small pieces of clay into long, thin coils. Curl each coil into a spiral and attach them to the opposite sides of the column's top.
   - Corinthian column: Complete the steps of a Doric column. Cut small pieces of clay into leaf shapes and layer them around the disc at the top of the column.
6. Finish your column off by adding a base! If you like, try creating all 3 types of columns.

7. Optional: Take a picture of your column(s). Keep it in your history notebook.

Classroom Adaptation: Have a model of each column type prepared beforehand that students can draw inspiration from or print pictures of each column type at each table.

Additional History Reading

Eyewitness: Ancient Greece, by DK Children (DK Children, 2023). This book is packed with information bites that make it a good reference. Descriptive of many aspects of ancient Greece, using pictures, drawings, costumed actors, and more. Fantastic pictures of artifacts! (Also recommended for chapters twelve, sixteen, twenty, and twenty-one) (RA)

Spend the Day in Ancient Greece! Projects and Activities that Bring the Past to Life, by Linda Honan (Jossey-Bass, 1998). Weave on a loom, paint an amphora, and build a racing chariot. These are a few of the fun projects taught in this book. Each section centers around a child in ancient Greece and the tasks he or she has to do. (Also recommended for Chapter Twenty) (RA and activity)

Where is the Parthenon? by Roberta Edwards (Penguin Workshop, 2016). This chapter book offers a deep dive into the story of the Parthenon. It includes a brief history of the building as well as explanations of the Parthenon's unique features, accompanied by illustrations. (IR 3-7)

Corresponding Literature Suggestions

Cupid and Psyche, by M. Charlotte Craft (HarperCollins, 1996). This child-appropriate retelling of the story of Cupid and Psyche has stunning illustrations. (RA)

Aesop's Fables for Children, by Milo Winter (Dover, 2020, and available in many other editions). The famous moral stories from Greek times in an illustrated, easy-to-read edition. (RA)

The Flying Horse: The Story of Pegasus (All Aboard Reading, Level 1), by Jane B. Mason, illus. Susan Swan (Grosset & Dunlap, 1999). A Greek story that most beginners can read alone. **Out of print, but worth looking for at your local library.** (IR)

CHAPTER TWENTY-EIGHT
Alexander the Great

Philip and His Son

Read & Review

Read pages 230–233 in the text. Afterward, check the student's understanding by asking the questions below.

1. **Who attacked the Greek cities?** *Philip*
2. **What country did he rule?** *Macedonia*
3. **What was the name of Philip's son?** *Alexander the Great*
4. **What does "Alexander" mean?** *Protector of men*
5. **Do you remember the name of Alexander's horse?** *Bucephalus*
6. **How did Alexander tame his horse?** *He turned the horse so that it couldn't see its shadow.*
7. **How did Alexander solve the problem of the Gordian Knot?** *He cut it in half.*

Narration Exercise

338–285 BCE

Tell me the story of Bucephalus.

Alexander's father was going to buy a horse. The horse was too wild for him. Alexander told his father that he would tame the horse. He did, and his father bought the horse for him.

or

Tell me the story of the Gordian Knot.

Alexander the Great saw a chariot with a huge knot on it. No one could untie the knot. So he cut it in half with his sword. This meant that he would conquer Asia.

Activities

Choose from the following activities:

- ☐ Coloring Page: Alexander the Great and Bucephalus
- ☐ Role Play: Bucephalus Obstacle Course
- ☐ Role Play: Tie a Gordian Knot
- ☐ Research Skills: Have the student look up a related topic in a history encyclopedia or another reliable source. Read the entry together and look at the pictures. Topics could include *Macedonia, Alexander the Great, Bucephalus*, and *the Gordian Knot*.

Coloring Page: Alexander the Great and Bucephalus (Student Page 90)

Together, Alexander the Great and his beloved horse Bucephalus rode into many battles.

Role Play

BUCEPHALUS OBSTACLE COURSE

Young Alexander bravely tamed his horse Bucephalus. Set-up an obstacle course in your backyard and try to get through it as fast as you can while riding a stick horse (if you don't have a stick horse, you can swap in a broom stick). A jump rope, blue blanket, or pool noodle on the ground could be a river you must jump over. Cones, chairs, or boxes could be mountains you must weave through. For an added challenge, try working through the horse while trotting, galloping, and then going as fast as you can. Time yourself to see how fast you can go!

Role Play

TIE A GORDIAN KNOT

Alexander cut the Gordian Knot because it was too complicated for him to untie. Pretend you don't have a sword and must untie a rope the hard way. Can you master tying and untying these special knots, without cutting?

MATERIALS:

- 2 heavy pieces of string or rope
- Student Page 91

DIRECTIONS:

1. Begin with the bowline knot—a knot in one piece of rope. First, make a loop in the rope and push the free end up through the loop from the bottom (Step 1). Next, pass the free end around the rope above the loop (Step 2). Finally, bring the free end back down through the loop and pull it tight (Step 3).
2. Now try a sheet bend. This knot ties two pieces of rope together. First, make a loop in one rope. Pass the end of the second rope through the end loop and then around the first rope further up (Step 1). Next, pull the end of the second rope through the loop in the first rope and tighten (Step 2).

Classroom Adaptation: Once a student has tied their knots, have them exchange their knots with another student to try untying.

Alexander's Invasions

Read & Review

Read pages 233–236 in the text. Afterward, check the student's understanding by asking the questions below.

1. **What four wonders of the ancient world have we learned about?** *The Hanging Gardens of Babylon, the Great Pyramid, the Statue of Zeus, the Pharos*
2. **What was the Pharos?** *A giant lighthouse*
3. **What was the name of the city Alexander built in Egypt?** *Alexandria*
4. **Why did Alexander stop before he conquered all of India?** *His soldiers refused to go any further.*

Narration Exercise

What three things did we learn about in this lesson? Note: Prompt as needed.

1. *Alexander didn't finish conquering India because his soldiers rebelled.*
2. *Alexander built a city in Egypt called Alexandria OR Alexander built many new cities.*
3. *The Pharos was a huge lighthouse in the harbor of Alexandria.*

Map Work: Alexander's Invasions (Student Page 92)

Read the instructions out loud to the student. After each step, pause and give time for the student to complete the task. Provide all necessary help.

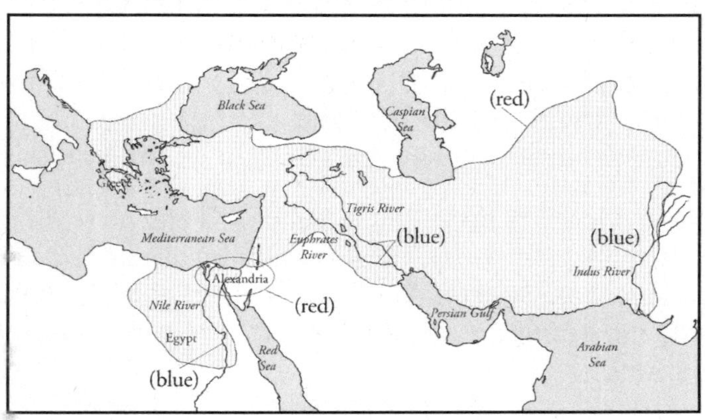

Note to Instructor: This chapter has two mapping activities. You do not need to complete both.

1. **Open to Student Page 92 and tear it out.**
2. **On your map, find the city that Alexander named for himself. Circle it in red. What country is it in?**
3. **Trace the *Nile River* in blue. Don't forget the *Nile Delta*!**

338–285 BCE

4. **Trace the borders of Alexander's empire in red.**
5. **Find and trace in blue the *Tigris*, *Euphrates*, and *Indus* rivers. How many rivers were inside Alexander's empire?**
6. **When you finish, place the completed map in your history notebook. You will use this map for the mapping activity in the next section. So keep it handy!**

Activities

Choose from the following activities:

- [ ] Role Play: Build Your Own City
- [ ] Art: Design Your Own Lighthouse
- [ ] Picture Study: Alexander Mosaic
- [ ] Research Skills: Have the student look up a related topic in a history encyclopedia or another reliable source. Read the entry together and look at the pictures. Topics could include *Alexander the Great*, *The Hellenistic Age*, *Pharos Lighthouse*, and *Alexandria*.

Role Play

BUILD YOUR OWN CITY

Alexander was famous for building cities in the lands he conquered. He named many of these cities Alexandria, after himself. He even named one city after his beloved horse, Bucephalus! Use toy building bricks or cardboard boxes to build a city! Then name your city by turning your own name into a city name by adding -andria, -burgh, or -ville. For example, if your name is Sam you could name the city Samandia, Samburgh, or Samville (or anything else, as long as your name is in it!). If you like, build a second city to name after your favorite pet, doll, or stuffed animal.

Note: Older students might enjoy building a city in a computer program or game like Minecraft. In fact, the book *Master Builder - Minecraft Ancient Wonders (Independent and Unofficial): A Step-By-Step Guide to Building Your Own Ancient Wonders*, by Sara Stanford (Welbeck Publishing Group, 2021) offers a step-by-step tutorial for building the Pharos Lighthouse. Role Play

Art

DESIGN YOUR OWN LIGHTHOUSE

Lighthouses have guided sailors safely to shore for thousands of years. Can you design your own lighthouse? Look up drawings of the Lighthouse of Alexandria and other famous lighthouses for Alexandria. What would your lighthouse look like? You can make it whatever shape and color you like. Just make sure that you have a place at the top for a light to shine bright to guide ships in the night!

If you like, you can build a model of your lighthouse using chip cans, tissue boxes, or any other materials you have around the house.

Art

THE ALEXANDER MOSAIC PICTURE STUDY

PARENTS, PLEASE PREVIEW. In this activity, you'll look closely at a famous piece of ancient art called the Alexander Mosaic, it depicts a real battle between Alexander the Great and King Darius III of Persia. This mosaic was created by Roman artists over 2,000 years ago, probably copying a Greek painting that no longer exists.

MATERIALS:

- Image of the Alexander Mosaic, House of Faun, Pompeii (We recommend viewing the mosaic digitally so that you can zoom in and look at the details. Find it by searching for "Alexander Mosaic, the House of the Faun, Pompeii." The mosaic is currently located in the Museo Archeologico Nazionale di Napoli. You can view the mosaic on the museum's website and other art websites.)

DIRECTIONS:

1. Give the student a few minutes to study the picture silently on their own, then ask the following questions:
   a. **This is an example of a special kind of art called a mosaic, which means it's made from thousands of tiny colored pieces of stone called tesserae. These little pieces were carefully placed to make a detailed picture. Can you look really close to the picture to see the tesserae?** Allow time for the student to look closely at the picture. Zoom in if you are viewing the picture digitally.
   b. **What are the people doing in the picture?** They are fighting a battle.

c. **What kind of armor or weapons do you see?** There are spears, shields, warhorses, helmets, armor, and a chariot.

d. **Does anyone seem like a leader? Why do you think so?** Answers will vary.

e. **The scene probably depicts a famous historical battle called the Battle of Issus. Alexander the Great surprised Darius and won. Can you point to Alexander the Great (he is the general on a horse).** Give the student time to point to Alexander the Great.

f. **Can you point to Darius? He is riding in a chariot.** Give the student time to point to Darius.

g. **Mosaics are extremely delicate. Over time, parts of the mosaic broke off or faded. Some of the tiles were lost when it was uncovered. That's why some spots are blank. Use your imagination to fill in the blanks. What do you think is in the missing sections?** Answers will vary.

The Death of Alexander

Read & Review

Read pages 236–237 in the text. Afterward, check the student's understanding by asking the questions below.

1. **How did Alexander the Great die?** *No one knows why he died. He got weak.*
2. **How many pieces did Alexander's empire get divided into?** *three*
3. **What did Ptolemy do in Egypt?** *Finished the city of Alexandria and built a library.*
4. **What is another name for the Seleucids?** *The Syrians*
5. **Did the three generals who ruled Alexander's kingdom make friends with each other?** *No, they fought.*

Narration Exercise

What happened when Alexander the Great died?

Alexander the Great had a huge kingdom. When he died, his generals split it into three parts. Then they all fought with each other.

Activities

Choose from the following activities:

- ☐ Sequencing Events: The Death of Alexander
- ☐ Game: Eleven Minutes to Conquer!
- ☐ Role Play: Sharing
- ☐ Research Skills: Have the student look up a related topic in a history encyclopedia or another reliable source. Read the entry together and look at the pictures. Topics could include *Alexander the Great*, *The Hellenistic Age*, and *Seleucids*.

338–285 BCE

Sequencing Events

THE DEATH OF ALEXANDER

In this activity, the student will put five events in the correct order, using the words **first, next, then, after that,** ***and*** **finally** ***to help her remember. The only supplies needed are paper or a white board to write on.***

DIRECTIONS:

1. We are going to list five events from the lesson in the correct order, using the words *first*, *next*, *then*, *after that*, and *finally* to help us remember.
2. We'll also use five words as a memory prompt, with each word representing a key action: *crowned*, *conquered*, *cried*, *died*, *divide*.
3. Before you begin, the instructor should write the words *first*, *next*, *then*, *after that*, and *finally* on a white board or piece of paper, and have the student chant them along with you.
4. Now have the student act out each event, emphasizing the underlined memory word in each step.
5. *First*, Alexander was crowned king (student mimes putting a crown on their heads).
6. *Next*, he conquered all of the ancient world (student marches across the room).
7. *Then*, he cried because there was nowhere left to conquer (student mimes crying).
8. *After that*, he got sick and died (student "dies" a dramatic death).
9. *Finally*, his generals had to divide the kingdom (student holds an imaginary sword and uses it to "divide" an imaginary kingdom).
10. Repeat steps 5 to 9.
11. Ask the student to chant the memory prompt words again: *crowned*, *conquered*, *cried*, *died*, *divide*.
12. Challenge the student to act out each event with only the memory word as a reminder.

Game

ELEVEN MINUTES TO CONQUER!

Alexander the Great built one of the largest empires in history in just eleven years! How many rooms in your house can you conquer in eleven minutes?

MATERIALS:

- a stopwatch or timer
- any items needed for tasks or games (see setup directions)
- a small prize (optional)

DIRECTIONS:

1. Choose a few rooms in your house to represent different regions of Alexander's empire. In each region, set up a mini-challenge. It could be physical, educational, or even a clean-up task. It does not need to be complicated! Examples for challenges include:
    a. Living Room (Macedonia): set up 3 cups and 3 ping pong balls. The student must throw one ball into each cup OR collect all of the library books from around the house and place them back in the library basket.
    b. Kitchen (Greece): using a straw, blow a piece of pasta across the table OR wipe down the table.
    c. Bedroom (Persia): stack 10 plastic cups into a pyramid with at least 3 layers (for younger students, have the pyramid set up so they can inspect it, knock it down, then recreate it) OR sort 10 pairs of unmatched socks and throw them, from a short distance, into a laundry basket.
    d. Bathroom (Egypt): use a large cup to transfer water (or bubbles) from the bathtub to the sink until the sink is full OR wipe down the sink, counter, and mirror.
    e. Hallway (India): do 20 jumping jacks OR sweep the floor.
2. Set a timer, then guide your student from room to room and have them complete each challenge as fast as they can (their goal is to complete all of the challenges in less than eleven minutes). When they complete the challenge for that room, say, "congratulations, you've conquered [insert region name];" then lead them to the next room/region. Once they have completed all of the challenges, tell them their total time and then celebrate! If you chose to do cleaning tasks instead of games, give your student a small prize.

Activity Directions (for the student):

1. There are challenges set up for you throughout the house; one challenge in each room. When the timer starts, start on the first challenge. Complete the challenge to "conquer" that room! See how many rooms you can conquer before the timer runs out!

Role Play

SHARING

After Alexander the Great died, his generals had to divide up his empire between them. The generals and their descendants fought each other for pieces of Alexander's empire for a hundred years!

Note to Instructor: This activity requires multiple students and works well with siblings of various ages.

Make or purchase a special treat (cake, pie, cookies, or even something non-edible, like stickers). Have students decide how to divide the treat up amongst family members (without adult help, if at all possible). Encourage them to discuss and negotiate—should everyone get the same size piece, or should some people get more based on age, hunger, or another reason? If they struggle to agree, ask them what might happen next—would they argue, compromise, or find a creative solution? Can they do better than Alexander's generals?

Additional History Reading

The Great and the Terrible: The World's Most Glorious and Notorious Rulers and How They Got their Names, by Joanne O'Sullivan (Running Press Kids, 2020). This book includes a short but engaging biography of Alexander the Great and other important rulers of the ancient world like Hatshepsut (chapter fourteen), Cyrus the Great (fhapter twenty-four), Asoka the Great (chapter twenty-nine) and Attila the Hun (chapter forty-one).(RA 1-2, IR 3-5)

The Greek News, by Anton Powell and Philip Steele (Candlewick Press, 1999). The cover story of this "Greek newspaper" (full of silliness and good information) is about Alexander the Great. **Out of print, but worth looking for at your local library.** (RA)

Who Was Alexander the Great? by Kathryn Waterfield and Robin Waterfield (Penguin Workshop, 2016). A chapter book biography of Alexander the Great with lots of illustrations. (IR 3-7)

Corresponding Literature Suggestions

Solomon and the Ant: And Other Jewish Folktales, by Sheldon Oberman (Boyds Mills Press, 2006). Forty-three traditional Jewish tales, written for reading out loud; include "The Seven Questions of Alexander the Great," a mythical encounter between Alexander and the wise men of Jerusalem. You can look for this book at the library or purchase it used or as an ebook. (RA 1-3, IR 3-6)

Corresponding Audiobook Suggestions

A Treasury of Wisdom, by Jim Weiss (Well-Trained Mind Press, 2015). This collection of inspiring biographies includes a story about Alexander the Great and the philosopher Diogenes.

CHAPTER TWENTY-NINE
The Mauryan Empire of India

The Empire United

Read & Review

Read pages 238–240 in the text. Afterward, check the student's understanding by asking the questions below.

1. **Are cities stronger if they are independent or if they're united together?** *United together*
2. **What was the name of the Indian empire that united the cities of India together?** *The Mauryan Empire*
3. **Who was its most famous ruler?** *Asoka*
4. **What religion did he follow?** *Buddhism*
5. **Can you tell me one of the kind things he did?** *He built hospitals, built animal hospitals, made laws against cruelty to animals, gave up violence, planted trees along roads, and gave up eating meat.*

Narration Exercise

How did the cities of India change, and why was this important?

268-232 BCE

Cities are stronger if they're all in one country. The cities of India were all separate. Then the Mauryan Empire made them into one country. Asoka ruled the empire.

Map Work: The Mauryan Empire (Student Page 93)

Read the instructions out loud to the student. After each step, pause and give time for the student to complete the task. Provide all necessary help.

1. **Open to Student Page 93 and tear it out.**

2. **In this chapter, you studied the Aryan Empire. The Mauryans came after the Aryans, and attempted to unite India. The two major rivers were still very important to this new empire. Find the *Ganges River* and the *Indus River*, and trace them in blue. Make sure that you trace the *Ganges Delta*.**
3. **The Mauryan Empire covered the whole northern part of India, and it is shown on your map as the area within the dashed lines. Shade the *Mauryan Empire* lightly in red.**
4. **Circle the names of the *Arabian Sea*, the *Indian Ocean*, and the *Bay of Bengal* in blue.**
5. **When you finish, place the completed map in your history notebook.**

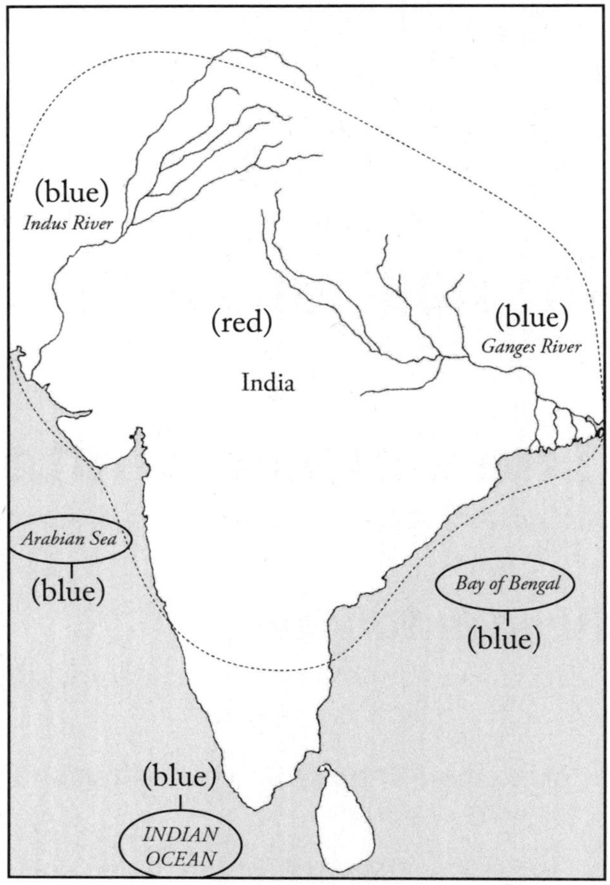

Activities

Choose from the following activities:

- [ ] Storytelling: Remind Yourself to Be Kind
- [ ] Role Play: Mindfulness
- [ ] Research Skills: Have the student look up a related topic in a history encyclopedia or another reliable source. Read the entry together and look at the pictures. Topics could include *the Mauryan Empire*, *Asoka*, *Buddhism*, and *Dharma*.

Storytelling

REMIND YOURSELF TO BE KIND

Even though Asoka was powerful, he chose to be kind in many ways, from taking care of animals to planting trees so travelers could walk in the shade.

He had monuments and pillars placed around his empire that reminded people of their duty to be kind and respectful to all living things. Make your own list of things you can do to be kind!

MATERIALS:

- paper
- pencil

DIRECTIONS:

1. Think of ways you can be kind, generous, and thoughtful.
   - If you see another kid sitting alone, ask if they'd like to play with you and your friends.
   - Give sincere compliments — for example, when someone makes a meal that you really enjoy.
   - Ask a parent if you can bring gloves and a trash bag to clean up any litter at the park, so everyone can enjoy it more.
   - Take your younger sibling outside to play or play their favorite game with them.
   - What are other ways you can be kind?
2. When you have decided on several ways to remind yourself to be kind, write *My Kindness Ideas* at the top of the paper, and then write or draw the ideas you want to remember.
3. Put the paper somewhere you will see it often, perhaps on the refrigerator or a bulletin board.
4. Go forth and be kind!

Classroom Adaptation: Asoka wrote messages about kindness and fairness on stone pillars and displayed them throughout his empire. Have each student write one short idea for being kind on a small piece of paper (for example: "Share with your friends," or "Don't hurt anyone."). If students are not writing yet, create short messages on small pieces of paper ahead of time and hand each student one message to color and decorate. Attach each student's "pillar" to a poster board and display it in the classroom or hallway.

Role Play

MINDFULNESS

After the war, Asoka was saddened by the pain he saw and decided to rule with peace and kindness. Asoka practiced mindfulness, which means sitting quietly, breathing slowly, and paying attention to your thoughts and feelings. Mindfulness is healthy for your brain and can help you calm down when you are stressed. Maybe mindfulness exercises helped Asoka lead with patience and compassion. Let's try a short mindfulness exercise and see how we feel afterward!

MATERIALS:

- a bell or chime
- optional: an audio player with soft instrumental music or nature sounds to play during the breathing exercise.

DIRECTIONS:

1. An instructor should introduce the mindfulness exercise with the following script:
    - **Find a comfy spot where you can sit quietly. You can sit on the floor or in a chair. Make sure your back is straight, and your hands are resting on your lap.**
    - **Close your eyes.**
2. An instructor should ring the bell or chime to start the mindfulness time. The instructor will read the instructions below to guide the meditation while the student or students sit with eyes closed:
    - **Imagine you are holding a beautiful flower. Take a deep breath in from your nose like you are smelling a flower, then breathe out slowly from your mouth like you're blowing the petals gently. Imagine the flower petals floating away. Keep blowing until all the petals are gone. Try that three times.**
    - **Now try breathing in through your nose for 1...2...3...4... seconds. As you breathe out through your mouth, make a "shhhhhhh" sound, like the sound of the ocean. Try that three times.**
    - **Now imagine you are a bear. Bears have big bellies. When they breathe, they fill up their bellies with air. Let's breathe in through our nose, feeling our bellies get big like a bear's tummy, and then breathe out through our mouth, feeling our bellies get soft. Ready? Big breath in... and let it out. Try that three times.**
3. To finish, the instructor should ring the bell or chime one more time and tell the student or students to keep their eyes closed and listen to the bell.
    - **When you cannot hear the bell sound any more, open your eyes. Stay silent until everyone in the meditation has opened their eyes.**
4. If you like, have a short discussion.
    - **When you are upset, what types of things can you do to calm yourself down? What types of activities make you feel peaceful?**

The Jataka Tales

Read & Review

Read pages 240–243 in the text. Afterward, check the student's understanding by asking the questions below.

1. **Why did the hare offer to roast himself?** *So that the priest wouldn't have to kill him*
2. **Was he rewarded for his generosity?** *Yes, he lived happily and was rewarded after death.*
3. **Who lived with the hare?** *An otter, a monkey, and a jackal*
4. **Were they as generous as the hare? Why or why not?** *No, because they stole the food they offered the priest.*

Narration Exercise

Draw a scene from the story. When you're done, tell me about it and I will write your description at the bottom of the page.

Activities

Choose from the following activities:

- ☐ Coloring Page: The Jataka Tales
- ☐ Storytelling: Pictures on the Moon (PREP)
- ☐ Game: Snakes and Ladders

Coloring Page: The Jataka Tales (Student Page 94)

Color a picture with lots of animal characters from the Jataka Tales.

268-232 BCE

Storytelling

PICTURES ON THE MOON

The story we read today attempts to explain why there is a picture of a hare on the moon. Different cultures see different shapes on the moon. In India and other parts of Asia, there is a tradition that the lines on the moon look like a rabbit or hare. In many European countries, the tradition is that the lines on the moon look like a man carrying a bundle of sticks. In some Vietnamese legends, the moon is supposedly holding a giant toad instead of a rabbit. In Polynesian mythology, the lines on the moon make up a woman called Rona who is fetching water. And in some African stories, the lines on the moon make up a buffalo or a cow.

Go out at night and look at the moon yourself. What do you see? If you like, make up your own story about how that person, animal, or object got onto the moon. Have an adult write your story down for you and place it in your history notebook (older students can write their story down by themselves) OR draw a picture of your moon.

Game

SNAKES AND LADDERS

Did you know that card games and the game of Chutes and Ladders both originated in ancient India?

If you have the game of Chutes and Ladders, get it out and look at it. If not, find an online board and print it out. Ancient Indians played a game like Chutes and Ladders—but they called it Snakes and Ladders! Each one of the slides in the game was a huge, scaly snake! Play the game of Chutes and Ladders, but whenever you slide down a chute, hiss like a snake.

Additional History Reading

A Coloring Book of Ancient India (Bellerophon Books, 1989). Uses images from ancient Indian culture. **Out of print, but worth looking for at your local library.** (RA and activity)

Hands on History: Ancient India, by Daud Ali (Armadillo, 2014). Illustrations, descriptions, and crafts, all related to ancient India. (RA)

Ashoka the Fierce: How an Angry Prince Became India's Emperor of Peace, by Carolyn Kanjuro, ill. Sonali Zohra (Bala Kids, 2021). This picture book biography of Asoka (spelled Ashoka in this book) adds more detail to the story told in the main text. It is entertaining and beautifully illustrated.

The Great and the Terrible: The World's Most Glorious and Notorious Rulers and How They Got their Names, by Joanne O'Sullivan (Running Press Kids, 2020). This book includes a short but engaging biography of Asoka the Great and other important rulers of the Ancient world like Hatshepsut (chapter fourteen), Cyrus the Great (chapter twenty-four), Alexander the Great (chapter twenty-eight) and Attila the Hun (chapter forty-one). (RA 1-2, IR 3-5)

Corresponding Literature Suggestions

Buddhist Stories for Kids: Jataka Tales of Kindness, Friendship, and Forgiveness, by Laura Burges (Bala Kids, 2022). Another well-done collection of tales. (RA)

I Once Was a Monkey: Stories Buddha Told, by Jeanne Lee (Farrar, Straus and Giroux, 2016). Each animal story has a moral about how we should treat others. (RA)

Nine Animals and the Well, by James Rumford (Houghton Mifflin, 2003). This traditional tale from India also covers the Indian origins of our nine number signs and our zero. **Out of print, but worth looking for at your local library.** (RA 1–2, IR 2–4)

The Monkey and the Crocodile: A Jataka Tale from India, by Paul Galdone (Clarion, 1987). A monkey manages to outwit the crocodile who decides to capture him (a retelling of one of the fables relating to Buddha). (RA)

CHAPTER THIRTY
The People of the Americas

The Nazca Drawings

Read & Review

Read pages 244–247 in the text. Afterward, check the student's understanding by asking the questions below.

1. **What is a continent?** *A big mass of land*
2. **There are three different "Americas." The first is South America; what are the other two?** *North America and Central America*
3. **South America has flat land in the middle. What does it have all down one edge?** *Mountains*
4. **Do you remember the name of the South American tribe that made drawings on the ground?** *The Nazca*
5. **How big were the drawings?** *Hundreds of feet across!*
6. **Do you remember what some of the drawings were?** *Spiders, pelicans, hummingbirds, flowers, spirals, squares, patterns.*
7. **Archaeologists don't know how the Nazca people made their drawings, but they have two guesses. What methods might the Nazca have used to draw these big lines?** *They may have used math or the position of the stars.*

Narration Exercise

Tell me about the Nazca.

The Nazca lived in South America. They made big drawings on the ground. Some of the drawings were of birds and flowers.

200 CE

or

Tell me what you learned about the Americas.

There are three Americas—North America, Central America, and South America. Tribes lived in South America a long time ago. They hunted and grew things like other people in ancient times. One tribe was called the Nazca.

Activities

Choose from the following activities:

- [ ] Art: Draw a Nazca Line Drawing
- [ ] Art: Chalk Nazca Lines
- [ ] Craft: Make a Seed Mosaic Map
- [ ] Research Skills: Have the student look up a related topic in a history encyclopedia or another reliable source. Read the entry together and look at the pictures. Topics could include *Nazca, ancient Peru, geoglyphs, the Andes mountains*, and *Ancient Americas*.

Art

DRAW A NAZCA LINE DRAWING

Do you remember reading about the huge Nazca line drawings that can only be seen from the air? How hard is it to draw a picture if you can't see what you are doing?

MATERIALS:

- white crayon
- white paper
- pan watercolor paints

DIRECTIONS:

1. Using the white crayon, draw a picture of your choice on white paper. Notice how difficult it is to draw a picture when you can't see exactly what you are doing. Be sure and press down hard with your crayon.
2. Using watercolor paints, paint over the entire sheet of paper.
3. Let it dry. How did your "invisible drawing" turn out?

Classroom Adaptation: If you like, have students swap drawings with a partner before revealing the image with watercolor. Each student must guess what is in their partner's picture. Afterward, hold a classroom discussion to discuss theories for how the Nazca drew their lines.

Art

CHALK NAZCA LINES

In this version, you will make your drawing as large as possible!

MATERIALS:

- pencil and paper for planning
- sidewalk chalk
- large outdoor space to draw, such as a sidewalk or cement patio

DIRECTIONS:

1. Plan your design on paper, keeping your outdoor drawing space in mind as you plan.
2. Take the paper with the design and your sidewalk chalk to your outdoor drawing space.
3. Compare your design to the available space; you want to make your drawing as large as possible.
4. Think about how you can scale up your design — what's the halfway point of your design, and what's the halfway point of your available space? Are there any landmarks, like a nearby tree, that might help you mentally divide the space?
5. Grab your chalk and start drawing! You can refer back to your design as you work.
6. When you're done, compare the design on your paper to your chalk drawing. Were you able to fit everything in or did you run out of room? How hard was it to keep the proportions correct when drawing in such a big space?

Classroom Adaptation: Have students work together to design and draw a phrase or symbol that represents their group (or school, co-op, family, etc...). Assign roles and have students work together to draw a large-scale version of their phrase or symbol in a place where parents and visitors will be able to see it. For example, draw a welcome message on the sidewalk in front of their school in their school's colors or draw a picture of their school's mascot, etc...

Craft

MAKE A SEED MOSAIC MAP

The foods we eat today come from different places all over the world. Many were first grown in the Americas! Some foods that originated in the Americas are: corn, many types of beans, sunflowers, tomatoes, peanuts, peppers, potatoes, pumpkins, squash, and strawberries.

MATERIALS:

- dried corn, beans, peanuts, as well as sunflower, tomato, pepper, pumpkin, and squash seeds
- copy of the map of the Americas on Student Page 95 (if you do not make a copy, you will not have a map available for the mapping exercise in the "Rabbit Shoots the Sun" lesson)
- glue

DIRECTIONS:

1. Brush glue all over your map.
2. Pick out which materials you want to use on each continent and glue them on. You can use smaller seeds for the flat land and larger seeds for the mountains.
3. Fill in the map with seeds and beans!

The Heads of the Olmecs

Read & Review

Read pages 247–249 in the text. Afterward, check the student's understanding by asking the questions below.

1. **What does "Meso" mean?** *Between*
2. **What does "Mesoamerica" mean?** *Between the Americas*
3. **What is the other name that we use for "Mesoamerica?"** *Central America*
4. **Do you remember the name of the tribe that lived in Central America?** *The Olmecs*
5. **Where did the rich Olmec people live?** *In the city, up on a hill*
6. **Where did the poor people live?** *Down on the plain below*
7. **What kind of pyramid did the Olmecs build in the middle of their city?** *A dirt pyramid*
8. **What kind of sculptures did they make?** *Giant heads of their rulers*

1200–900 BCE

Narration Exercise

Tell me about the Olmecs.

Central America is in the middle between North America and South America. The Olmec people lived there. They made huge giant stone heads that didn't have any bodies.

or

The Olmecs lived in a place called Central America. They built a dirt pyramid at the center of their city. The rich people lived up in the city, and the poor people lived down on the ground.

Activities

Choose from the following activities:

- [ ] Art: Build the Olmec Heads out of Clay
- [ ] Game: No Hands Ball
- [ ] Research Skills: Have the student look up a related topic in a history encyclopedia or another reliable source. Read the entry together and look at the pictures. Topics could include *Ancient Americas*, *Olmecs*, *giant heads* or *colossal heads*, *Mexico*, and *Mesoamerica*.

Art

BUILD THE OLMEC HEADS OUT OF CLAY

The Olmecs carved massive stone heads, likely to honor their rulers, just as we create statues of important leaders today.

MATERIALS:

- air-dry clay or salt dough (recipe on page 414)
- plastic knives, toothpicks, and other sculpting tools
- images of Olmec heads for reference (or use the illustration on page 249 of the main text)
- craft paint (optional)

DIRECTIONS:

1. Look at a picture of the giant Olmec heads. Point out the key features.
2. Build your own clay heads out of clay. Roll dough into a large ball; then flatten the bottom so it stands upright. Then use tools to shape the eyes, nose, and mouth. Many Olmec heads also had helmet-like headgear.
3. If you like, paint your heads once they dry.

Low-Prep Adaptation: Instead of carving the Olmec heads out of clay, draw them instead. Remember that they were big, so each head should take up a whole sheet of paper!

Classroom Adaptation: Portion the clay ahead of time to reduce mess and waste. Provide reference images at each table. If time is short, you could use Play-Doh instead of clay for younger students. However, if you use Play-Doh or salt dough, the completed project will not last as long.

Game

NO-HANDS BALL

The Olmecs played a special ball game where two teams tried to keep a ball in the air. The trick was that they could only hit the ball with their hips, thighs, knees, and upper arms. In some parts of Mesoamerica, indigenous people still play a version of this game today. In this activity, you will try a simplified version of this game.

MATERIALS:

- a large outdoor play area
- cones or other objects to mark the boundaries of the play area
- a large balloon (or lightweight ball for older students)
- a hula hoop (optional)
- string (optional)

DIRECTIONS:

1. Mark a large play area with cones or other items. If available, stretch a string across the ground in the middle to divide the area into two sides. If you don't have string, use cones or markers to divide the play area into two sides.
2. Toss a balloon into the area. Everyone must work together to keep the balloon off the ground. Players cannot touch the balloon with their hands or their heads. They can use their hips, knees, thighs, upper arms, and elbows.
3. Once everyone has some practice, it is time to play the game. Divide students into two teams — each team stays on one side of the play area (if you have only one student, the instructor and the student can play one-on-one). If the ball lands on the ground on your team's side, the other team earns a point. The first team to earn 5 points wins.
4. In the ancient game, some versions included a small stone hoop that players could try to pass the ball through for an automatic win. To add this challenge, have an instructor or student hold a hula hoop on the edge of the playing area, between the two sides. If a player gets the ball through the hoop, their team wins instantly.

Rabbit Shoots the Sun

Read & Review

Read pages 249–253 in the text. Afterward, check the student's understanding by asking the questions below.

1. **What two countries are now in North America?** *Canada and the United States*
2. **Way up in the northern part of North America, where it is too cold to grow crops, what did ancient people eat?** *Seals, polar bears, birds, caribou, mosses, lichens, and whales*
3. **How about people in the middle part of North America—what did they eat?** *Corn, buffalo, fish*
4. **Did the people of North America live in cities?** *No, they were nomads.*
5. **In the story of "Rabbit Shoots the Sun," why did Rabbit decide to shoot the sun?** *Because it was so hot and dry*
6. **What happened when Rabbit's arrow hit the sun?** *Fire came out and started to burn up the world.*
7. **What color did the bush turn when the fire scorched it?** *Yellow*
8. **Was Rabbit still brave and bold at the end of the story?** *No, he was timid and shy.*
9. **Did the sun still jump over the edge of the world in a hurry?** *No, it crept up a little at a time.*

Narration Exercise

500 BCE

Tell me two things about the people who lived in the far northern parts of North America, and two things about the people who lived down in the warmer part of North America.

People in the cold part of North America hunted seals and gathered moss to eat. People where it was warmer hunted buffalo and grew corn.

or

People in North America were nomads. Up where it was cold, they hunted whales and polar bears. Further down they grew corn and wheat, and they went fishing and hunting.

or

Tell me the story of "Rabbit Shoots the Sun."

Rabbit was mad at the sun for making it so hot and dry. He shot the sun with an arrow, but fire poured out all over the world and made it brown. Rabbit had to hide. Now Rabbit is very shy and the sun is afraid to jump up over the edge of the world.

Map Work: Rabbit Shoots the Sun (Student Page 95)

Read the instructions out loud to the student. After each step, pause and give time for the student to complete the task. Provide all necessary help.

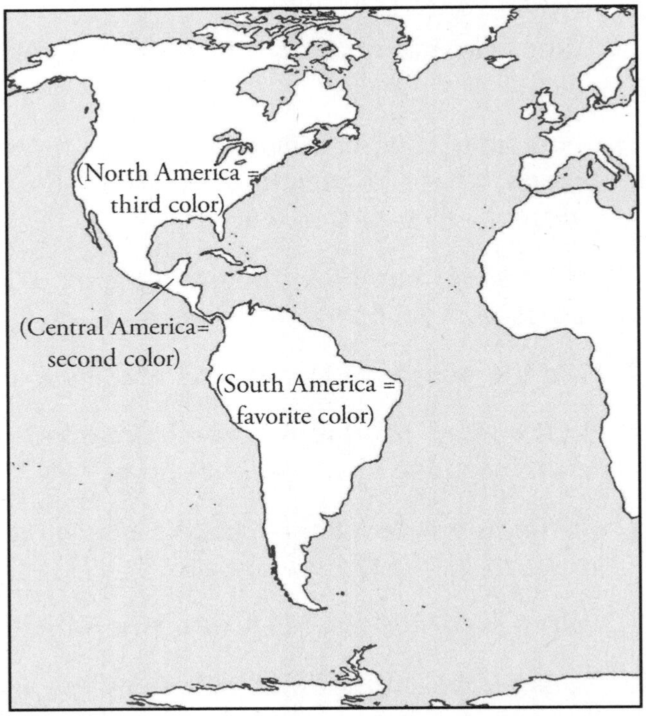

Note: If you want to complete the mosaic seed map activity, listed above, you will need two copies of this map.

1. **Open to Student Page 95 and tear it out.**
2. **On your map, find *South America*. Color it with your favorite color.**
3. **Choose another color and shade in *Central America*.**
4. **Choose a third color to shade in *North America*.**
5. **When you finish, place the completed map in your history notebook.**

Activities

Choose from the following activities:

- ☐ Coloring Page: Rabbit Shoots the Sun
- ☐ Cooking: Make Corn Cakes
- ☐ Celebration: Complete all of the activities in this chapter to celebrate what you've learned about ancient North and South America! Cook up some tasty corn cakes and invite your friends over to eat them with you. Read a story from the Ancient Americas or play the "No-Hands Ball" game. Finally, choose one of the craft activities to complete (Nazca Lines, Olmec Heads, or Seed Map) for a full afternoon of fun!

Coloring Page: Rabbit Shoots the Sun (Student Page 96)

For the Student: Color the "Rabbit Shoots the Sun" comic strip while your parent reads the story aloud. Then cut out each frame, shuffle them, and see if you can tell the story while you put the frames back in order.

Cooking

MAKE CORN CAKES

We don't know exactly what the ancient people of North America ate, but we do know that they grew corn! This recipe mimics something that ancient North Americans might have eaten, long ago.

INGREDIENTS:

- 2 cups cornmeal
- 1 cup water (or milk for a richer texture)
- 1 tablespoon honey
- 1 pinch of salt
- 1 tablespoon butter or oil
- optional: additional honey or berries (for serving)

DIRECTIONS:

1. Mix the cornmeal, water, salt, and honey into a thick batter.
2. Heat a pan or griddle over a fire or stove and lightly grease it with oil.
3. Drop spoonfuls of batter onto the pan, flattening slightly.
4. Cook for 3-5 minutes per side until golden brown.
5. Eat plain or with honey or berries.

Additional History Reading

DK Eyewitness: Ancient Civilizations, by Joseph Fullman (DK Children, 2013). Short sections on a wide range of civilizations, including America's first civilizations. Lots of color pictures and photographs of actual artifacts.

Lady of the Lines: How Maria Reiche Saved the Nazca Lines by Sweeping the Desert, by Michaela Maccoll, illus. Elisa Chavarri (Astra Young Readers, 2025). A picture-book biography about Maria Reiche, an archeologist and mathematician whose dedication, hard work, and ingenuity saved the Nazca lines from being destroyed. (RA)

What Do We Know About the Nazca Lines? By Ben Hubbard (Penguin Workshop, 2024). An easy-to-read chapter book that explores the mystery of the Nazca lines. (IR 3-6)

A Coloring Book of Incas, Aztecs, and Mayas (Bellerophon Books, 1985). All Bellerophon coloring books use a simplified adaptation of actual images from the culture under study.

Life in Ancient Mexico Coloring Book, by John Green (Dover, 1991). Detailed scenes of ancient Central American culture.

The Lost World of the Anasazi: Exploring the Mysteries of the Chaco Canyon, by Peter Lourie (Boyds Mills Press, 2003). The Anasazi were an ancient North American people; this well-photographed volume, a supplement to the stories of South and Central American peoples found in *The Story of the World*, shows the ruins they left behind. **Out of print, but worth looking for at your local library.** (RA 1–3, IR 4–6)

Corresponding Literature Suggestions

Note: Numerous North, Central, and South American tales have been published as picture books; you can use many books other than those listed below for this chapter.

Ancient Night, by David Alvarez, illus. David Bowles (Levine Querido, 2017). A short, poetic story adapted from a variety of famous Mesoamerican legends.

Feathered Serpent and the Five Suns: A Mesoamerican Creation Myth, by Duncan Tonatiuh (Abrams Books for Young Readers, 2020). This picture book tells the story of Quetzalcoatl, or feathered serpent, a figure who has appeared in Mesoamerican legends, buildings, and monuments for over 2,500 years.

How the Raven Got His Crooked Nose: An Alaskan Dena'ina Fable, by Barbara J. Atwater and Ethan J Atwater, illus. Mindy Dwyer (Alaska Northwest Books, 2018). A short, brilliantly illustrated trickster tale from North America.

Jabuti the Tortoise, by Gerald McDermott (Voyager, 2005). This very brightly colored picture book version of a South American legend tells how the tortoise's shell was cracked and why the toucan is so bright, and explains a host of other natural phenomena. (RA)

Keepers of the Earth: Native American Stories and Environmental Activities for Young Children, by Michael J. Caduto and Joseph Bruchac (Fulcrum Publishing, 1997). Retellings of 25 legends from 20 different cultures combined with scientific information and hands-on activities. Joseph Bruchac has written many other books about Native Americans. (RA)

Thirteen Moons on Turtle's Back: A Native American Year of Moons, by Joseph Bruchac (Putnam, 1997). Tales from a wide range of Native American traditions are beautifully illustrated with watercolors; each story explains the importance of a season to a particular tribe. (RA)

CHAPTER THIRTY-ONE
The Roman Republic

The Roman Builders

Read & Review

Read pages 254–256 in the text. Afterward, check the student's understanding by asking the questions below.

1. **Can you tell me three things that the Romans built?** *Roads, aqueducts, and apartment buildings*
2. **What were the Roman roads made out of?** *Sand, gravel, stone, concrete*
3. **Can you still see Roman roads today?** *Yes*
4. **What did aqueducts do?** *Carried water into the city*
5. **What did the Romans use the water for?** *Drinking, cooking, and public baths*

Narration Exercise

Tell me three things that the Romans built, and one fact about each of these things.

- *Roads. They were made of sand and gravel.*
- *Aqueducts. They carried water.*
- *Apartments. They were made of concrete.*

300-50 BCE

Activities

Choose from the following activities:

- ☐ Make a Model: Roman Archway and Aqueduct
- ☐ Cooking & Make a Model: Make (and Eat) a Roman Road
- ☐ Research Skills: Have the student look up a related topic in a history encyclopedia or another reliable source. Read the entry together and look at the pictures. Topics could include *Ancient Rome, the Roman Republic, the Appian Way, Roman roads, insulae (Roman apartment buildings), ancient concrete*, and *aqueducts*.
- ☐ Field Trip Idea: Check your local art museum to see if they have an exhibit on Roman artifacts or try a virtual tour of a large museum—for example, The British Museum (search "virtual field trip Ancient Rome")

Make a Model

ROMAN ARCHWAY AND AQUEDUCT

As the Roman towns grew, the architects put their beautiful archways to use as water-conduits, in structures known as aqueducts. The aqueducts were a series of connected archways built to bring the water from its source to a holding tank in the town which would distribute the water to a piping network, like those in use today.

Note to Instructor: This is a more complicated activity best suited for older students.

MATERIALS:

- photocopy of aqueduct template (Student Page 97)
- sand dough or your favorite kind of clay (recipe on page 414)
- rolling pin
- table knife
- baking sheet
- cardboard roll from paper towels
- empty yogurt cup
- plastic straw
- scissors
- full glass of water

DIRECTIONS:

1. Pre-heat oven to 250 degrees.
2. Cut out the archway pattern.

3. Divide your sand dough into 2 parts. Wrap up the dough you are not using to prevent drying. Pat or roll out the first ½-inch to 1-inch thickness and place the archway pattern on top. Using a table knife, cut around the pattern. Save the scraps with the rest of the dough not being used.
4. Carefully lift your first arch onto a baking sheet.
5. Repeat with the other slab of dough, but with the second arch, add ¼-inch more dough on the bottom, or base. This is so that when the archways are hooked together, there is a gradual sloping down to the water tank. (You can make additional archways as long as each is slightly taller than the last.)
6. Bake the archways for 20 minutes. Let them cool for 15 minutes.
7. To make your archways stand, lift them one at a time and stand them on the baking sheet. Brace the bottoms with more sand dough built up on the sides slightly. When all are standing, bring them together and smooth in sand dough between them, hooking them securely.
8. Gather a glob of sand dough the size of 2 jumbo marbles. Pat it down in the palm of your hand and press it on to the side of a rolling pin. This will create a kind of cradle for the cardboard tube to sit on. Add these cradles to the top of each archway, checking to make sure there is a gradual sloping downward. Bake the aqueduct for another 20 minutes.
9. After your aqueduct has cooled, lay the cardboard tube on the top.
10. On the bottom of the yogurt cup, poke scissors through on 3 sides. Cut the straw into 3 parts and insert into the bottom holes of the cup. This is the water tank for the Roman town. Place it under the lower end of your aqueduct.
11. Pour water into the tube at the top of your aqueduct and watch as it travels to your holding tank and out the different pipes to the parts of the town that need it. You are hired as a Roman architect!
12. Optional: Take a picture of your completed project. Keep it in your history notebook.

Optional: Embellish your Roman archway with columns or scroll work on the top. Use a toothpick to etch decorative borders or use the sand dough and make heads of lions, bears or eagles on the top of the arch.

Cooking & Make a Model

MAKE (AND EAT) A ROMAN ROAD

The Romans were well known for their roads. One of the most famous Roman roads was known as the Appian Way. You can make an edible model with all of the layers of a Roman road!

MATERIALS:

- a clear 9x12 dish
- 2 cups graham crackers (about 16 sheets)
- 6 tablespoons butter
- 20 Oreo cookies
- 3 cups chocolate pudding (prepared)
- whipping cream or whipped topping
- 1-2 packs of rectangular shortbread cookies, like Lorna Doones (for paving stones)
- a print out picture of a Roman road with all of the layers showing (optional)

DIRECTIONS:

1. First layer: The first layer of a Roman road was sand. Crumble the graham crackers and mix with 6 tablespoons of melted butter. Press the mixture in the bottom of your dish.
2. Second layer: The second layer in a Roman road was made of small stones mixed with mortar. You can crumble up Oreo cookies and mix them with your prepared chocolate pudding mix. Layer this mixture on top of the sand.
3. Third layer: The third layer was concrete. To recreate this, whip your whipping cream and use a spatula to layer it over the pudding mixture.
4. Fourth layer: The fourth layer was paving stones. Carefully layer your shortbread or rectangular cookies over the whipping cream in a neat road-like pattern.
5. Chill the dessert for about 30 minutes.
6. Take pictures for your history notebook and/or explain each layer to a parent or friend before eating it. Then dig in!

Alternative Idea: Instead of providing specific instructions for what ingredient to use for each layer, provide the student with all of the materials. Read the description of Roman roads in the main text (page 255). For each layer, let the student decide what ingredients he wants to use to represent that layer. Have him explain his reasoning as he goes.

The Roman Gods

Read & Review

Read pages 256–259 in the text. Afterward, check the student's understanding by asking the questions below.

1. **Whose gods did the Romans worship?** *The Greek gods, with different names*
2. **Can you tell me any of their names?** *Jupiter, Ceres, Proserpine, Pluto, Neptune, Mars*
3. **Why did Proserpine have to stay with Pluto for six months of the year?** *Because she ate some seeds from a pomegranate*
4. **What season of the year comes when Proserpine is underground with Pluto?** *Winter*

Narration Exercise

Draw a person or scene from the story. When you're done, tell me about it and I will write your description at the bottom of the page.

Activities

Choose from the following activities:

- [ ] Craft: Make an Olympus Family Tree. If you have already completed the Olympus Family Tree project in chapter twenty-one, add the names of the Roman gods using a different-colored paper leaf. If you have not yet completed the activity, do so now (instructions are on page 188). Use a green leaf for the Greek names and an orange leaf for the Roman names.
- [ ] Memory Work: Greek vs Roman Gods
- [ ] Game: Greek vs. Roman Gods
- [ ] Craft: Proserpine's Seasons
- [ ] Research Skills: Have the student look up a related topic in a history encyclopedia or another reliable source. Read the entry together and look at the pictures. Topics could include *Ancient Rome, Roman gods, Roman mythology*, and *Roman religion*.

Memory Work

GREEK VS ROMAN GODS

Memorizing the difference between Greek and Roman gods will help the student understand how cultures have adapted and transformed religious beliefs to fit their worldview. In addition, the student will recognize Roman gods' names because they are used for our planets!

Note to Instructor: For detailed guidance on using memory work activities, see Appendix Two. The student's memory work reference page is available on Student Page 98. Below, you'll find the list of items to memorize, along with additional teaching ideas for your convenience.

1. Zeus (ZOOS) - King of gods becomes Jupiter
2. Hera (HEER uh or HAIR uh) - Queen of the gods, wife of Zeus becomes Juno (JOO no)
3. Poseidon - (po SYE din) God of the sea becomes Neptune
4. Athena (ath EE nuh) - Goddess of wisdom and warfare becomes Minerva (mih NUR vuh)
5. Apollo - (uh POL oh) God of the sun, music, and poetry stays Apollo
6. Artemis - (AR tuh miss) Goddess of the hunt, wilderness, and childbirth becomes Diana (dye AN uh)
7. Hestia - (HESS tee uh) Goddess of the hearth and fire becomes Vesta (VES tuh)
8. Demeter - (duh MEE ter) Goddess of the harvest becomes Ceres (SEER eez)
9. Hermes - (HER meez) Messenger of the gods, god of trade becomes Mercury
10. Ares - (AIR eez) God of war becomes Mars
11. Aphrodite (A fro DITE ee or AH fro DITE ee) - Goddess of love and beauty becomes Venus
12. Hephaestus (heh FESS tuss) - God of fire, metalworking, and sculpture becomes Vulcan

Suggested Activity: Use the matching game in the activity below to practice your memory work!

Related Reading: *The Romans: Gods, Emperors, and Dormice*, by Marcia Williams (Candlewick, 2013).

Game

GREEK VS. ROMAN GODS

The Romans took Greek gods and gave them their own names! Some of those names we still use for our planets. Can you match the Greek god to his or new Roman name?

MATERIALS:

- 24 flash cards or equal-sized pieces of card stock
- Student Page 98
- Crayons, markers, or colored pencils

DIRECTIONS:

1. Make one set of flashcards for the Olympians with their Greek name on it. Write down their name and title on one side of the card, using Student Page 98 as a reference. Add an illustration if you like.
2. Make a second set of flashcards with the Olympians' Roman names. Write down their Roman name and their title, and add an illustration if you like.
3. Place all 24 cards, blank side up, in a grid in front of the players. On your turn, turn up 2 flashcards. If you turn up 2 cards that have Roman and Greek names for the same god or goddess, pull the cards out of the grid and keep them. If not, turn the cards back over to their blank side.
4. Take turns until all of the cards have been matched. Whoever collects the most matches is the winner!

Alternative Idea: If you have a computer, an instructor or older student could design the cards digitally, print them out, and paste them to cardstock or cardboard squares.

Craft

PROSERPINE'S SEASONS

Create a spinning seasons wheel to visually represent how the story of Pluto (the god of the underworld) and Proserpine (his captive bride) explains the changing of the seasons.

MATERIALS:

- 2 paper plates
- crayons, markers, or colored pencils
- scissors
- glue or tape
- 1 brass fastener (brad pin)
- stickers, cotton balls, leaves, glitter, or tissue paper for decoration (optional)

DIRECTIONS:

1. Have the student draw a big "X" on their paper plate to divide it into four equal sections.
2. Label each section Spring, Summer, Fall, and Winter (the instructor should help younger students with this).
3. Draw or decorate a picture in each season's section:

- Spring: Draw flowers blooming, a happy Ceres, and Proserpine returning from the underworld.
- Summer: Show a bright sun, lots of plants, and a joyful Ceres and Proserpine together.
- Fall: Draw leaves changing colors and Proserpine going underground.
- Winter: Show bare trees, snowflakes, and a sad Ceres missing her daughter.

4. Cut out a quarter of the second plate in a pie shape to reveal one season at a time when laid across the bottom plate. Use a brass pin (brad) to attach the top plate to the bottom decorated plate.

5. Turn the spinner to show when Proserpine is underground (Fall/Winter) and when she returns to Ceres (Spring/Summer). You can use your spinner to retell the story of Proserpine to your family and friends! Make sure to explain how the Greeks used her story to explain the seasons.

The Roman Gladiators

Read & Review

Read pages 260–262 in the text. Afterward, check the student's understanding by asking the questions below.

1. **What did gladiators do?** *Fought with each other or with wild animals while an audience watched*
2. **Why did Servius have to be a gladiator?** *He didn't have any choice because he was a prisoner.*
3. **Where did Servius learn how to fight?** *In the gladiator school*
4. **Did he want to be a fighter?** *No*
5. **What happened when he fought in the arena?** *He didn't kill his opponent.*

Narration Exercise

Can you tell me the story of Servius very briefly—in just a couple of sentences? Begin with "Servius was captured..." and go from there. Note: This exercise is developing your student's ability to summarize the main points of a story. Offer guidance as needed.

Servius was captured by Roman soldiers. They took him to Rome and forced him to go to gladiator school.

Activities

Choose from the following activities:

- ☐ Coloring Page: Gladiators in the Arena
- ☐ Activity Page: Match Each Gladiator to Their Weapon!
- ☐ Research Skills: Have the student look up a related topic in a history encyclopedia or another reliable source. Read the entry together and look at the pictures. Topics could include *Ancient Rome*, *the Roman Republic*, *the Colosseum*, *spectacles*, and *gladiators*.

Coloring Page: Gladiators in the Arena
(Student Page 99)

PARENTS, PLEASE PREVIEW. The Romans watched gladiators fight each other for sport. Some people, like Servius, were forced into becoming gladiators.

Activity Page

MATCH EACH GLADIATOR TO THEIR WEAPON!

(Student Page 100)

Can you match the gladiators to their weapons?

Note to Instructor: Read the description of each gladiator out loud to your student. As she listens, the student should draw a line between each gladiator and their matching weapons.

The two-sword man (Dimachaerus) wore padding or small guards on both arms. He did not carry a shield. Instead, he held two small swords, one in each hand.

The net-fighter (retiarius) wore only a loincloth, a belt, and armor on one arm and shoulder. He carried a weighted fishnet to throw over his enemy, and a long, three-pronged spear called a trident.

The chaser (secutor) wore a smooth, round helmet with only two tiny eye-holes and no mouth opening, making him look almost sealed inside. He protected his left leg with a metal guard, and he carried a short sword and a tall, rectangular shield.

The fish man (murmillo) wore a large helmet with a crest on top shaped like a fish's fin. The front of the helmet had a metal grill for breathing. He fought with a short sword and carried a big, round, shield.

Once you have matched the gladiator to their weapons, you can use the page as a reference for the next section, where you will hear more about these types of gladiators.

The Gladiator School

Read & Review

Read pages 263–266 in the text. Afterward, check the student's understanding by asking the questions below.

1. **Did Servius feel lucky to be a gladiator?** *No, he hated it.*
2. **Do you remember what a secutor is?** *Prompt student if necessary: a fighter who chases net-fighters*
3. **What did Servius do in his first match when the net-fighter stumbled?** *Let him live, let him get away*
4. **Did the Romans like to see gladiators die?** *Most of them did. A few, like Seneca, did not.*

Narration Exercise

Can you tell me the end of Servius' story? First, let's read what you told me last time.

Read the student's summary of the first part of the story.

Now can you finish the story? Note: Aim for two to three sentences.

Servius learned how to fight. But when he went to the arena, he didn't want to kill the other man. So he let him live.

Map Work: The Gladiator School (Student Page 101)

Read the instructions out loud to the student. After each step, pause and give time for the student to complete the task. Provide all necessary help.

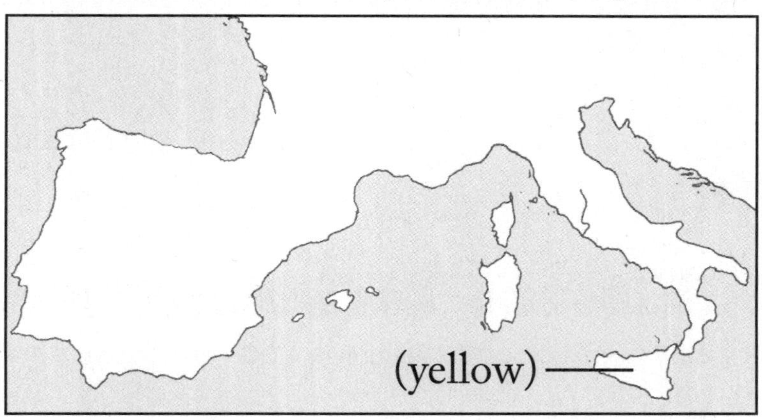

1. **Open to Student Page 101 and tear it out.**
2. **Find the island of *Sicily*. Color it yellow.**
3. **What is Italy shaped like?**

4. **What does it look like it is doing to the island of Sicily?**
5. **When you finish, place the completed map in your history notebook.**

Activities

Choose from the following activities:

- ☐ Role Play: Make a Roman Chariot
- ☐ Role Play: Gladiator Training School
- ☐ Research Skills: Have the student look up a related topic in a history encyclopedia or another reliable source. Read the entry together and look at the pictures. Topics could include *Ancient Rome, the Roman Republic, the Colosseum, secutor*, and *gladiators*.

Role Play

MAKE A ROMAN CHARIOT AND RACE!

There were many types of gladiators; one type, the essedarius, fought from a chariot. Make your own chariot and complete your very own chariot race!

MATERIALS:

- cardboard box large enough to fit around your student
- packaging tape
- scissors
- paints
- construction paper
- markers and anything else you may want to decorate the "chariot" with
- paper plates
- glue
- gold or silver paint or gold or silver foil (optional)

DIRECTIONS:

1. Use a cardboard box that will fit around your student and provide a little extra "running" room.
2. Cut out the bottom and top of the box. Cut a half-circle shape into the front of the box, similar to a Roman racing chariot. Cut off the back of the box.

3. For handles, cut two 4-inch lines, one about 1½ inches above the other, on each side of the box. Reinforce the handles with packaging tape.
4. Make two "wheels" by gluing two paper plates on the chariot, one per side (these are just decorative).
5. Decorate your chariot however you like! Roman chariots were often painted red, gold, or silver, with symbols like eagles, lightning bolts, or laurel wreaths.
6. Optional: Use metallic foil to add additional decorative details.
7. Let the races begin! Try racing across your yard as fast as you can! Time yourself and see if you can beat your time with practice. You can even shout "Jupiter, conserva me!" ("Jupiter, protect me!) like real Roman charioteers did!

Role Play

GLADIATOR TRAINING SCHOOL

Servius had to go to gladiator training school to prepare for his big fight. In today's activity, you will try some gladiator training school activities.

MATERIALS:

- a wide-open area outside
- a measuring tape
- pool noodles or soft swords
- a soft ball or small net
- two scraps of paper, one with "net fighter" written on it and one with "sword fighter" written on it
- a bowl

DIRECTIONS:

1. Use cones or other objects to designate a play area. This is your battle zone.
2. Now it is time for your gladiator fitness test. Run the battle zone. Time yourself as you run from the start to the finish line and back. Write down the total time on your paper.
3. Now we will test your endurance. How many sit-ups can you do in a row? Write down your total. How long can you last in a plank position? Write down your time. How many jumping jacks can you do? Write down your total. Add other fitness tests if you like.
4. Optional extension if you have only one student: Now it is time to test your gladiator skills. Choose which kind of gladiator you want to be: a net-fighter or a sword-fighter. If you choose net-fighter, practice throwing a net or ball to hit a target. If you choose sword-fighter, practice hitting a target with a play sword.
5. Optional extension if you have more than one student: Now it is time to find out what kind of gladiator you will be! Will you be a net-fighter or a sword-fighter? Close your eyes and draw a piece of paper from the prepared bowl.

a. If you draw the net-fighter card: You will have a ball (the ball represents the net). You must throw your ball at your opponent. If you hit your opponent with your ball 5 times, before they hit you with their sword 7 times, you win.

b. If you draw the sword-fighter card: You will be armed with a sword (pool noodle or foam sword). If you can poke your opponent with your noodle or foam sword 7 times, before the net-fighter hits you 5 times, you win.

c. If either gladiator steps out of the zone of the play area, they lose one "hit."

d. To try to make things as fair as possible, the instructor can adjust the amount of hits needed depending on the players' age and abilities. So, if a younger student is playing against an older student, the older student will need to complete more hits to win.

e. If you like, switch roles with your opponent and try again!

f. For an extra challenge, give the net-fighter a pool noodle to represent his trident and give the sword-fighter a shield (play shield or a piece of cardboard) to help her deflect attacks.

g. You can come up with your own versions of different types of gladiators. Test them out!

Additional History Reading

Ancient Rome for Kids, by Oldrich Ruzicka, illus. Tomas Tuma (Albatross, 2024). Explore ancient Rome, the Roman Republic, the Roman Empire, the Roman gods, the Roman army, and Roman gladiators with this book of six fully-illustrated fold-out maps.

Eyewitness: Ancient Rome, by Dr. Simon James (DK Children, 2022). This book is packed with short information bites and pictures of artifacts. It focuses on daily life in Rome, including going to the theater, arts, entertainment, life for children and families, crafts, cooking, and more. (Also recommended for chapters twenty-two and forty-two) (RA)

Aqueduct of Segovia (Extreme Engineering), by Brienna Rossiter (North Star Editions, 2024). This book explains how aqueducts work, using pictures and descriptions of the largest Roman aqueduct still standing. (IR 2-3)

City: A Story of Roman Planning and Construction, by David Macaulay (Houghton Mifflin, 1983). Follow the development of a Roman town from its earliest days. (RA)

Rome Antics, by David Macaulay (Abbeville, 2025). Macaulay takes a pigeon's-eye view and leads young readers through the streets of early Rome. Beautifully done, like all of Macaulay's books. (RA)

The Roman Colosseum (Wonders of the World), by Elizabeth Mann (Mikaya, 1998, 2006). This book is to be "explored," not necessarily read word-for-word; look at the pictures, read the captions, and read those pages that the child finds most interesting. You can look for this book at the library or purchase it used or as an ebook. (RA)

You Wouldn't Want to Be a Roman Gladiator, by John Malam (Franklin Watts, 2000). An entertaining guide to the life of a Gallic captive trained to be a gladiator, with cartoon-like illustrations. Good historical information. You can look for this book at the library or purchase it used or as an ebook. (RA 1–2, IR 3–5)

Corresponding Literature Suggestions

Classic Myths to Read Aloud, by William F. Russell (Crown, 1992). A collection of Greek and Roman myths, designed to be read aloud to children five and older. (RA)

Asterix the Gladiator, by Rene de Goscinny (Orion, 2004). This comic-strip tale of adventure is as much fun for grown-ups as for children. (RA)

Danger in Ancient Rome (Ranger in Time Series), by Kate Messner (Scholastic Press, 2015). A time-traveling dog has to help a boy escape from being a gladiator. (RA 1-2, IR 3-4)

See You Later, Gladiator (Time Warp Trio), by Jon Scieszka (Puffin, 2004). Gratias tibi ago quia me gladio tuo non fodisti. That's "thank you for not poking me with your sword," a useful phrase for the hapless time-traveling trio, Sam, Fred, and Joe, when they find themselves flunking out of gladiator school in ancient Rome. (RA)

OPTIONAL LESSON

The Story of Spartacus, The Rebel Gladiator

Read & Review

Read pages 267–271 in the text. Afterward, check the student's understanding by asking the questions below.

1. **How did Spartacus the gladiator rebel?** *He assembled an army to fight the Romans.*
2. **After winning many victories, what did Spartacus want to do instead of fighting the Romans?** *He wanted to leave Rome and go home.*
3. **What happened to Spartacus?** *He was killed by the Romans.*

Activities

Choose from the following activities:

- ☐ Coloring Page: Spartacus (Student Page 102)
- ☐ Creative Writing Prompt: Imagine you were Spartacus. What is one thing you would have done differently? (If needed, review the instructions on how to use the creative writing prompts in Appendix One.)

103–71 BCE

CHAPTER THIRTY-TWO Rome's War with Carthage

The Punic Wars

Read & Review

Read pages 272–276 in the text. Afterward, check the student's understanding by asking the questions below.

1. **What city did Rome fight?** *Carthage*
2. **What did they fight over?** *They wanted to trade with the same cities.*
3. **Was it a long war or a short war?** *A long war!*
4. **Do you remember what the wars were called?** *The Punic Wars*
5. **Where did they fight—on land or on water?** *Mostly on water*
6. **What are soldiers who fight on water called?** *A navy*
7. **What did Hannibal do?** *He fought the Romans with elephants.*
8. **How did General Scipio get Hannibal out of Italy?** *He attacked Carthage.*
9. **Who won—Carthage or Rome?** *Rome*
10. **What did Hannibal do when Carthage surrendered?** *He drank poison*

264-202 BCE

Narration Exercise

Tell me what happened during The Punic Wars.

Rome and Carthage fought a long war. They fought with each other on ships. One Roman general had chickens for good luck! Then Hannibal attacked Rome with elephants. But he lost and drank poison.

or

Rome wanted to rule more land. So did Carthage. They fought the Punic Wars. Hannibal went into Italy with elephants. Then Scipio attacked Carthage, and Hannibal came back to fight him. But Carthage lost.

Map Work: The Punic Wars (Student Page 103)

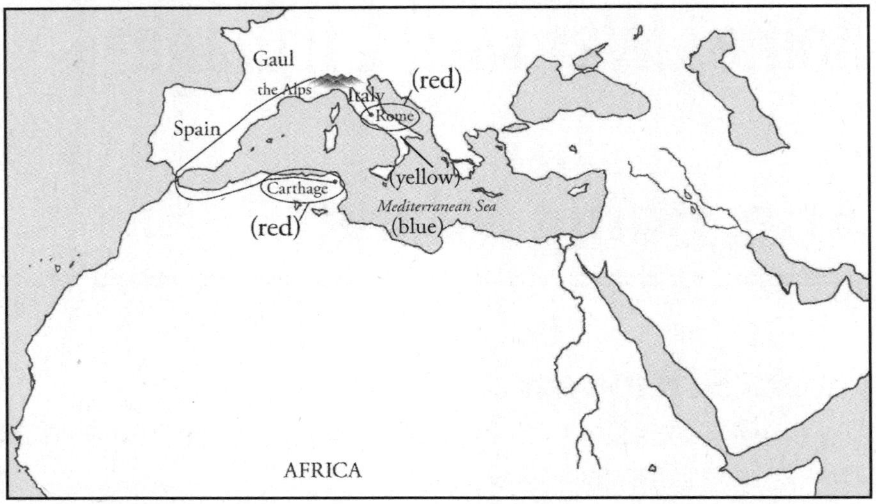

Read the instructions out loud to the student. After each step, pause and give time for the student to complete the task. Provide all necessary help.

1. **Open to Student Page 103 and tear it out.**
2. **Find *Rome* and circle it with a red crayon. Color Italy yellow.**
3. **Color the *Mediterranean Sea* with a blue crayon.**
4. **Find *Carthage* and circle it with a red crayon. What continent is Carthage in?**
5. **Draw a line showing how Hannibal and the Carthaginians got to the Alps by going through North *Africa*, *Spain*, and *Gaul*.**
6. **Now draw a line from the Alps down to Rome. This is the path that Hannibal tried to take with his elephants.**
7. **When you finish, place the completed map in your history notebook.**

Activities

Choose from the following activities:

- ☐ Coloring Page: Hannibal's War Elephants
- ☐ Coloring Page: Hannibal
- ☐ Storytelling: Sacred Chickens or Charging Elephants
- ☐ Craft: Make a Cuff Bracelet
- ☐ Craft: Make a Centurion's Helmet
- ☐ Research Skills: Have the student look up a related topic in a history encyclopedia or another reliable source. Read the entry together and look at the pictures. Topics could include *the Punic Wars* or *Carthaginian Wars*, *Carthage*, *war elephants*, *Scipio Africanus*, and *Hannibal*.

Coloring Pages: Hannibal's War Elephants (Student Page 104) or Hannibal (Student Page 105)

Hannibal was a famous Carthaginian general who led his army, including elephants, across the alps to fight the Romans. Choose to color either Hannibal or one of his elephants, or both!

Storytelling

SACRED CHICKENS OR CHARGING ELEPHANTS

Imagine you are one of the sacred chickens brought onto the Roman ship before a big battle. Describe your day. Do you like the attention the soldiers give you, or are you nervous about what might happen next? What is the real reason you won't eat?

OR

Imagine you are one of Hannibal's elephants, marching through the snowy Alps to surprise Roman soldiers. Describe what the march was like. Is it hard to march through the snow with a soldier on your back? What do the Roman soldiers' faces look like when they see you coming (remember, many Romans may have never seen an elephant before!).

Younger students could narrate their answer to an adult or act out the scenario based on the prompt. Older students can write their answers down on their own. If your student wants to, have her draw a picture to illustrate her story.

Craft

MAKE A CUFF BRACELET

Roman soldiers wore these bracelets to show their commitment to Rome.

MATERIALS:

- poster board or lightweight cardboard
- aluminum foil
- permanent marker

DIRECTIONS:

1. Cut the poster board so that it is about 2 inches wide and fits around the wrist of your student.
2. Cover the poster board with aluminum foil.
3. Write S-P-Q-R on the bracelet with a permanent marker.
4. Staple the bracelet together so it fits your student's wrist.

Note: SPQR stands for *Senatus Populus que Romanus*, which means "The Senate and People of Rome" in Latin. Roman soldiers were supposed to remember that they served Roman citizens and the Senate.

Craft

MAKE A CENTURION'S HELMET

The Roman centurion was an army officer, and his helmet had a special plume on top so he could be easily identified by his foot soldiers in battle. In this craft project, you'll make your own centurion's helmet.

MATERIALS:

- Student Page 106 and Student Page 107 (Centurion Helmet Template)
- 1 gallon plastic milk jug, rinsed and dried
- scissors
- cardboard (a cereal box would work)
- 2 sheets of red construction paper
- glue stick
- sharp knife or craft knife
- silver paint suitable for plastic or aluminum foil*

* You have several options: (1) Use Paint for Plastic, available at craft stores, and apply with a brush. You must use the Paint for Plastic Primer as a base coat. (2) Use spray paint available at craft and home improvement stores. Wipe the plastic down with paint thinner first for best results. (3) You can skip the paint and cover the helmet with aluminum foil, but prepare yourself for some complicated wrapping. (4) Or you can leave the helmet unpainted. Pretend that it has been through many battles and that its original metallic sheen has faded to the color of a milk jug.

DIRECTIONS:

1. Cut out Plume Template A from Student Page 106. Trace the template onto the cardboard twice and cut out both pieces.
2. Cut out Plume Template B from Student Page 107. Trace the template onto each piece of construction paper and cut out both pieces. Cut the fringe into the paper plumes.
3. Fit the two cardboard plumes back to back so they match perfectly. Glue a red paper plume to the inside of each piece (so the red plume is sandwiched by the cardboard pieces and the fringe of the plume sticks up above the cardboard). Set aside.
4. Use the first image in the diagram below to cut the milk jug so that it is shaped like a helmet (an instructor or older student should complete this step):

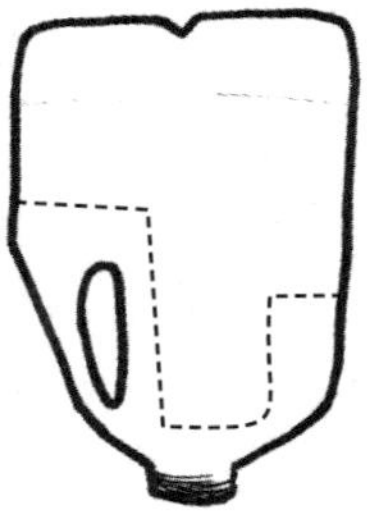

5. Using the sharp knife or craft knife, cut a slit in the top of the helmet wide enough to stick in the stem of the cardboard plume. [This step should be completed by an adult!]

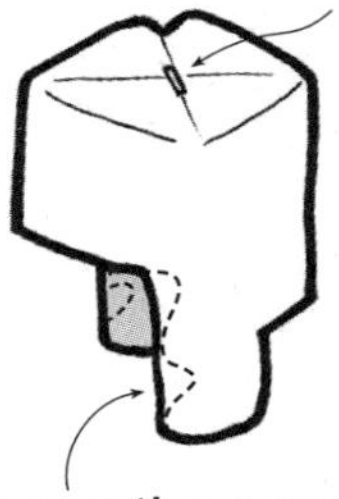

6. Stick the cardboard plume into the helmet so 1 inch of the cardboard stem is on the inside of the helmet. Fold back each of the cardboard pieces inside the helmet so they lie flat against the helmet interior.

Insert the cardboard stems (with plumes attached) into the slit. On the inside of the helmet, fold back each cardboard flap so that they lie flat and hold the plume in place.

7. Paint the helmet silver or cover it with aluminum foil. The helmet will sit high up on the head, but the ear flaps will keep it in place. If you wish to widen the helmet, cut a slit up the back of the helmet to the crown.

Additional History Reading

Roman Soldiers: Discover the World of the Ancient Roman Army, by Tegen Evans, illus. Tom Froese (Nosy Crow, 2024). Lots of fun illustrations and simple explanations of what it was like to be a Roman soldier. (RA)

The Magnificent Book of Treasures: Ancient Rome, by Stella Caldwell, illus. Eugenia Nobati (Welden Owen Children's Books, 2022). Reading this book is like going to a museum. Each page has an enlarged illustration of a real artifact from Ancient Rome and bullet points about what that artifact tells us about the history of Rome. (RA)

The Roman Army, by John Wilkes (Cambridge, 1973). A good illustrated guide to the arms and organization of the Roman military. (RA)

Hannibal, by Robert Green (Franklin Watts, 1997). The life and military exploits of the famous Carthaginian general. Really too much text for young children, but this is the only "junior biography" of Hannibal available. (RA)

Corresponding Literature Suggestions

Hannibal and His 37 Elephants, by Marilyn Hirseh (Holiday House, 1977). The only available picture book related to the Punic Wars. **Out of print, but worth looking for at your local library.** (RA)

The Young Carthaginian, by G.A. Henty (Kessinger, 2004). This historical novel, set during the times of Hannibal and the Punic Wars between Carthage and Rome, is for older children, but could be an extended read-aloud project (especially if you have an older student who could read to the younger ones). An adventure story that describes the campaigns of Hannibal in Iberia, Cisalpine Gaul, and at Rome's doorstep through the experiences of a young Carthaginian noble. (RA)

Corresponding Audiobook Suggestions

The Young Carthaginian, by G.A. Henty, read by Jim Weiss (Well-Trained Mind Press 2004). The struggle between Rome and Carthage was at first a struggle for empire, and then—on the part of Carthage—a struggle for existence. Mr. Henty's classic work tells the story of this struggle and the attempt of Hannibal to conquer Rome. Malchus, the young hero, a cousin of Hannibal, becomes involved in political intrigue and joins Hannibal in Spain and Italy, sharing for a time in his adventures.

CHAPTER THIRTY-THREE
The First Dynasties of China

The First Emperor and the Great Wall

Read & Review

Read pages 277–281 in the text. Afterward, check the student's understanding by asking the questions below.

221–100 BCE

1. **What Warring State conquered the rest?** *Qin (pronounced "Chin")*
2. **How did Qin Zheng keep control of his new empire?** *He made his rivals move into his own city, executed anyone who was planning rebellion, and had books burned.*
3. **Did the Chinese people love their new emperor?** *No; many disliked him for his cruelty.*
4. **Qin Zheng changed his name to Shi Huangdi. What does this name mean?** *The First Emperor*
5. **Why did Shi Huangdi want to build a wall?** *To keep the Mongols out*
6. **What is the full name for the wall he built?** *The Great Wall of China*
7. **How long is the wall?** *Almost 3000 miles, or as long as the United States is wide*
8. **What is the wall made out of?** *Stone in some places, packed dirt in others*
9. **Was it finished during Shi Huangdi's lifetime?** *No, it took hundreds of years to finish.*
10. **Can you still see the wall today?** *Yes*

Narration Exercise

Tell me about the wall this lesson talks about.

The emperor of China wanted to keep the Mongols out. So he built a huge wall. It was made out of stone and out of dirt packed hard. It is called the Great Wall of China.

Activities

Choose from the following activities:

- [ ] Coloring Page: The Great Wall of China
- [ ] Geography: How Long Was the Wall?
- [ ] Make a Model: The Great Wall of China
- [ ] Research Skills: Have the student look up a related topic in a history encyclopedia or another reliable source. Read the entry together and look at the pictures. Topics could include *Qin Zheng, Shi Huangdi, Period of the Warring States, Mongols*, and *The Great Wall of China*.

Coloring Page: The Great Wall of China
(Student Page 108)

The Great Wall of China was built over many centuries to protect China from invaders.

Geography

HOW LONG WAS THE WALL?

At its longest, the Great Wall of China was about 5,500 miles long. During the time period in this lesson, the Great Wall of China was about 2,000 miles long. Use a mapping program or physical map to figure out what city or landmark is 2,000 miles from where you live. Then find a city or landmark that is 5,500 miles from where you live. That's a long wall!

Make a Model

THE GREAT WALL OF CHINA

Some parts of The Great Wall of China were built on steep mountainsides, but had to be sturdy and steady enough for soldiers, horses, and chariots to travel on. Today, you will try to make a section of the wall that is stable enough for a "chariot" to roll along.

Note to Instructor: Try to let the student(s) come up with ideas for materials to help stabilize and hold the wall together; the idea is to use what is available and make it work, just as the ancient architects had to come up with new ideas because there wasn't enough stone for such a long wall.

MATERIALS:

- cardboard building blocks OR a variety of cardboard boxes
- pillows or cushions, enough to make three separate "mountains"
- a lightweight playball to serve as the "chariot"
- common items to help stabilize and hold the wall together; this might include: blankets, jump ropes, chairs, bins, whatever is available and approved by the parent/instructor
- measuring tape

DIRECTIONS:

1. Use pillows or cushions to make three separate "mountains"— they can be touching each other, but it shouldn't be one stack of pillows as a single mountain.
2. Start experimenting with the cardboard bricks/boxes and other materials. If your wall isn't stable enough, it will fall apart when you roll your "chariot" across. If it's too bumpy, the "chariot" won't roll.
3. When you are ready to test it, start at one end of the "wall" and give the ball a push.
4. Did it make it all the way across? How far did it go?
5. You can try different variations and see which one works the best.
6. Optional: Take a picture of your wall. Keep it in your history notebook.

The First Emperor's Grave

Read & Review

Read pages 282–284 in the text. Afterward, check the student's understanding by asking the questions below.

1. **How was the tomb of Shi Huangdi discovered?** *Two farmers uncovered clay pieces while digging a well.*
2. **What was found inside the underground city?** *Thousands of life-sized clay horses and soldiers*
3. **Why did Shi Huangdi build such a huge city?** *Because he hoped to live forever*
4. **Can you tell me two things that might be inside the burial mound?** *Rivers of mercury, treasure, crossbows, stars, and planets*

Narration Exercise

Tell me about the grave that Shi Huangdi built for himself.

Shi Huangdi built an underground city. It had soldiers and horses in it, made out of clay. He is buried in the city, but no one has found his tomb yet.

Map Work: The First Emperor's Grave
(Student Page 109)

Read the instructions out loud to the student. After each step, pause and give time for the student to complete the task. Provide all necessary help.

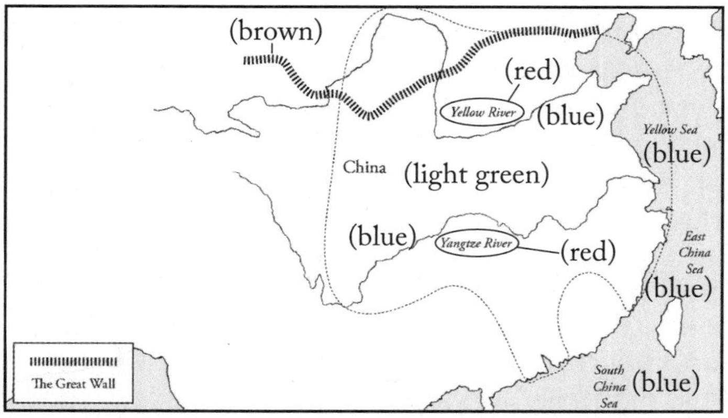

1. **Open to Student Page 109 and tear it out.**
2. **Find the *Great Wall of China*. Color it light brown.**
3. **On your map, find the *Qin Empire*. Remember that Qin Zeng, later known as Shi Huangdi, conquered all the Warring States until he ruled all of China. His empire, the Qin Empire, is shown within the dashed lines on your map. Shade it lightly in green.**
4. **Look back at the Great Wall you already colored. The Chinese built this wall to keep the Mongols out of China. Do you remember how the Great Wall was built?**

5. **Find the names of the *two important rivers* in the Qin Empire and circle their names in red. Then, trace the rivers in blue.**
6. **What *three seas* are next to China? Find them on your map, and shade them lightly in blue.**
7. **When you finish, place the completed map in your history notebook.**

Activities

Choose from the following activities:

- [ ] Art: Draw or Sculpt the Terra Cotta Warriors
- [ ] Geography: Latitude and Longitude
- [ ] Research Skills: Have the student look up a related topic in a history encyclopedia or another reliable source. Read the entry together and look at the pictures. Topics could include *Qin Dynasty*, *Shi Huangdi*, *terracotta warriors*, *terracotta*, and *funerary art*.

Art

DRAW OR SCULPT THE TERRA COTTA WARRIORS

Each one of the thousands of life-size terra cotta warriors in Emperor Shi Huangdi's tomb was unique! Discovered in 1974 in Xi'an, China, these warriors were part of a vast underground army meant to protect China's first emperor in the afterlife. Archaeologists believe that over 700,000 workers labored for decades to create this massive burial complex, which includes life-sized statues of soldiers, chariots, horses and other members of his court, like officials, acrobats, and musicians.

Try drawing (or sculpting) 5 or more small figures for Shi Huangdi's tomb. You can find a salt dough recipe on page 414. Make sure each figure has its own unique size, features, and facial expressions. The terra cotta warriors were once painted in bright colors, with lifelike details that faded over time. Imagine how much effort it took to sculpt, paint, and arrange thousands of figures in formation!

Classroom Adaptation: Combine all of the students' models or pictures to create your own classroom terra cotta army!

Geography

LATITUDE AND LONGITUDE

Latitude and longitude are a special grid system that helps us find exact locations on Earth.

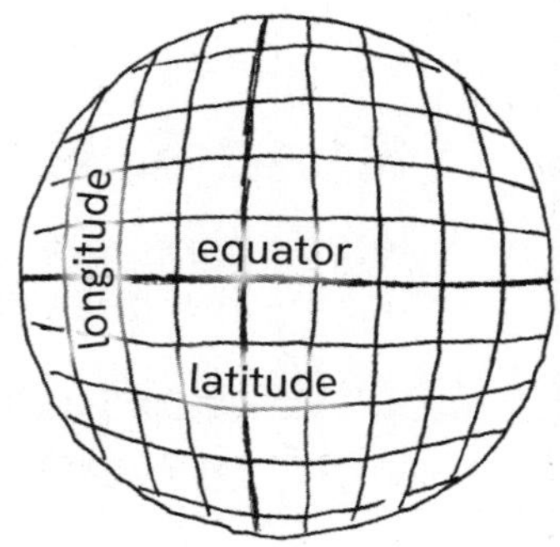

- **Latitude** measures how far north or south a place is from the equator. These lines run horizontally (side to side, like the rungs of a ladder).
- **Longitude** measures how far east or west a place is from the Prime Meridian. These lines run vertically (up and down, like the poles of a ladder).

In this activity, you will find the exact locations of major cities in China and your home country.

MATERIALS:

- A globe or world map with longitude and latitude lines
- A ruler (optional)

DIRECTIONS:

1. Find latitude and longitude on the map:
   - Look at the lines running across the map (latitude) and up and down (longitude).
   - Notice the numbers on the edges of the map. These numbers tell you how far north/south (latitude) or east/west (longitude) a place is.
2. Locate major cities in China:
   - Use your globe or map to find big cities in China like Beijing, Shanghai, and Guangzhou.
   - Write down the latitude and longitude of each city.
3. Find a match!
   - Look across the map at the same latitude line and find a major city in the United States that has a similar latitude.
   - Find the latitude of your city or town and see if there is a city or town in China with a similar latitude.
4. **Bonus Challenge:** Find out if the weather in your city and its Chinese match are similar! Does being at the same latitude mean the two places have the same weather? What other factors impact climate?

Note to Instructor: This activity works best if you live in the United States.

Classroom Adaptation: Have students work in pairs to find U.S. cities with similar latitudes to major Chinese cities and find a Chinese city with a similar latitude to their own city. Once everyone has a chance to try to find the answers on their own, bring the class together to discuss their answers.

The Han Dynasty and the Silk Road

Read & Review

Read pages 284–288 in the text. Afterward, check the student's understanding by asking the questions below.

1. **What did Liu Bang's soldiers do when he told them he wanted to keep the Warring States together in one nation?** *His men followed him and fought by his side.*
2. **What did Emperor Liu Bang do to his conquered enemies?** *He pardoned them.*
3. **What do we call the paths travelers took from Europe into China?** *The Silk Road*
4. **What are some things that merchants from Europe bought in China?** *silk, perfumes, gold, jade, lacquer, rare and beautiful flowers, spices like cloves and ginger, cinnamon, and rugs*

Narration Exercise

How did the Han Dynasty emperors change China?

The first Han emperor made China a stable country. European merchants went to China to buy and sell goods. We call the roads they traveled on "The Silk Road."

Activities

Choose from the following activities:

- ☐ Coloring Page: Liu Bang
- ☐ Game: Silk Road Senses
- ☐ Research Skills: Have the student look up a related topic in a history encyclopedia or another reliable source. Read the entry together and look at the pictures. Topics could include *the Han Dynasty*, *Liu Bang* or *Gao Zu*, *Wendi*, *Wu Di* or *Wudi*, *silk*, *trade caravans*, and *the Silk Road*.

221–100 BCE

Coloring Page: Liu Bang (Student Page 110)

Liu Bang was a peasant who worked his way into becoming a general and eventually the emperor of China!

Game

SILK ROAD SENSES

During the Han Dynasty, traders from India and Persia brought spices like cinnamon, pepper, and cloves as well as many other goods to China along the Silk Road. In this activity you will smell, touch, and taste a few goods that were commonly traded along the Silk Road. Can you guess what they are? If you play with multiple students, keep track of who makes the most correct guesses!

MATERIALS:

- small cups or bowls with spices or essential oils (cinnamon, pepper, cloves, cardamom, ginger, nutmeg, frankincense or myrrh) for smelling
- cloth bags or boxes with one item inside each bag or box. Ideas include:
  - silk fabric
  - a few pieces of dried fruit like apricots, figs, or raisins
  - wool or wool fabric
  - tea bags
  - glass beads or marbles
  - gold or silver jewelry
  - dry chickpeas or lentils
- a few tasty Silk Road treats with a plate covering them so the student cannot see what they are. Ideas include:
  - pomegranate seeds
  - dried figs
  - dried apricots
  - almonds
  - walnuts
  - pistachios
  - grapes
  - cooked barley
  - cooked lentils
  - cooked chickpeas

DIRECTIONS:

1. Start with a Silk Road smell test. Have the student close her eyes and smell a spice. Ask her to describe the scent (spicy, sweet, strong, etc.) and guess what it might be. Explain that traders carried these spices along the Silk Road to sell in distant lands.

2. Next, move on to the touch test. Pass the student mystery bags or small boxes containing different textures. Prompt the student to describe how each one feels, and guess what it might be.

3. Finally, have the student close her eyes. Give her samples of foods traded on the Silk Road to try eating. Encourage her to describe the flavors and textures. Can she tell what she is eating?

4. Finish with a discussion. Ask: why do you think spices were so valuable in ancient times? How would it feel to travel for months carrying these goods? What was your favorite smell, touch, or taste from the Silk Road?

Classroom Adaptation: If you have multiple students, track each student's correct guesses. The student who makes the most correct guesses wins!

Additional History Reading

The Great Wall, by Elizabeth Mann (Mikaya Press, 1997). Covers the building of the Great Wall of China and the thousands of years of conflict that preceded it. (RA)

The Great Wall of China, by Leonard Everett Fisher (Aladdin, 1995). A brief history of the Great Wall of China, with detailed, large pictures. (RA)

The Great Wall Through Time: A 2,700-Year Journey Along the World's Greatest Wall, illus. Du Fei (DK Children, 2022). This book depicts scenes from the Great Wall of China across time. The illustrations are fun to look at and there are interesting annotations in the margins. (RA)

You Wouldn't Want to Work on the Great Wall of China!, by Jacqueline Morley, illus. David Antram (The Salariya Book Company, 2020). A humorous picture book that discusses life for workers on the Great Wall of China.

Corresponding Literature Suggestions

Riding on a Caravan, by Laurie Krebs, illus. Helen Cann (Barefoot Books, 2017). A simple rhyming story that follows a family as they travel along the ancient Silk Road. (RA)

The Ch'I-Lin Purse: A Collection of Ancient Chinese Stories, by Linda Fang (Farrar, Straus and Giroux, 1997). Stories of ancient China, from several different traditions. (RA)

The Dragon Prince: A Chinese Beauty and the Beast Tale, by Laurence Yep (HarperCollins, 1999). A poor farmer's youngest daughter agrees to marry a fierce dragon to save her father's life. (RA)

The Lost Horse: A Chinese Folktale, by Ed Young (Silver Whistle, 1998). This tale, based in the "barbarian" lands of northern China, comes with paper puppets so that young readers can act out the story. (RA 1, IR 2–4)

OPTIONAL LESSON
The Story of Zhang Qian, Hero of the Silk Road

Read & Review

Read pages 289–293 in the text. Afterward, check the student's understanding by asking the questions below.

1. **What were Zhang Qian's two tasks?** *He was supposed to stop the barbarians and create a map for travelers.*
2. **What happened to Zhang Qian when the Xiongnu caught him?** *They made him their prisoner.*
3. **Once Zhang Qian and his followers helped make the roads safe, what are two things that people brought from China to the West?** Acceptable answers include: *silk, jade stones, beads, oils and spices, tea, stoneware and porcelain dishes, vases, plates, bowls, and cups*

Activities

Choose from the following activities:

- ☐ Coloring Page: Zhang Qian (Student Page 111)
- ☐ Creative Writing Prompt: If you were a merchant on the Silk Road, what would you sell? What would you want to buy? (If needed, review the instructions on how to use the creative writing prompts in Appendix One.)

138-126 BCE

CHAPTER THIRTY-FOUR
The Rise of Julius Caesar

Caesar is Kidnapped

Read & Review

Read pages 294–297 in the text. Afterward, check the student's understanding by asking the questions below.

1. **What city was Julius Caesar from?** *Rome*
2. **Who did Julius Caesar's family say they were descended from?** *Romulus*
3. **Why did the people of Rome like Caesar?** *He was a good speaker; he threw parties for people; he was brave; he defeated the pirates.*
4. **The pirates told Caesar that they wanted a lot of money from his relatives before they would let him go. What did Caesar tell them?** *That he was worth more than that*
5. **What did Caesar do when the pirates let him go?** *He gathered an army together, hunted down the pirates, and defeated them.*

Narration Exercise

Tell me three things you learned about Julius Caesar.

Julius Caesar was from an important family. He lived in Rome. He was captured by pirates, but when they set him free he punished them.

100-50 BCE

or

Julius Caesar was captured by pirates. Pirates sailed on the sea and stole things. Julius Caesar told the pirates to let him go. Finally they did.

Map Work: The Rise of Julius Caesar
(Student Page 112)

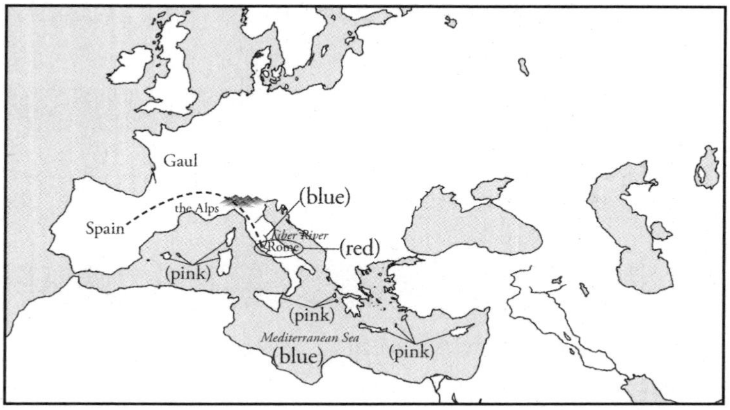

Read the instructions out loud to the student. After each step, pause and give time for the student to complete the task. Provide all necessary help.

1. **Open to Student Page 112 and tear it out.**
2. **On your map, find the *Mediterranean Sea* and color it blue. Then, color the islands in the sea pink. Do you remember what happened to Julius Caesar in the Mediterranean Sea?**
3. **Find the *Tiber River* and trace it in blue.**
4. **Find *Rome* and circle it in red.**
5. **The consuls made Julius Caesar a leader of the colony of Spain. Find *Spain* on your map. Use a dotted line and draw a route that Caesar and his men might have taken from Rome to Spain.**
6. **When you finish, place the completed map in your history notebook.**

Activities

Choose from the following activities:

- ☐ Game: Ransom Caesar Board Game
- ☐ Research Skills: Have the student look up a related topic in a history encyclopedia or another reliable source. Read the entry together and look at the pictures. Topics could include *Julius Caesar, the Roman Republic, pirates in ancient times, consuls, rhetoric,* and *the Roman Senate.*

Game

RANSOM CAESAR BOARD GAME

Julius Caesar was kidnapped by pirates. Help him escape with this game!

MATERIALS:

- 2 copies of the "Ransom Caesar" game board (Student Page 113)
- 2 pennies
- a handful of dry beans

DIRECTIONS:

1. Each player hides Julius Caesar (the penny) on their game board. Don't let your opponent see your game board!
2. Taking turns, pick a row letter and a column number (for example, R3). Call the number out to your opponent.
3. If your opponent's penny is on that number, you've found Caesar! But if it isn't, mark that square on your own board with a bean, so that you'll remember not to call it again.
4. The first person to rescue Julius Caesar from the pirates wins.

The Consuls of Rome

Read & Review

Read pages 297–299 in the text. Afterward, check the student's understanding by asking the questions below.

1. **What did a consul do?** *Governed (or ruled) Rome*
2. **What country did Caesar govern, before he became a consul?** *Spain*
3. **Why did Caesar weep when he read the story of Alexander the Great?** *Because he hadn't accomplished anything great*
4. **Did Caesar become a consul?** *Yes*
5. **Once Caesar became consul, how many consuls were there?** *Three*
6. **The three consuls were called the "triumvirate." What does "tri" mean?** *Three*

Narration Exercise

What are three things you learned in this lesson?

Caesar wanted to be important in Rome. He went to Spain, but he didn't like it there. Finally he got to be a consul in Rome.

or

Consuls ruled Rome. Caesar wanted to be a consul. Finally he got to be one. There were two other consuls, too.

Activities

Choose from the following activities:

- [ ] Craft: Make a Crown of Leaves
- [ ] Game: Triumvirate Tug of War
- [ ] Research Skills: Have the student look up a related topic in a history encyclopedia or another reliable source. Read the entry together and look at the pictures. Topics could include *Julius Caesar, the Roman Kingdom, the Roman Republic, consuls,* and *Roman rulers*.

Craft

MAKE A CROWN OF LEAVES

Roman leaders liked to wear crowns on their heads. This was to show their importance or rank in society. The crowns were made from leaves and formed into the shape of a wreath. Julius Caesar liked to wear wreaths of gold leaves.

MATERIALS:

- ¾″ wide strip of posterboard, long enough to fit around student's head
- leaves (real, fake, or made from construction paper)
- tape or glue
- scissors

DIRECTIONS:

1. Form the posterboard into a circle that will fit on the student's head. Tape or glue into place.
2. Glue leaves onto crown form and let dry.

Game

TRIUMVIRATE TUG OF WAR

This game helps students understand the power dynamics in the First Triumvirate by illustrating how Caesar, Pompey, and Crassus each competed for influence and control.

MATERIALS:

- a large open space
- a long rope or jump rope
- 3 small cones or flags
- 3 or more players

DIRECTIONS:

1. Tie the rope into a loop. Place it on the ground in the shape of a triangle.
2. Position one player at each corner of the triangle - each student represents one of the leaders of the triumvirate: Caesar, Pompey, and Crassus.
3. Place a cone or flag about 6 feet behind each player.

4. When the instructor shouts "go!" each player should pull on their corner of the rope while stepping backwards, trying to reach their flag or cone by dragging the other two players in their direction.
5. The player that gets to their flag or cone first is the winner and should be crowned Caesar, because Caesar was the strongest of the three consuls in the triumvirate.

Classroom Adaptation: Have students take turns playing the game; or for larger groups, connect the ends of three ropes or jump ropes in the center. Then, divide the class into teams, with each team lining up at one of the ropes.

Caesar and the Senate

Read & Review

Read pages 299–302 in the text. Afterward, check the student's understanding by asking the questions below.

1. **What did the Senators think Caesar wanted to be?** *King of Rome*
2. **What was Caesar doing that made the Senators angry?** *He ignored them and did whatever he wanted.*
3. **What did Cincinnatus do when the people wanted him to be king?** *He went back to his fields.*
4. **Do you think Caesar was like Cincinnatus?** *No*

Narration Exercise

Tell me about Caesar and the Senate.

The Senate didn't want Caesar to be king. They thought he should be like Cincinnatus. Cincinnatus didn't want to be king of Rome.

or

The people of Rome liked Caesar. But the Senate didn't. They were men who ran Rome. They thought Caesar wanted to be king.

Activities

Choose from the following activities:

- ☐ Craft: Make a Roman Mosaic
- ☐ Role Play: Vote in the Roman Senate
- ☐ Research Skills: Have the student look up a related topic in a history encyclopedia or another reliable source. Read the entry together and look at the pictures. Topics could include *Julius Caesar, the Roman senate*, and *Cincinnatus*.

100-50 BCE

Craft

MAKE A ROMAN MOSAIC

A Roman mosaic was made by pressing small tiles, or tesserae, of stone into plaster or cement in the shape of a picture. Romans often used mosaics to decorate the floors of their homes, instead of carpets. You can make your mosaic in the pattern of a sun, flower, or cloud, or just make an interesting design.

MATERIALS:

- posterboard or heavy construction paper
- a variety of dried beans (you can also use small squares of colored paper)
- glue
- pencil, for drawing outline

DIRECTIONS:

1. Draw the outline of your picture on the posterboard or construction paper. Erase and redraw until you have it just right.
2. Squeeze out a line of thin glue onto the pencil lines.
3. Lay beans or colored paper squares along the lines of glue.
4. Now fill in the middle of your picture. You can arrange the beans or colored paper squares into patterns to complete your mosaic!

Role Play

VOTE IN THE ROMAN SENATE

In Ancient Rome, the Senate made decisions about what to do for the good of the people. Today you get to help make decisions that will guide our day. Roman senators voted in two ways: For smaller decisions, they raised their hands or used their voices. For important decisions, they moved to different spots in the room to show their vote.

MATERIALS:

- Friends or family members to act as Roman senators
- A leader (could be the instructor or a responsible student)

- A few simple decisions to vote on related to the rest of the day's schedule; for example: "Should we have hot dogs or hamburgers for lunch?," "Should we do math or reading after we finish history?," "Should we go to the park or the library after nap time?" (Note to Instructor: prepare the options ahead of time and do not offer options that you are unwilling or unable to fulfill. For example, do not make going to the library an option if you don't have a car available; do not offer to make hot dogs for lunch if you don't have hot dogs.)

DIRECTIONS:

1. Assemble the senators! The leader of the senate should read out a choice for the senate to vote on.
2. After reading out the choices, the leader should call for a vote. Senators voting "yes" should move to one corner of the room, while those voting "no" should move to the opposite corner.
3. The majority wins!
4. Repeat the process 2-3 times, making decisions about how you will carry out the rest of your day.

Classroom Adaptation: Here are a couple classroom-friendly ideas for things to vote on: "should we do a dance party or story time after lunch?" or "should we color with crayons or pencils?"

Caesar Fights the Celts

Read & Review

Read pages 302–305 in the text. Afterward, check the student's understanding by asking the questions below.

1. **Why were Caesar's soldiers so loyal to him?** *He treated them well, paid them money, and made sure they had plenty of food to eat.*
2. **What country did Caesar want to conquer?** *Britain*
3. **What do we call the people who lived in Britain?** *Celts*
4. **Did Caesar ever completely conquer Britain?** *No*
5. **What did he tell the people of Rome about his wars with the Celts?** *That he was winning*
6. **Do you remember the name of the book Caesar wrote about his wars?** *The Gallic Wars*

Narration Exercise

What did Caesar want, and what did he try to do, in this lesson?

Caesar wanted to conquer Britain. It was hard because the Celts were very good fighters. He told the Romans that he was winning, but he didn't win all his battles.

Activities

Choose from the following activities:

- [ ] Art: Design and Defend Your Own Flag
- [ ] Storytelling: Be Your Own Superhero
- [ ] Research Skills: Have the student look up a related topic in a history encyclopedia or another reliable source. Read the entry together and look at the pictures. Topics could include *Julius Caesar*, *ancient Britain*, *the Celts*, and *the Gallic Wars*.

Art

DESIGN AND DEFEND YOUR OWN FLAG

In this lesson, the flag bearer jumped into the water to fight the Celts, and the other soldiers followed him so they could protect the flag. The flag, also known as a vexillum, was a symbol that reminded the soldiers of their purpose. The flag was not to be destroyed or captured by the enemy. In this activity, you will design and make a flag of your own.

MATERIALS:

- ruler
- 11″x14″ white posterboard or similar
- a piece of sturdy cardboard approximately 1″x12″ (just a bit wider than your flag)
- a second piece of sturdy cardboard (approximately 3″x24″)
- pencil
- permanent markers
- packing tape
- scissors
- additional craft supplies for further decoration (optional)

DIRECTIONS:

1. Roman flags were square, so cut your poster to 11″x11.″
2. They often had fringe across the bottom. To make fringe, mark a line all the way across about 1″ up from the bottom of the back of the posterboard, then make cuts up to the line about ¼″ apart. If you do this first, you won't cut into any of the decorated parts of your flag.
3. Think about what colors, shapes, numbers, and symbols you want to use.
4. If you want your flag divided into sections, do that now, using light pencil lines (a diagonal line to divide it into 2 triangles, one vertical and one horizontal line to divide it into 4 squares, or just mark off any shapes you want).
5. Draw any symbols, shapes, and numbers you want on your flag, using light pencil lines.
6. Use your markers to go over your pencil lines, and to color in as you wish.
7. Add any additional decorations until you are satisfied with your flag.
8. Tape the 1 inch by 12 inch piece of cardboard horizontally across the back of the top of your flag, so that it is showing on each end.

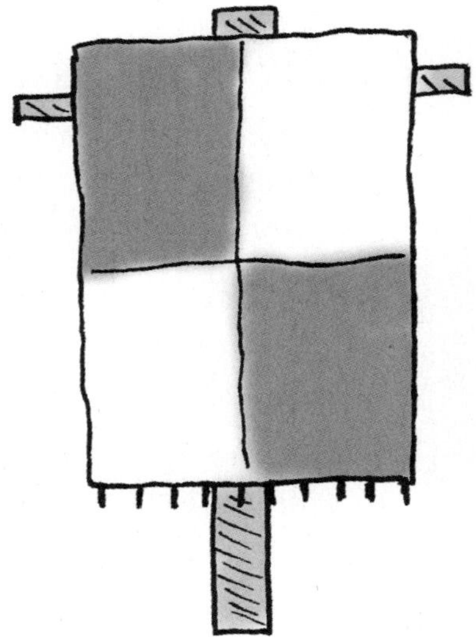

9. Tape the longer piece of cardboard vertically to the middle of the back of the flag, so that a bit is showing on the top and there is enough at the bottom to hold. Use several strips of packing tape going across the cardboard and onto the poster board so that it is secure.

10. Be a proud standard-bearer and march around the house with your flag! If you have siblings or friends who also made this project, you can go outside and play Capture the Flag.

Classroom Adaptation: Have students work in groups to create a flag with symbols that represent their classroom and values. Once the flags are made, use them to play Capture the Flag!

Storytelling

BE YOUR OWN SUPERHERO

Caesar was known for exaggerating or even lying in his accounts of the Gallic Wars to make himself look more heroic and successful. He wanted to make sure the people of Rome thought he was the best. Exaggerating means making something sound much bigger, better, or more exciting than it really was! For example, instead of saying "I ran fast" you could say, "I ran so fast that I almost broke the sound barrier!" Can you tell me a story of something you did, like play at the park, help your dad cook dinner, or finish a school assignment, but exaggerate how great you are so that you sound like a superhero?

If needed, provide a sentence starter to help the student get started:

- "In just one second, I managed to..."
- "The world had never seen anyone cook like I did when I helped my dad..."
- "Even superheroes would be amazed at how fast I..."
- "The ground shook as I..."
- "Crowds cheered when I..."

Younger students can narrate their answer to an adult. Older students can write their answers down on their own. If you like, draw a picture to illustrate their story. Give the picture a title that has your name and then "The Great" after it, so if your name is Sarah, put "Sarah the Great."

Additional History Reading

A Pirate's Life for Me, by Julie Thompson and Brownie Macintosh (Charlesbridge Publishing, 1996). A fun, fact-filled book about all kinds of pirates. **Out of print, but worth looking for at your local library.** (RA)

Roman Soldiers: Discover the World of the Ancient Roman Army, by Tegen Evans, illus. Tom Froese (Nosy Crow, 2024). Lots of fun illustrations and simple explanations of what it was like to be a Roman soldier. Also recommended for chapter thirty-two. (RA)

The Life and Times of Julius Caesar (Biography from Ancient Civilizations series), by Jim Whiting (Mitchell Lane Publishers, 2005). A fairly advanced junior biography of Julius Caesar, readable and well illustrated. Sections are suitable as read-alouds. (RA 1–3, IR 4–7)

Corresponding Literature Suggestions

Famous Men of Rome: Annotated, by John Haaren and A.B. Poland (Cedar Lake Classics, 2020). Stories of famous Roman figures, including Cincinnatus and Caesar. (RA)

Rome Antics, by David Macaulay (Abbeville Press, 2025). A messenger pigeon takes readers on a tour of Rome, including both ancient sites and modern areas of the city. (RA)

The Wadjet Eye, by Jill Rubalcaba (Clarion, 2000). The story of Damon, a medical student living in Egypt, who journeys to Spain to locate his father, who is serving in the Roman army led by Julius Caesar. Written for slightly older children; a good read-aloud project over several weeks, particularly if an older student can read to the younger child. **Out of print, but worth looking for at your local library.** (RA)

CHAPTER THIRTY-FIVE
Caesar, Ruler of Rome

Caesar Crosses the Rubicon

Read & Review

Read pages 306–308 in the text. Afterward, check the student's understanding by asking the questions below.

1. **Which senator married Caesar's daughter and then became jealous of Caesar?** *Pompey*
2. **When Caesar heard that he was going to be arrested, what did he do?** *He marched his army towards Rome.*
3. **What river did Caesar cross over with his army?** *The Rubicon*
4. **Did Pompey and the Senators fight against Caesar?** *No, their soldiers ran away.*
5. **Was Caesar the king yet?** *No, but he was very powerful.*
6. **What does "crossing the Rubicon" still mean?** *Doing something you can't undo*

Narration Exercise

Tell me what happened with Caesar and Pompey.

The Senators made Pompey jealous of Caesar. Pompey tried to arrest Caesar. But Caesar marched into Rome with his army, and Pompey and the Senators ran away.

49 BCE-14 CE

Map Work: Caesar Crosses the Rubicon
(Student Page 114)

Read the instructions out loud to the student. After each step, pause and give time for the student to complete the task. Provide all necessary help.

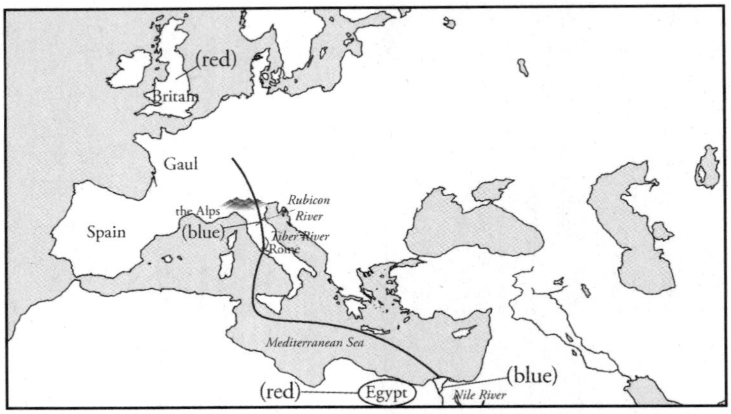

1. **Open to Student Page 114 and tear it out.**
2. **On your map, find *Gaul* and color it with a red crayon.**
3. **Trace the *Rubicon River* in blue.**
4. **Find *Egypt* and circle it in red. Then, trace the *Nile River* in blue.**
5. **Draw a line from Gaul down to Rome, to show the route Caesar might have taken when he returned to Rome with his army. Make sure that your line crosses the *Rubicon River*!**
6. **Now draw another line from Rome down to the *Nile Delta*. This route might be the one Caesar would have taken when he went down to Egypt to Cleopatra.**
7. **When you finish, place the completed map in your history notebook.**

Activities

Choose from the following activities:

- ☐ Coloring Page: Julius Caesar
- ☐ Research Skills: Have the student look up a related topic in a history encyclopedia or another reliable source. Read the entry together and look at the pictures. Topics could include *Julius Caesar*, *Pompey*, *the Rubicon*, and *Gaul*.

Coloring Page: Julius Caesar (Student Page 115)

Caesar and Cleopatra

Read & Review

Read pages 309–312 in the text. Afterward, check the student's understanding by asking the questions below.

1. **What country did Pompey run to?** *Egypt*
2. **What queen ruled Egypt?** *Cleopatra*
3. **How did Cleopatra's brother try to make friends with Caesar?** *He killed Pompey.*
4. **Why did Cleopatra want Caesar to be on her side?** *She wanted to get rid of her brother and rule Egypt all alone.*
5. **Did Caesar help her rule Egypt alone?** *Yes, he did.*
6. **What does "Veni, Vidi, Vici" mean?** *I came, I saw, I conquered.*
7. **What language is this in?** *Latin*

Narration Exercise

What important things happened in this lesson?

Pompey went to Egypt. Caesar went after him. Cleopatra was the queen of Egypt. She got Caesar to stay and help her in Egypt.

or

Caesar was mad at the Egyptians when he heard that they killed Pompey, but then he fell in love with Cleopatra. He wasn't mad anymore. He even fought her brother so she could rule Egypt by herself.

Activities

Choose from the following activities:

- ☐ Craft: Mint Your Own Coins Out of Clay
- ☐ Research Skills: Have the student look up a related topic in a history encyclopedia or another reliable source. Read the entry together and look at the pictures. Topics could include *the Roman Empire*, *Cleopatra*, and *Ptolemy XIII*.

Note to Instructor: there are a variety of activities about life in ancient Rome in the final lesson for this chapter, "Augustus Caesar." These activities are relevant to all sections in this chapter and could be completed all at once or spread out between the lessons.

Craft

MINT YOUR OWN COINS OUT OF CLAY

Julius Caesar was the first politician to place his likeness on the coins of Rome. Prior to that time, coins were decorated with pictures of animals, ships, buildings, and pictures of the gods. Many coins were minted to commemorate a special event, such as Caesar winning the Gallic Wars. Today you will make coins that will commemorate something special that has happened in your life, such as learning to read or ride a bike.

MATERIALS:

- air-dry clay or salt dough (recipe on page 414)
- rolling pin, sculpting tool, sharpened pencil or toothpick
- round plastic lids (hair spray, starch) in assorted sizes (round biscuit and cookie cutters would also work).
- copper, silver, and gold metallic paint
- paint brush

DIRECTIONS:

1. Roll out the air-dry clay into a rectangle that is about ¼"-½" thick. Use the varying sizes of plastic tops or cookie cutters to cut out your coins. It might be easier for younger students to work with larger, rather than smaller, circles.
2. Use the sculpting tool, pencil, or toothpick to draw a picture on your clay circle. If it is to commemorate the day you learned to ride a two-wheel bike, don't forget to add the year you did it in.
3. Place the coins aside and allow them to dry completely (follow the instructions on your clay).
4. When the coins have dried, take your different colored paints and paint each coin. This will need to be done in a two-step process: paint one side, let dry, paint the other side.

The Death of Caesar

Read & Review

Read pages 312–314 in the text. Afterward, check the student's understanding by asking the questions below.

1. **When Caesar became dictator, what could he do?** *Anything he wanted*
2. **Can you name one thing that Caesar did when he became dictator?** *He took power away from the Senate; he could declare war, pass laws, and raise taxes; he made money with his picture on it; he paid for gladiator fighting and chariot racing.*
3. **What did Caesar want to be called?** *King Caesar*
4. **Who did he want to be king after him?** *His nephew Octavian*
5. **Why did the Senate decide to kill Caesar?** *They were afraid of his power; they didn't want him to pass his power on to another king.*
6. **Can you remember one strange thing that happened to Caesar on the fifteenth of March?** *His horses were crying; a fortune-teller told him to be careful; his wife had a strange dream.*
7. **What did Caesar say when he died?** *Et tu, Brute?*
8. **What does this mean?** *You, too, Brutus?*

Narration Exercise

What did Julius Caesar do and what happened to him afterwards?

Caesar became a dictator. He could do whatever he wanted. But he wanted to be called "king." So the Senators decided to kill Caesar. They stabbed him to death.

Map Work: The Death of Caesar (Student Page 116)

Read the instructions out loud to the student. After each step, pause and give time for the student to complete the task. Provide all necessary help.

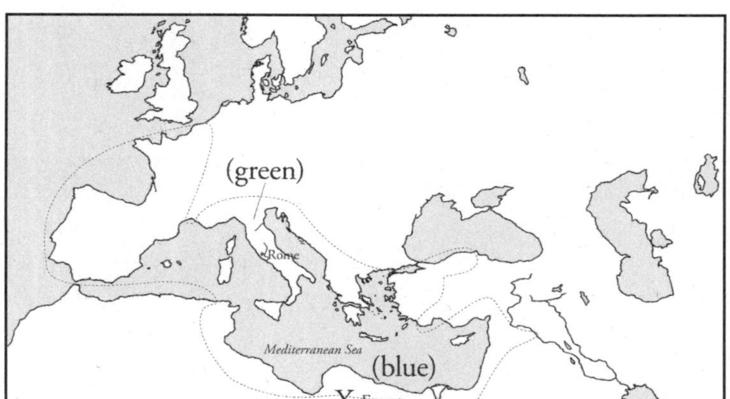

1. **Open to Student Page 116 and tear it out.**
2. **On your map, color in green the area that made up the Roman Empire when Julius Caesar was killed. The dashed lines on your map show you the borders of the Empire.**
3. **What is the name of the sea that the Roman Empire surrounded? Find this sea on your map, and shade it lightly in blue.**
4. **Find Cleopatra's home of *Egypt* on your map, and mark it with an X.**
5. **When you finish, place the completed map in your history notebook.**

Activities

Choose from the following activities:

- ☐ Memory Work: Roman Numerals
- ☐ Research Skills: Have the student look up a related topic in a history encyclopedia or another reliable source. Read the entry together and look at the pictures. Topics could include *Julius Caesar, the Roman Senate, Brutus, the Ides of March, and the Roman Empire.*

Note to Instructor: there are a variety of activities about life in ancient Rome in the final lesson for this chapter, Augustus Caesar. These activities are relevant to all sections in this chapter and could be completed all at once or spread out between the lessons.

Memory Work

ROMAN NUMERALS

The Romans didn't use the numbers we use today. Instead, they had their own special number system made from letters—like I, V, and X. You can still spot Roman numerals today! They are used in all kinds of places; for example: on clocks, on buildings, or for numbering the chapters in a book.

MATERIALS:

- 15 blank index cards
- black marker

DIRECTIONS:

1. On side 1, write the Arabic numbers 1, 2, 3, 4, 5, 6, 7, 8, 9, 10, 50, 100, 500, and 1000.
2. On side 2, write each corresponding Roman numeral: I, II, III, IV, V, VI, VII, VIII, IX, X, L, C, D, and M respectively.
3. After you create the cards, turn them over with the Roman numeral face up and see if you can guess the correct value for each card.
4. When you have learned the Roman numerals well, use them to write out the ages of all your family members. Be sure to include grandma and grandpa, since their ages will probably use the L (50) numeral.

49 BCE-14 CE

Augustus Caesar

Read & Review

Read pages 314–317 in the text. Afterward, check the student's understanding by asking the questions below.

1. **Who was Octavian's uncle?** *Julius Caesar*
2. **How did Octavian make himself popular with the people of Rome?** *He threw a big party with Caesar's money; he gave presents and money to the poor families.*
3. **Did Octavian ask to be king?** *No, he said that he would quit.*
4. **What title did the Senate give Octavian?** *First Citizen, or "princeps"*
5. **What was Octavian's new name?** *Augustus Caesar*
6. **Which month is named after Augustus Caesar?** *August*
7. **Which month is named after Julius Caesar?** *July*

Narration Exercise

What did you learn about Octavian?

Octavian was Caesar's nephew. The people of Rome liked him because he was generous. He said that he would not be king, but the Senate wanted him to rule. They gave him a title that means 'prince.'

Activities

Choose from the following activities:

- [ ] Coloring Page: Augustus Caesar
- [ ] Role Play: Make a Roman Toga
- [ ] Role Play: Run a Roman Hair Salon
- [ ] Cooking & Role Play: Run a Thermopolium (Roman Take-Out Restaurant)
- [ ] Research Skills: Have the student look up a related topic in a history encyclopedia or another reliable source. Read the entry together and look at the pictures. Topics could include *Octavian, Augustus Caesar, the months of the calendar*, and *the Roman Empire.*
- [ ] Celebration: Complete all of the activities in this lesson for a full-day celebration of Roman history and culture! If possible, have friends or siblings help you build your own Roman town! Have one group run a Roman clothing store and help kids get into togas; have one group run the hair salon; and have one group run the Thermopolium. Students can take turns visiting each other's shop and paying for services with "Roman Coins" (either use coins made in the "Caesar and Cleopatra" lesson, or make pretend coins out of aluminum foil, or use pennies).

Coloring Page: Augustus Caesar (Student Page 117)

This picture of Augustus Caesar is based on a marble statue located in the Vatican Museum in Rome.

Role Play

MAKE A ROMAN TOGA

A toga was a very complicated outfit to wear and was usually only worn on very special or important occasions. Traditionally the toga was 2 ½ times as long as the person was tall and about 2 times as wide as the person. Slaves were forbidden from ever wearing a toga, because the toga was considered to be a sign of power and prestige. Only the most important people of the Roman Empire were allowed to use the color purple.

MATERIALS:

- one old white sheet
- 3 yards of wide purple ribbon
- double-sided tape
- length of cord
- an oversized adult t-shirt

DIRECTIONS:

1. Fold the sheet in half lengthwise. Sew, or use the double-sided tape to attach the purple ribbon along one side of the long edge. Trim away any excess ribbon.
2. Put on the large t-shirt and use a piece of cord to tie a belt around your waist.
3. Have a partner stand behind you, holding the toga by the long straight edge. Have her drape a quarter of the toga over your left shoulder and arm. Push the toga up your arm, so that your hand is free.
4. Bring the rest of the toga around your body, making sure that you go under your right arm. Gather a couple of folds in the toga and tuck them into the waistband securely.
5. Last of all, fold the remaining loose fabric over your left arm. You will need to keep your left arm close to your body to hold it in position. Don't forget to wear the cuff bracelet from chapter thirty-two, the crown of leaves from chapter thirty-four, and a pair of sandals for the full effect!

Storytelling

RUN A ROMAN HAIR SALON

In Ancient Rome, elaborate hairstyles were a symbol of wealth and status. In this activity, you will create simple versions of Roman hairstyles using natural hair or a wig. Both Roman men and women were known to wear wigs and toupees made of blonde, red, or black hair.

MATERIALS:

- a hairbrush
- hairpins, bobby pins, ribbons, etc.
- curling iron (optional)
- a blonde, black, or red wig or hair piece OR a doll with long hair (optional)

DIRECTIONS:

Hairstyle ideas for long hair:

1. Seni Crines: Part hair in the center. Create a small roll or curl of hair along the forehead line by rolling a small strand of hair from the top of your head away from the face, adding hair as you roll until you reach the nape of your neck. Hold the hair so that the curl does not unfurl and repeat on the opposite side of the part. Place both strands of hair and all of your hair into a low ponytail and secure with a hair band. Divide the ponytail into 6 sections and braid each section. Pin each braid into a circle shape on the top of your head, stacking each braid on top of the next (pin the stacked braids together with u-shape hairpins). Add ribbons and bows as you please.
2. Tutulus: Separate hair into 3 sections: a small amount on each side of the front of the face and the largest amount on the back of the head. Take the hair on the back of the head and separate out a small amount of hair at the nape of the neck from the main section of hair. Lift the main section of back hair and comb upwards. Twist the main section of back hair into a bun on the top of the head. Fix the bun with bobby pins, a bodkin needle, or hair tie. Braid the strand of hair left at the nape of the neck. Lift that braid up and over the bun, wrap any extra hair around the bun, and pin into place. Divide the hair on the front part of the head into 3 sections on either side. Twist each section and wrap it around the bun, alternating sides as you go (top left, top right, middle left, middle right, bottom left, bottom right).
3. Simple Bun: Gather hair into a low bun at the nape of the neck and secure it with a hair tie and bobby pins. Pull out 2 strands of hair, one on each side of the face, and curl them into a ringlet. Make sure to get an adult to help with the curling iron.

Hairstyle idea for short hair:

1. Classic Caesar Cut: This hairstyle was named after Julius Caesar. Boys often grew their hair down to their shoulders during Roman times. However, Julius Caesar cropped his hair to be about 1-2 inches long all over his head. His bangs were straight in the front. Because this style requires actually cutting your hair, you may want to use a wig. This hairstyle is still popular today! You can ask for a "caesar cut" at your local barber or hair salon.

Cooking & Role Play

RUN A THERMOPOLIUM (ROMAN TAKE-OUT RESTAURANT)

In Ancient Rome, you could grab a quick bite to eat at the local thermopolium, similar to our fast food restaurants today. In this activity, you can set-up your own thermopolium to serve your friends or family members.

MATERIALS:

- posterboard and markers
- canned lentil soup
- bread
- olives
- fruit
- grape juice
- bowls, spoons, glasses, serving utensils
- large pot for soup (or crock-pot)

DIRECTIONS:

1. Paintings outside the thermopolium advertised what was on the menu. Make posters with pictures of the items you will be selling (bread, soup, fruit, grape juice, olives, etc.)
2. Heat the soup in a pan or crock-pot (adult help needed!).
3. Cut up fruit and bread and arrange it on a platter or plate (adult help needed!).
4. Open for business (maybe a family dinner). Be sure to bring lots of coins to pay for the hard work!
5. If you want to, serve the Roman dish below:

Cecina

INGREDIENTS:

- olive oil
- salt
- basil leaves (dried or fresh)
- 2 cans chickpeas

DIRECTIONS:

1. Heat oven to 375 degrees.
2. Drain beans, but save the liquid. Mash beans in a bowl.
3. Add 2 tablespoons of olive oil and enough liquid as needed to make a smooth paste.
4. Oil a cookie sheet or pizza pan with olive oil. Spread batter on the pan, shaping into a circle.
5. Drizzle on a tablespoon of olive oil. Sprinkle with basil. Bake for 45 minutes. Cut into slices.

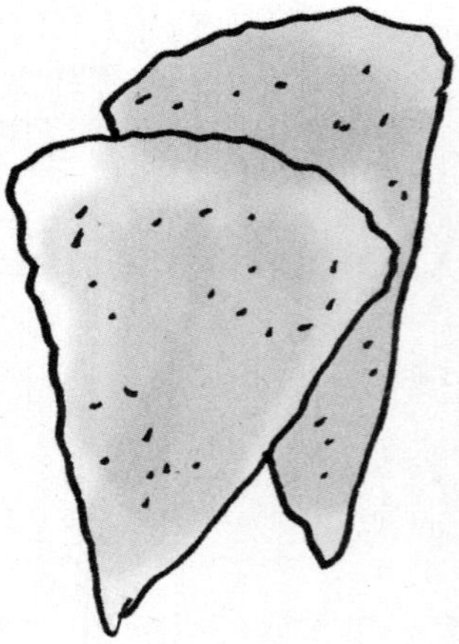

Additional History Reading

Roman Numerals I to MM, by Arthur Geisert (Sagebrush, 2001). Introduces Roman numerals; by counting pigs in the illustrations, the reader can practice Roman math! (RA)

Who Was Julius Caesar? by Nico Medina (Grosset & Dunlap, 2014). A simple chapter book about the life and legacy of Julius Caesar (there are short asides that discuss aspects of life in Ancient Rome). (IR 3-6)

Cleopatra, by Diane Stanley (HarperTrophy, 1997). Slightly more detailed and serious account of Cleopatra's life. (RA)

The Story of Clocks and Calendars: Marking a Millenium, by Betsy Maestro (HarperTrophy, 2004). Discusses the evolution of the calendar. (RA)

The Ancient Romans, by Allison Lassieur (Franklin Watts, 2004). A colorful guide to the Roman empire after Augustus, with a focus on daily life. **Out of print, but worth looking for at your local library.** (RA 1–3, IR 4–6)

Corresponding Literature Suggestions)

Cleopatra Tells All!, by Chris Naunton, illus. Guilherme Karsten (Thames & Hudson, 2022). A humorous and upbeat biography of Cleopatra written as if Cleopatra is telling her own story and setting the record straight. (RA 1-3, IR 3-5)

Sun-day, Moon-day: How the Week Was Made, by Cherry Gilchrist (Barefoot Books, 1998). Presents the stories behind the names of the days of the week. **Out of print, but worth looking for at your local library.** (RA)

Leon Garfield's Shakespeare Stories by Leon Garfield (NYR Children's Collection, 2015). A read-aloud, story version of twenty-one of Shakespeare's plays, including Julius Caesar. (RA)

Corresponding Audiobook Suggestions

Julius Caesar and the Story of Rome, adapted by Jim Weiss (Well-Trained Mind Press, 2015) This is an adapted and abridged version of Shakespear's famous play, *Julius Caesar*, brought to life by the passionate performance of storyteller Jim Weiss.

CHAPTER THIRTY-SIX
Israel Under Roman Rule

Herod, "The Great"

Read & Review

Read pages 318–321 in the text. Afterward, check the student's understanding by asking the questions below.

1. **Why did the Romans trust Herod to rule the Jews?** *His father had been a trusted advisor to Julius Caesar.*
2. **What does it mean that Herod was a "client king"?** *He acted like a king in Israel, but he also had to obey the emperor of Rome.*
3. **What are two important structures that Herod built?** *The temple, a new harbor, and fortresses*
4. **Did the Jews like Herod, their king?** *No.*

Narration Exercise

Tell me three things about King Herod.

King Herod was not a real king. He had to do whatever the Romans told him to do. He became famous for building many great buildings.

37–4 BCE

Activities

Choose from the following activities:

- [ ] Coloring Page: Herod's Temple
- [ ] Role Play: Herod's Building Projects
- [ ] Research Skills: Have the student look up a related topic in a history encyclopedia or another reliable source. Read the entry together and look at the pictures. Topics could include *Herod, Judea, Herod's Temple, Solomon's Temple, the Second Temple*, and *Roman Palestine*.

Coloring Page: Herod's Temple (Student Page 118)

Herod wanted to prove his greatness by building massive structures—including his grand reconstruction of the Temple.

Note to Instructor: If you plan to complete the "Destruction of the Temple" craft in the final section of this chapter, make a copy of this coloring page OR save your student's completed coloring page.

Role Play

HEROD'S BUILDING PROJECTS

Herod was famous for his many building projects, but he didn't actually do any of the work. He gave orders while others did all the building. In this activity you will practice giving good instructions.

MATERIALS:

- a set of blocks, toy building bricks, or another building toy
- a flat surface for working
- pencil and paper
- a blindfold (optional)
- a timer (optional)

DIRECTIONS:

1. Start by planning a simple building project on a piece of paper. It could be a harbor, a temple, a fortress, a palace, or any other great building that you choose. Don't make it too complicated. If you have multiple students, everyone should plan their own building without showing their plan to anyone else. No peeking! This is Herod's great vision, but will it turn out as planned?
2. Choose roles and put a blindfold on whoever is going to be "Herod" first (if you don't have a blindfold, have "Herod" sit facing away from the blocks or toy building bricks).
3. "Herod" must give careful, specific instructions on how to build the project that he designed. He cannot look at the project and he cannot touch any of the blocks; he can only direct everyone else in what to do. The builders must follow Herod's instructions exactly! For an optional challenge, set a time limit!
4. When the building is finished (or the timer runs out), have Herod take off his blindfold or turn around. Compare the final building to the plan on the piece of paper. How did you do?
5. Take turns being "Herod." When you finish, follow-up with the discussion questions:
    a. How did it feel to be Herod versus a builder?
    b. What does this tell us about Herod's leadership?
    c. Even though Herod built great things, did it make him a beloved leader?

Classroom Adaptation: Have each student sit at his or her desk and draw a building. Then pair students up. Student A is "Herod" and should describe her drawing carefully to Student B, the "builder," without showing the builder the picture. The "builder" must draw his own picture of the building, trying to make it as similar as possible to the original picture (by following "Herod's verbal instructions). Once the builder finishes his drawing, compare it to the original then switch roles and go again. Who did the best job following instructions? If you like, name the student with the best drawing "Herod the Great," then create new titles for other builders like "Herod the Confused" (for the most chaotic structure), "Herod the Tyrant" (for the bossiest "Herod"), or "Most Loyal builder" (for the builder that followed the instructions the best).

A Prophet Named Jesus

Read & Review

Read pages 321–326 in the text. Afterward, check the student's understanding by asking the questions below.

1. **What do we call the time of peace and safety in the Roman empire?** *The Pax Romana*
2. **According to the story from the Gospel of Luke, where was Jesus born?** *In Bethlehem*
3. **What holiday celebrates the birth of Jesus?** *Christmas*
4. **What is Jesus' most famous teaching called?** *The Sermon on the Mount*
5. **What does the Gospel of Luke say happened after Jesus was buried?** *He rose from the dead.*
6. **What are followers of Jesus called?** *Christians*

Narration Exercise

Tell me what Jesus did OR Tell me what happened to Jesus.

Jesus taught people and many followed him. The Romans were afraid that people wouldn't listen to the emperor. They put Jesus to death, but Christians believe he rose from the dead.

or

Jesus was put to death because the Romans and some of the religious leaders didn't want him teaching the people any more. The Gospel says that he rose from the dead. People who believe in Jesus are called Christians.

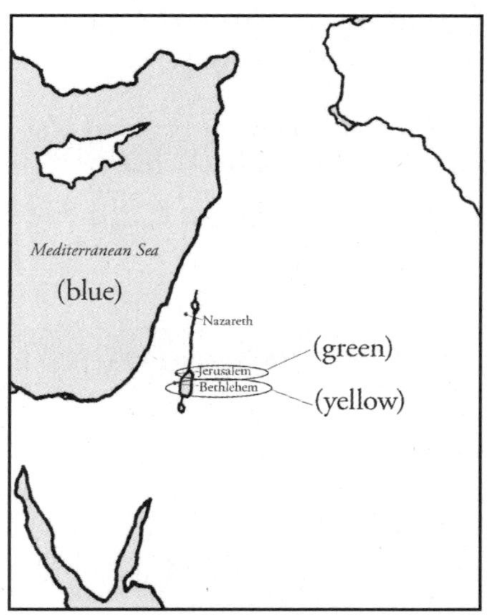

Map Work: A Prophet Named Jesus (Student Page 119)

Read the instructions out loud to the student. After each step, pause and give time for the student to complete the task. Provide all necessary help.

1. **Open to Student Page 119 and tear it out.**

3 BCE–35 CE

2. **Find the *Mediterranean Sea* on your map. Color it in blue.**
3. **Judea was near the coast of the Mediterranean Sea. Jesus was born in Bethlehem, which is in Judea. Circle *Bethlehem* in yellow.**
4. **Jesus was crucified in Jerusalem. Find *Jerusalem* on your map, and circle it in green.**
5. **When you finish, place the completed map in your history notebook.**

Activities

Choose from the following activities:

- [ ] Math: Census Activity
- [ ] Art: Nativity Picture Study
- [ ] Storytelling: The Life of Jesus
- [ ] Research Skills: Have the student look up a related topic in a history encyclopedia or another reliable source. Read the entry together and look at the pictures. Topics could include *Christianity*, *Jesus*, *the Gospels*, *the Pax Romana*, and *Christians*.

Math

THE CENSUS

People had to travel to their ancestral towns for the census ordered by Caesar Augustus. This is the journey that Mary and Joseph took to Bethlehem for the birth of Jesus. Imagine you were living during this time and had to travel to an ancestor's birthplace for the census.

MATERIALS:

- map or online distance tool (like a GPS)
- calculator (optional)
- paper and pencil

DIRECTIONS:

1. Pick one of your relatives' (grandmother, grandfather, or any other relative) hometown.
2. Use a map or an online tool to find out how far the town is from where you live. Write down the distance in miles. You can ask a parent to help you with this step.

3. Plan your journey: Now imagine you have to walk to your destination. In ancient Rome, people traveled mostly by foot or on animals, and they could walk about 15 miles per day.
4. Divide the total number of miles by 15 (the number of miles you could walk in a day). How many days would it take you to get there? For younger students who have not yet learned to divide, have an adult help with this and/or use a calculator.
5. Finish with a discussion: "How would traveling without modern technology or transportation be different from how we travel today?" and "What would you need to bring with you on a long journey like this?"

Art

NATIVITY BY JEAN-BAPTISTE MARIE PIERRE PICTURE STUDY

PARENTS, PLEASE PREVIEW. In this activity, you will look closely at a painting that depicts the story of Jesus' birth. This is Nativity, *painted by a French artist called Jean-Baptiste Maire Pierre in 1789.*

MATERIALS:

- Image of *Nativity* by Jean-Baptiste Marie Pierre (Find it by searching for "Nativity painting by Jean-Baptiste Marie Pierre." It is available on multiple art websites.)

DIRECTIONS:

1. Give the student a few minutes to study the picture silently on their own, then ask the following questions:
   a. **In the lesson, we learned that Jesus was born in a cave where animals were kept. What animals can you see in the painting?** *A lamb, a cow*
   b. **We also learned that angels appeared in the sky. Can you find the angels?** Give the student time to point out the angels.
   c. **What time do you think it is in the painting? How can you tell?** *It is night time, because you can see the moon in a dark sky.*
   d. **Where is the brightest part of the painting? Why do you think the artist painted it that way?** *It is brightest all around baby Jesus; the artist is showing that he is the most important part of the painting, showing that he is holy/divine.*
   e. **Looking at the painting and remembering the lesson, who do you think the different people in the painting are?** *Mary (Jesus is resting his head on her lap), Joseph (behind Mary), shepherds on the other side (because the lesson told us shepherds went to see him).*

Role Play

A NIGHT AT THE STABLE

Imagine you are with Mary, Joseph, and baby Jesus on the night of Jesus' birth. You've been traveling a long way, and when you arrive in Bethlehem, there's no room at the inn. You have to spend the night in a humble stable. Use blankets, pillows, furniture, and stuffed animals to create your own "stable" in the living room. Drape blankets over chairs, couches, or tables to make a cozy shelter. Turn off the bright lights and use a flashlight or battery-powered candle to create a quiet, peaceful atmosphere. You might even play soft music or read the nativity story aloud. If your family is up for it, bring sleeping bags or blankets and spend the night in your "stable."

The Destruction of the Temple

Read & Review

Read pages 326–328 in the text. Afterward, check the student's understanding by asking the questions below.

1. **What did Caligula want to put inside the Jewish temple?** *A statue of himself.*
2. **What city did the Romans destroy?** *Jerusalem*
3. **What did the Romans do to the Temple?** *They burned it.*
4. **What was the name of the fortress the Jewish fighters fled to?** *Masada*
5. **What happened to the Jewish people then?** *They were scattered through all the countries of the world.*

Narration Exercise

Tell me at least two things that happened in today's lesson.

The Romans made the Jews pay taxes and obey them, so the Jews attacked them. Then the Romans burned Jerusalem and knocked the Temple down. The Jews had to leave their country and didn't come back for a long time.

Activities

Choose from the following activities:

- [ ] Craft: The Destruction of the Temple
- [ ] Craft: Make Your Own Dreidel
- [ ] Cooking: Make Hanukkah Latkes
- [ ] Research Skills: Have the student look up a related topic in a history encyclopedia or another reliable source. Read the entry together and look at the pictures. Topics could include *Caligula*, *Herod the Great*, *Masada*, and *Judea*.

66-73 CE

Craft

THE DESTRUCTION OF THE TEMPLE

(Student Page 118)

In the lesson, we learned that the temple contained many beautiful objects made of silver and gold. Some old stories say that when the temple burned down, the gold and silver melted and ran into the cracks between the huge stones of the temple's foundation.

MATERIALS:

- Student Page 118
- blank piece of paper
- scissors
- glue stick
- gold and silver crayons

DIRECTIONS:

1. *Color in the temple on Student Page 118.*
2. *Now cut the temple into several large pieces.*
3. *Glue the pieces onto a blank piece of paper, leaving a bit of space between each piece.*
4. *Use your gold and silver crayons to color in the spaces, representing the melted gold and silver that ran into the cracks of the temple!*

Craft

MAKE YOUR OWN DREIDEL

Hanukkah means "dedication." It is an eight-day holiday that celebrates the victory of Judas Maccabee and his followers over the Syrian King Antiochus (see the biography of Judas Maccabee in the main text pages 329-333).

A traditional game played during this holiday is called Dreidel. The Hebrew letters written on each side of the square top stand for the words "A great miracle happened there."

There is an old legend as to why this game is played during Hanukkah. Even though King Antiochus forbade the Jews to study their sacred books, young Jewish boys would gather together and study them anyway. When they heard soldiers approaching, the boys would hide their scriptures, take out their tops, and pretend that they were playing games instead.

MATERIALS:

- paper
- scissors
- glue
- markers and pencil
- dreidel pattern (Student Page 120)
- 10-15 pieces of candy per player

DIRECTIONS:

1. Cut out the dreidel. If you like, use colored markers to decorate.
2. Fold along each of the solid lines. This will make it easier to glue the tabs down when you shape the dreidel. Place glue on all of the tabs and form into a 4-sided top.
3. Insert a pencil in the middle of the X at the top of the dreidel. Get ready to play!

GAME INSTRUCTIONS:

1. All players need to start out with 10–15 pieces of candy. Each player puts one piece of candy in the middle (or the pot) to start the game off.
2. Then each player takes a turn spinning the dreidel and does what each letter stands for. The "N" stands for *nisht* and means "nothing." If you land on this you do nothing and pass the dreidel on to the next player. The "G" stands for *ganz* and means "all." If you land on this you get to take everything that is in the pot. The "H" stands for *halb* and means "half." If you land on "H", you get to take half of the candy out of the pot (take an extra one if there is an odd number of pieces of candy in the pot). The "S" stands for *shtel* and means "to put in." When you land on this, you must add a piece of your candy to the pot.
3. When there is only one piece of candy or none left in the pot, each player must add a piece of candy to the pot so the game can continue. The game ends when one person has all the candy.

Cooking

MAKE HANUKKAH LATKES

Latkes, or potato pancakes, are another Jewish tradition at Hanukkah. Latkes became part of the tradition because they are fried in oil, and that helps remind the Jewish people that a little jar of oil burned miraculously for eight days so very long ago.

INGREDIENTS:

- 4 large potatoes, peeled, grated, and well drained
- 1 medium onion, grated
- 2 beaten eggs
- 1½ teaspoons of salt
- dash of white pepper
- 2 tablespoons all-purpose flour
- vegetable oil

DIRECTIONS:

1. In a large bowl, combine the potatoes, onions, eggs, salt, pepper, and flour.
2. Heat 1″ of oil in a 12″ skillet. When the oil is hot, slowly drop a heaping tablespoon of the potato mixture into the oil. For a crisper latke, gently flatten with the back of a spoon. Fry over medium heat for about 3–4 minutes on each side, or until the pancakes are golden brown and crispy.
3. Drain the cooked latkes on paper towels and set them aside in a warm oven. Finish frying the rest of the batter. You may need to add extra oil between batches.
4. When the cooking is completed, sprinkle the hot latkes with sugar or cinnamon, and serve with applesauce, jam, or sour cream.

Additional History Reading

DK Read and Listen: First Bible Story Book, by Mary Hoffman (DK Publishing, 2000). A simplified biblical account; includes several stories about Jesus from the New Testament. (RA)

Religion Around the World: A Curious Kid's Guide to the World's Great Faiths, by Sonja Hagander, Matthew Maruggi, and Megan Borgert-Spaniol (Beaming Books, 2022). Pages 24-31 cover Judaism and pages 32-39 cover Christianity. (RA)

The Bible, whichever version your family prefers (try the New International Version for up-to-date language). The story of the birth of Jesus is found in Matthew 1:18–2:18 and Luke 2:1-20; the Beatitudes are found in Matthew 5:1-12; and the story of the death and resurrection of Jesus is found in Matthew 26:47–28:20, Mark 14:43–16:20, Luke 22:47–24:53, and John 18:1–21:25.

The World Jesus Knew: A Curious Kid's Guide to Life in the First Century (Curious Kid's Guides, 4), by Marc Olson (Beaming Books, 2023). A series of eye-pleasing infographics and information on life in the first century. It covers everything from the structure of Roman society, to plants that grew in the Roman Empire, to the Jewish calendar. (IR 4-6)

Corresponding Literature Suggestions

The Very First Christmas, by Paul Maier (Concordia Publishing House, 1998). Following the Luke narrative, this beautifully illustrated look at the first Christmas draws readers into each scene. (RA)

The Miracles of Jesus, by Tomie dePaola (Holiday House, 1996). Simple, one-page stories about the miracles of Jesus. (RA)

The Parables of Jesus, by Earnest Graham (Olive Branch Books, 2013). A graphic novel adaption of the parables of Jesus.

The Very First Easter, by Paul Maier (Concordia Publishing House, 2004). Full-page illustrations and a simple story. (RA)

OPTIONAL LESSON
The Story of Judas Maccabee, Champion of the Jewish People

Read & Review

Read pages 329–333 in the text. Afterward, check the student's understanding by asking the questions below.

1. **What did Antiochus Epiphanes tell the Jews they had to do?** *He said they must worship Zeus.*
2. **What did Judas and his family do when Antiochus made Judaism illegal?** *They started a war against him.*
3. **How long did the oil burn in the temple, even though there was only enough for one day?** *It burned for eight days.*

Activities

Choose from the following activities:

- ☐ Coloring Page: Judas Maccabee (Student Page 121)
- ☐ Writing Prompt: After Judas won, the people celebrated by lighting the menorah. Imagine you were there. How would you celebrate? What food, music, and decorations would you have? (If needed, review the instructions on how to use the creative writing prompts in Appendix One.)

167–164 BCE

CHAPTER THIRTY-SEVEN
Rome and the Christians

Nero, the Evil Emperor

Read & Review

Read pages 334–336 in the text. Afterward, check the student's understanding by asking the questions below.

1. **Where was Nero when Rome burned?** *At a party, at a house in the country*
2. **Did he come back to Rome when he heard about the fire?** *No, he stayed in the country a little while longer.*
3. **Did Nero help the families who lost their homes?** *No*
4. **What did he do instead?** *He decided to build a bigger palace where the fire had burned.*
5. **What did the people of Rome think about this?** *They were angry with Nero.*
6. **Whom did Nero blame for the fire?** *The Christians*

Narration Exercise

Tell me what happened to the city of Rome when Nero was emperor, and what Nero did in response.

Nero was a bad emperor. He thought he was a good musician. When Rome burned down, he decided to build a bigger palace. He blamed the Christians for the fire.

54–100 CE

or

A big fire burned down the poor part of Rome. It burned down some of the rich parts too. The emperor Nero blamed Christians for starting the fire. He had them arrested.

Map Work: Nero, the Evil Emperor (Student Page 122)

Read the instructions out loud to the student. After each step, pause and give time for the student to complete the task. Provide all necessary help.

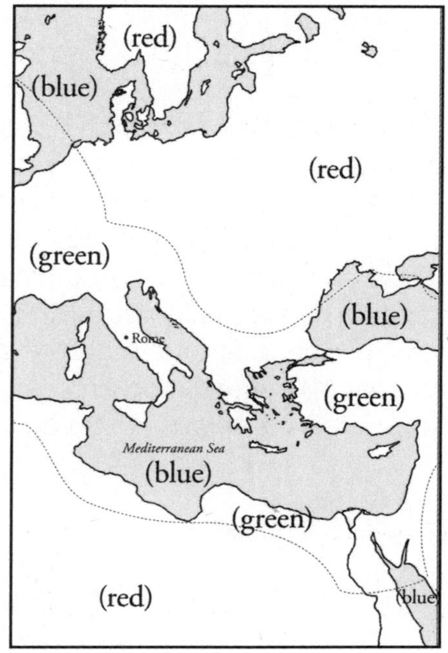

1. **Open to Student Page 122 and tear it out.**
2. **At the time of Nero, the Roman Empire was still very large. On your map, use a green pencil to color in the area that made up the *Roman Empire*. The dashed lines on your map show the borders of the Roman Empire.**
3. **Color the rest of the land on your map with a red pencil. This shows you the land around the Mediterranean Sea that was not part of the Roman Empire.**
4. **Shade the seas and oceans on your map lightly in blue.**
5. **Can you find *Rome*, in Italy, on your map? Some of the catacombs you read about—the ones the Christians hid in—were in Rome.**
6. **When you finish, place the completed map in your history notebook.**

Activities

Choose from the following activities:

- [ ] Storytelling: Nero's Legacy
- [ ] Role Play: Silly Laws
- [ ] Cooking: Host a Roman Banquet
- [ ] Research Skills: Have the student look up a related topic in a history encyclopedia or another reliable source. Read the entry together and look at the pictures. Topics could include *Caligula* and *Nero*.

Storytelling

NERO'S LEGACY PLAY

Create your own dramatic skit about the life of Emperor Nero! Choose several key moments from Nero's story. You may want to read a biography or encyclopedia entry about Nero to find more inspiration. You and your siblings, friends, or even stuffed animals can act out scenes like Nero playing his lyre while Rome burns, blaming the Christians for the fire, and his court pretending to praise his terrible lyre playing out of fear. Other ideas include Nero declaring plans to build a grand palace in the ruins of the city, or the dramatic moment of his death. Be sure to get creative with costumes and props! Afterward, perform your skit for your family and discuss what these events say about Nero's reign and legacy.

Role Play

SILLY LAWS

Emperors could make up whatever laws, or rules, that they wanted. Caligula and Nero were not good rulers and they made up some very silly laws! According to legend, Caligula tried to make his horse a senator, and he declared war on the ocean. Nero bribed his way into the Olympics and was declared the winner, even though he fell out of his chariot! According to rumor, after the fire in Rome, he tried to rename Rome "Neropolis!"

Today, you are the emperor of Rome! You can make your own silly law. Remember, once you make a law, everyone must follow it (at least for a little while)! It can be as silly as you want, but it should be fun and kind. Some ideas include: "nobody is allowed to walk – they must hop!" or "everyone must call me 'your royal awesomeness,'" or "all sentences must end with 'meow.'"

Classroom Adaptation: Give students time to each come up with their own law. Let students take turns whispering their law to the instructor. Once it is approved, have the student declare their law by saying "As Emperor, I declare that __________ must ___________!" For one minute, the class must follow the law! Rotate through the students until everyone has had a turn. Or, assign each student a different law to follow. If you like, finish with a discussion. Discussion questions could include: "What would happen if real rulers made silly laws all the time?," "Why is it important for leaders to make fair laws?," "Do you think laws would be more fair if they had to be approved by other people, or more fair if just one person made them all?"

Cooking

HOST A ROMAN BANQUET

Powerful Romans, including emperors like Nero, hosted elaborate parties for their friends and political allies. Guests would lay on couches or cushions and share food that had been set on a low table between them.

To experience a taste of ancient Rome, carefully arrange finger foods on a platter. Some Roman favorites included cheese, boiled eggs, olives, apples, pears, figs, grapes, and bread. The Romans drank wine at their banquets, but for your feast, you can use grape juice or a Roman-style drink made with water mixed with honey and a touch of cinnamon.

To eat like a Roman, place a picnic blanket down on the floor and arrange comfy pillows and cushions around the eating area. Wealthy Romans often reclined on their left side and ate with their fingers.

If you like, make this popular Roman treat to serve at your feast:

MATERIALS AND INGREDIENTS:

- chopping board
- frying pan
- food processor or grinder
- pitted dates
- walnuts, pecans, and almonds,
- ½ cup of honey

DIRECTIONS:

1. Carefully slit open the side of each date. Be careful not to cut all the way through the date.
2. Use the food processor or grinder to chop the nuts into fine pieces. Stuff a small amount of the nut mixture into each date.
3. Pour some salt on the chopping board and lightly roll each date in it. Make sure that you don't use too much salt.
4. One low heat, melt the honey in the frying pan. Lightly fry the dates for about 5 minutes, turning them with a spoon while they cook.
5. Place the fried dates on a serving dish and sprinkle with more of the chopped nuts.

Christians in the Catacombs

Read & Review

Read pages 336–338 in the text. Afterward, check the student's understanding by asking the questions below.

1. **What man were Romans supposed to worship?** *The emperor*
2. **Did Christians worship the emperor?** *No*
3. **How were Christians punished?** *They were put in prison or forced to fight wild animals.*
4. **Where did Christians have their meetings?** *Underground, in secret passages*
5. **What were those secret passages called?** *Catacombs*
6. **What secret symbol did the Christians use?** *The symbol of a fish*

Narration Exercise

What can you tell me about the Christians in this lesson?

Christians were supposed to worship the emperor, but they said that they wouldn't. Some of the emperors had them arrested or made them fight animals. So the Christians met in secret places called catacombs.

Activities

Choose from the following activities:

- ☐ Coloring Page: The Catacombs Beneath Rome
- ☐ Art: Draw a Secret Symbol
- ☐ Role Play: Read the Chapter in Your Own "Catacomb"
- ☐ Research Skills: Have the student look up a related topic in a history encyclopedia or another reliable source. Read the entry together and look at the pictures. Topics could include *Nero*, *catacombs*, and *Christianity*.
- ☐ Field Trip Idea: Visit a local pedestrian tunnel or cavern. Imagine what it would be like if you had to hide there, like the early Christians had to hide in catacombs. Or find an online video tour or virtual tour of the catacombs beneath Rome.

Coloring Page: The Catacombs Beneath Rome
(Student Page 123)

The catacombs beneath Rome are a network of underground burial sites built by early Christians.

Art

DRAW A SECRET SYMBOL

The Christians in Rome used the fish as their secret symbol. You can make your own secret symbol!

MATERIALS:

- paper
- crayons or pencils
- tape
- scissors

DIRECTIONS:

1. Think about what you want your symbol to be.
    - It could have to do with your last name, like this: Long—a long line; Rainey—rain drop; Wise—owl; Johnson—a man ("John") and his little boy ("son"); Smith—a hammer (like a blacksmith uses).
    - It could have to do with where you live, for example: desert—cactus; seashore—wave; woods—tree; city—skyscraper.
    - It could be a favorite hobby, for example: music—musical note; chess—pawn; fitness—barbell; or a character or symbol from a video game.
2. Draw your symbol on several pieces of paper.
3. In ancient Rome, the Christians drew a fish symbol to let other Christians know that they were present. What will you use your symbol for? Maybe you will leave one in your parents' room as a sign that you want to talk to them. You can put one on your door to show when you're in your room, and remove it when you leave. What else can you do?

Classroom Adaptation: Once students have drawn their symbols, collect them. Hold up one symbol, covering the student's name, and have the class guess whose symbol it is. Have the student explain the meaning behind their symbol.

Role Play

READ THIS CHAPTER IN YOUR OWN "CATACOMB"

The Christians in Rome had to meet secretly in their catacombs. What would it be like to have a secret meeting?

MATERIALS:

- text
- Instructor Guide
- sheets
- flashlight
- tape
- secret symbol from previous project (optional)

DIRECTIONS:

1. Set up your own catacomb (or cave) using sheets draped over tables and chairs.
2. If you like, tape your secret symbol (from the activity above) onto your catacomb so others can find the meeting.
3. Dim the lights in that room and gather inside of the catacomb. Use flashlights or electric lanterns to read the chapter in the main text or, if you have already read the chapter, read one of the books in the additional history reading list. Read in a hushed tone, as if you are having a secret gathering and are afraid of being discovered. Older students may want to take turns reading.
4. Every now and then, pause and listen: do you hear anyone coming, or is your secret meeting still safe?
5. Answer your review questions or do your narration in the same hushed tone.

Additional History Reading

A Coloring Book of Rome (Bellerophon, 1988). Uses actual images from Roman art and architecture. (RA and activity)

The Roman Record: Hot News from the Swirling Mists of Time, by Paul Dowswell (EDC Publications, 1998). A slightly tongue-in-cheek look at Roman history, set up like a tabloid sheet. **Out of print, but worth looking for at your local library.** (RA)

The World of the First Christians: A Curious Kid's Guide to the Early Church, by Marc Olson (Beaming Books, 2020). This book uses infographics, charts, and illustrations to explain the historical context of the New Testament and the history of the early Christian church.

Corresponding Literature Suggestions

Mystery of the Roman Ransom, by Henry Winterfeld (Odyssey Classics, 2002). The purchase of a slave for their teacher leads a group of Roman schoolboys into a dangerous intrigue. A good book, but intended for slightly older readers; this would be a good, long read-aloud project, especially if older children can read to the younger students.

The Thieves of Ostia (Roman Mysteries #1), by Caroline Lawrence (Orion Children's, 2002). This book follows four children who solve a mystery together during Emperor Titus's reign. It is the first in a series of well-researched mystery books. This particular mystery involves someone who is beheading watchdogs, so if that theme is too violent you may also want to try a different book in the series. (IR 3-5)

Saint Valentine, by Robert Sabuda (Aladdin, 1999). The story of Saint Valentine, in which a blind girl receives her sight through a Christian miracle. This book has beautiful mosaic-style illustrations and touches on Roman persecution of Christians. There is an author's note at the end that explains a little bit about the origins of Valentine's Day. (RA 1-2, IR 3-5)

Corresponding Audiobook Suggestions

Beric the Briton, by G.A. Henty, read by Jim Weiss (Well-Trained Mind Press, 2023). Beric, a dashing young British chieftain, must fight for liberty from the forests of his homeland, where he defies legendary Roman legions, to the Roman Colosseum, where he must employ gladiatorial skills to defend a persecuted Christian girl. G.A. Henty provides fascinating details of life in a Roman villa, in the imperial palace, and in the villages of the tribal Britons; and accurately shows the strengths that allowed the Romans to conquer their empire and the weaknesses that would end it.

CHAPTER THIRTY-EIGHT
Rome Begins to Weaken

The British Rebellion

Read & Review

Read pages 339–341 in the text. Afterward, check the student's understanding by asking the questions below.

1. **Do you remember the names of two strong, powerful leaders of Rome?** *Julius Caesar and Caesar Augustus*
2. **Were the emperors after them strong too?** *No, many were weak.*
3. **Who lived in Britain?** *The Celts*
4. **Did Rome control all of Britain?** *No, only part of it.*
5. **Who was the leader of the rebellious Celts in our story?** *Boadicea*
6. **Why were the Romans embarrassed to be beaten by Boadicea?** *Because she was a woman*
7. **Do you remember any of the strange things that were supposed to have happened when the Celts were attacking the Romans?** Acceptable answers include: *The statue of Victory fell face down, the sea turned red, a ghost town in ruins was seen near Londinium, yells came from an empty theater*
8. **Were there more Romans or more Celts?** *Celts*
9. **Why did the Romans win?** *They obeyed their general and fought together.*

60–61 CE

Narration Exercise

Tell me two things you learned about the Celts in this lesson.

The Romans tried to rule Britain. But the people who lived there didn't like the Romans. They were Celts. Their leader was a woman. The Celts fought Rome, but they lost.

or

The Celts lived in Britain. One of their leaders was named Boadicea. She led them against Rome. They lost, but Rome had to leave Britain anyway.

Activities

Choose from the following activities:

- [ ] Coloring Page: Boadicea in Her Chariot
- [ ] Art: Design and Draw a Celtic Border
- [ ] Cooking: Host a Celtic Feast
- [ ] Research Skills: Have the student look up a related topic in a history encyclopedia or another reliable source. Read the entry together and look at the pictures. Topics could include *the Roman Empire*, *Celts*, *Ancient Britain*, *Cassius*, *British rebellion*, and *Boadicea* or *Boudicca*.

Coloring Page: Boadicea in Her Chariot
(Student Page 124)

Boadicea, the fierce queen of a Celtic tribe, led a powerful revolt against Roman rule in Britain.

Art

DESIGN AND DRAW A CELTIC BORDER

The Celtic people were known for beautiful, intricate patterns. In this activity, you can design your own pattern and use it to decorate!

MATERIALS:

- scratch paper
- white paper
- crayons or markers
- scissors
- glue stick
- optional: photograph

DIRECTIONS:

1. Look at the examples of Celtic patterns below:

2. Use your scratch paper to practice making your own simple design out of swirls, spirals, zigzags, or circles.
3. Have an adult or older sibling help you draw a 4-inch border on your paper.
4. Draw your design or shape over and over again inside the border. You can alternate two or more designs/shapes, if you want to.
5. Cut a piece of paper so that it fits inside of your border. Draw a note or a picture on that smaller piece of paper.
6. Use the glue stick to paste your note/drawing inside of the border. Alternatively, you could paste a photograph that you like inside of your border. Optional: you can use this artwork as decor for your Celtic feast (listed below).

Cooking

HOST A CELTIC FEAST

The Celts had great feasts for their warriors to celebrate victories in battle. Legend has it that Celtic warriors painted themselves blue. If you like, use body paint to paint blue markings on yourselves.

A Celtic feast should have music, storytelling, and good food. If you like, decorate your party room with Celtic borders that you draw yourself (see activity above). Borrow some traditional Celtic music from the library or find some on the internet. Take turns reading Celtic tales (see reading list for additional ideas) or retell the story of Boadicea from your memory.

Finally, enjoy some simple food: roasted chicken from the store, wine (better use grape juice), berries, and plain bread with butter. This would be a feast to the Celts! **Be sure to eat it with your hands! No silverware allowed!**

Rome Divided in Two

Read & Review

Read pages 341–343 in the text. Afterward, check the student's understanding by asking the questions below.

1. **Why couldn't the Roman soldiers defend all the borders of Rome?** *It was too big!*
2. **How did the emperor Diocletian try to protect the huge empire of Rome?** *He divided it into two pieces.*
3. **What were the two parts of the Roman empire called?** *The Western Roman Empire and the Eastern Roman Empire*
4. **What city was the capital of the Western Roman Empire?** *Rome*
5. **What city was the capital of the Eastern Roman Empire?** *You can look on your map as you answer. Constantinople*
6. **Which city got to be rich and powerful?** *Constantinople*
7. **Which city grew poor and shabby?** *Rome*
8. **Who invaded the Western Roman Empire?** *Barbarians*

Narration Exercise

What happened when Rome got very big?

Rome got too big for one emperor. So it was split into two parts. The two parts were the Eastern Roman Empire and the Western Roman Empire. Barbarians invaded the west.

or

Rome got so big that it split into two parts. Rome was the capital of the west part. Constantinople was the capital of the east part. The east got richer and the west got poorer.

Map Work: The British Rebellion (Student Page 125)

Read the instructions out loud to the student. After each step, pause and give time for the student to complete the task. Provide all necessary help.

1. **Open to Student Page 125 and tear it out.**

250–305 CE

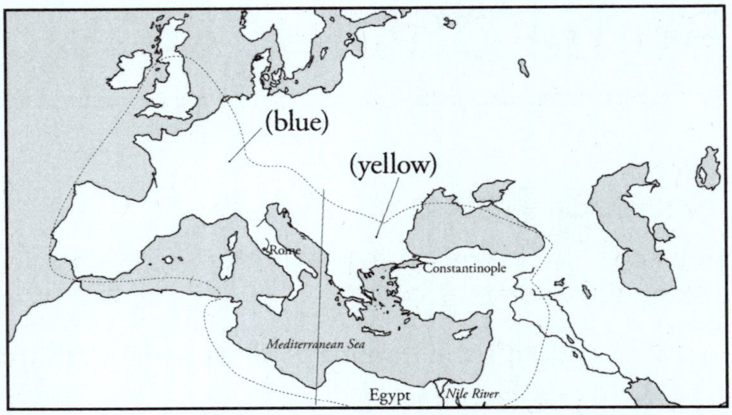

2. **On your map, color the *Eastern Roman Empire* yellow. East is *right* on your map.**
3. **Do you remember the capital city of the Eastern Roman Empire? It was Constantinople. Find *Constantinople* on your map.**
4. **Color the *Western Roman Empire* blue. West is to your *left*.**
5. **Do you remember the capital city of the Western Roman Empire? It was Rome. Find *Rome* on your map.**
6. **Which half of the Roman Empire became the richer one? Which became the poorer, weaker one?**
7. **When you finish, place the completed map in your history notebook.**

Activities

Choose from the following activities:

- [ ] Geography: North, South, East, West
- [ ] Game: Roman Collapse
- [ ] Game: Defend the Empire!
- [ ] Research Skills: Have the student look up a related topic in a history encyclopedia or another reliable source. Read the entry together and look at the pictures. Topics could include *the Roman Empire*, *Diocletian*, *Maximian*, *Western Roman Empire*, *Eastern Roman Empire*, *Constantinople*, and *the decline of Rome*.

Geography

NORTH, SOUTH, EAST, WEST

The Roman Empire was divided into two sections, the Eastern Roman Empire and the Western Roman Empire. Can you find east and west?

MATERIALS:

- chalk
- a sunny day
- a compass (optional)

DIRECTIONS:

1. Outside in an open area, draw a large circle in chalk. Early in the morning, stand in the center of the circle and face the sun. Mark an E for east on the side of the circle that you are facing.
2. West is behind you. Turn all the way around and face west. Mark a W on that side of the circle.
3. Now turn so that the E is on your right hand, and the W is on your left. You are facing north. Mark an N on the north side of the circle.
4. Now south is behind you. Turn completely around and mark an S on the circle behind you.

5. Optional challenges:
   - Compare your directions to a real compass. It won't be exactly right, but it should be close.
   - Have the instructor call out a direction and a task, for example "run to the West!" or "hop on one foot to the East," etc...
   - Have the student track his shadow's direction at different times during the day to see how the sun's position changes.

Classroom Adaptation: Take students outside on a sunny day and create a large directional circle with chalk. Before you begin, stand in the middle of the circle and have students guess which direction is north by standing at that spot in the circle. Guide students through identifying East, West, North, and South using the sun's position. See which of the students were the closest to getting it right!

Game

ROMAN COLLAPSE

In this chapter, we learned about a few of the reasons why Rome collapsed. Play a block-stacking game, like Jenga. Each time someone removes a block from the tower, the instructor should read off another reason why Rome collapsed. Play until your tower collapses!

- The Roman Empire got too big.
- Its borders were too long for one army to protect.
- The soldiers couldn't keep the invaders out.
- More and more invaders came to Rome.
- The emperors had to fight invaders constantly.
- Romans had to hire outside soldiers who weren't always loyal to Rome
- The government spent a lot of money on wars!
- Diocletian split the Roman Empire into two parts, the Western Roman Empire and the Eastern Roman Empire.
- The Western Roman Empire grew poorer and poorer.
- The people in the west had trouble finding food. Many became sick.
- The city of Rome became shabby.
- Invaders from the north attacked the Western Roman Empire. They were called barbarians.
- The barbarians invaded Britain.
- The barbarians invaded Gaul.
- The barbarians invaded Spain.
- Barbarians were coming for Rome!

If you finish the prompts and your tower still hasn't fallen, start at prompt 1 and continue playing until the tower falls.

Game

DEFEND THE EMPIRE

Barbarians came to steal Rome's riches. It was difficult to defend Rome's wide borders. That's why Diocletian decided to split the Roman Empire into two halves. In this game, you will feel what it is like to protect a large area from invaders!

MATERIALS:

- 5-10 small items to represent Roman riches (beanbags, cones, or small toys)
- a large outdoor play area
- cones, rope, or chalk to mark the empire's borders
- a timer

DIRECTIONS:

1. Use cones, rope, or chalk to mark a large "Roman Empire" zone and scatter the "riches" (beanbags, cones, or small toys) across it.
2. Choose 1 player to defend Rome. The rest are barbarian invaders. The defender stands inside the empire. The defender cannot step outside the empire's boundary line. Invaders start outside the boundary. They cannot enter the boundary line until the instructor gives them a signal.
3. The instructor should set a timer for 60 seconds, then signal to the invaders to begin their invasion. Invaders try to run in, grab riches, and run out of the zone without being tagged by the defender. If they're tagged, they freeze in place for the rest of that round.
4. At the end of the round, shrink the empire (make the zone smaller) and play again. Repeat until the empire is very small and easy to protect.
5. Afterward, debrief with the following discussion questions:
    - "Which size was hardest to defend?"
    - "Did it feel easier when the borders were smaller?"
    - "Why do you think Diocletian split the empire?"

Classroom Adaptation: If you have more than five students playing at once, have two students be defenders instead of one.

The Emperor Is a Christian!

Read & Review

Read pages 343–347 in the text. Afterward, check the student's understanding by asking the questions below.

1. **What god did Constantine worship at first?** *Apollo*
2. **Why did he stop persecuting Christians?** *He didn't think people should be put in jail because of the god they worshipped.*
3. **What did he see a vision of?** *A cross made out of light*
4. **Do you remember what the words underneath the cross said?** *By this sign, you will be victor.*
5. **What battle did Constantine's army win?** *The Battle of Milvian Bridge*
6. **What happened to Constantine after the victory?** *He became a Christian* OR *He built a new capital city.*
7. **Constantine built a new capital city and named it after himself. Do you remember what it was called?** *Constantinople*

Narration Exercise

Tell me about Constantine and the Christians.

Roman emperors persecuted Christians. But Constantine thought that was wrong. He said that Christians should be left alone. Then he had a vision of a cross and became a Christian too.

or

Constantine and his army were going to a battle. They were very tired and discouraged. Then Constantine saw a cross in the sky. He put the cross on his soldiers' shields, and they won the battle. Then Constantine became a Christian.

312–337 CE

Activities

Choose from the following activities:

- ☐ Craft: Make Constantine's Shield
- ☐ Research Skills: Have the student look up a related topic in a history encyclopedia or another reliable source. Read the entry together and look at the pictures. Topics could include *Apollo, Christianity, Constantine, the Milvian Bridge*, and *Constantinople*.

Craft

CONSTANTINE'S SHIELD

According to the story, Constantine made all of his soldiers paint the Greek letters for Christ's name on their shields.

MATERIALS:

- cardboard
- scissors
- glue
- stapler (use brads if cardboard is too thick)
- construction paper
- black marker

DIRECTIONS:

1. Cut out a large rectangle or circle from the cardboard for the shield.
2. Cut 2 long strips of cardboard for the handles. One should be just large enough for the student to grip; the other should be slightly larger to fit their forearm through.
3. Constantine ordered all of his soldiers to put the monogram for Christ on their shields. The monogram for Christ is Chi Rho, which are the first two letters, in Greek, of the word "Christ." These Greek letters look like the letters "X" and "P" in the English alphabet. Use a black marker to draw this symbol on the shield or create your own design.
4. Cut out designs in the construction paper and decorate the rest of the shield.
5. Take the smaller handle strip and bend it into an arch. Flatten about an inch on each end and glue these sections to the back of the shield, positioning it vertically at the center. This will be the grip handle. Attach the larger strip in the same way, slightly below the first handle, to serve as the forearm strap.
6. Let dry completely before use.

Classroom/Movement Adaptation: Once each student has made their own shield, put them to use! Divide students into 2 teams. One team pretends to "defend" while the other "attacks" using pool noodles or another soft "weapon" to tag defenders. Defenders must use their shields to block the attacks. Switch roles after a few minutes. At the end of each round, have all students raise their shields and cheer, "By this sign, we will be victors!" just like Constantine.

Additional History Reading

Life in Celtic Times Coloring Times, by A.G. Smith (Dover, 1997). Focuses on the culture of the ancient Celts. (RA)

The Ancient Celts, by Patricia Calvert (Franklin Watts, 2005). An excellent guide to the Celts during Roman times, with many illustrations and a good clear explanation of the earliest Celtic tribes and their origins. (RA 1–3, IR 3–6)

What Was Pompeii?, by Jim O'Connor (Grosset & Dunlap 2014). A non-fiction chapter book that tells the story of the eruption of Vesuvius with lots of illustrations. The book includes information on the science of volcanoes, references Pliny the Younger, details how archeologists discovered the remains of Pompeii, and discusses what life would have been like in ancient Pompeii. (IR 3-7).

Corresponding Literature Suggestions

Celtic Fairy Tales, by Joseph Jacobs (Kessinger, 2003). A standard collection of wonderful tales. (RA)

Celtic Fairy Tales: 20 Classic Stories Including The Black Cat, Lutey and the Mermaid, and The Fiddler in the Cave by Neil Philip (Armadillo, 2021). A more recent collection, beautifully illustrated in the style of the Book of Kells, with gold-leaf borders. (RA)

I Survived the Destruction of Pompeii, by (2024). A graphic-novel style story of a boy escaping the eruption of Mount Vesuvius.

Pompeii ... Buried Alive, by Edith Kunhardt (Random House, 1987). A simple retelling of the fateful days in 79 AD when Mt. Vesuvius erupted and the people in the ancient town of Pompeii perished. (IR for most readers, RA for beginners)

Bodies from the Ash: Life and Death in Ancient Pompeii, by James M. Deem (Houghton Mifflin, 2017). Deem aims his retelling of the story toward older students. Parents should preview this book because of the excellent yet graphic photographs of the plaster casts. (IR 4–7)

Corresponding Audiobook Suggestions

Celtic Treasures, by Jim Weiss (Well-Trained Mind Press, 2021). An award-winning collection of ancient Celtic stories performed by Jim Weiss.

OPTIONAL LESSON
The Story of Pliny the Younger, Survivor of Mount Vesuvius

Read & Review

Read pages 348–351 in the text. Afterward, check the student's understanding by asking the questions below.

1. **What was Pliny the Younger famous for?** *He wrote lots of letters about ancient Rome.*
2. **What big event did Pliny the Younger describe in the letter we read?** *He described a volcano erupting.*
3. **What are two things he saw during the eruption?** Answers may vary. Acceptable answers include: *The ground moved, buildings crumbled, carts moved by themselves, the sea was sucked backward, dark clouds appeared, and ash fell from the sky.*

Activities

Choose from the following activities:

- ☐ Coloring Page: Mount Vesuvius Erupts (Student Page 126)
- ☐ Creative Writing Prompt: Imagine you were with Pliny the Younger when Mount Vesuvius erupted. What did you see? What did you smell? How did you feel? Write a letter to your friends describing the experience. (If needed, review the instructions on how to use the creative writing prompts in Appendix One.)

CHAPTER THIRTY-NINE
Troubles in China

The End of the Han Dynasty

Read & Review

Read pages 352–355 in the text. Afterward, check the student's understanding by asking the questions below.

1. **What types of disasters swept across China during the end of the Han Dynasty?** *Famine, violent storms, epidemics of disease, floods, locusts*
2. **What was the name of the band of warriors who fought against the Han government?** *The Yellow Turbans*
3. **What did General Dong Zhuo do instead of fighting the Yellow Turbans?** *He marched into the capital city, captured the emperor, and declared himself ruler.*
4. **Who did General Ts'ao Ts'ao force the emperor to marry?** *His daughter*

Narration Exercise

Tell me about the end of the Han Dynasty.

The Han generals fought each other. One general took control. The Han Dynasty ended.

or

The Yellow Turbans rebelled against the Han government. Instead of fighting the rebels, the Han generals fought each other. One general took control of the empire by forcing the emperor to marry his daughter.

184–300 CE

Activities

Choose from the following activities:

- ☐ Sequencing Events: The End of the Han Dynasty (Student Page 127)
- ☐ Art: Yellow Turban Recruitment Poster
- ☐ Research Skills: Have the student look up a related topic in a history encyclopedia or another reliable source. Read the entry together and look at the pictures. Topics could include *the Han Dynasty*, *Yellow Turbans*, *Chang Chueh*, *Dong Zhuo*, *epidemics in ancient times*, and *Ts'ao Ts'ao*.

Sequencing Events

THE END OF THE HAN DYNASTY

A lot happened in this lesson! We will put five of the main events in chronological order, using the words first, next, then, after that, and finally to help us remember them. This time, we will also use pictures to help us remember.

MATERIALS:

- Student Page 127
- crayons
- scissors

DIRECTIONS:

1. The instructor should write the words *first*, *next*, *then*, *after that*, and *finally* on a white board or piece of paper.
2. Let the student color the Student Page.
3. Cut out each square and put them in random order.
4. Tell the student to lay out the squares in the correct order as she listens. The instructor should read out the following prompts:
   - First, a strange thing happened: children began inheriting the throne! (The student should choose the square with three young emperors.)
   - Next, more disasters kept happening! (The student should line up the square depicting flooding and locusts.)
   - Then, the Yellow Turbans tried to take over but lost. (The student should line up the card with the band of Yellow Turbans on it.)

- After that, two of the generals fought each other to take over. (The student should line up the card with two generals fighting.)
- Finally, after so many disasters and battles, there was no kingdom left to rule. (The student should line up the final card, the one with a palace broken into three pieces.)

Art

YELLOW TURBAN RECRUITMENT POSTER

Have the student create a poster to try to recruit people to join the Yellow Turban rebellion. What are some reasons someone might want to join the Yellow Turbans? You could include a drawing of the leader, Chang Chueh, or his promise that magic could save his followers from disease or battle wounds. Use bright colors and bold persuasive language!

Note to Instructor: If the student is not familiar with recruitment posters, show her a few examples, like Uncle Sam or Smokey the Bear. Explain that a recruitment poster is like a big sign that asks people to join or help with something. Imagine if a school made a poster saying, "Come join our soccer team!" It would show pictures of kids playing soccer, and maybe it would say things like, "We need players!" or "Have fun and be part of the team!"

Classroom Adaptation: Display all of the recruitment posters and have students vote anonymously for the one they think is "most persuasive." You can add other voting categories if you like, for example "most beautiful," "most historically accurate," etc... Place ribbons on the winning posters.

The Three Kingdoms, The Jin, and the Sixteen Kingdoms

Read & Review

Read pages 355–358 in the text. Afterward, check the student's understanding by asking the questions below.

1. **How many pieces did the Han kingdom fracture into after the emperor fled?** *Three*
2. **Why did Wei Yuandi agree to abdicate the throne to his general, Sima Yan?** *He was surrounded by Sima Yan's soldiers.*
3. **What did Sima Yan decide to do after becoming emperor?** *Sima Yan decided to conquer the last remaining kingdom.*
4. **What did Jin Wudi's army do to get around the iron chains on the river?** *They sent fiery rafts down the river to melt the chains.*

Narration Exercise

Tell me at least two things that happened in this lesson.

The first Jin emperor united China. He had many sons. His sons split the empire apart again.

or

After the Han Dynasty, China split into three kingdoms. The first Jin emperor united China once again. After he died, his sons fought each other and weakened the empire.

Map Work: The Three Kingdoms, The Jin, and the Sixteen Kingdoms (Student Page 128)

Read the instructions out loud to the student. After each step, pause and give time for the student to complete the task. Provide all necessary help.

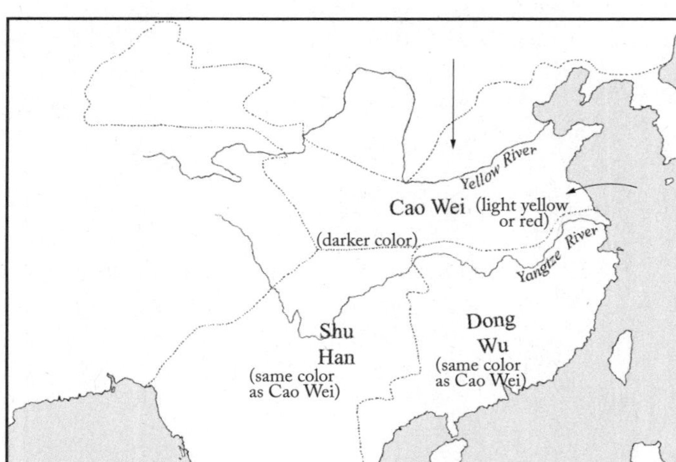

184-300 CE

1. **Open to Student Page 128 and tear it out.**
2. **On your map, find the Three Kingdoms. Color *Cao Wei* light yellow or light red.**
3. **Cao Wei conquered Shu Han. Color *Shu Han* with the same color you used for Cao Wei.**
4. **Eventually, Jin Wudi, the emperor, took over the final kingdom, Dong Wu. Color *Dong Wu* over with the same color you used for the other two kingdoms. China is united again!**
5. **Uh oh! When Jin Wudi died, his many sons fought to take control of China. Barbarians from the North began to steal Jin lands. Draw an arrow coming from the North (above China) down into China. If you like, draw a barbarian next to the arrow.**
6. **Pirates sailed along the coast and began to steal and kidnap. Draw an arrow from the coast into China. If you like, draw a pirate flag next to that arrow.**
7. **The Jin lost everything above the Yangtze River. Take a darker color crayon and color in everything above the *Yangtze River*.**
8. **What was left became split up into many small warring kingdoms. These were called the Sixteen Kingdoms (even though sometimes there were fewer than sixteen and sometimes there were more than sixteen).**
9. **When you finish, place the completed map in your history notebook.**

Activities

Choose from the following activities:

- [ ] Memory Work: First Dynasties of China
- [ ] Game: Chinese Playground Games
- [ ] Cooking: Chinese Dumplings
- [ ] Celebration: Celebrate learning about China by having a dumpling party! Dumplings are a lot of work, so it can be fun to invite friends over to help. Before you eat, try out some popular Chinese schoolyard games (listed below). Then fold your dumplings while listening to traditional Chinese music!
- [ ] Research Skills: Have the student look up a related topic in a history encyclopedia or another reliable source. Read the entry together and look at the pictures. Topics could include *the Three Kingdoms, Cao Wei, Dong Wu, Shu Han, Sima Yan* or *Jin Wudi, Jin Dynasty*, and *the Sixteen Kingdoms.*

Memory Work

FIRST DYNASTIES OF CHINA

Memorizing the major dynasties of Ancient China will give the student pegs she can hang information on as she dives deeper into the study of this region.

Note to Instructor: For detailed guidance on using memory work activities, see Appendix Two. The student's memory work reference page is available on Student Page 129. Below, you'll find the list of items to memorize, along with additional teaching ideas for your convenience.

1. Xia (Shee-ah) Dynasty - mythical beginnings
2. Shang (SHANG) Dynasty - first historical dynasty
3. Zhou (JOH, like the English name Joe) Dynasty - longest dynasty
4. Warring States Period
5. Qin (CHIN) Dynasty - unified China
6. Han (HAN) Dynasty - established Silk Road
7. Three Kingdoms Period - China fractured

Although the following dynasties occurred *after* the period covered in this volume, interested older students can still learn them:

8. Sui (SWAY) Dynasty
9. Tang (TAHNG) Dynasty
10. Song (SUNG) Dynasty
11. Yuan (YOU-AHN) Dynasty
12. Ming (MING) Dynasty
13. Qing (CHING) Dynasty

Suggested Activity: Have the student create an illustrated timeline of Ancient China on Student Page 129. For example, the student could draw a shape broken into two pieces next to "Zhou Dynasty" or a road next to "Han Dynasty."

Related Reading: *All About China: Songs, Crafts, and Games for Kids*, by Allison Branscombe (Tuttle Publishing, 2018)

Game

CHINESE PLAYGROUND GAMES

Celebrate learning about China by playing games that are popular in China! These games require multiple students, so if you don't have siblings, you will need to go to the park to play or invite friends over.

Dragon's Tail

Players form a line, holding onto the waist or shoulders of the person in front. The line must not break. The first person is the head, the last is the tail. The head tries to catch the tail while the rest of the body moves to prevent it. When the head catches the tail, the head moves to the back of the line and becomes the new tail.

Shuttlecock

Players use their feet, knees, and head to keep a shuttlecock in the air. The game can be played alone or in a group, counting how many times they can keep it up.

Cat and Mouse

One player is the cat and one is the mouse. The rest form a circle, holding hands. The mouse starts inside the circle, and the cat starts outside. The players forming the circle raise or lower their arms to block the cat from entering or to allow the mouse to escape. The cat must chase the mouse in and out of the circle, but can only enter the circle if the circle opens. The game ends when the cat catches the mouse. Then kids can switch roles for a new round.

Cooking

CHINESE DUMPLINGS

Celebrate learning about China by making your own traditional dumplings! Making dumplings is a lot of work! You can make a party out of it. Or, if you need something a little easier, most grocery stores sell frozen dumplings you can cook up. For an extra challenge, try using chopsticks to eat them!

Today, China has many different cuisines, each with unique flavors and styles. Dumplings are just one delicious example of a food that is popular in China.

Note to Instructor: If you go to an international grocery store to pick up some of these ingredients, buy extra chopsticks, soy sauce, sesame oil, and some sweet potato noodles (dangmyeon) so that you are prepared for the Japchae recipe in the next chapter.

MATERIALS:

Dumpling Ingredients:

- 1 pack of pre-made dumpling wrappers (you can make these yourself, but having them prepped beforehand makes the entire process much simpler. You can purchase them from international grocery stores.)
- small bowl of water (for sealing dumplings)
- 1 lb (450g) ground pork or chicken
- 2 cups Napa cabbage or bok choy, finely chopped (you can omit this and add 5-6 extra green onions instead)

- 2 green onions, finely chopped
- 2 cloves garlic, minced
- 1 tbsp ginger, grated (or you can use ginger paste)
- 1 tbsp soy sauce
- 1 tsp sesame oil
- ½ tsp salt
- ½ tsp sugar
- 1 tsp cornstarch
- 2 tbsp cooking oil (if pan frying)

Dipping Sauce Ingredients:

- 2 tbsp soy sauce
- 1 tsp minced garlic
- ½ tsp grated ginger (or ginger paste)
- 1 tsp sugar

Optional: purchase chopsticks to eat your dumplings with!

DIRECTIONS:

1. **Prepare the Filling:** Sprinkle a little salt over the chopped cabbage and let it sit for 10 minutes. Squeeze out excess water with your hands or a clean towel. In a bowl, mix the ground meat with soy sauce, sesame oil, salt, sugar, and cornstarch. Stir in one direction until sticky. Add the cabbage, green onions, garlic, and ginger. Mix until well combined.

2. **Wrap the Dumplings.** Place a wrapper in your palm. Add about 1 teaspoon of filling in the center. Dip your finger in water and lightly wet the edges of the wrapper. Fold the wrapper in half to create a half-moon shape, pressing the edges together firmly. You can pleat for a traditional look or simply press shut. Repeat until all filling is used.

3. **Mix sauce.** Combine all of the dipping sauce ingredients together in a small bowl and set aside.

4. **Cook the Dumplings:**

   Pan fried (recommended):

   1. Heat 1 tbsp oil in a non-stick pan over medium heat. Arrange dumplings in a single layer, pleat side up.

   2. Cook for 2-3 minutes until the bottoms are golden brown.

   3. Carefully add ½ cup water and cover immediately. Steam for 5-6 minutes or until the water evaporates.

   4. Uncover and let cook for another minute to crisp up. Serve with dipping sauce.

   Boiled:

   1. Bring a pot of water to a rolling boil.

   2. Add dumplings in batches, stirring gently to prevent sticking.

3. When they float, cook for another 2-3 minutes. Drain then serve with dipping sauce.

Steamed:

1. Line a steamer basket with parchment or cabbage leaves.
2. Arrange dumplings in a single layer without touching.
3. Steam over boiling water for 8-10 minutes.
4. Serve with the dipping sauce.

Additional History Reading

A Coloring Book of Ancient China (Bellerophon Books, 1984). Uses actual images from ancient Chinese art. **Out of print, but it can be ordered online.** (RA and activity) (Also recommended for chapter thirty-three)

All About China: Stories, Songs, Crafts and Games for Kids (Tuttle Publishing, 2018) by Allison "Aixin" Branscombe. This book has lots of great information about China's geography and culture, modern and ancient. There is a timeline with a quick overview of each of the major dynasties. There are also recipes, games, activities, and stories. (Also recommended for chapter ten) (RA)

Zhang Heng And the Incredible Earthquake Detector, by Randel McGee, (Familius LLC, 2022). A picture book story about one of Zhang Heng's inventions, the seismoscope. (RA 1-5)

Corresponding Literature Suggestions

Cao Chong Weighs an Elephant, by Songju Ma Daemicke, illus. Christina Wald (Arbordale Publishing, 2017). How did the young son of a Han Dynasty official use the science of buoyancy to figure out how to weigh an elephant? Find out in this fun picture book. There are two science demonstrations in the back of the book.

Chinese Menu: The History, Myths, and Legends Behind Your Favorite Foods (Little, Brown and Company, 2023), by Grace Lin. This unique book offers an illustrated legend or historical story for a variety of common Chinese foods. There is an outline in the front so that you can find food stories connected to whatever dynasty you are studying. Recipes are not included, but can easily be found online. (Also recommended for chapter twenty-six) (RA)

Lon Po Po, by Ed Young (Puffin Books, 1989). A Caldecott Award book that tells a version of "Little Red Riding Hood" set in China. (RA)

OPTIONAL LESSON
The Story of Zhang Heng: Astronomer, Poet, Mathematician, Geographer, and More

Read & Review

Read pages 359–363 in the text. Afterward, check the student's understanding by asking the questions below.

1. **Why did Zhang Heng go to Chang'an?** *He wanted to study at the college.*
2. **What is something Zhang Heng invented or discovered?** Answers may vary. Acceptable answers include: *He discovered the earth was round, he built a model of the earth and planets, he invented a device that could detect earthquakes, he invented a new kind of clock, he drew accurate maps, he invented an odometer, he learned how to paint on silk.*
3. **Zhang Heng was a polymath. What does polymath mean?** *Someone who knows a lot about many different subjects*

Activities

Choose from the following activities:

- [ ] Coloring Page: Zhang Heng's Earthquake Detector (Student Page 130)
- [ ] Creative Writing Prompt: Imagine you are Zhang Heng. Write a diary entry describing how you spent your day. What amazing things did you learn about? (If needed, review the instructions on how to use the creative writing prompts in Appendix One.)

CHAPTER FORTY
Lands East of China

The Three Kingdoms of Korea

Read & Review

Read pages 355–358 in the text. Afterward, check the student's understanding by asking the questions below.

1. **What were the names of the three kingdoms on the peninsula of Korea?** *Goguryeo, Baekje, and Silla*
2. **How did the Goguryeo respond to Han rule in Korea?** *They fought hard against the Han.*
3. **What happened to the lands ruled by the Goguryeo after King Micheon died?** *They were invaded by the armies of the "Sixteen Kingdoms."*
4. **How did young King Sosurim help the country of Goguryeo survive?** *He welcomed visitors from China and India, rewarded soldiers for joining his army, strengthened his borders, and rebuilt damaged cities.*
5. **Why did they call King Guanggaeto "The Great Expander"?** *He came close to uniting the Korean kingdoms.*

Narration Exercise

Tell me two things you learned in this lesson.

The peninsula we now call Korea was once divided into three kingdoms. King Guanggaeto spent his rule fighting. He came close to uniting the three kingdoms. He was given the nickname "The Great Expander."

300–413 CE

Activities

Choose from the following activities:

- ☐ Cooking: Japchae
- ☐ Storytelling: Read the Lesson with Character Cards!
- ☐ Game: Chicken Fight
- ☐ Research Skills: Have the student look up a related topic in a history encyclopedia or another reliable source. Read the entry together and look at the pictures. Topics could include *Ancient Korea*, *King Micheon*, *Pyongyang*, and *Guanggaeto*.

Cooking

JAPCHAE

Japchae is a delicious and colorful noodle dish from Korea that's fun to make and even more fun to eat! For an extra challenge, try eating it with chopsticks!

MATERIALS:

For the noodles:

- 12 oz (340g) sweet potato starch noodles (dangmyeon). You can purchase these online or at an Asian grocery store.
- 2 tbsp sesame oil
- 2 tbsp soy sauce

For the meat:

- 8 oz (170g) beef (ribeye or sirloin) or chicken breast (or use 6-8 shiitake mushrooms for a vegetarian option)
- 2 tbsp soy sauce
- 2 tbsp sesame oil
- 1 tsp sugar
- 2 cloves garlic, minced

For the veggies:

- 1 one small onion, thinly sliced
- 1 carrot, julienned
- 1 red or yellow bell pepper, thinly sliced
- 6 oz (170g) fresh spinach
- 1 tbsp sesame oil
- 1 tbsp soy sauce
- 2 tbsp sesame oil
- sesame seeds
- minced garlic
- 1 tbsp sugar

For the sauce:

- 3 tbsp soy sauce
- 1.5 tbsp sugar
- 1.5 tbsp sesame oil
- 2 tsp sesame seeds
- 2 cloves of garlic (minced)

DIRECTIONS:

1. Boil the noodles in water according to the package instructions (about 6-8 minutes). Drain and rinse under cold running water. Toss with soy sauce and sesame oil to prevent sticking.
2. In a bowl, mix the meat or mushrooms with the soy sauce, sesame oil, sugar, and minced garlic. Let them marinate together for 10-15 minutes.
3. While the meat (or mushrooms) marinates, cook the vegetables. Heat sesame oil in a large pan or wok over medium heat. Add the onion and stir-fry for 1-2 minutes. Add the carrots and bell peppers and stir-fry until they are slightly softened. Add the spinach and cook until it is wilted (it will not take long). Remove from the pan and set aside.
4. Cook the marinated meat (or mushrooms) in the same pan you used to cook the vegetables.
5. Mix all of the sauce ingredients together in a small bowl.
6. Once the veggies are tender, mix together the noodles, meat (or mushrooms), and vegetables. Toss with the sauce and serve warm.

Storytelling

READ THE LESSON WITH CHARACTER CARDS!

This lesson had lots of important characters in it! Use these character cards as you read to keep track of who is who.

MATERIALS:

- Student Page 131
- scissors
- colored pencils or crayons
- popsicle sticks (optional)
- tape or glue (optional)

DIRECTIONS:

1. Color the Character Cards on Student Page 131. Then cut them out.
2. If you like, tape or glue each colored picture onto a popsicle stick.
3. Each student chooses (or is assigned) a character card.
   - If working with a single student, you may want to re-read the story (or key sections) multiple times, allowing them to take turns using different character cards each time.
   - If you have fewer than 4 students, older students can manage multiple character cards; younger students should focus on one character card.
   - If you have more than 4 students, multiple students can share the same character. Have each student color their own copy of their character's card.
4. Use the pronunciation guide in the main text to help your student say their character's name correctly.
5. As you read the lesson, pause when you say a character's name.
6. The student assigned to that character should hold up their card and project the name out loud. (i.e. when you read "King Sosurim had to figure out how to help his country survive," any student with the Sosurim card should stand up and say "SOSURIM!"). Continue reading after each response.
7. When you finish reading the lesson, ask the student to summarize what happened to just their character.

Classroom Adaptation: Place students into 4 groups and assign each group a character. Each student should color their own picture of their character and learn the pronunciation for their character's name. Whenever a character is mentioned in the lesson, every student from that character's group should stand, raise their card, and boldly declare their character's name in unison. Once you complete the story, have students from each group take turns retelling what happened to their particular character.

Game

CHICKEN FIGHT (DAK-SA-UM)

To celebrate learning about Korea, let's try a popular children's game from Korea that allows you to test your strength and agility against your opponents!

MATERIALS:

- A soft space for playing
- 2 or more players

DIRECTIONS:

1. Find a safe, open, space free of obstacles. Designate a small area that players must stay inside during the match.
2. Players should wear comfortable clothing and shoes to avoid slipping. If there are more than 2 players, pair up with a player of a similar size.
3. Each player must lift one leg and hold their ankle with their hand. The other foot remains on the ground.
4. Players hop toward each other and try to knock their opponent off balance using their body (shoulders, arms, or torso).
5. Hands cannot be used to push or grab the opponent—only body contact is allowed.
6. A player loses if:
    - They put both feet on the ground.
    - They fall over.
    - They release their raised foot from their hand.
    - They step out of bounds.
7. The last player remaining on one leg wins the game!

Classroom Adaptation: Play with 2 teams. The last standing member of either team wins for their group.

The Yamato of Japan

Read & Review

Read pages 368–373 in the text. Afterward, check the student's understanding by asking the questions below.

1. **How many large islands make up Japan?** *four*
2. **The Yamato emperors said they were descendants of who?** *Amaterasu, the Sun Goddess*
3. **What made Amaterasu's brother, the sea-god Susano, jealous?** *The sky is larger than the sea.*
4. **Where did Susano flee after losing the war against his sister?** *Earth*
5. **Why were the old man and the old woman weeping?** *A serpent was coming to eat their daughter.*
6. **To keep the girl hidden from the serpent, what did Susano change her into?** *A comb*
7. **After Susano chopped the servant into eighty pieces, what did he find inside its body?** *A magical sword*
8. **When Amaterasu saw that Japan was noisy and full of battles, what did she do?** *She sent her favorite grandson to bring peace.*
9. **Name at least two of the sacred objects that Amaterasu gave her grandson, Ninigi.** *A string of beads, a mirror, and Susano's magical sword*

Narration Exercise

Tell me about the Yamato of Japan.

Japan was ruled by many clans. The Yamato clan wanted to rule all of Japan. They said they were descendants of the sun goddess. Over time, the other clans agreed to obey the Yamato.

or

What happened to Susano, the sea god, after he lost the war against his sister, the sun goddess?

The sea god fled to earth after he lost the war to his sister. He met an old man and woman who were crying because a giant serpent was going to eat their daughter! He hid the girl by changing her into a comb, and then chopped the serpent into pieces. He found a magical sword inside the serpent.

Map Work: The Yamato of Japan (Student Page 132)

Read the instructions out loud to the student. After each step, pause and give time for the student to complete the task. Provide all necessary help.

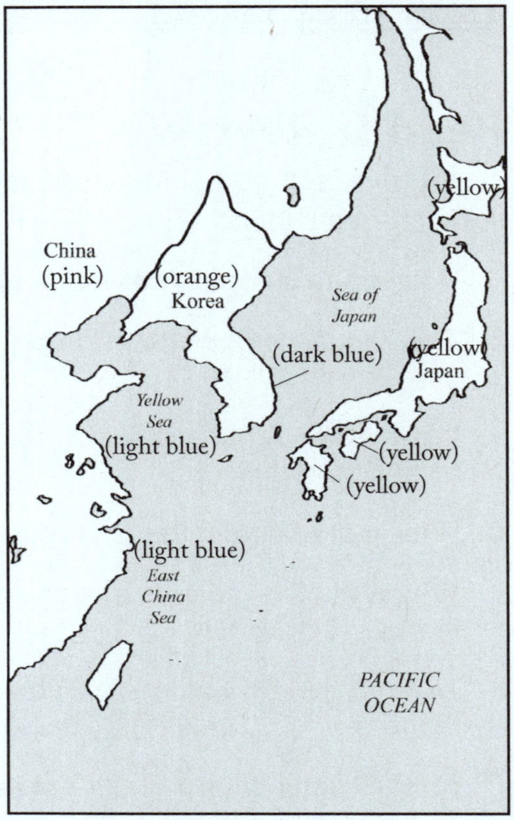

1. **Open to Student Page 132 and tear it out.**
2. **Color *Korea* orange.**
3. **Korea is a peninsula, meaning that it is surrounded by water on three sides. Outline the coast of Korea dark blue.**
4. **Color the water in the *Sea of Japan*, the *Yellow Sea*, and the *East China Sea* in light blue.**
5. **Japan is made up of four large islands. Color those islands yellow.**
6. **Color *China* pink.**
7. **When you finish, place the completed map in your history notebook.**

Activities

Choose from the following activities:

☐ Coloring Page: Susano

☐ Art: Design a Kimono

☐ Research Skills: Have the student look up a related topic in a history encyclopedia or another reliable source. Read the entry together and look at the pictures. Topics could include *Japan*, *the Yamato*, *Ojin*, *Susano*, and *Amaterasu*.

Coloring Page: Susano (Student Page 133)

Color the picture of Susano, the spirit of the sea.

Art

DESIGN A KIMONO

Colorful kimonos were a sign of wealth and power in Ancient Japan. Try your hand at designing your own beautiful kimono.

MATERIALS:

- Student Page 134
- colored pencils or crayons
- fabric scraps, glossy magazine pictures, and glue (optional)

DIRECTIONS:

1. Pull out Student Page 134.
2. Lightly sketch your kimono design.
3. Gather up your art supplies and fill in the kimono. Designs from nature and mythical animals were very popular. You can color in your kimono with colored pencils and crayons or fill it in with scraps of fabric or strips from magazines.

Additional History Reading

All About Korea: Stories, Songs, and Games for Kids, by Ann Martin Bowler (Tuttle Publishing, 2011). An introduction to the geography and culture of modern Korea. This book includes folktales, modern stories, games, activities, and recipes.

All About Japan: Stories, Songs, and Games for Kids, by Willamarie Moore (Tuttle Publishing, 2011). An introduction to the geography and culture of modern Japan. This book includes folktales, modern stories, games, activities, and recipes. It is mostly about modern Japan, but includes a two page spread on the history of Japan.

Corresponding Literature Suggestions

Korean Children's Favorite Stories, by Kim So-un (Tuttle Publishing, 2019). An illustrated collection of Korean folktales. (RA)

Tap Dancing on the Roof, by Linda Sue Park, illus. Istvan Banyai (Clarion Books, 2015). A collection of short poems in a traditional Korean style called Sijo. Like haikus, these poems are short and easy to memorize. Each poem has a set of stressed and unstressed syllables and a twist at the end (RA 1, IR 2-5).

The Green Frogs: A Korean Folktale, by Yumi Heo (Houghton Mifflin Harcourt, 1996). A retelling of a sad Korean story about two naughty frogs. (RA 1-2, IR 3-5).

A Carp for Kimiko, by Virginia Kroll (Charlesbridge Publishing, 1996). A little girl wishes for a calico carp kite, just like the one her brothers fly on Children's Day. But Japanese tradition dictates that only boys have colorful kites on that day. The story introduces the readers to the Japanese customs and traditions surrounding the celebrations of Children's Day and Doll's Day. (RA 1-2, IR 3-5).

Japanese Children's Favorite Stories, by Florence Sakade (Tuttle Publishing, 2013). An illustrated collection of Japanese folktales.

CHAPTER FORTY-ONE
The Attacking Barbarians

Stilicho, Roman and Barbarian

Read & Review

Read pages 374–376 in the text. Afterward, check the student's understanding by asking the questions below.

1. **What barbarian tribe invaded the Western Roman Empire?** *The Visigoths*
2. **How long did it take them to fight the barbarians?** *Years and years*
3. **Were the Romans able to beat the Visigoths?** *No*
4. **How did they finally convince the Visigoths to go away?** *The Romans paid them 4,000 pounds of gold.*
5. **Why were people suspicious of Stilicho?** *Because his father was a barbarian*
6. **Was he a good Roman, or not?** *Yes, he was.*
7. **What happened to him?** *He was executed.*

Narration Exercise

Tell me about Stilicho and the Visigoths.

The Visigoths invaded Rome. Stilicho fought against them. He had to pay them to leave. But the Romans had him killed.

or

Stilicho was part barbarian and part Roman. He fought the Visigoths. But people didn't like him because he was a barbarian. He was executed.

390-408 CE

Activities

Choose from the following activities:

- ☐ Role Play: Reassemble a Roman Pot
- ☐ Game: Stilicho Says
- ☐ Research Skills: Have the student look up a related topic in a history encyclopedia or another reliable source. Read the entry together and look at the pictures. Topics could include *Stilicho, barbarians, the Visigoths, the Danube River*, and *Germanic peoples*.

Role Play

REASSEMBLE A ROMAN POT

When the barbarians invaded, they destroyed much of Rome—they broke everything they could get their hands on! Centuries later, archaeologists dug in the ruins of Rome to find out more about the invasion. They had to put back together the things that the barbarians broke! Try to be an archaeologist and reassemble a Roman artifact.

MATERIALS:

- pot or dish that your parents will let you break (NOT glass—pottery is best; an old flowerpot works very well. Be sure not to look at it before it is broken! Ask your parents to choose it.)
- glue
- paintbrushes

DIRECTIONS:

1. Archaeologists don't know what their artifacts will look like—all they see are the ruined pieces! So don't look at the dish or pot. Ask your mother to take it away and break it. She should be careful to pick out tiny splinters that might hurt you.

   Note to Instructor: Wrap the pot in a towel before you break it. That way, all the pieces will stay in one place.

2. Now it's your turn! Try to figure out how the pot looked before the "barbarian" broke it! Can you reassemble the pieces with your glue? You can use a paintbrush to apply the glue. Ask your mother whether your reassembled pot or dish looks like the original.
3. For an extra challenge, have an adult break two or three pots and mix up the pieces! Sort the fragments and try to determine which pieces go together. The adult could even add a "fake" piece that doesn't belong to any of the pots to make it more challenging.

Game

STILICHO SAYS

Stilicho was in charge of the entire Roman army! In this game, you will practice being Stilicho. Play it like Simon Says. One player is Stilicho and gives Roman army commands. For example:

- "Stilicho says march like a Roman soldier!" (students must march in place)
- "Stilicho says blow the horn!" (cup hands around your mouth and make a deep horn sound)
- "Stilicho says ride your horse into battle!" (gallop in place)
- "Stilicho says throw your spear!" (mime throwing a spear)
- "Stilicho says defend the gates!" (all players lock arms)

Practice each command once or twice before you begin. Once the game begins, if you move without "Stilicho" saying, "Stilicho says," you're out! The last player standing becomes the next Stilicho.

The Coming of the Visigoths

Read & Review

Read pages 377–379 in the text. Afterward, check the student's understanding by asking the questions below.

1. **What was the first barbarian tribe to invade the city of Rome?** *The Visigoths*
2. **What was the second tribe?** *The Vandals*
3. **Which tribe was worse?** *The Vandals*
4. **Why didn't the Visigoths burn the churches of Rome?** *Because some of them were Christian*
5. **Where was the Emperor when Rome was invaded?** *He had gone away to a city in a swamp.*
6. **Why didn't the Eastern Roman Emperor send help?** *He was afraid of the barbarians invading his own city.*

Narration Exercise

Tell me two or three important things that happened in this lesson.

The Visigoths invaded Rome and took gold. Then the Vandals came and destroyed Rome. They were worse.

or

Barbarians invaded Rome. The Eastern Roman Emperor wouldn't help. The Western Roman Emperor ran away to a swamp where he was safe.

410 CE

Activities

Choose from the following activities:

- [ ] Coloring Page: A Visigoth Invader
- [ ] Role Play & Science: Walking in the Swamp
- [ ] Game: Barbarian Tag
- [ ] Research Skills: Have the student look up a related topic in a history encyclopedia or another reliable source. Read the entry together and look at the pictures. Topics could include *barbarians, the Visigoths, ancient Goths, the Western Roman Empire, Eastern Roman Empire*, and *vandals/vandalism*.

Coloring Page: A Visigoth Invader (Student Page 135)

The Visigoths were fierce warriors.

Role Play & Science

WALKING IN THE SWAMP

Why couldn't the Visigoths get through the soft, muddy ground of the swamp with their horses? Let's experiment with this messy project!

MATERIALS:

- a watertight container
- mud (if it hasn't been raining, start with dirt and add water; an adult should check the dirt/mud and remove any harmful debris)
- popsicle sticks or similar
- additional water

DIRECTIONS:

1. Mix dirt and water to make mud as needed (make it thick at first, so you can experiment with more water).
2. The Romans had many good roads that made it easy to travel; think about walking on the sidewalk or driving on a paved street.
3. Using a table or floor, try a few things: "walk" with your fingers, tap your fingers, tap with a popsicle stick, slide your hand, slide a popsicle stick.
4. Now try the same things in the container of mud. What differences can you feel? What

might make it harder for a horse to walk across mud rather than a good Roman road? Mud is slippier, stickier, softer; it resists movement and creates a feeling of being stuck or pulled down. Horses are very heavy, so they will sink farther into the mud and have a harder time overcoming the resistance to movement.

5. If you like, you can experiment with adding more water to make different thicknesses of mud, and feeling the differences each time

Game

BARBARIAN TAG

Just like the Romans had to flee from the Visigoths when their city was no longer safe, in this game, you must escape to Ravenna before being caught.

MATERIALS:

- a large play area
- cones or items to mark off the area
- friends!

DIRECTIONS:

1. Mark off a large play area with cones or other items.
2. Decide who will be the Visigoth and who will be Stilicho. All other players are Romans.
3. Have the Romans and Stilicho line up on one side of the play area (Rome). The Visigoth starts on the opposite side.
4. When the Visigoth is ready, he should call out, "The Visigoths are coming!" The Romans and Stilicho must run from Rome to the opposite side of the play area (Ravenna) without being tagged.
5. If a Roman is tagged, they must sit down or freeze where they were caught.
6. The round continues until all Romans have either escaped to Ravenna or been caught.
7. Stilicho's Rescue: Once all the Romans have either escaped or been tagged, Stilicho has 30 seconds to run back and tag as many frozen Romans as possible to unfreeze them. Stilicho must avoid being tagged by the Visigoth—if he is caught, the Romans are on their own!
8. Any Romans who escape after being rescued may continue running to Ravenna. Any Romans still frozen when time runs out remain caught.
9. All captured Romans become Visigoths in the next round. The game continues until all Romans, including Stilicho, have been caught.
10. If you want to play again, the last Roman to get caught becomes the first Visigoth for the next game.

Attila the Hun

Read & Review

Read pages 379–382 in the text. Afterward, check the student's understanding by asking the questions below.

1. **What do we call the barbarians who came from central Asia?** *Huns*
2. **Who was their leader?** *Attila*
3. **Who was Honoria?** *The sister of the Western Roman Emperor*
4. **Why did she send Attila a letter, offering to marry him?** *Because she wanted to get away from the Roman court*
5. **What did Attila do when he got the letter?** *He invaded Italy.*
6. **Why did Attila agree to leave Italy?** *The Western Roman Emperor paid him to leave.*

Narration Exercise

Tell me about Attila the Hun.

Attila the Hun was the leader of the Huns. He tried to conquer the Western Roman Empire, but the Emperor paid him to leave. He died of a nosebleed.

or

The Huns were barbarians. Their leader was Attila. The Emperor's sister wanted to marry him, but she didn't. Attila came all the way to Italy.

Map Work: Attila the Hun (Student Page 136)

Read the instructions out loud to the student. After each step, pause and give time for the student to complete the task. Provide all necessary help.

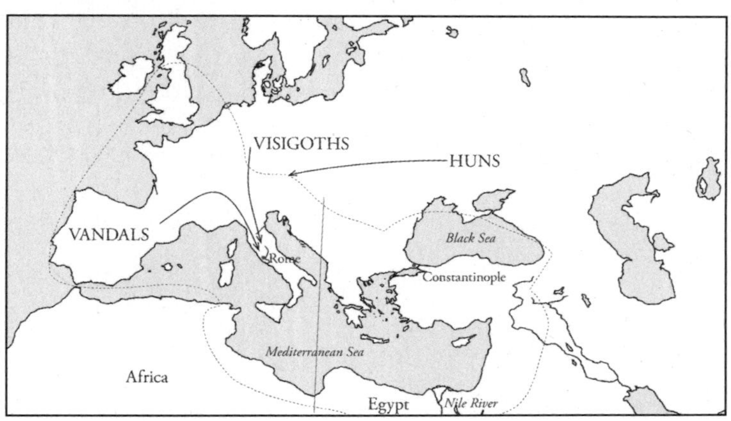

1. **Open to Student Page 136 and tear it out.**

440–453 CE

2. **Look back at your map from the last chapter. The Huns attacked the Roman Empire from the area north of the Black Sea. (North is up on your map.) Find *"HUNS"* in this area on your map. Draw an arrow from the word HUNS to the border of the Western Roman Empire (to the north of Rome).**
3. **The Visigoths came from the area we now call Germany. Find *"VISIGOTHS"* on your map. Draw a line from VISIGOTHS down to Rome.**
4. **The Vandals captured parts of France and North Africa. Find *"VANDALS"* next to France, and find Africa on your map. Draw lines from the VANDALS down to Rome.**
5. **When you finish, place the completed map in your history notebook.**

Activities

Choose from the following activities:

- [ ] Art: Draw Attila the Hun
- [ ] Research Skills: Ask the student to look up one or more related topics in a history encyclopedia or another reliable source. Read the entry together and look at the pictures. Topics could include *barbarians*, *the Huns*, *Attila the Hun*, and *Honoria*.

Art

DRAW ATTILA THE HUN

The great historian Edward Gibbon wrote this description of Attila the Hun in his book *The Decline and Fall of the Roman Empire*. Listen: "[Attila had] a large head, a swarthy complexion, small, deep-seated eyes, a flat nose, a few hairs in the place of a beard, broad shoulders, and a short square body, of a nervous strength, though of a disproportioned form. The haughty step and demeanor of the king of the Huns expressed the consciousness of his superiority above the rest of mankind; and he had a custom of fiercely rolling his eyes, as if he wished to enjoy the terror which he inspired."

Can you draw a picture of Attila that fits this description?

Additional History Reading

Note: Many of the previously recommended titles also contain sections on the barbarian invasions.

The Great and the Terrible: The World's Most Glorious and Notorious Rulers and How They Got their Names, by Joanne O'Sullivan (Running Press Kids, 2020). This book includes a short but engaging biography of Attila the Hun and other important rulers of the Ancient world like Hatshepsut (chapter fourteen), Cyrus the Great (chapter twenty-four), Alexander the Great (chapter twenty-eight), and Asoka the Great (chapter twenty-nine). (RA 1-2, IR 3-5)

Corresponding Literature Suggestions

Why Are You Calling Me a Barbarian? by Birgitta Petren (J. Paul Getty Museum Publications, 2000). A Roman child makes friends with the child of a barbarian. **Out of print, but worth looking for at your local library.** (RA)

CHAPTER FORTY-TWO
The End of Rome

The Last Roman Emperor

Read & Review

Read pages 383–385 in the text. Afterward, check the student's understanding by asking the questions below.

1. **Why did the Roman people call Romulus Augustus "Little disgrace"?** *They didn't want to obey a child who was also a barbarian.*
2. **What happened to him after he was removed from the throne?** *He was sent to live in another city.*
3. **Was there another Roman Emperor after him?** *No. He was the last Roman emperor.*
4. **What happened to the Western Roman Empire?** *It disappeared. Barbarians lived there.*
5. **The Eastern Roman Empire continued. What is the other name for that empire?** *The Byzantine Empire*

Narration Exercise

Tell me about the last Roman emperor.

The last Roman emperor was only a little boy. Nobody wanted to obey a kid! After he left his throne, there were no more emperors. That was the end of the Roman empire.

or

Tell me what happened to the Western Roman empire, and what happened to the Eastern Roman empire.

The Western Roman Empire ended and the barbarians lived there. The Eastern Roman Empire survived but it was called a different name. It was now the Byzantine Empire.

475–476 CE

Activities

Choose from the following activities:

- ☐ Game: Find the Emperor!
- ☐ Research Skills: Have the student look up a related topic in a history encyclopedia or another reliable source. Read the entry together and look at the pictures. Topics could include *the decline of Rome*, *The fall of Rome*, and *Romulus Augustus*.

Game

FIND THE EMPEROR!

The Last Roman Emperor is on the run, trying to evade capture by the invading barbarians! The barbarians must follow the emperor's trail through the wilderness and capture him before time runs out.

MATERIALS:

- a large outdoor play area, preferably with structures or trees
- 15 small tokens (craft sticks, pieces of paper or material, etc...)
- a timer

DIRECTIONS:

1. Choose one older (or trustworthy) student to be the Last Roman Emperor.
2. The emperor is given 15 small tokens (craft sticks, pieces of cloth, or paper slips) and a 3-minute head start.
3. All the players close their eyes except the emperor. The emperor runs into the forest or designated play area. As he runs, he must drop a token periodically along his trail (about every 10 feet). He can try to use the tokens to confuse the barbarian tracking team, so he might change directions, retrace his steps, jump over logs, etc... Once all of the tokens are dropped, he must find a place nearby to hide.
4. When the 3-minute head start ends, the rest of the players (the barbarians) begin searching for the emperor, using the trail of tokens he left behind. They are given a rough idea of where the emperor entered the wilderness but must rely on the tokens to track him.

5. If they find the emperor within a set time limit (3, 6, or 10 minutes depending on the size of the play area), the barbarians win. If time runs out and the emperor remains hidden, the emperor wins!
6. Pick up all of the tokens and start over with a new emperor. Remember, in the real story the emperor escaped and the barbarian Orestes installed his own son as a replacement emperor!

The Gifts of Rome

Read & Review

Read pages 385–387 in the text. Afterward, check the student's understanding by asking the questions below.

1. **Can you tell me three things that we got from the Romans?** *Books, swimming pools, coins, names of months, names of planets*
2. **Can you tell me two words that come from Latin?** *Flower, P.S., ship, library, family, refrigerator* (Names of months and planets are also acceptable.)

Narration Exercise

What are some ways the Roman Empire still influences us today?

The Roman Empire is gone, but we still use Roman words. We also use Roman things like books and swimming pools.

or

The Romans spoke Latin. Some of our English words come from Latin, like flower, navy, and ship.

Map Work: The Gifts of Rome (Student Page 137)

Read the instructions out loud to the student. After each step, pause and give time for the student to complete the task. Provide all necessary help.

1. **Open to Student Page 137 and tear it out.**
2. **Let's review what we've learned. On your map, can you identify the continents of *North America*, *South America*, *Europe*, *Asia*, and *Africa*?**
3. **Can you find the *Mediterranean Sea*?**
4. **Where is *Italy*?**
5. **Where is *Britain*?**
6. **Where is *China*?**
7. **Where is *India*?**
8. **Where is the *Nile River*?**
9. **Where is *Central America*?**

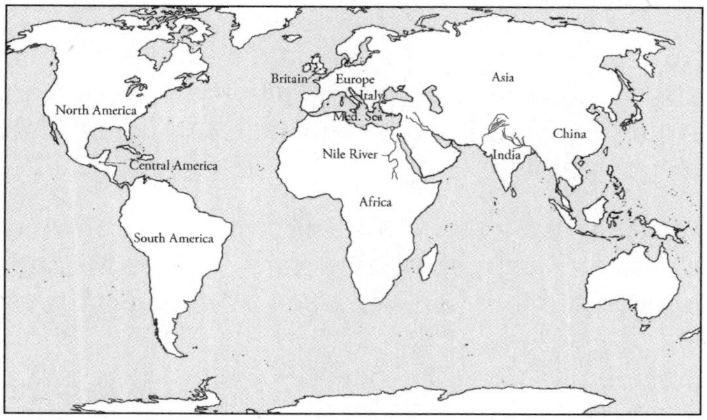

Activities

Choose from the following activities:

- [ ] Game: "The Gifts of Rome" Bingo
- [ ] Craft: Make a "Gifts of Rome" Collage
- [ ] End of Book Celebration: You have just completed your study of ancient history, and it is time to celebrate! If you like, invite some family and friends. You could make the invitations look like they came from the ancient past by writing on a hieroglyphic scroll (page 35) or a cuneiform tablet (page 334). Choose a costume to wear. You may have already created Hatshepsut's beard (page 122), no-sew Greek clothes (page 177), a Roman cuff bracelet (page 294), a centurion's helmet (page 294), or a Roman toga (page 329). Encourage guests to dress up as well (you could award a prize to the best dressed!). Create a gallery walk to display all of your saved projects from previous chapters. Choose one of your favorite recipes from the year to cook again. Choose one of your favorite games from the year to play again.

Game

"THE GIFTS OF ROME" BINGO

Pull out Student Page 138. Check off each box on the bingo card as you find the gift of Rome that's listed. It doesn't matter if you find it on purpose or by accident. You might see a Latin phrase on American money, or hear the name of a Roman god on a show you're watching. You might spot arches, fountains, or the names of planets around your neighborhood or town. There's no time limit, so take your time and enjoy finding the gifts of Rome!

Note to Instructor: Romans did not invent books, but they did develop the codex - the bound-book format we still use today. Instead of just finding a book (that's too easy), students should find a reference to Ancient Rome in a book in order to claim that bingo space.

You can also make this a field trip! Visit a town center or university campus with classically inspired architecture or drive around town (visit the library, a public pool, a park with a fountain, etc.). See how many gifts of Rome you can find!

Craft

MAKE A "GIFTS OF ROME" COLLAGE

Celebrate the many "gifts" we still use from Rome today with a colorful collage!

MATERIALS:

- poster board
- scissors
- glue
- magazines (or images printed from the internet)
- crayons or markers
- colored paper, fabric scraps, stickers, or other decorative materials (optional)

DIRECTIONS:

1. Lay out your poster board on a flat surface. Write "The Gifts of Rome" at the top.
2. Make a collage depicting the gifts of Rome. Using the list in *The Story of the World*, find and cut pictures depicting the gifts of Rome out of magazines or off the internet. You can also draw your own pictures, if you like. Arrange them in a visually appealing way. You can create sections for Roman architecture, food, technology, etc... Get creative and make it your own!

Classroom Adaptation: Set up a Roman Innovations Gallery Walk by having students display their Gifts of Rome collages around the room. Assign different student groups a category to focus on. For example, one group might focus on Roman influence on modern culture, one group might focus on Roman technology, and one group might focus on Latin words. Half the class starts as presenters, standing by their work to briefly explain their favorite Roman "gift," while the other half walks around, listening, and asking questions. After a set time, switch roles so everyone gets a chance to present and a chance to explore.

Additional History Reading

Note: Many of the previously recommended titles also contain sections on the barbarian invasions.

Ancient Rome: See Through History, by Simon James (Viking, 1992). Peel-away sheets reveal the insides of Roman buildings. **Out of print, but worth looking for at your local library**. RA)

Eyewitness: Ancient Rome by Dr. Simon James (Dk Children, 2022). This book is packed with short information bites and pictures of artifacts. It focuses on daily life in Rome, including going to the theater, arts, entertainment, life for children and families, crafts, cooking, and more. There is a two-page spread on the "Twilight of Rome" as well as links and references to resources for diving deeper into a study of Rome. (Also recommended for chapter twenty-two and thirty-one) (RA)

The Genius of the Romans: Innovations from Past Civilizations, by Izzi Howell (Crabtree Publishing, 2020). Each page has an easy-to-read summary of a different major innovation invented in Ancient Rome. (IR 3-6)

Corresponding Literature Suggestions

Cattus Petasatus: The Cat in the Hat in Latin, by Dr. Seuss and Jennifer Morish Tunberg (Bolchazy Carducci, 2000). Just for fun, look through this book together and see if you can spot familiar words that are almost the same in Latin as in English. English borrowed those words from Latin! **Out of print, but worth looking for at your local library.** (RA)

Quomodo Invidiosulus Nomine Grinchus Christi Natalem Abrogaverit: How the Grinch Stole Christmas in Latin, by Dr. Seuss and Terence O. Tunberg (Bolchazy Carducci, 1998). Try the same experiment with this familiar book. (RA)

APPENDIX ONE

Instructions for optional creative writing prompts

Creative writing prompts are not for every kid! Only do these if your student enjoys creative writing. Do not require it.

For younger students: read your student the creative writing prompt and have them verbally narrate their answer to you. Write down the first sentence of their narration (modifying when necessary to simplify or shorten). Have your student carefully copy the model sentence onto a separate sheet of paper (or a copy of Student Page 1) and place it in their history notebook.

For older students: have students write down their answers to the creative writing prompt. This is just for fun! Don't worry about correcting grammar.

If students like, have them draw an illustration to accompany their creative writing piece.

APPENDIX TWO

Instructions for optional memory work activities

Throughout first grade, students should aim to memorize one list of twenty facts or two lists of ten facts across all of their school subjects. A second grader should aim for two lists of fifteen to twenty items. Third and fourth graders should aim for three lists of twelve to eighteen items. You can always do more if your student enjoys memory work!

We strongly recommend that you choose your own memory work based on your student's interests. For example, if students are particularly interested in ancient technology, look up and have them memorize a list of ten important ancient inventions and where the inventions came from. If they show a particular interest in Hammurabi, have them memorize a few of Hammurabi's laws.

Once you have decided what to memorize, experiment with different fun ways to review the information. You can come up with your own creative ideas or try one of the activities below:

1. Have students recite their memory work while jumping up and down to a beat.
2. Write the memory work down on your own paper.
3. Have students recite memory work while catching and throwing a ball. Give a clue—for example, the title of an Egyptian god—throw the ball, and have them say back the name of the god before catching the ball.
4. Create a tune and sing out the memory work.
5. Create illustrated flash cards.
6. Create a matching game.

If you do not choose your own memory lists, you can choose from the memory work lists provided in the Instructor Guide. For each list of memory work in the Instructor Guide, there is an accompanying reference sheet for students in the Student Workbook.

Build Your Own Memory Work Routine

If you already have a memory work system in place, simply add in your history selections. If not, a memory work routine might look like this (routines will vary based on the students' ages and the length of the material):

Stage One: Start by reading the memory work out loud daily until students are very familiar with the material.

Stage Two: Once students are familiar with the material, incorporate activities to practice and test their memory two to three times a week.

Stage Three: After students have fully memorized the material, shift to review. Start by reviewing once a week, then gradually decrease the frequency to once a month or once a quarter to help keep it in long-term memory.

APPENDIX THREE
Supplies

The supply lists in each chapter tell you what is needed to complete each activity as written. For most activities, you don't need to use the exact materials listed and can substitute what you have on hand. For instance, if you don't have craft dowels, grab wooden barbeque skewers or the chopsticks from your last takeout order. Fresh out of googly eyes? Draw eyes on paper and cut them out. Encourage students to be resourceful and think of their own substitutions — and improvements! — for activities.

Frequently used supplies include:

- Adhesives: glue, glue stick, tape
- Coloring materials: crayons, colored pencils, markers, paint, paintbrushes
- Craft sticks: craft sticks, dowels, lollipop sticks, wooden sticks
- Cutting tools: scissors, hole punch
- Embellishments: fabric scraps, ribbon, yarn
- Found and recycled materials: Cardboard tubes, boxes, plastic containers
- Paper: paper, construction paper, stiff paper or cardboard
- Ruler
- Scissors
- Toys: Building bricks, blocks, or other building toys; stuffed animals

Special note on Chapter 4, Make a Chicken Mummy: this activity uses common items such as salt and baking powder, but it uses a large amount of them and takes several weeks to complete. If you want to mummify a chicken, it's helpful to read through all of the instructions ahead of time.

So that you can plan ahead, here are some additional supplies and the corresponding chapters:

Cardboard & cardboard boxes

- Chapter 4, Make a Model: Sugar Cube Step Pyramid (flat cardboard for base, at least 5″x5″; a cake board is easy and works well but isn't necessary)
- Chapter 10, Art: Draw Your Own Pictograms (white cardboard OR construction paper)
- Chapter 12, Role Play: Bull Jumping Practice (medium cardboard box OR stuffed animal)
- Chapter 14, Role Play: Make One of Hatshepsut's Monuments (cardboard boxes OR other materials)
- Chapter 16, Craft: Make a Mycenaean Shield (large piece of cardboard, ideally about the same height as the student)
- Chapter 28, Role Play: Build Your Own City (multiple cardboard boxes OR building bricks)
- Chapter 28, Role Play: Make a Roman Chariot and Race! (cardboard box large enough to fit around student)

- Chapter 33, Make a Model: The Great Wall of China (a variety of cardboard boxes OR cardboard building blocks)
- Chapter 34, Art: Design Your Own Flag (one piece approximately 1″x12″ and a second piece approximately 3″x24″)
- Chapter 35, Craft: Constantine's Shield (one piece approximately 16″x16″ or bigger)

Clay (see salt dough recipe in Appendix Five)

- Chapter 1, Make a Model & Science: Shaduf (optional)
- Chapter 2, Make a Model: Nile River (optional)
- Chapter 3, Storytelling & Craft: Make Cuneiform Tablets
- Chapter 5, Craft & Role Play: Make a Sumerian Cylinder Seal
- Chapter 9, Make a Model: Mohenjo-Daro Dwelling
- Chapter 12, Science & Make a Model: Erupting Volcano
- Chapter 13, Craft: Make an Incense Holder
- Chapter 20, Role Play: Write on an Athenian Wax Tablet (non-hardening OR lard)
- Chapter 21, Craft: Make an Olympus Family Tree (OR sand OR small rocks)
- Chapter 22, Craft: Make a Saturnalia Gift Out of Clay
- Chapter 27, Make a Model & Art: Build Greek Columns Out of Clay
- Chapter 30, Art: Build the Olmec Heads out of Clay
- Chapter 31, Make a Model: Roman Archway and Aqueduct
- Chapter 35, Craft: Mint Your Own Coins Out of Clay

Paint (specialty paint)

- Chapter 6, Craft: Make Joseph's Coat of Many Colors (fabric paint OR markers OR tempera paint OR permanent markers)
- Chapter 13, Craft: Make a Golden Bracelet (gold paint)
- Chapter 13, Craft: Make an Incense Holder (paint; optional gold or gilded paint)
- Chapter 16, Craft: Make a Mycenaean Helmet (paint; optional bronze paint)
- Chapter 30, Art: Draw a Nazca Line Drawing (pan watercolor paints)
- Chapter 32, Craft: Make a Centurion's Helmet (optional silver paint suitable for plastic)
- Chapter 35, Craft: Make Your Own Coins Out of Clay (copper, silver, and gold metallic paint)
- Chapter 38, Host a Celtic Feast (optional blue body paint)

Papier-mâché Paste

- Chapter 14, Craft: Make an Egyptian Death Mask (this can be purchased or made with the recipe in the chapter)

APPENDIX FOUR
Activities by Type

If you love certain kinds of activities, the category lists on this page will let you easily find them. Some chapters have more than one section, so the section name is used after the chapter number. Note that some activities will appear in more than one category.

Activity Page

These engaging activity pages are perfect for a quick challenge!

- Chapter 5, Sargon and the Akkadians: Sumerian Inventions Word Search
- Chapter 6, Joseph Goes to Egypt: The Jewish People Word Search
- Chapter 7, Hammurabi's Code: Name That Place Crossword Puzzle
- Chapter 12, King Minos and the Minotaur: The Minotaur's Maze
- Chapter 19, Greece Gets an Alphabet: Write Your Name in Greek Letters
- Chapter 21, The Golden Apple: Greek Gods & Goddesses Word Search
- Chapter 31, The Roman Gladiators: Match Each Gladiator to Their Weapon!

Art

- Chapter 1, The First Nomads: Making a Cave Painting
- Chapter 7, Hammurabi's Code: Make Your Own Law Code Stele
- Chapter 8, The Story of Gilgamesh: Draw a Picture of Enkidu
- Chapter 10, The Pictograms of Ancient China: Draw Your Own Pictograms
- Chapter 19, The Stories of Homer: Illustrate or Dramatize One of Homer's Stories
- Chapter 21, The Golden Apple: Draw a Home for the Greek Gods
- Chapter 22, Romulus and Remus: Illustrate a Story Book
- Chapter 23, The Hanging Gardens of Babylon: Draw the Hanging Gardens of Babylon
- Chapter 26, Calligraphy in China: Practice Chinese Calligraphy
- Chapter 26, Confucius: China's Wise Teacher: The Golden Rule Poster
- Chapter 27, The Greeks Fight Each Other: Build Greek Columns Out of Clay
- Chapter 28, Alexander's Invasions: Design Your Own Lighthouse
- Chapter 30, The Nazca Drawings: Draw the Nazca Lines; Chalk Nazca Lines
- Chapter 30, The Heads of the Olmecs: Build the Olmec Heads Out of Clay
- Chapter 33, The First Emperor's Grave: Draw or Sculpt the Terra Cotta Warriors
- Chapter 34, Caesar Fights the Celts: Design Your Own Flag
- Chapter 36, A Prophet Named Jesus: Nativity Picture Study
- Chapter 37, Christians in the Catacombs: Draw a Secret Symbol
- Chapter 38, The British Rebellion: Design and Draw a Celtic Border
- Chapter 39, The End of the Han Dynasty: Yellow Turban Recruitment Poster
- Chapter 40, The Yamato of Japan: Design a Kimono
- Chapter 41, Attila the Hun: Draw Attila the Hun

Celebration

Celebrations will be listed in the last section for each chapter, and often include completing and combining multiple activities. It's easier to prepare if you read the Celebration activity first.

- Chapter 19, Greece Gets Civilized Again
- Chapter 25, The Aryans of India
- Chapter 30, The People of the Americas
- Chapter 35, Caesar, Ruler of Rome

- Chapter 38, The British Rebellion
- Chapter 39, Troubles in China
- Chapter 42, The End of Rome: End of Book Celebration!

Classroom Option

Don't feel limited by the activities listed here; many of the other activities can be used in the classroom! Low prep ideas are marked LP. Email support@welltrainedmind.com for licensing information.

- Each chapter includes at least one map and coloring page (LP)
- Each lesson includes related topics to look up in a history encyclopedia or other reliable source (LP)
- Each optional mini-lesson includes a creative writing prompt (LP)
- Check out our field trip ideas (in-person and virtual)
- Explore our Additional Reading suggestions to find new classroom favorites
- Introduction, What is History?: Make a Timeline of Your Life
- Introduction, What is Archaeology?: A Dirty Dig!
- Chapter 1, The First Nomads: Making a Cave Painting; Make a Shaduf
- Chapter 3, The First Writing: Make a Hieroglyphic Scroll
- Chapter 5, Sargon and the Akkadians: Sumerian Inventions Word Search (LP); Make a Sumerian Cylinder Seal
- Chapter 6, God Speaks to Abraham: Trade in Haran
- Chapter 6, Joseph Goes to Egypt: The Jewish People Word Search (LP)
- Chapter 7, Hammurabi's Code: Name That Place Crossword Puzzle (LP); Make Your Own Law Code Stele; Hammurabi's Court (LP)
- Chapter 8, Shamshi-Adad, King of the Whole World: Dictator for the Day (LP)
- Chapter 8, The Story of Gilgamesh: Draw a Picture of Enkidu (LP); Compose Your Own Fairy Tale (LP)
- Chapter 9, The Mystery of Mohenjo-Daro: What Happened at Mohenjo-Daro? (LP)
- Chapter 10, Lei Zu and the Silkworm: Life Cycle of a Silkworm; The Story of Lei Zu (LP)
- Chapter 10, The Pictograms of Ancient China: Draw Your Own Pictograms (LP)
- Chapter 10, Farming in Ancient China: Sequencing Events (LP)
- Chapter 11, Anansi and Turtle: Act Out an Anansi the Spider Story (LP)
- Chapter 12, Bulljumpers and Sailors: Bull-Jumping Practice (LP)
- Chapter 12, King Minos and the Minotaur: The Minotaur's Maze (LP)
- Chapter 13, Egypt Invades Nubia: Make a Golden Bracelet
- Chapter 13, The Middle Kingdom of Egypt: Make an Incense Holder
- Chapter 13, The Hyksos Invade Egypt: Make an Egyptian War Chariot
- Chapter 14, Amenhotep and King Tut: Be an Archaeologist!
- Chapter 15, The Baby Moses: Will It Float? Science Challenge
- Chapter 16, The Greek Dark Ages: Tell a Story Without Writing (LP); Iron vs. Bronze (LP)
- Chapter 17, The Founding of Carthage: Sequencing Events (LP); Queen Dido's Perimeter Trick (LP)
- Chapter 18, The Library of Nineveh: Record a Family Story (LP)
- Chapter 19, Greece Gets an Alphabet: The Greek Alphabet; Write Your Name with Greek Letters (LP)
- Chapter 19, The Stories of Homer: Make a Simple Cyclops Puppet
- Chapter 19, The Stories of Homer: Illustration or Dramatic Reading (LP)
- Chapter 19, The First Olympic Games: Host the Olympic Games
- Chapter 20, Life in Athens: Vote at an Agora
- Chapter 21, The Golden Apple: Greek Gods and Goddesses Word Search (LP); The Greek Gods; Draw A Home for the Greek Gods (LP)
- Chapter 22, Romulus and Remus: Illustrate a Story Book
- Chapter 22, The Power of Rome: Make a Saturnalia Gift Out of Clay

- Chapter 23, Nebuchadnezzar's Madness: Nebuchadnezzar's Charades (LP)
- Chapter 23, The Hanging Gardens of Babylon: The Seven Wonders of the Ancient World (LP); Draw The Hanging Gardens of Babylon (LP)
- Chapter 24, Cyrus the Great: Make the Persian Ruler's Silver Plate
- Chapter 25, The Castes of Ancient India: Make a Rakhi
- Chapter 26, Calligraphy in China: Practice Chinese Calligraphy (LP when using pens/ markers)
- Chapter 26, Confucius: China's Wise Teacher: Confucius's Teachings (LP); The Golden Rule Poster (LP)
- Chapter 27, Greece's War with Persia: Run a Marathon! (LP)
- Chapter 27, The Greeks Fight Each Other: Build Greek Columns out of Clay
- Chapter 28, Philip and His Son: Bucephalus Obstacle Course (LP); Tie a Gordian Knot (LP)
- Chapter 28, Alexander's Invasions: Design Your Own Lighthouse (LP); Alexander Mosaic Picture Study
- Chapter 28, The Death of Alexander: Sequencing Events (LP)
- Chapter 29, The Empire United: Remind Yourself To Be Kind (LP); Mindfulness (LP)
- Chapter 30, The Nazca Drawings: Draw a Nazca Line Drawing (LP); Chalk Nazca Lines
- Chapter 30, The Heads of the Olmecs: Build the Olmec Heads out of Clay; No Hands Ball
- Chapter 31, The Roman Gods: Greek vs Roman Gods; Proserpine's Seasons
- Chapter 31, The Roman Gladiators: Match Each Gladiator to Their Weapon! (LP)
- Chapter 31, The Gladiator School: Gladiator Training School
- Chapter 32, The Punic Wars: Sacred Chickens or Charging Elephants (LP)
- Chapter 33, The First Emperor and the Great Wall: How Long Was the Wall?
- Chapter 33, The First Emperor's Grave: Draw or Sculpt the Terra Cotta Warriors (LP); Latitude and Longitude (LP)
- Chapter 33, The Han Dynasty and the Silk Road: Silk Road Senses
- Chapter 34, The Consuls of Rome: Triumvirate Tug of War
- Chapter 34, Caesar and the Senate: Vote in the Roman Senate (LP)
- Chapter 34, Caesar Fights the Celts: Design Your Own Flag
- Chapter 35, The Death of Caesar: Memorize the Roman Numerals (LP)
- Chapter 35, Augustus Caesar: Make a Roman Toga; Run a Roman Hair Salon; Run a Thermopolium
- Chapter 36, Herod, "The Great": Herod's Building Projects (LP)
- Chapter 36, A Prophet Named Jesus: Census Activity (LP); Nativity Picture Study
- Chapter 36, The Destruction of the Temple: The Destruction of the Temple (LP)
- Chapter 37, Nero, the Evil Emperor: Nero's Legacy; Silly Laws (LP)
- Chapter 37, Christians in the Catacombs: Draw a Secret Symbol (LP)
- Chapter 38, The British Rebellion: Design and Draw a Celtic Border (LP)
- Chapter 38, Rome Divided in Two: North, South, East, West (LP); Defend the Empire! (LP)
- Chapter 39, The End of the Han Dynasty: Sequencing Events (LP); Yellow Turban Recruitment Poster (LP)
- Chapter 39, The Three Kingdoms, The Jin, and the Sixteen Kingdoms: Memorize the First Dynasties of China (LP); Chinese Schoolyard Games (LP)
- Chapter 40, The Three Kingdoms of Korea: Read the Lesson with Character Cards (LP); Chicken Fight (LP)
- Chapter 40, The Yamato of Japan: Design a Kimono (LP)
- Chapter 41, Stilicho, Roman and Barbarian: Stilicho Says (LP)
- Chapter 41, The Coming of the Visigoths: Barbarian Tag
- Chapter 41, Attila the Hun: Draw Attila the Hun (LP)
- Chapter 42, The Last Roman Emperor: Find the Emperor! (LP)

Cooking

- Chapter 1, The First Nomads: Lizard Stew
- Chapter 11, Ancient Peoples of West Africa: African Recipes
- Chapter 11, Anansi and the Make-Believe Food: African Food Taste Tests
- Chapter 19, The First Olympic Games: Host a Greek Feast
- Chapter 25, Siddhartha: Indian Recipes
- Chapter 26, Confucius: China's Wise Teacher: Chinese Tea
- Chapter 27, Greek's War with Persia: Make an Ice Cream Boat
- Chapter 30, Rabbit Shoots the Sun: Make Corn Cakes
- Chapter 31, The Roman Builders: Make (and Eat) a Roman Road
- Chapter 35, Augustus Caesar: Run a Thermopolium (Roman take-out restaurant)
- Chapter 36, The Destruction of the Temple: Make Hanukkah Latkes
- Chapter 37, Nero, the Evil Emperor: Host a Roman Banquet
- Chapter 38, The British Rebellion: Host a Celtic Feast
- Chapter 39, The Three Kingdoms, The Jin, and the Sixteen Kingdoms: Chinese Dumplings
- Chapter 40, The Three Kingdoms of Korea: Japchae
- Chapter 42, The Gifts of Rome: Choose One of Your Favorite Recipes to Cook Again

Craft

- Chapter 2, Two Kingdoms Become One: Make Your Own Double Crown of Egypt
- Chapter 3, The First Writing: Make Cuneiform Tablets; Make a Hieroglyphic Scroll
- Chapter 4, Making Mummies: Make Scented Oil
- Chapter 5, Sargon and the Akkadians: Make a Sumerian Cylinder Seal
- Chapter 6, Joseph Goes to Egypt: Make Joseph's Coat of Many Colors
- Chapter 11, Anansi and Turtle: Make Anansi the Spider; Make Anansi's Friend, Turtle
- Chapter 12, King Minos and the Minotaur: Build Your Own Maze
- Chapter 13, The Middle Kingdom of Egypt: Make a Golden Bracelet; Make an Incense Holder
- Chapter 14, The General and the Woman Pharaoh: Make Hatsheput's False Beard
- Chapter 14, Amenhotep and King Tut: Make an Egyptian Death Mask
- Chapter 15, The Baby Moses: Make Baby Moses' Basket
- Chapter 15, The Exodus from Egypt: Make a Red Sea Diorama
- Chapter 16, The Mycenaeans: Make a Mycenaean Shield
- Chapter 17, Phoenician Traders: Faux Colored Glass; Make a Colored Pasta Necklace (requires making purple dye from Science section first)
- Chapter 19, Greece Gets an Alphabet: Make a Greek Loom
- Chapter 19, The Stories of Homer: Make a Simple Cyclops Puppet
- Chapter 19, The First Olympic Games: Make Greek Instruments; Make an Olympic Wreath
- Chapter 20, Life in Sparta: Make Spartan and Athenian Paper Dolls
- Chapter 21, The Golden Apple: Make an Olympus Family Tree
- Chapter 22, The Power of Rome: Make the Fasces; Make a Saturnalia Gift Out of Clay
- Chapter 24, Cyrus the Great: Make the Persian Ruler's Silver Plate
- Chapter 25, Life on the Ganges River: Shiva and the Ganges River
- Chapter 25, The Castes of Ancient India: Make a Rakhi
- Chapter 30, The Nazca Drawings: Make a Seed Mosaic Map
- Chapter 31, The Roman Gods: Make an Olympus Family Tree; Proserpine's Seasons
- Chapter 32, The Punic Wars: Make a Cuff Bracelet; Make a Centurion's Helmet
- Chapter 34, The Consuls of Rome: Make a Crown of Leaves
- Chapter 34, Caesar and the Senate: Make a Roman Mosaic
- Chapter 35, Caesar and Cleopatra: Mint Your Own Coins Out of Clay

- Chapter 35, Augustus Caesar: Make a Roman Toga
- Chapter 36, The Destruction of the Temple: The Destruction of the Temple; Make Your Own Dreidel
- Chapter 38, The Emperor Is a Christian: Make Constantine's Shield
- Chapter 42, The Gifts of Rome: Make a "Gifts of Rome" Collage

Field Trip

Field trips usually have a virtual option listed as well.

- Chapter 10, Farming in Ancient China: Local Farm
- Chapter 12, Bull-Jumpers and Sailors: Marina
- Chapter 17, Phoenician Traders: Glass Studio
- Chapter 18, The Library of Nineveh: Library Challenge
- Chapter 23, The Hanging Gardens of Babylon: Botanical Garden
- Chapter 25, The Castes of Ancient India: Hindu Temple
- Chapter 25, Siddhartha: Buddhist Temple
- Chapter 27, The Greeks Fight Each Other: The Parthenon Replica
- Chapter 31, The Roman Builders: Art Museum with Roman Artifacts
- Chapter 37, Christians in the Catacombs: Pedestrian Tunnel or Cavern
- Chapter 42, The Gifts of Rome: Town Center or University Campus

Game

- Chapter 5, Sargon and the Akkadians:The Royal Game of Ur
- Chapter 8, Shamshi-Adad, King of the Whole World: Assyrian Battle!
- Chapter 18, The Library of Nineveh: Library of Nineveh Scavenger Hunt
- Chapter 24, Cyrus the Great: Mesopotamian Conquest Board Game
- Chapter 25, Life on the Ganges River: Catch Ganga!
- Chapter 25, The Castes of Ancient India: Play Tiger Hunt
- Chapter 29, The Jataka Tales: Snakes and Ladders
- Chapter 30, The Heads of the Olmecs: No Hands Ball
- Chapter 31, The Roman Gods: Greek vs Roman Gods
- Chapter 33, The Han Dynasty and the Silk Road: Silk Road Senses
- Chapter 34, Caesar is Kidnaped: Ransom Caesar!
- Chapter 34, The Consuls of Rome: Triumvirate Tug of War
- Chapter 38, Rome Divided in Two: Roman Collapse; Defend the Empire!
- Chapter 39, The Three Kingdoms, The Jin, and the Sixteen Kingdoms: Chinese Playground Games
- Chapter 40, The Three Kingdoms of Korea: Chicken Fight
- Chapter 41, Stilicho, Roman and Barbarian: Stilicho Says
- Chapter 41, The Coming of the Visigoths: Barbarian Tag
- Chapter 42, The Last Roman Emperor: Find the Emperor!
- Chapter 42, The Gifts of Rome: The Gifts of Rome Bingo

Geography

- Map work in every chapter; 43 maps total
- Check the reading lists for great books that cover the geography of various regions
- Chapter 22, Romulus and Remus: Make a Salt Dough Map of Italy
- Chapter 33, The First Emperor and the Great Wall: How Long Was the Wall?
- Chapter 33, The First Emperor's Grave: Latitude and Longitude
- Chapter 38, Rome Divided in Two: North, South, East, West

Low Prep/No Prep

- All of the optional mini-lessons are low prep
- Most of the field trip suggestions have a low prep virtual option
- Chapter 1, The First Nomads: Build Your Own Hut
- Chapter 2, The Gods of Egypt: Memorize the Gods of Egypt
- Chapter 4, Making Mummies: Make Scented Oil

- Chapter 4, Egyptian Pyramids: Step Pyramid (with toy building bricks)
- Chapter 5, Sargon and the Akkadians: Sumerian Inventions Word Search
- Chapter 6, Joseph Goes to Egypt: Memorize The Twelve Sons of Jacob or The Twelve Tribes of Israel; The Jewish People Word Search
- Chapter 7, Hammurabi's Code: Name That Place Crossword Puzzle; Court Roleplay
- Chapter 8, Shamshi-Adad: Dictator of the Day Roleplay; Assyrian Battle
- Chapter 8, The Story of Gilgamesh: Draw Enkidu; Compose Your Own Fairytale
- Chapter 9, The First Cities of India, The River Road: Memory Work: Rivers and Their Civilizations
- Chapter 9, The Mystery of Mohenjo-Daro: What Happened at Mohenjo-Daro?
- Chapter 10, Lei Zu and the Silkworm: Life Cycle of a Silkworm; The Story of Lei Zu
- Chapter 10, Pictograms: Draw Your Own Pictograms (with pens or markers)
- Chapter 10, Farming in Ancient China: Sequencing Activity
- Chapter 11, Anansi and Turtle: Act Out a Story (using stuffed animals)
- Chapter 12, Bull Jumpers and Sailors: Bull-Jumping Practice
- Chapter 12, King Minos and the Minotaur: The Minotaur's Maze
- Chapter 14, The General and the Woman Pharaoh: Make One of Hatshepsut's Monuments
- Chapter 14, Amenhotep and King Tut: Pharaoh for Dinner
- Chapter 16, The Greek Dark Ages: Tell a Story Without Writing; Iron vs. Bronze
- Chapter 17, The Founding of Carthage: Sequencing Events; Queen Dido's Perimeter Trick
- Chapter 18, Ashurbanipal's Attack: Make an Assyrian Siege Tower
- Chapter 18, The Library of Nineveh: Record a Family Story; Library of Nineveh Scavenger Hunt
- Chapter 19, Greece Gets an Alphabet: The Greek Alphabet; Write Your Name with Greek Letters
- Chapter 19, The Stories of Homer: Make a Simple Cyclops Puppet; Illustration or Dramatic Reading
- Chapter 20, Life in Athens: Write on an Athenian Wax Tablet; Vote at an Agora
- Chapter 21, The Golden Apple: Greek Gods and Goddesses Word Search; Memorize the Greek Gods; The Golden Apple: Draw a Home for the Greek Gods
- Chapter 22, Romulus and Remus: Illustrate a Storybook
- Chapter 23, Nebuchadnezzar's Madness: Nebuchadnezzar's Charades
- Chapter 23, The Hanging Gardens of Babylon: The Seven Wonders of the Ancient World; Draw the Hanging Gardens of Babylon
- Chapter 24, A New Empire: Persian Puppets Storytelling (using stuffed animals)
- Chapter 24, Cyrus the Great: Make the Persian Ruler's Silver Plate; Play Mesopotamian Conquest!
- Chapter 25, Life on the Ganges River: Catch Ganga!
- Chapter 25, The Castes of Ancient India: Tiger Hunt
- Chapter 26, Calligraphy in China: Practice Chinese Calligraphy (using pens or markers)
- Chapter 26, Confucius, China's Wise Teacher: Chinese Tea (using common tea); Storytelling; The Golden Rule Poster
- Chapter 27, Greece's War with Persia: Run a Marathon!
- Chapter 28, Philip and His Son: Bucephalus Obstacle Course; Tie a Gordian Knot
- Chapter 28, Alexander's Invasions: Build Your Own City; Alexander Mosaic Picture Study
- Chapter 28, The Death of Alexander: Sequencing Events; Eleven Minutes to Conquer; Sharing
- Chapter 29, The Empire United: Remind Yourself to Be Kind; Mindfulness
- Chapter 29, The Jataka Tales: Pictures on the Moon
- Chapter 30, The Nazca Drawings: Draw a Nazca Line Drawing

- Chapter 31, The Roman Gods: Greek vs Roman Gods
- Chapter 31, The Roman Gladiators: Match Each Gladiator to Their Weapon!
- Chapter 32, The Punic Wars: Sacred Chickens or Charging Elephants
- Chapter 33, The First Emperor and the Great Wall: How Long Was the Wall?
- Chapter 33, The First Emperor's Grave: Draw/Sculpt the Terra Cotta Warriors; Latitude and Longitude
- Chapter 34, Caesar is Kidnaped: Ransom Caesar
- Chapter 34, Caesar and the Senate: Vote in the Roman Senate
- Chapter 35, The Death of Caesar: Memorize the Roman Numerals
- Chapter 36, Herod the Great: Herod's Building Projects
- Chapter 36, A Prophet Named Jesus: The Census; Nativity Picture Study; A Night At the Stable
- Chapter 36, The Destruction of the Temple
- Chapter 37, Nero the Evil Emperor: Silly Laws
- Chapter 37, Christians in the Catacombs: Draw a Secret Symbol; Read the Chapter in Your Own "Catacomb"
- Chapter 38, The British Rebellion: Design and Draw a Celtic Border
- Chapter 38, Rome Divided in Two: North, South, East, West
- Chapter 39, The End of the Han Dynasty: Sequencing Events; Yellow Turban Recruitment Poster
- Chapter 39, The Three Kingdoms, The Jin, and the Sixteen Kingdoms: Memorize the First Dynasties of China ; Chinese Playground Games
- Chapter 40, The Three Kingdoms of Korea: Read the Lesson with Character Cards; Chicken Fight
- Chapter 40, The Yamato of Japan: Design a Kimono
- Chapter 41, Stilicho, Roman and Barbarian: Stilicho Says
- Chapter 41, The Coming of the Visigoths: Barbarian Tag
- Chapter 41, Attila the Hun: Draw Attila the Hun
- Chapter 42, The Last Roman Emperor: Find the Emperor!

Make a Model

- Chapter 1, The First Nomads Become Farmers: Shaduf
- Chapter 2, The Gods of Egypt: Nile River
- Chapter 4, Egyptian Pyramids: Sugar Cube Step Pyramid
- Chapter 9, The Mystery of Mohenjo-Daro: Mohenjo-Daro Dwelling
- Chapter 12, The Mysterious End of the Minoans: Erupting Volcano
- Chapter 12, The Hyksos Invade Egypt: Egyptian War Chariot
- Chapter 18, Ashurbanipal's Attack: Make an Assyrian Siege Tower
- Chapter 22, Romulus and Remus: Make a Salt Dough Map of Italy
- Chapter 27, Greek's War with Persia: Make an Ice Cream Boat
- Chapter 27, The Greeks Fight Each Other: Build Greek Columns Out of Clay
- Chapter 31, The Roman Builders: Roman Archway and Aqueduct; Make (and Eat) a Roman Road
- Chapter 33, The First Emperor and the Great Wall: The Great Wall of China

Math

- Chapter 6, Joseph Goes to Egypt: Seven Years of Famine
- Chapter 17, The Founding of Carthage: Queen Dido's Perimeter Trick
- Chapter 36, A Prophet Named Jesus: Census Activity

Memory Work

- Chapter 2, The Gods of Egypt: The Gods of Egypt
- Chapter 6, Joseph Goes to Egypt: The Twelve Sons of Jacob or The Twelve Tribes of Israel
- Chapter 9, The River-Road: Rivers and Their Civilizations
- Chapter 19, Greece Gets an Alphabet: The Greek Alphabet

- Chapter 21, The Golden Apple: The Greek Gods
- Chapter 23, The Hanging Gardens of Babylon: The Seven Wonders of the Ancient World
- Chapter 31, The Roman Gods: Greek vs Roman Gods
- Chapter 35, The Death of Caesar: Roman Numerals
- Chapter 39, Troubles in China: First Dynasties of China

Movement

Keep students energized and focused with these active and out-of-seat activities!

- Introduction, What is Archaeology?: A Dirty Dig!
- Chapter 6, God Speaks to Abraham: Trade in Haran
- Chapter 8, Shamshi-Adad, King of the Whole World: Dictator for the Day
- Chapter 12, Bull-Jumpers and Sailors: Bull Jumping Practice
- Chapter 14, Amenhotep and King Tut: Be an Archaeologist!
- Chapter 16, The Greek Dark Ages: Iron vs. Bronze
- Chapter 18, The Library of Nineveh: Scavenger Hunt
- Chapter 19, The Stories of Homer: Simple Cyclops Puppet (with stuffed animals or action figures)
- Chapter 19, The First Olympics: Host the Olympic Games
- Chapter 23, Nebuchadnezzar's Madness: Nebuchadnezzar's Charades
- Chapter 25, Life on the Ganges River: Catch Ganga!
- Chapter 25, The Castes of Ancient India: Tiger Hunt
- Chapter 27, Greece's War with Persia: Run a Marathon!
- Chapter 28, Philip and His Son: Bucephalus Obstacle Course
- Chapter 28, The Death of Alexander: Eleven Minutes to Conquer!
- Chapter 30, The Heads of the Olmecs: No Hands Ball
- Chapter 31, The Gladiator School: Make a Roman Chariot; Gladiator Training School
- Chapter 34, The Consuls of Rome: Triumvirate Tug of War
- Chapter 34, Caesar and the Senate: Vote in the Roman Senate
- Chapter 34, Caesar Fights the Celts: Design (and defend!) Your Own Flag
- Chapter 38, Rome Divided in Two: North, South, East, West; Defend the Empire!
- Chapter 39, The Three Kingdoms, The Jin, and the Sixteen Kingdoms: Chinese Playground Games
- Chapter 40, The Three Kingdoms of Korea: Chicken Fight
- Chapter 41, Stilicho, Roman and Barbarian: Stilicho Says
- Chapter 41, The Coming of the Visigoths: Barbarian Tag
- Chapter 42, The Last Roman Emperor: Find the Emperor!

Picture Study

- Chapter 28, Alexander's Invasions: Alexander Mosaic
- Chapter 36, A Prophet Named Jesus: Nativity Picture Study

Research Skills

- Chapters 1-42 all have prompts for looking up relevant topics in a history encyclopedia or other reliable source

APPENDIX FIVE

Salt Dough Recipe

This recipe makes about 1lb of salt dough.

Note to Instructor: Salt dough is a budget-friendly alternative to air-dry clay. It can be molded, shaped, and dried to create sturdy craft projects, wherever air-dry clay is called for. Just remember that the final product may be a bit grainier and more brittle than if you had used air-dry clay. It may also be a bit more difficult to paint, as salt dough absorbs moisture. Because it can absorb moisture over time, projects may not last as long.

INGREDIENTS:

- 2 cups all-purpose flour
- 1 cup salt
- ¾ cup water (add more if needed)

DIRECTIONS:

1. In a mixing bowl, combine the flour and salt.
2. Gradually add the water, stirring until a dough forms.
3. Knead the dough for about 5 minutes until it becomes smooth and pliable. If too dry, add a tiny bit more water; if too sticky, add a little more flour.
4. Shape the dough as desired.
5. If air-drying, leave the pieces in a dry place for 24-48 hours.
6. For faster drying, bake at 200°F (93°C) for 2-3 hours or until hardened.

APPENDIX SIX
Suggested Schedules

The main text has 42 chapters, split into 98 sections. One way to divide up the program into a 36-week school year is to complete one chapter per week on most weeks, and choose seven weeks where you will double-up chapters. We recommend pairing:

1. Chapters 2 and 3
2. Chapters 5 and 6
3. Chapters 7 and 8
4. Chapters 15 and 16
5. Chapters 17 and 18
6. Chapters 21 and 22
7. Chapters 23 and 24

OR if you complete roughly 3 subsections a week, you can get through the program in one school year (with time to spare to slow down where children are particularly interested in a topic).

There is one map work activity in each chapter. Complete as much map work as you can, without stressing too much about it.

Each subsection has "Read & Review" questions, a narration exercise, and optional interactive activities. We recommend completing either the "Read & Review" questions OR the narration exercise for each subsection. You do not need to complete both. Each exercise requires different, equally important skills, so we recommend alternating between these two types of review exercises.

All other activities are optional, but they make history fun and interactive, and thus memorable.

The following plans are just examples. Tailor your schedule to meet your family's needs. For example, if you are taking a trip in the middle of the year, you can switch up the flow and spend a week or two just reading the book. If you have a busy week with a lot of time riding in the car, you can listen to the audiobook as you ride around town and have an older student call out the "Read & Review" questions. If you have a day where you are free to complete a fun optional activity, you don't have to do the activity from that day's reading. You can go back and complete an activity from a previous section or chapter.

Work through the program flexibly! If your student finds a topic particularly fascinating, slow down. Complete more of the optional activities and order library books from the recommended reading lists. You can move through other sections more quickly to make up the time. It is more important to enjoy the experience of learning about faraway lands and times than to adhere perfectly to a rigid schedule.

2-Day a Week Schedule for 35-36 Weeks

If you spend two days a week on history, your flow could look something like this:

- **Day 1:** Read or listen to two subsections (some students enjoy working on the coloring page while they listen). Complete the read & review questions and the map work activity, if there is one.
- **Day 2:** Read or listen to one subsection. Complete the narration exercise. When you have time, add in an interactive activity.
- Explore additional history reading and corresponding literature books as part of your language arts and reading program.
- If you like, incorporate more interactive activities into different parts of your day to encourage students to make connections between disciplines (art, math, science, etc.). Appendix Four can help with this!

4-Day a Week Schedule for 35-36 Weeks.

If you spend four days a week on history, your flow could look something like this:

- **Day 1:** Read or listen to one or two subsections (some students enjoy working on the coloring page while they listen). Complete the read & review questions. Complete the map work, if there is one.
- **Day 2:** Complete an optional activity.
- **Day 3:** If you read two subsections on day 1, read or listen to 1 subsection. If not, read or listen to 2 subsections. Complete the narration exercise/s. Complete the map work, if there is one.
- **Day 4:** Complete an optional activity.
- Explore additional history reading and corresponding literature books as part of your language arts and reading program.

Co-Op/Classroom Schedule Ideas.

If you cover history in a classroom 2-3 times a week:

- **Day 1:** Listen to two subsections (some students enjoy working on the coloring page while they listen). Complete the read & review questions as a class, as a Turn and Talk, or (for older students) as a Quick Write exercise. Have students complete the map work activity individually or in small groups.
- **Day 2:** Listen to one subsection. Complete the narration exercise as a class, then have each student write down one sentence about what they remember. Older students can complete the narration on their own.
- **Day 3:** Choose a classroom adaptable activity (labeled in the instructor guide, and listed in Appendix Four) to complete.
- Explore additional history reading and corresponding literature books as part of your language arts and reading program.
- If you want to do more activities, incorporate them into other areas of your school day (art, math, science, etc.). Appendix Four can help with this!

If you meet with a co-op group once a week or cover history once a week:

- During the week, have families read through 2-3 sections of the main text on their own (or listen to the audiobook) and complete the read & review questions OR narration exercises.
- On Fridays, or whenever you meet, complete one set of maps together as a class and 1-2 classroom-adaptable activities (each lesson has at least one activity labeled as classroom adaptable and has special notes on how to complete the activity in a group setting).

If you meet with a co-op group less than once a week:

- Agree to a reading schedule for each family to complete at home. Encourage families to complete the narration exercises and map work at home.
- When you meet, review the portion of the text assigned for that segment of time, using the Read & Review questions. Then choose 1-3 classroom-adaptable activities to complete.

Detailed 36-Week Schedule

This is an adaptable example! You can swap activities in and out and adjust the pacing as you see fit. If you do history two days a week instead of four, merge days 1-2 and days 3-4. This schedule was designed with families of multi-level students in mind and is set at about a third-grade level. If you have younger students, remove at least two activities per week. If you have older students, check out the reading lists in each chapter, which include suggested titles for slightly older students.

WEEK 1

Day 1:

- Read or listen to the first part of the introduction: "What is History?"
- Complete the read & review questions.

Day 2:

- Complete either the "Conduct an Interview" OR the "Make a Timeline of Your Life" activity.

Day 3:

- Read or listen to the second part of the introduction: "What is Archaeology?"
- Complete the narration exercise.

Day 4:

- Complete the "A Dirty Dig!" activity OR read *What is an Archaeologist?* by Libby Romero (or a different book from the reading list).

WEEK 2

Day 1:

- Read or listen to the first section of chapter one: "The First Nomads."
- Complete the read & review questions.
- Complete the map work.

Day 2:

- Complete the "Making a Cave Painting" activity, or a different optional activity.

Day 3:

- Read the second section of chapter one: "The First Nomads Become Farmers." Optional: your student can color "A Farmer Using a Shaduf" (Student Page 4) as she listens.
- Complete the narration exercise.

Day 4:

- Complete the "Shaduf" activity or a different optional activity OR read *Discovery in the Cave* by Mark Dubowski (or a different book from the reading list).

WEEK 3

Note to Instructor: This is one of seven weeks in which we will cover two chapters from the main text in one week.

Day 1:

- Read or listen to the first section from chapter two: "Two Kingdoms Become One."
- Complete the read & review questions.
- Read or listen to the second section from chapter two: "The Gods of Egypt." Optional: your student can color "Osiris and Set" (Student Page 6) as he listens.
- If you have time, complete the map work.

Day 2:

- Read or listen to the first section from chapter three: "Hieroglyphs and Cuneiform." Optional: your student can color "Carving Hieroglyphs" (Student Page 9) as she listens.
- Complete the narration exercise.
- Complete the "Make a Hieroglyphic Scroll" activity (from chapter three).

Day 3:

- Complete the map work for chapter three.
- Complete the "Make a Cuneiform Tablet" activity

Day 4:

- Complete the "Clay Tablet vs Paper Scroll" activity OR read *Hieroglyphs* by Joyce Milton (or a different book from the reading list).

WEEK 4

Day 1:

- Read or listen to the first section from chapter four: "Making Mummies."
- Complete the read & review questions.
- Gather materials for either the "Make a Chicken Mummy" or the simpler "Make an Apple Mummy" activity.

Day 2:

- Complete the "Make a Chicken Mummy" or the "Make an Apple Mummy" activity. If you choose "Chicken Mummy," you will continue to work on this for a few weeks. It is a lot of effort, but we think it is worth it to get a great understanding of the mummification process.

Day 3:

- Read the second section from chapter four: "Egyptian Pyramids." Optional: your student can color "Pyramids of Egypt" (Student Page 13) as he listens.
- Complete the narration exercise.

Day 4:

- Complete the map work.
- Complete the "research skills" activity OR read *Mummies Made in Egypt* by Aliki (or a different book from the reading list).

WEEK 5

Note to Instructor: This is the second of seven weeks in which we will cover two chapters from the main text in one week.

Day 1:

- Read or listen to the first section of chapter five: "Sargon and the Akkadians." Optional: your student can color "Sargon, King of Mesopotamia" (Student Page 15) as she listens.
- Complete the narration exercise.
- Complete the map work.

Day 2:

- Play "The Royal Game of Ur" or complete a different optional activity.

Day 3:

- Read or listen to the first section of chapter six: "God Speaks to Abraham." Optional: your student can color "The Ziggurat of Ur" (Student Page 18) as he listens.
- Complete the read & review questions.
- Read the second section of chapter six: "Joseph Goes to Egypt."
- Complete the read & review questions.

Day 4:

- If you have a large group of students, complete the "Trade in Haran" activity. If not, try the "Seven Years of Famine" activity, or a different optional activity.

WEEK 6

Note to Instructor: This is the third of seven weeks in which we will cover two chapters from the main text in one week.

Day 1:

- Read or listen to the first section of chapter seven: "Hammurabi's Code."
- Complete the narration exercise.
- Complete the map work.

Day 2:

- Complete the "Hammurabi's Court" activity or a different optional activity.

Day 3:

- Read or listen to the first section of chapter eight: "Shamshi-Adad, King of the Whole World."
- Complete the read & review questions.
- Complete the map work.
- Optional: if you have time, try the "Dictator for the Day" activity or the "Assyrian Battle!" activity.

Day 4:

- Read the second section of chapter eight: "The Story of Gilgamesh." Optional: your student can color "Gilgamesh and the Lion" (Student Page 28) as she listens.
- Complete the read & review questions.
- If you have time, read *Gilgamesh The King* by Ludmila Zeman (or a different book from the reading list).

WEEK 7

Day 1:

- Read or listen to the first section of chapter nine: "The First Cities of India."
- Complete the read & review questions.

Day 2:

- Complete the "Rivers and Their Civilizations Memory Work" or a different optional activity.

Day 3:

- Read the second section of chapter nine: "The Mystery of Mohenjo-Daro." Optional: your student can color "A Statue from Mohenjo-Daro" (Student Page 31) as he listens.
- Complete the narration exercise.
- Review "Rivers and Their Civilizations" memory work.

Day 4:

- Complete the map work.
- Complete the "research skills" activity OR read *The Indus Valley* by Madeline Tyler (or a different book from the reading list) and *Once a Mouse* by Marcia Brown (or a different book from the reading list).
- Review "Rivers and Their Civilizations" memory work.

WEEK 8:

Day 1:

- Read or listen to the first section of chapter ten: "Lei Zu and the Silkworm."
- Complete the read & review questions.
- Complete the map work.
- Review "Rivers and Their Civilizations" memory work.

Day 2:

- Read the second section of chapter ten: "The Pictograms of Ancient China."
- Complete the narration exercise.
- Complete the "Draw Your Own Pictograms" activity.
- Review "Rivers and Their Civilizations" memory work.

Day 3:

- Read the third section of chapter ten: "Farming in Ancient China."
- Complete the read & review questions.
- Complete the "Sequencing Events" activity.
- Review "Rivers and Their Civilizations" memory work.

Day 4:

- Read the relevant sections in *DK Eyewitness Books: Ancient China* by Arthur Cotterell (or a different book from the reading list).
- Review "Rivers and Their Civilizations" memory work.

WEEK 9

Day 1:

- Read or listen to the first section of chapter eleven: "Ancient Peoples of West Africa."
- Complete the read & review questions.
- Complete the map work.

Day 2:

- Read the second section of chapter eleven: "Anansi and Turtle." Optional: your student can color "Anansi and Turtle" (Student Page 35) while she listens.
- Complete the narration activity.
- Complete the "Anansi the Spider" activity.
- Review "Rivers and Their Civilizations" memory work.

Day 3:

- Read the third section of chapter eleven: "Anansi and the Make-Believe Food."
- Complete the read & review questions.
- Complete the "Anansi's Friend, Turtle" activity.

Day 4:

- Read one story from *The Pot of Wisdom: Ananse Stories* by Adwoa Badoe or a different book from the reading list.
- Use your new puppets to complete the "Act out an Anansi the Spider" activity OR if you didn't make puppets earlier in the week, try the "African Foods Taste Test" activity.

- Review "Rivers and Their Civilizations" memory work.

WEEK 10

Day 1:

- Read or listen to the first section of chapter twelve: "Bull-Jumpers and Sailors." Optional: your student can color "Bull Jumper" (Student Page 37) as he listens.
- Complete the read & review questions.
- Complete the map work.

Day 2:

- Complete the "Bull-Jumping Practice" activity
- If you have time, read *The Palace of Knossos* by Emily Rose Oachs (or a different book from the reading list).

Day 3:

- Read the second section from chapter twelve: "King Minos and the Minotaur."
- Complete the narration exercise.
- Complete the "Research Skills" activity OR read a story from *D'Aulaires' Book of Greek Myths* or a different Greek myth from the reading list.

Day 4:

- Read the third section from chapter twelve: "The Mysterious End of the Minoans."
- Complete the read & review questions.
- Review memory work.

WEEK 11

Day 1:

- Read or listen to the first section of chapter thirteen: "Egypt Invades Nubia." Optional: your student can color "Nubians" (Student Page 40) as she listens.
- Complete the read & review questions.

Day 2:

- Read or listen to the second section of chapter thirteen: "The Hyksos Invade Egypt."
- Complete the narration exercise.
- Complete the map work.

Day 3:

- Complete the "Egyptian War Chariot" activity, or a different optional activity.

Day 4:

- Complete the "Research Skills" activity OR read *Be A Scribe: Working for a Better Life in Ancient Egypt* by Michael Hoffen, Christian Casey, and Janet Thum (or a different book from the reading list).
- Review memory work.

WEEK 12

Day 1:

- Read or listen to the first section of chapter fourteen: "The General and the Woman Pharaoh."
- Complete the read & review questions.

Day 2:

- Complete the "Be an Archaeologist" activity (from the upcoming section), or a different optional activity.

Day 3:

- Read the second section of chapter fourteen: "Amenhotep and King Tut." Optional: your student can color "The Mask of King Tut" (Student Page 42) while she listens.
- Complete the narration exercise.
- Complete the map work.

Day 4:

- Complete the "Pharaoh for Dinner" activity. Choose a biography of your chosen Pharaoh to read before you complete the activity. It will help you prepare.
- Review memory work.

WEEK 13:

Note to Instructor: This is the fourth of seven weeks in which we will cover two chapters from the main text in one week.

Day 1:

- Read or listen to the first section of chapter fifteen: "The Israelites Leave Egypt."
- Complete the read & review questions.
- Read or listen to the second section from chapter fifteen: "The Exodus from Egypt." Optional: your student can color "Moses Parting the Red Sea" (Student Page 44) as he listens.
- Complete the read & review questions.
- If you have time, complete the map work.

Day 2:

- Read the first section of chapter sixteen: "The Mycenaeans." Optional: your student can color "Greek War Chariot" (Student Page 46) as she listens.
- Complete the narration exercise.
- Complete the map work.

Day 3:

- Read the second section of chapter sixteen: "The Greek Dark Ages." Optional: your student can color "A Greek Vase" (Student Page 47) as she listens.
- Complete the read & review questions.

Day 4:

- Complete an optional activity OR read *The Trojan Horse* by Emily Little (or a different book from the reading list).

- Review memory work.

WEEK 14

Note to Instructor: This is the fifth of seven weeks in which we will cover two chapters from the main text in one week.

Day 1:
- Read or listen to the first section of chapter seventeen: "Phoenician Traders." Optional: your student can color "A Phoenician Ship" (Student Page 49) as he listens.
- Complete the map work.
- If you have time, start reading *Ox, House, Stick: The History of Our Alphabet*, by Don Robb (or another book from the reading list).

Day 2:
- Read or listen to the second section of chapter seventeen: "The Founding of Carthage." Optional: your student can color "Queen Dido" (Student Page 50) as she listens.
- Complete the narration exercise.
- If you have time, complete either the "Sequencing Events: Founding of Carthage" activity OR the "Queen Dido's Perimeter Trick" activity.

Day 3:
- Read the first section of chapter eighteen: "Ashurbanipal's Attack." Optional: your student can color "A Bas-Relief from Ancient Assyria" (Student Page 52) as he listens.
- Complete the read & review questions.

Day 4:
- Read the second section of chapter eighteen: "The Library of Nineveh."
- Complete the map work.
- Review memory work.

WEEK 15

Day 1:
- Read or listen to the biography of Queen Shammuramat. Optional: your student can color "Queen Shammuramat" (Student Page 54) as she listens.
- Complete the read & review Questions.
- Read or listen to the first section of chapter nineteen: "Greece Gets an Alphabet."
- Complete the read & review questions.
- If you have time, complete the "Write Your Name in Greek Letters" activity page OR finish reading *Ox, House, Stick: The History of Our Alphabet*, by Don Robb.

Day 2:
- Read the second section of chapter nineteen: "The Stories of Homer." Optional: your student can color "The Cyclops" (Student Page 59) as she listens.
- Complete the narration exercise.
- Complete the map work.

Day 3:

- Read the third section from chapter nineteen: "The First Olympic Games."
- Complete the read & review questions.
- If you like, prepare for your "Olympic Games" by completing the "Greek Instruments," "Olympic Wreath," OR "Greek Feast" activity.

Day 4:

- Complete the "Host the Olympic Games" activity!
- Review memory work.

WEEK 16

Day 1:

- Read or listen to the first section of chapter twenty: "Life in Sparta." Optional: your student can color "A Spartan Warrior" (Student Page 60) as he listens.
- Complete the read & review questions.

Day 2:

- Read or listen to the second section of chapter twenty: "Life in Athens."
- Complete the narration exercise.
- Complete the map work.

Day 3:

- Complete the "Vote at an Agora" activity, or a different optional activity.

Day 4:

- Read "The Story of Draco and Salon, the Two Lawgivers of Athens." Optional: your student can color "Draco Flees Athens" (Student Page 65) as she listens.
- Complete the read & review questions.

WEEK 17

Note to Instructor: This is the sixth of seven weeks in which we will cover two chapters from the main text in one week.

Day 1:

- Read or listen to the first section of chapter twenty-one: "The Golden Apple." Optional: your student can color "Athena and Zeus" (Student Page 67) as he listens.
- Complete the read & review questions.
- Complete the map work.

Day 2:

- Read the first section of chapter twenty-two: "Romulus and Remus." Optional: your student can color "Romulus and Remus" (Student Page 70) as she listens.
- Complete the read & review questions.

Day 3:

- Complete the "Salt Dough Map of Italy" activity, or a different optional activity.

Day 4:

- Read or listen to the second section of chapter twenty-two: "The Power of Rome."
- Complete the narration exercise.
- Complete the map work.
- Review memory work.

WEEK 18

Note to Instructor: This is the seventh and final week in which we will cover two chapters from the main text in one week.

Day 1:

- Read or listen to "The Story of Tullia Minor and Tarquin the Proud, the Last King and Queen of Rome." Optional: your student can color "The King and the Queen of Rome" (Student Page 73) as he listens.
- Complete the read & review questions.
- Complete the "Seven Wonders of the Ancient World" memory work activity from the upcoming chapter (or a different optional activity).

Day 2:

- Read the first section of chapter twenty-three: "Nebuchadnezzar's Madness." Optional: your student can color "The Ishtar Gate" (Student Page 75) as she listens.
- Complete the map work.
- Read the second section of chapter twenty-three: "The Hanging Gardens of Babylon." Optional: your student can color "Marduk and Tiamat" (Student Page 76) as she listens.
- Practice the "Seven Wonders of the Ancient World" memory work.

Day 3:

- Read the first section of chapter twenty-four: "A New Empire." Optional: your student can color "Cyrus the Great " (Student Page 79) as he listens.
- Complete the narration exercise.
- Complete the map work OR Read the section about Cyrus the Great in *The Great and the Terrible: The World's Most Glorious and Notorious Rulers and How They Got Their Names*, by Joanne O'Sullivan (or a different book from the reading list).
- Practice the "Seven Wonders of the Ancient World" memory work.

Day 4:

- Read the second section of chapter twenty-four: "Cyrus the Great."
- Complete the read & review questions.
- Practice the "Seven Wonders of the Ancient World" memory work activity.
- If you have time, play the "Mesopotamian Conquest" board game (a great way to review a lot of what you've learned so far), or complete a different optional activity.

WEEK 19

Day 1:

- Read or listen to the first section of chapter twenty-five: "Life on the Ganges River."
- Complete the read & review questions.

- Complete the map work.

Day 2:
- Read the second section of chapter twenty-five: "The Castes of Ancient India."
- Complete the narration exercise.
- Complete the "Make a Rakhi" activity and save it for Friday.

Day 3:
- Read or listen to the third section of chapter twenty-five: "Siddhartha."
- Complete the read & review questions.
- Read or listen to "The Story of Ajatashatru the Expander, The First Empire-Builder of India." Optional: your student can color "Ajatashatru Travels to Meet the Buddha" (Student Page 82) as she listens.
- Complete the read & review questions.

Day 4:
- Celebrate your study of Ancient India! Complete the "Indian Recipes" activity. Exchange your rakhis. Play ancient Indian music and dance! Finish off by reading some stories about Ancient India from the reading list or play the "Catch Ganga!" game.
- Review memory work.

WEEK 20

Day 1:
- Read or listen to the first section of chapter twenty-six: "Calligraphy in China."
- Complete the read & review questions.
- Complete the "Practice Chinese Calligraphy" activity.

Day 2:
- Read the second section of chapter twenty-six: "Confucius: China's Wise Teacher." Optional: your student can color "Confucius: China's Wise Teacher" (Student Page 84) as he listens.
- Complete the narration exercise.

Day 3:
- Complete the "Golden Rule Poster" activity, or a different optional activity.
- Read *Confucius: Great Teacher of China*, by Demi or a different book from the reading list.

Day 4:
- Read "The Story of Mencius, The Greatest Follower of Confucius." Optional: your student can color "Mencius" (Student Page 85) as she listens.
- Complete the read & review Questions.
- Review memory work.

WEEK 21

Day 1:
- Read or listen to the first section of chapter twenty-seven: "Greece's War with Persia."

- Complete the read & review questions.
- Complete the map work.

Day 2:
- Complete the "Make an Ice Cream Boat" activity, or a different optional activity.

Day 3:
- Read or listen to the second section of chapter twenty-seven: "The Greeks Fight Each Other." Optional: your student can color "The Parthenon" OR "Design a Greek Temple" (Student Page 88 OR 89) as he listens.
- Complete the narration exercise.

Day 4:
- Complete the "Build Greek Columns out of Clay" activity, or a different optional activity OR read a book from the reading list.
- Review memory work.

WEEK 22

Day 1:
- Read or listen to the first section of chapter twenty-eight: "Philip and His Son." Optional: your student can color "Alexander the Great and Bucephalus" (Student Page 90) as she listens.
- Complete the read & review questions.

Day 2:
- Read or listen to the second section of chapter twenty-eight: "Alexander's Invasions."
- Complete the narration exercise.
- Complete the map work.

Day 3:
- Read or listen to the third section of chapter twenty-eight: "The Death of Alexander."
- Complete the read & review questions.
- Complete the "Sequencing Events: The Death of Alexander" activity.

Day 4:
- Complete the "Picture Study: Alexander Mosaic" activity.
- If you have time, read the section about Alexander the Great in *The Great and the Terrible: The World's Most Glorious and Notorious Rulers and How They Got Their Names*, by Joanne O'Sullivan (or a different book from the reading list) OR complete the "Role Play: Sharing" activity.
- Review memory work.

WEEK 23

Day 1:
- Read or listen to the first section of chapter twenty-nine: "The Empire United."

- Complete the read & review questions.
- Complete the map work.

Day 2:
- Complete the "Role Play: Mindfulness" activity, or a different optional activity.
- Read *Ashoka the Fierce: How an Angry Prince Became India's Emperor of Peace*, by Carolyn Kanjuro (or choose a different book from the reading list).

Day 3:
- Read or listen to the second section of chapter twenty-nine: "The Jataka Tales." Optional: your student can color "The Jataka Tales" (Student Page 94) as he listens.
- Complete the narration exercise.

Day 4:
- Read an ancient Indian tale from *Nine Animals and the Well* by James Rumford, or a different book from the reading list.
- Play "Snakes and Ladders," or complete a different optional activity.
- Review memory work.

WEEK 24

Day 1:
- Read or listen to the first section of chapter thirty: "The Nazca Drawings."
- Complete the read & review questions.
- Read *Lady of the Lines: How Maria Reiche Saved the Nazca Lines by Sweeping the Desert* by Michaela Maccoll (or a different book from the reading list)

Day 2:
- Read or listen to the second section of chapter thirty: "The Heads of the Olmecs."
- Complete the narration exercise.

Day 3:
- Read or listen to the third section of chapter thirty: "Rabbit Shoots the Sun." Optional: your student can color "Rabbit Shoots the Sun" (Student Page 96) as she listens.
- Complete the read & review questions.
- Complete the map work.

Day 4:
- Celebrate what you've learned about Ancient America! Cook up some corn cakes. Play "no-hand ball" OR read a story from the Ancient Americas (from the reading list). If you have time, choose one of the crafts from this chapter to complete (Nazca Lines, Olmec heads, or Seed Map).
- Review memory work.

WEEK 25

Day 1:
- Read or listen to the first section of chapter thirty-one: "The Roman Builders."

- Complete the read & review questions.
- Complete the "Make a Model: Make (and eat) a Roman Road" activity, or a different optional activity OR read *Aqueduct of Segovia (Extreme Engineering)* by Brienna Rossiter (or a different book from the reading list).

Day 2:
- Read or listen to the second section of chapter thirty-one: "The Roman Gods."
- Complete the review questions.
- Play the "Greek vs Roman Gods" game OR complete the "Proserpine's Seasons" activity OR read another Greek myth from the reading list.

Day 3:
- Read or listen to the third section of chapter thirty-one: "The Roman Gladiators." Optional: your student can color "Gladiators in the Arena" (Student Page 99) as he listens.
- Complete the narration exercise.
- Complete the "Match Each Gladiator to Their Weapon" activity page, or a different optional activity.

Day 4:
- Read or listen to the fourth section of chapter thirty-one: "The Gladiator School."
- Complete the narration exercise.
- Complete the map work.
- Review memory work.

WEEK 26

Day 1:
- Read or listen to "The Story of Spartacus, The Rebel Gladiator." Optional: your student can color "Spartacus" (Student Page 102) as she listens.
- Complete the read & review questions.

Day 2:
- Complete the "Gladiator Training School" activity, or a different optional activity from the previous chapter OR read *See You Later, Gladiator* by Jon Scieszka (or a different book from the reading list).

Day 3:
- Read or listen to the first section in chapter thirty-two: "The Punic Wars." Optional: your student can color "Hannibal's War Elephants" (Student Page 104) or "Hannibal" (Student Page 105) as she listens.
- Complete the read & review questions.

Day 4:
- Complete the map work.
- Read *Roman Soldiers: Discover the World of the Ancient Roman Army* by Tegen Evans (or a different book from the reading list) OR complete the "Research Skills" activity.
- Review memory work.

WEEK 27

Day 1:

- Read or listen to the first section of chapter thirty-three: "The First Emperor and the Great Wall." Optional: your student can color "The Great Wall of China" (Student Page 108) as he listens.
- Complete the read & review questions.
- Complete the "How Long Was the Wall" activity, or a different optional activity.

Day 2:

- Read or listen to the second section of chapter thirty-three: "The First Emperor's Grave."
- Complete the map work.
- Complete the "Draw or Sculpt the Terra Cotta Warriors" activity, or a different optional activity.

Day 3:

- Read or listen to the third section of chapter thirty-three: "The Han Dynasty and the Silk Road." Optional: your student can color "Liu Bang" (Student Page 110) as he listens.
- Complete the narration exercise.

Day 4:

- Read "The Story of Zhang Qian, Hero of the Silk Road." Optional: your student can color "Zhang Qian" (Student Page 111) as she listens.
- Complete the read & review questions.
- If you have time, play the "Silk Road Senses" game.
- Review memory work.

WEEK 28

Day 1:

- Read or listen to the first section of chapter thirty-four: "Caesar is Kidnapped."
- Complete the read & review questions.
- Complete the map work.

Day 2:

- Read or listen to the second section of chapter thirty-four: "The Consuls of Rome."
- Complete the read & review questions.
- If you have time, play "Triumvirate Tug of War," or complete a different optional activity.

Day 3:

- Read or listen to the third section of chapter thirty-four: "Caesar and the Senate."
- Complete the read & review questions.

Day 4:

- Read the fourth section of chapter thirty-four: "Caesar Fights the Celts."
- Complete the "Design Your Own Flag" activity, or a different optional activity (some students may enjoy working on their flags as they listen).

- Review memory work.

WEEK 29

Day 1:

- Read or listen to the first section of chapter thirty-five: "Caesar Crosses the Rubicon." Optional: your student can color "Julius Caesar" (Student Page 115) as he listens.
- Complete the read & review questions.
- Complete the map work.

Day 2:

- Read or listen to the second section of chapter thirty-five: "Caesar and Cleopatra."
- Complete the narration exercise.
- If you have time, complete the "Mint Your Own Coins Out of Clay" activity to prepare for Friday's celebration.

Day 3:

- Read or listen to the third section of chapter thirty-five: "The Death of Caesar."
- Complete the read & review questions.
- Read or listen to the fourth section of chapter thirty-five: "Augustus Caesar." Optional: your student can color "Augustus Caesar" (Student Page 117) as she listens.
- Complete the read & review questions.

Day 4:

- Celebrate what you've learned about Roman history and culture! If possible, have friends or siblings help you build your own Roman town! Have one group run a Roman clothing store and help kids get into togas (use the "Make a Roman Toga" activity); have one group run the hair salon (use the "Run a Roman Hair Salon" activity); and have one group run the Thermopolium (use the "Run a Thermopolium" activity). Students can take turns visiting each other's shop and paying for services with "Roman Coins" (either use coins made in the "Caesar and Cleopatra" lesson, or make pretend coins out of aluminum foil, or use pennies). If you have only one student, choose one of the activities from the chapter to complete.

WEEK 30

Day 1:

- Read or listen to the first section of chapter thirty-six: "Herod,'The Great'." Optional: your student can color "Herod's Temple" (Student Page 118) as she listens.
- Complete the read & review questions.
- If you have time, complete the "Herod's Building Projects" activity, or a different optional activity.

Day 2:

- Read or listen to the second section of chapter thirty-six: "A Prophet Named Jesus."
- Complete the narration exercise.
- Complete the "*Nativity* by Jean-Baptiste Marie Pierre" Picture Study activity, or a different optional activity.

Day 3:

- Read or listen to the third section of chapter thirty-six: "The Destruction of the Temple."
- Complete the read & review questions.
- Read "The Story of Judas Maccabee, Champion of the Jewish People." Optional: your student can color "Judas Maccabee" (Student Page 121) as he listens.

Day 4:

- Review the relevant section in *The Kids Book of World Religions* by Jennifer Glossop (or read a different book from the reading list).

WEEK 31

Day 1:

- Read or listen to the first section of chapter thirty-seven: "Nero, the Evil Emperor."
- Complete the read & review questions.
- Complete the map work.

Day 2:

- Complete the "Silly Laws" activity or a different optional activity.
- If you have time, review *The Roman Record: Hot News from the Swirling Mists of Time*, by Paul Dowswell (or another book from the reading list).

Day 3:

- Build your catacomb using the instructions in the "Read this Chapter in Your Own Catacomb" activity.
- Read the second section of chapter thirty-seven: "Christians in the Catacombs," inside your catacomb.
- Complete the narration exercise.

Day 4:

- Complete the "Host a Roman Banquet" activity, or a different optional activity.

WEEK 32

Day 1:

- Read or listen to the first section of chapter thirty-eight: "The British Rebellion." Optional: your student can color "Boadicea in Her Chariot" (Student Page 124) as she listens.
- Complete the read & review questions.

Day 2:

- Complete the "Celtic Feast" activity, or a different optional activity.

Day 3:

- Read or listen to the second section of chapter thirty-eight: "Rome Divided in Two."
- Complete the read & review questions.
- Complete the map work.
- If you have time, try the "Roman Collapse" activity (if you have 1-3 students) or the "Defend the Empire" activity (if you have more than 3 students).

Day 4:

- Review memory work.
- Read "The Story of Pliny the Younger: Survivor of Mount Vesuvius." Optional: your student can color "Mount Vesuvius Erupts (Student Page 126) as he listens."

WEEK 33

Day 1:

- Read or listen to the first section of chapter thirty-nine: "The End of the Han Dynasty."
- Complete the "Sequencing Events: The End of the Han Dynasty" activity, or a different optional activity.

Day 2:

- Read or listen to the second section of chapter thirty-nine: "The Three Kingdoms, The Jin, and the Sixteen Kingdoms."
- Complete the map work.

Day 3:

- Read or listen to "The Story of Zhang Heng: Astronomer, Poet, Mathematician, Geographer, and More." Optional: your student can color "Zhang Heng's Earthquake Detector" (Student Page 130) as she listens. Complete the read & review questions.

Day 4:

- Celebrate what you've learned about Ancient China! Complete the "Chinese Dumplings" activity (or buy and cook dumplings at the store). Play "Chinese Playground Games." Check out *All About China: Stories, Songs, Crafts and Games for Kids* (Tuttle Publishing, 2018) by Allison "Aixin" Branscombe for more activity ideas and information about the history, culture, and geography of China.
- Review memory work.

WEEK 34

Day 1:

- Read or listen to the first section of chapter forty: "The Three Kingdoms of Korea."
- Complete the "Read the Lesson with Character Cards" activity.

Day 2:

- Complete the "Japchae" activity, or a different optional activity OR read *All About Korea: Stories, Songs, and Games for Kids* by Ann Martin Bowler (or a different book from the reading list).

Day 3:

- Read or listen to the second section of chapter forty: "The Yamato of Japan." Optional: your student can color "Susano" (Student Page 133) as he listens.
- Complete the narration exercise.

Day 4:

- Complete the map work.

- Read *All About Japan: Stories, Songs, and Games for Kids* by Willamarie Moore, or a different book from the reading list.
- Review memory work.

WEEK 35

Day 1:
- Read or listen to the first section of chapter forty-one: "Stilicho, Roman and Barbarian."
- Complete the read & review questions.
- If you have time, play "Stilicho Says" or complete a different optional activity.

Day 2:
- Read or listen to the second section of chapter forty-one: "The Coming of the Visigoths." Optional: your student can color the Visigoth (Student Page 135) as she listens).
- Complete the narration exercise.
- If you like, play "Barbarian Tag," or complete a different optional activity.

Day 3:
- Read or listen to the third section of chapter forty-one: "Attila the Hun."
- Complete the read & review questions.
- Complete the map work.

Day 4:
- Complete the "Research Skills" activity OR Read the section about Attila the Hun in *The Great and the Terrible: The World's Most Glorious and Notorious Rulers and How They Got Their Names*, by Joanne O'Sullivan (or a different book from the reading list).
- Review memory work.

WEEK 36

Day 1:
- Read or listen to the first section of chapter forty-two: "The Last Roman Emperor."
- Complete the read & review questions.
- If you have a group of students, play the "Find the Emperor" game. If you have just one student, complete the "research skills" activity.

Day 2:
- Read or listen to the second section of chapter forty-two: "The Gifts of Rome."
- Complete the map work.
- Play "The Gifts of Rome Bingo," or complete a different optional activity.

Day 3:
- Prepare your End of Book celebration!

Day 4:
- Host your End of Book celebration!